T0259799

Improving the Quality of ABAP Code

Striving for Perfection

Paul David Hardy

apress®

Improving the Quality of ABAP Code

Paul David Hardy
North Strathfield, NSW, Australia

ISBN-13 (pbk): 978-1-4842-6710-3   ISBN-13 (electronic): 978-1-4842-6711-0
https://doi.org/10.1007/978-1-4842-6711-0

Managing Director, Apress Media LLC: Welmoed Spahr
Acquisitions Editor: Divya Modi
Development Editor: Laura Berendson
Coordinating Editor: Divya Modi

Cover designed by eStudioCalamar

Cover image designed by Pixabay

Distributed to the book trade worldwide by Springer Science + Business Media New York, 1 New York Plaza, New York, NY 10004. Phone 1-800-SPRINGER, fax (201) 348-4505, email orders-ny@springer-sbm.com, or visit www.springeronline.com. Apress Media, LLC is a California LLC, and the sole member (owner) is Springer Science + Business Media Finance Inc (SSBM Finance Inc). SSBM Finance Inc is a **Delaware** corporation.

For information on translations, please e-mail booktranslations@springernature.com; for reprint, paperback, or audio rights, please e-mail bookpermissions@springernature.com.

Apress titles may be purchased in bulk for academic, corporate, or promotional use. eBook versions and licenses are also available for most titles. For more information, reference our Print and eBook Bulk Sales web page at http://www.apress.com/bulk-sales.

Any source code or other supplementary material referenced by the author in this book is available to readers on GitHub via the book's product page, located at www.apress.com/978-1-4842-6710-3. For more-detailed information, please visit http://www.apress.com/source-code.

Printed on acid-free paper

I dedicate this book to my loving wife, Vikki,
who has to make so many sacrifices whilst I am locked
away in my own world writing books!

Table of Contents

About the Author

Paul David Hardy joined Heidelberg Cement in the United Kingdom in 1990. For the first seven years, he worked as an accountant. In 1997, a global SAP rollout came along, and he jumped on board and has never looked back. He has worked on country-specific SAP implementations in the United Kingdom, Germany, Israel, and Australia.

After starting off as a business analyst configuring the good old IMG, Paul swiftly moved on to the wonderful world of ABAP programming. After the initial run of data-conversion programs, ALV reports, interactive Dynpro screens, and SAPscript forms, he yearned for something more, and since then has been eagerly investigating each new technology as it comes out, which culminated in his writing the book *ABAP to the Future*.

Paul became an SAP Mentor in March 2017 and can regularly be found blogging on the SAP Community site and presenting at SAP conferences in Australia (Mastering SAP Technology and the SAP Australian User Group annual conference) and at SAP TECHED Las Vegas. If you happen to be at one of these conferences, Paul invites you to come and have a drink with him at the networking event in the evening and to ask him the most difficult questions you can think of, preferably about SAP.

About the Technical Reviewer

 **James E. McDonough** received a degree in music education from Trenton State College. After teaching music for only two years in the New Jersey public school system, he changed careers. He's spent the past 38 years as a computer programmer while also maintaining an active presence as a freelance jazz bassist between New York and Philadelphia. Having switched from mainframe programming to ABAP in 1997, he now works as a contract ABAP programmer designing and writing ABAP programs on a daily basis. An advocate of using the object-oriented programming features available with ABAP, he has been teaching private ABAP education courses over the past few years, where his background in education enables him to present and explain complicated concepts in a way that makes sense to beginners.

Acknowledgments

I wrote this book mainly in two pubs in Sydney—the Woolpack in Parramatta (which opened in 1796 and is thus the oldest pub in Sydney) and the Horse and Jockey in Homebush. So many thanks go to all the bar staff in both establishments (especially Molly in the Horse and Jockey) for keeping me fueled whilst book writing!

I am also grateful to my wife Vikki for allowing me to sneak off to these pubs to write the book.

My favorite part of the book-writing process is the editing phase, when one can literally feel the book getting better. To this end, I am grateful to Jim McDonough for the technical review and Laura Berendson from Apress for her suggestions. I would also like to thank Divya Modi from Apress for inviting me to write the book in the first place.

On the technical side, I could not have come so far so fast without the incredible quality of the blogs on the SAP Community website. I have endeavored to reference the important blogs in the "recommended reading" part at the end of some chapters. As always, for any useful information I used from those blogs the author should take the credit—any mistakes are all down to me!

Introduction

In 2015, the American SAP Users Group (ASUG) wanted my opinion on a new survey that had been put out by a company called CAST, which had analyzed about 70 large custom ABAP applications from organizations all across the United States and Europe and come to the conclusion that all that custom code was a load of old baloney, ludicrous, rubbish, hopeless, and fit only for the dustbin.

The clear implication was that the ABAP programmers who had written these applications could not touch their own nose, let alone write a program containing even one ounce of quality. Nonetheless, the programs worked—they solved the business problems they were created to solve.

How can this be? How can we get to the stage where 100 percent of code is "no good" and yet 100 percent of code appears to work? It is because the two things are unrelated to an extent—but only to an extent.

What is meant by the code's being "no good" is that the analyzed programs were "big balls of mud"—prone to breaking for no apparent reason, and so complicated it would be impossible for any programmer other than the creator (and often even the creator) to understand what was going on and how to fix things or make a change. Sadly, this did not surprise me at all.

For Whom This Book Is Applicable

This book is aimed at all ABAP developers, whether they started yesterday or have been programming for 20 years. In fact, the ones who have been programming for 20-plus years probably need this book more, as a lot of them have fallen into bad habits or have never even heard of modern programming concepts like object-oriented programming or test-driven development.

Why This Book Was Written

If I were to boil this book down to one sentence, it would be: "How did we get to the terrible situation where the vast majority of custom code is of poor quality, and what can we (realistically) do to solve this problem?"

How Did We Get Here?

So the next question is, how did we get here? It is not because the programmers lack skill. Most programs usually start off perfect with no quality issues at all. Then, somehow, they get worse over time as more and more changes and additions are made.

I would say that programs degrade as a result of the false belief that code quality really does not matter at all. I imagine that in 99 percent of organizations, what the programmer is instructed to do is to make the exact change(s) required and ignore the fact that the program is (a) already a horrible mess or (b) your current change will make a fairly good program into more of a mess than it was before. The fact that you are actually making the problem worse over time is neither here nor there, as long as the requirement is met, really quickly.

Most management would say this approach is the only possible way to get things done. Time (and money) is always tight and getting tighter. Therefore, the idea is to make our changes as quickly as possible. In real life, over a protracted period quality code is actually cheaper than poor-quality code because the maintenance effort is so much lower, but that is a very difficult concept to convey.

How Do We Get Back?

Fear is always a killer—when changing a program, if you find an obvious existing bug, do you fix it, even if that is not what you are actually supposed to be doing? In some companies, you could get sacked for that.

You probably have heard the following famous quote:

> *The only thing necessary for the triumph of evil is for good men to do nothing.*
>
> *— Edmund Burke (in a letter addressed to Thomas Mercer)*

I could rephrase this as follows:

All it takes for poor quality to triumph is for good programmers to leave obviously bad code the way it is because they are scared of it.

This book is going to be about confronting and overcoming that fear, gradually increasing the quality of your code. This could be described as doing a favor to yourself, and to your colleagues both current and future. Robert C. Martin has an approach he calls "The Boy Scout Rule" regarding what to do with the area of code you have just fixed or enhanced:

It's not enough to write the code well. The code has to be kept clean over time. We've all seen code rot and degrade as time passes. So we must take an active role in preventing this degradation.

The Boy Scouts of America have a simple rule that we can apply to our profession.

Leave the campground cleaner than you found it.

If we all checked-in our code a little cleaner than when we checked it out, the code simply could not rot. The cleanup doesn't have to be something big. Change one variable name for the better, break up one function that's a little too large, eliminate one small bit of duplication, clean up one composite if statement.

Can you imagine working on a project where the code simply got better as time passed? Do you believe that any other option is professional? Indeed, isn't continuous improvement an intrinsic part of professionalism?

When I showed this to one of my colleagues, he responded thusly:

The boy scouts also have a saying: "Be Prepared."

In the case of (other external contractors) and myself, that might mean Be Prepared for (the CIO) to march us out the door if we introduce a bug in an area that is not in the scope that we are meant to be working on.

That is a reasonable counter-argument—any change you make, no matter how trivial, has a chance of causing a bug, and when the finger pointing starts you will get asked, "Why EXACTLY did you change that? Was that change in the specification?"

As a specific example, I once found a custom program where an internal table was emptied, then there were half a million lines of commented-out code, and then a loop full of logic done over that empty table.

After that loop (which obviously did nothing) there was a comment saying the above code did not seem to be working, and a helpdesk reference, from 2001. After that came some code to fill up the table again, followed by the exact same loop full of the exact same code.

As might be imagined, when debugging this, the identical second loop worked a lot better than the first. I can only presume that whoever tried to fix this 12 years ago did not want to touch the existing code, for fear of breaking something, so wrote some extra code below it to get the data from the database, then did a big copy and paste and everything worked, problem over.

However, I wouldn't let it lie. I could have let it lie, but I didn't. I deleted all the commented-out code, as well as the loop over the empty table. I might have broken something. I didn't, but I might have.

My crimes don't end there. It gets worse. Sometimes I even change the technology, like replacing WRITE statements with the ALV.

Each change should make more obvious what is going on, should reduce the complexity rather than just add endless extra chunks of conditional logic, or should increase the separation of concerns so a change in one place is less likely to break something far away.

The idea is that whenever you find that something you have to do in regard to custom program maintenance could be placed in the "difficult to change" basket and so could take a lot of work, ask yourself why it was difficult and how you can redesign things, such that the next change is not so hard.

This could be described as an "antimatter" idea—instead of the normal situation where every change makes the program more complicated, so the next change is more difficult, every change makes the next one easier. Also, just like antimatter, when this sort of idea meets traditional ways of doing things, the entire universe explodes.

Thus, another main focus of this book will be how to make such gradual changes in a safe manner. It is, after all, no consolation when you are standing in the unemployment line that you were trying to do the "right" thing when you brought down the production system on the busiest day of the year.

Credentials of the Author

I feel a burning need to point out that I have no formal training in the IT area at all—an O level (type of exam you take in the United Kingdom when you are 16) in computer science from 1983 just does not cut the mustard.

My actual degree was in economics, and I worked in financial accounts for the first seven years in my organization, and then when the SAP projects started I was a FI/CO consultant for two years before finally starting with ABAP in the year 1999 in Israel. In effect, I taught myself to program in assorted languages—BASIC in 1981 when I was 13, Pascal at university, Visual Basic when I started as an accountant in 1990, and lastly ABAP.

So, why read a book by me rather than one by someone with a formal education in IT?

In 2012, the SAP Community website started allowing anyone to write blogs. At that point, I had been programming in ABAP for 13 years, so I knew the reality. I had the idea of reading all those textbooks that "proper" computer science people would have known all their careers—*Clean Code, Working Effectively with Legacy Code, Head First Design Patterns*, and the like—and writing blogs where I compared the theory with the reality.

That worked so well that a few years later, when world-famous SAP programming guru Thomas Jung "retired" from writing books about ABAP, I was invited to take his place by SAP Press. A few years after *that* I was invited to become an SAP Mentor, and before you knew it I was attending meetings inside SAP HQ in Walldorf advising on the future of the ABAP language and giving speeches at SAP TechEd in Las Vegas and at SAP Inside Track events all over Europe.

Structure of the Book

The ideal structure of any book is that each chapter logically follows on from the preceding one and that there is a "golden thread" that runs through all the chapters linking them together. It will come as no great shock that the underlying thread is that of code quality, and the first six (long) chapters follow on from each other, and the remaining four (short) chapters sit on their own as specialist topics.

Chapter 1: OO Programming in General — There is nothing magical about object-orientated programming that makes it higher quality than procedural programming, but it does help. More important, this topic goes first because it enables the subject of the second chapter.

Chapter 2: Test-Driven Development — The idea is that by using TDD for all new development you can increase the quality of your programs over time in a rock-solid, safe manner. All subsequent chapters relate to activities you perform in the so-called blue phase of the TDD cycle, which is all about improving code quality.

Chapter 3: Clarity — This is the first of the three pillars of code quality. This goes before the other pillars because code needs to be understandable before you can address the other problems.

Chapter 4: Stability — This is the second pillar of code quality and what some consider the only measure, though hopefully this book will convince you otherwise.

Chapter 5: Performance — The first two pillars were developer facing; now you move on to user-facing aspects. In this case, that means making the code run quickly.

Chapter 6: User Friendliness — This is not one of the three "pillars" as this area has its own TDD cycle, and yet it is a violently important aspect of code quality that is often totally ignored.

Chapter 7: User Exits — This subject stands on its own to an extent. The point of the chapter is that user exits can be programmed using a TDD methodology as well.

Chapter 8: Conversion to S/4HANA — This is not applicable to everyone (yet) but it will be one day and so is worth investigating.

Chapter 9: Conversion to ABAP in the Cloud — This area is even further into the future than S/4HANA but is still worth looking at for the same reasons.

Chapter 10: How to Create Your Own Code Inspector Check — The rest of the book focuses on what is available today and how you add quality checks that you require but that do not yet exist in the standard system.

CHAPTER 1

Why Object-Oriented Programming Is a Must for Code Quality

Did you know that object-oriented (hereafter OO) programming was introduced to SAP as far back as the year 2000 in the form of ABAP Objects? Ergo, there are some people at work who are younger than the ABAP Objects language.

Let us say for the sake of argument that a programming career lasts 50 years. Furthermore, you would expect during the 20 years that OO ABAP has been around that every new programmer joining would want to program in an OO language, as that is what they encountered at university. Given those two "facts," you would expect that even if zero percent of die-hard ABAP people had decided to switch to OO programming in 2000, nevertheless at least 40 percent of new code would be written in an OO manner purely because of all the new people. However, things don't work like that in real life.

Something that might surprise you is this screenshot from the "questions" section of the SAP Community website shown in Figure 1-1.

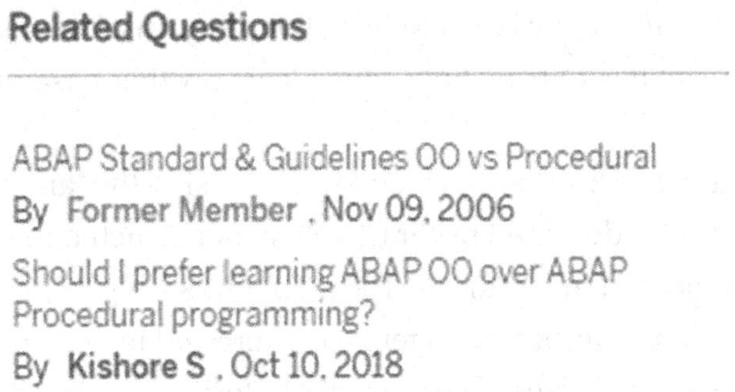

Related Questions

ABAP Standard & Guidelines OO vs Procedural
By Former Member . Nov 09, 2006

Should I prefer learning ABAP OO over ABAP Procedural programming?
By Kishore S . Oct 10, 2018

Figure 1-1. SAP Community website questions

© Paul David Hardy 2021
P. D. Hardy, *Improving the Quality of ABAP Code*, https://doi.org/10.1007/978-1-4842-6711-0_1

Clearly even in 2018 new programmers were unsure whether or not to learn procedural or OO programming techniques in ABAP. Even in the year 2021, you still get blogs on the SAP Community website with titles like, "I have a hard time getting my head around anything OO."

As another example, last month my boss came to me with a question about test-driven development (a subject you will hear about in Chapter 2). What he wanted to know was this: "Can this approach be used with 'normal' programming?" You might be horrified to hear that he considers procedural programming to be "normal." Even worse—he is 100 percent correct. It is still the normal way that ABAP programs get written.

To try and explain why this is the case, this chapter starts with possible reasons why OO has never really taken off in the ABAP world, then moves on to a discussion of the theoretical benefits of OO programming, centered around the example of a global SAP rollout. Next comes my personal journey in regard to making the switch from procedural to OO programming. The chapter ends with how you can benefit from making a similar switch, based on some concrete practical (as opposed to theoretical) benefits OO programming can bring, and therefore why it is a must to really improve your code quality.

Why OO Has Never Taken Off in ABAP World

Sometimes you read a statement that you disagree with for some reason or another. Sometimes you read a statement you disagree with so much it makes you laugh out loud, and you wonder how anyone could say such a thing and keep a straight face. In my case, the least true statement I ever read was, "ABAP Objects is better than procedural programming because it is easier to learn." That quote came from the SAP Press book *ABAP Programming Guidelines* by Horst Keller. Obviously, just because I don't believe something, doesn't mean it isn't true, but I can at least say that has not been my personal experience.

I learned procedural programming when I was 14, using the language BASIC on the UK computer the ZX81, designed by Sir Clive Sinclair, which had a grand total of 1K memory and was released in, naturally, 1981. That was a big thing in the United Kingdom that year; a load of young teenagers got interested in computers when they would never have even thought about such things before.

Anyway, grasping the idea of procedures rather than writing every command in a big, long line—which some people still do in ABAP to this very day—made perfect sense to my young self; I got the idea within the hour.

Fast forward from 1981 to 1999, when I first encountered ABAP on an SAP implementation in Tel Aviv. I was a functional consultant back then, and my assigned ABAP person got sacked, so I asked the powers that be if I could finish off the data-conversion programs he was writing. ABAP did not look that different from BASIC to me. Naturally, everything was procedural back then, and by the end of the first day I had gotten my head around SAP-specific features like internal tables, header lines, and FORM routines. The learning curve was not steep in the slightest.

Conversely, I made my first attempts at OO programming about the year 2006 and made a right mess of it. After six years, I was still struggling with the basics. If I look back at some of the OO code I wrote then, I am horrified. Even in 2020 I am still discovering new things. Maybe my brain has become fossilized; when you are 14 you are much more open to new ideas.

One thing I can say for sure is that poorly written OO code is a million times worse than poorly written procedural code. I recall a colleague who had never heard of OO looking at my terrible OO code at the time and saying, "Mr. Paul, this is not the way forward!" He got put off by looking at the rubbish I had written, thought that must be what OO code is like always, and thus never looked twice at OO again.

However, not all OO code is terrible, so the question becomes—why is it so difficult to explain the benefits of OO to people? If something is clearly better than something else, then it should be obvious—it should sell itself.

Perhaps it is down to some of the articles I have read entitled, "Ten Reasons to Use OO ABAP Programming," where a lot of the reasons come down to "because I said so" or "because it is better, but I won't tell you why because it is obvious." Neither of those reasons on their own is going to entice someone to make the jump.

It has been a source of great frustration to many in the SAP world that most programmers have stuck with procedural programming and refuse to convert to OO programming despite the "obvious" benefits. They feel like they are trying to convince people the Earth is not flat. That reminds me of the time I was at an SAP conference in Melbourne and an SAP expert came up with the ever-popular theory that there were no moon landings.

As another, non-moon-related example, I have seen my fair share of business analysts debugging, and one (in Germany) even told me, "I can follow whatever you write as long as it is not that object-oriented nonsense." They actually used a somewhat stronger term than "nonsense."

I think procedural programming will be with us for a *long* time, as the longer something sticks around the harder it becomes to dislodge.

A common claim is that OO programs are more difficult to maintain. Since 99 percent of development effort revolves around the maintenance of existing programs, if that statement were true then of course no one would use OO programming. However, all the academic articles claim that the entire benefit of OO is that it makes programs *easier* to maintain.

You cannot have it both ways—either OO programming does in fact make existing programs easier to fix or enhance, or it doesn't.

I will make my position clear: After many experiments and actual use cases in my live system—as opposed to any sort of theory—I have become a convert. However, I am not going to say, "It is good because I said so." I am hopefully going to give some real-life examples as to what influenced my thinking and, more important, what I have actually seen working in a live system and concrete reasons why this works better than what I used to do before (which also worked well). That last one is often the killer; i.e., it works fine, so no need to change, a.k.a. "do not mess with a running system." The running system in this case is not a given program but rather the methodology of writing new programs.

If you try to explain a concept to someone and they just do not understand, then often the best approach is to try again using some sort of analogy—that is just how the human brain works.

I once had a work colleague who was a quarry manager. When his daughter got to the age where she was able to ask what he did for a living, he said, "I dig big holes in the ground." That's accurate enough and something a child can clearly understand. However, then he got put on the project team for the global SAP rollout—how do you explain that to a young child? His answer was thus: "Now I invent ways to dig BETTER holes in the ground."

That worked a treat. Is it possible to convince anyone that object-oriented programming is a better way to dig a hole?

Any sort of proposed solution makes no sense without a concrete example. I could invent an artificial one, but it occurred to me that it would be better if I used one from my own company, provided I don't expose any trade secrets. The example I picked was one that most SAP people would be very familiar with—that of global SAP rollouts.

I could describe my career as seven years as an end user, followed by two years as a business analyst followed by twenty-one years as a developer. During that time, I have been on assorted SAP implementation projects all around the world. Here, at least, I am on solid ground. Everywhere I went I saw the same thing, and no doubt anyone who has been through a global SAP rollout will have as well.

There is a nice big word I like called *dichotomy* where two things are totally different. In this case, the global head office moves heaven and earth to come up with a global template that will describe the business process all around the world and cater for all eventualities. This, in theory, cannot go wrong, because in the best case "we asked every country and they told us what they do," or in the worst case "they will have to accept the global template, like it or not, as it is best practice."

I can see people shuddering whenever they hear the words *best practice*, but leaving that aside, what you end up with is some sort of diagram in VISIO or some such, which you give to a project team in each country and say, "This is what your system should do, implement this as close as you can." You know what happens. Each country feels the global diagram is not for them, creates their own, and implements based upon that. Or you can have a model like Nestlé used to have where all changes are done in a central place. That has problems of its own, but just say you do not want to do that—soon you have ten countries all on the "global template," each with its own program for doing the same business process, all within the same SAP instance.

You may say there is no such animal, but I have seen this again and again.

And then you are halfway through, or even finished, and it occurs to you that having all these duplicates is not optimal. Well, it's too late, is it not? Too late to recover the situation without a major, incredibly risky rework. Or is it?

If there is something you do not know, then there is always someone who does, and this is one of the major bonuses of the internet. If you can filter out the nonsense, there is always useful advice about anything, and advice as to how using OO can help out in such situations is no exception.

At the end of this chapter, you will find the "recommended reading"—books and articles that I read that enabled me to get my head around what OO was really about and why it was good.

After about the twentieth IT article I read on the subject, I was reminded of when I was 16 and studying A-level economics in the United Kingdom. All the exercises were on different parts of the economy, and one day it suddenly popped into my head how they all fit together, and I shouted to the world, "*NOW I UNDERSTAND HOW THE ECONOMY WORKS!*" Wonderful. So why have I never been chancellor of the Exchequer?

Obviously, what we were studying then was a very simplified model of the economy, so getting my head around it was not such a huge achievement as I imagined. I had a similar revelation about how OO programming fits into the grand scheme of things, and that is the "A-ha!" moment I want every single procedural ABAP programmer to encounter.

OO Benefits: The Theory

In the very first SAP ABAP training course I attended, when OO programming was (very briefly) mentioned, the instructor made much of the fact that OO was a code-based representation of the real world. I find it is more like a cartoon version of the real world, one in which all the objects like materials and sales orders "talk" to each other.

Modeling the real world in a program is supposed to be a good thing as it makes the program easier to understand—even by (gasp) a businessperson. It's all well and good to make such a claim, but it's a bit abstract. In this section, I am going to try to explain the idea using an example that many ABAP programmers would find familiar: designing programs for use in a global SAP rollout.

We'll start off by talking about how you describe the design of an OO program using a diagram, and then move on to the theory of how to use this to design an OO ABAP program that reflects a business process that exists in the real world.

Describing OO Programs: UML

After I posted my first blog on the SAP Community website in 2012 expressing a desire to get my head around OO programming, one of the responses was that as a first step I should learn the UML. What's that? It stands for Unified Modeling Language. That is not a programming language but rather a way of describing the various moving parts of an OO program and how they all fit together to solve a business problem.

Oh no! This is moving out of the programming silo and looking at the entire business process as a whole. It is often said that programmers should not care about the high-level details, should not care about the "big picture," as Americans describe it, but should just blindly obey the technical specification. That's a bit glib, but I have met programmers who feel just that way, and business analysts who feel that is the way programmers should behave.

There was no separate "language" (apart from flowcharts, which are not really a language) to describe procedural programming, because some procedural languages were invented specifically to read like a book, hence the programming language was self-documenting. COBOL, parts of PL/I, and ABAP all exhibit this characteristic. Because of this, it may seem really strange that there *is* a "language" you need to know to properly understand OO programming. Nonetheless, I did want to have such an understanding, so UML sounded like a good place to start. Thus, I downloaded the book *UML Distilled* by Martin Fowler. Luckily, it was really funny as well as informative.

As of the year 2020, the UML is 23 years old— happy birthday to it—but clearly reading things from "ages" ago still helps one to understand the way SAP (amongst others) has designed things, and indeed the way OO programs should be designed in theory.

As an example, when I tried to design a program (to let a user in SAP create purchase orders via SAP Ariba) according to the guidelines in all the SAP press books I had read, and then put the result into a pseudo-UML diagram, it came out looking like the one in Figure 1-2.

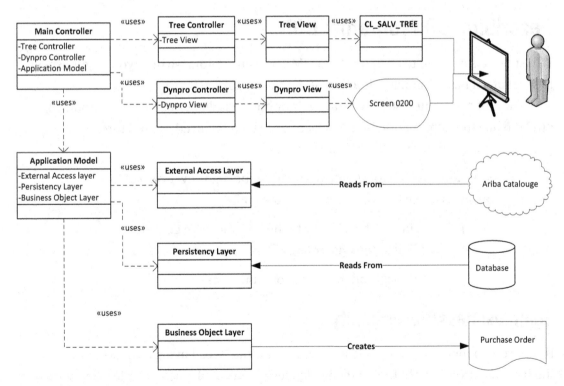

***Figure 1-2.** Pseudo UML diagram*

Without going into minute detail, what this diagram is supposed to show is the "separation of concerns"—the rectangular boxes represent classes dealing with one thing only, while the other shapes (e.g., human in front of a screen) are non-OO artifacts that the classes interact with.

As I am never satisfied and always curious, I noticed that UML was once, a long time ago, only one of many competing standards on how to draw pretty pictures of OO programs. This is somewhat like BETAMAX competing with VHS and VIDEO2000 (for younger readers, these were all different technologies to record TV programs onto video cassettes back around 1985). There is only ever one winner in these cases, and UML won that battle, in the same way VHS did despite BETAMAX's being deemed better by many people. There were also three competing flat-screen TV technologies, if that makes it any easier, though of course some people will ask, "Haven't TVs always been flat?" I think I will give up.

Still, I had a look at one of the competitors to UML from that period called BON (Business Object Notation), and I am very glad I did, as it revolves around some important concepts.

Describing OO Programs: BON

Whilst BON is claimed to be better than UML by its inventors—whom you might expect to say that—it has never had a fraction of the success of UML.

I was not much interested in a way to draw business diagrams that never took off, but I did like the introduction in the BON book, which revolved around three principles—also embodied in UML, no doubt:

1. Seamlessness, or how to make sure that the high-level view of the business process related directly to the code.

2. Reversibility, in which a change to the lower level (e.g., code) could be applied to the higher level.

3. Design by contract (and, by extension, unit tests)

Seamlessness/Reversibility

If you were to mention the seamless/reversible points—i.e., having a consistent view of the business process right from a really high level down to the actual code—SAP would tell you they have this nailed. They would have told you this for quite a long time, as it turns out. I could not say whether this is a true statement, either now or in the past. In all but one of the SAP implementations I have been on, VISIO was the tool of choice for the business process diagrams, the exception being the last one I was on, where I did not see one flowchart of any form; everything was described in text in big, thick documents.

Like many things at SAP, the representation of high-level business processes within a computer has gone through quite a lot of iterations. A product called ARIS by IDS Scheer was the business process modeling tool of choice for a long while, with integration into Solution Manager, which in turn integrated into the operational SAP system. Nowadays, you have SAP BPML (Business Process Master List) or whatever it is called this week, based on an open-standards business process modeling language.

Seamlessness via an Automated Tool

The utopian idea is that you have some sort of automated software whereby you can generate a code template out of the high-level design, or conversely generate the high-level diagram out of the source code. The idea of all this is that if the system (source code) changes then the high-level diagram also has to change and vice versa, and if you can easily push the changes from one to the other then everything is seamless.

People will say, "Of course you can do that." One of my colleagues tells me that "they" were claiming that was possible in the days that he programmed by using punch cards. Certainly, I have encountered two different tools that are supposed to generate ABAP classes from a UML model, and from SE80 you can call up a UML diagram of an existing program.

However, neither of the two tools to generate ABAP code from a UML diagram worked as well as one might hope, and there was never enough interest from the ABAP community in such a concept, so they never caught on, and both were abandoned.

So, it looks like even if you have the most wonderful UML diagram in the world, you have to write the code for it yourself.

One of the principles we are talking about—seamlessness—says that the most important thing is that the names of classes in the code match the names in the big diagram (which they would if they were automatically generated), and when those class names in turn match names in the real world, fine. Then the obvious questions is this: What are those names exactly?

Seamlessness via Naming Conventions

In Chapter 3, you will hear about Clarity. I have always been a big advocate of making the code self-documenting by naming things clearly, from variables up to class names.

It has been said there are only two difficult things in programming: what to name things, caching, and off-by-one errors. If you understood that joke then you are already a programmer at heart, but the problem with naming things is not a trivial one.

At the very minimum, if you can get the class names the same as boxes in the very highest-level business process design, then hooray. If everything is named something different, then that would make the automatic propagation of one level forward or backward difficult, one would think.

Design by Contract

The third aspect of BON was "design by contract," which is all to do with what each part of a system expects before it can execute and what it promises to deliver. Initially, I thought that was more to do with how you write the code than the higher-level design, but apparently this is supposed to be done right at the start. The "contract" is an integral part of what the high-level object does and it can and should be defined right at the start as a real-world concept, as opposed to the actual implementation in a software system.

At the end of the chapter there is a link to the original article about design by contract by Bertrand Mayer, which I strongly advise you to read. I will give a brief summary here.

In essence, the "contract" defines what any given routine needs to be given in order to function properly, and what that routine needs to give back in return. This concept is built into the EIFFEL programming language and is an integral part of the signature of a method; i.e., in effect, a check is done at the start and end of every routine, and those checks are written by the programmer in special sections before the code starts and just before it ends inside the routine.

The checks in the "contracts" are not looking for behavioral errors (that's what unit tests look for) but are instead looking for clear errors in the structure of the program; i.e., whether the various parts of the program are not working together correctly.

It may seem strange that I only started learning about computer science 15 years after programming day-to-day in a real business environment, but I find it fascinating and picked up all sorts of useful things. I thought the design by contract thing was so good I instantly tried to work out how to apply it in an ABAP environment; more on that in Chapter 2, but most of the concepts can be used.

To most ABAP programmers, this may seem like a back-to-front way of doing things. Normally, you code all your checks whilst writing the actual code in the routines. Now the idea is that such checks are written first, and as you will see the same concept applies to unit tests, because both the checks and the tests define the high-level nature of your overall system.

Design by Unit Tests

Some people (e.g., Robert Martin) have said the best way to come up with a high-level design is by writing unit tests.

You will hear a lot more about unit tests in Chapter 2, but in this context the idea is that you can tell if your high-level design is correct because you can compose tests for it—on paper or in your head. The logic seems to be that if you can't think of what tests to write then you can't visualize how the finished system will look even vaguely, so most likely you don't actually know what it is that you want. I'd like to stress the word *vaguely*, as in my experience a lot of people don't really know exactly what they want until you show them a prototype based on their initial specification, and after looking at the prototype become 100 percent sure they want the opposite.

In this case—looking at an existing process that has been in place for ages—we know what we want because it is what we do at the moment. In addition, we have hundreds of tests that we perform every time we have a support-stack application, or an upgrade, don't we? I hope we do. These tests may be automated, e.g., via HPQC or ECATT; or may be manual, i.e., written down on Word documents or spreadsheets; or may be in people's heads, but they are known.

So, if taking existing tests into account gives you a better higher-level system design, then we should be laughing.

What if we haven't got any existing tests? Another thing that I do on every project I go through is to get a list of the areas that are different, because those differences had to be programmed, and all such changes were documented (weren't they?). So, for every difference, the test is "can this program do THIS here and THAT there and choose the correct option in the correct situation?"

In one sense you have the highest-level design, which you would expect to be considered at the very start of the project, based on what is often considered the very last step in the process—i.e., testing. I stress once again that the tests are all designed before anyone has even dreamed about looking at thinking about how the requirements will be realized. This sort of backward thinking can make certain people's heads spin so hard they fall off. It's like saying that the Earth rotates around the sun, and Copernicus will tell you the price you have to pay for suggesting such heretical ideas.

However, if we can avoid being burnt at the stake, then using our vast catalog of existing test cases we can build the best high-level UML model in the world.

Once again, we have the idea of seamlessness—if you base the high-level design upon a set of tests written on paper, and at the very end of the process have the low-level code validated by the code equivalents of those very same tests, then you have hit the first two aspects of the BON design: seamlessness and reversibility. The latter comes because if you change a low-level test you are in effect changing the high-level design.

Anyway, at one stage there were competing standards as to how to describe an OO program using a diagram, and there was one clear winner, which was UML. What the various approaches agreed on is that you start the OO program design ball rolling by drawing a high-level diagram. So, let's apply this to the global SAP rollout example.

Designing a Worldwide OO Program

In my experience, however you model the high-level business process, even if it is just in your head, you can be 100 percent certain of one thing. As soon as you present the "global business process" to any country they will say:

"We don't do it like that here."

Then, the target country will move Heaven and Earth to prove to you how different they really are, often coming up with "laws" you cannot find in any statute book, and which are different from the way their competitors do the same thing in that country, and which mysteriously match the way they have always done things. I wonder how much effort hundreds of companies have expended over the years fighting this battle. It's like trying to get accountants to stop using Excel.

At one SAP conference in Melbourne, Australia, the CIO of Pabst Brewing Company in the United States (who was an Australian, by the way) talked about "shadow IT" and how the business goes off behind the backs of the real IT department and does its own thing. His point seemed to be no matter how hard you try you can't stop this, so you may as well turn around and harness it and try to turn it to your own advantage. This is the martial arts approach of using your enemy's strength to benefit yourself.

So, to recap the central problem, the head office would like everything the same, but each country would like everything different. There are lots of ways you can deal with this; e.g., fire everyone who disagrees. This could be rather like hitting moles over the head though, with the new "loyal" people reverting to country-specific behavior the moment your back is turned.

You would think that from an IT perspective I would be shouting out about having everything the same—the good old "best practice" that SAP always talked about; i.e., "Do it this way, it does not fit your business process at all, but it is *BEST PRACTICE*." It must be best practice because that is the way SAP wrote it, like not being able to expense a purchase order with multiple account assignments at time of goods receipt. They called this best practice, but every single accountant in the world vehemently disagreed, and so after many years SAP was forced to change the software to match the real business process.

In real life you have to accept that in the end each country is going to be implementing their processes inside SAP very differently regardless of how similar the processes are in real life, so the question becomes, how can you code that in the best way? It helps that *really* the differences are nowhere near as big as everyone thinks.

The next step is finding common ground.

There are some people who would argue with you if you told them grass was green, but generally there must be something people will agree on that is the same between countries. How about the name of the company?

I am lucky in my industry—building materials. If I worked making 3D printers or in some such industry where the product did not even exist until recently then the variances would be quite dramatic. Luckily, concrete has been made the same way since the days of the Roman empire, and when it comes to quarries the ancient Egyptians, or even Fred Flintstone, were not doing anything dramatically different than what we do today, leaving technology aside. I do not, however, get to slide down a brontosaurus neck when I finish work for the day. I have to take the elevator. And they call that progress?

In a quarry, the high-level business process could be described as shown in Figure 1-3.

Figure 1-3. *High-level business process*

For 30 years I have been to quarries all over the United Kingdom, Australia, and Israel, and the preceding diagram looks right to me based on my observations. Most probably everyone from every country would agree this is how they do things; you are not really giving them anything to argue with. So it is just a question of expanding one box at a time, as shown in Figure 1-4.

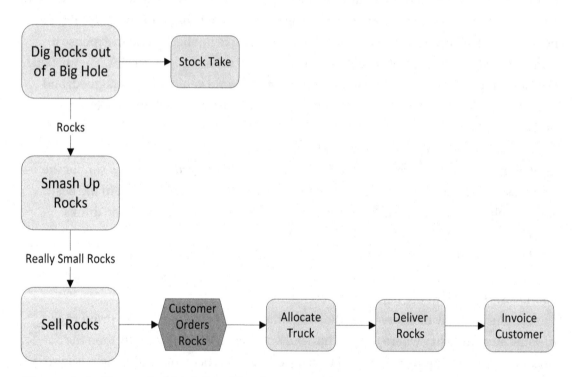

Figure 1-4. *Expanded high-level business process*

A stock take is a physical inventory of goods, by the way. Anyway, when presenting the expanded process to someone you most likely would not get much argument about that either, but as you expand the level of detail, at some point, sooner rather than later, someone will shout, "STOP—I don't do things that way." So, as a gross oversimplification, you could say that one level above that point is your global unified business process.

At that point, you have reached what is known as an inflection point—what could be described as the calm bit on a rollercoaster before it drops a hundred feet in one second. That is, if we move our lovely simple diagram down one level, it is going to fragment into a million different variations on the theme.

I stress once again that I am oversimplifying, but as you will see I am aiming this more at writing programs than project management, on the grounds that in my own mind at least I know how to write programs but have about as much knowledge of project management as a penguin has about the Large Hadron Collider.

If you encounter any sort of really complicated problem, then the first step is to see if anyone before you has had the same sort of problem, and, if so, whether they solved it and how. This is why you have SAP customers at events like SAPPHIRE get up on stage to share their "war stories" with anyone else thinking about going down the same path.

One evening, I read something that I imagine most people who know about object-oriented design read on their first day studying the subject. It was called "Heuristics and Coffee" by Robert C. Martin from his book *UML for Java Programmers*. There is a link to this in the "Recommended Reading" section at the end of the chapter.

That article made perfect sense to me, even if the language used is Java. Java is a lot less verbose than ABAP, but after a quick browse through the book *Thinking in Java* by Bruce Eckel, Java no longer seems that alien. Some Java constructs even look the same as the BASIC language I used in 1981, which is quite ironic as it means I have come full circle.

Examples that everyone can understand are the strength of articles like "Heuristics and Coffee," where the author is using the example of designing a program to control a specific type of coffee machine, and thus is talking about how in OO programming you have an intrinsic separation of core and details. I have heard this expressed as separating the "things that change from the things that stay the same."

I think that is a perfect match for my situation, where you would want to design the whole system with the so-called best practice logic that never changes in the middle and the gritty details of each country hovering around the outside, as shown in Figure 1-5.

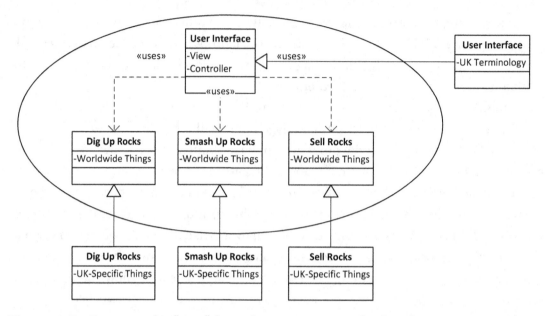

Figure 1-5. *Separate the "core" from the country-specific details*

I apologize for my haphazard use of UML. No doubt the preceding diagram breaks all the rules, but hopefully you get the idea—this is my version of the coffee-maker diagram. The "user interface" box at the top is a compressed view of what could be dozens of different programs dealing with assorted areas of the business. Some would be standard SAP; some would be site-customized programs. As we will see, these can be treated in the exact same way. I specifically mention "UK Terminology" as many countries call the exact same thing by a different name; more on this later.

As far as I can see, the whole OO concept is about trying to move things either inside or outside the ellipse with no two-way dependency between them, so that you can change the details of one box outside the ellipse without affecting anything else. In some senses, the whole point of good OO design is to remove dependencies; this is known as dependency inversion, in which the concrete implementation (e.g., UK way of smashing rocks) depends on the abstract idea and not vice versa; i.e., the WHAT is 100 percent independent from the HOW.

Now, unless you are a startup and there is no existing code, you will find you are in a position where you have to change the existing system state to the newly designed "utopian" state, and, as the Irish like to say, "You can't get there from here."

In this theoretical example (which is not really theoretical at all as I am basing everything on something I actually had to do in real life), you start off with a system that is nothing like the preceding diagram and have to move it from one country to another, with consideration for many more countries to come. To achieve that task, you have to look at the following three areas:

- What is the existing system state?

- Why is the existing system state not "portable"?

- What can be done about fixing that portability problem?

What Is the Existing System State?

After reading all the articles offering high-level visions of how to structure a system full of computer programs in a wonderfully elegant manner using assorted design patterns until you get a utopian vision of perfection, I was quite happy to read an article called "Big Ball of Mud" (reference at the end of the chapter), which notes that in real life 99 percent of computer systems are big, sprawling messes that violate every one of these academic rules.

I was quite relieved to hear that, as virtually every type of system I had seen was like that big ball, and thus typical in every way. It is not even bad, in and of itself—after all, it works, but it can be improved, which is what this book is about.

The next question becomes, "Why is a big ball of mud bad?" to which the answer is, "It is not portable." What does that mean?

Why Is the Existing System State Not Portable?

The best way to answer that is to use an example from a 100 percent standard SAP system.

Older standard SAP programs could be described as big balls of mud as well, with monolithic programs like the sales order creation program (SAPMV45A) having tentacles out to totally unrelated parts of the system. For example, one of my colleagues was puzzled to discover that one of the form-based user exits from SAPMV45A was called during the MM transaction MIRO whilst verifying a supplier invoice. Who would have thought the two areas of the system were related?

It is very common to find a standard SAP function module that looks standalone and does something really useful, think "that is just what I want," and reuse it in a custom program. SAP will say, "Don't do that, that function module is not released for customers," but the developer will think, "Hardly any function modules are released for customers, and they don't change much after an upgrade, and anyway this WORKS and my deadline is next week," so in it goes. A fine example is module VIEW_KUAGV, which gives you a list of ship-tos for a customer. A really useful module, it has worked a treat for 12 years in one of our custom programs. It is not released for customer use, but, as I said, it works so all was well.

Then one day, out of the blue, in the development system, that function stopped returning any values at all, seemingly at random. That new (wrong) behavior was only in development, which meant something had changed, and when that change made it to production we would be sunk. It took me weeks of tinkering to find a pattern, and when I did find a pattern I could not believe my eyes.

It turned out that this "standalone" SD function module started returning no values directly after I released a certain sort of purchase order. Two seemingly unrelated areas of the standard SAP system were influencing each other. I found if I logged off and logged back on again then the problem vanished, so it must have been something in memory. It turned out that function VIEW_KUAGV uses a PARAMETER ID to determine if the system is running in batch, in conjunction with system variables like SY-BATCH, but if the PARAMETER ID says you are running batch, then no list is returned if you are online. In standard SAP code, the module is never called without expressly setting the PARAMETER ID to online when you are online. If your site-customized program tries to call some BAPIs online (there is no pattern), you are supposed to clear the parameter first by calling function DIALOG_SET_NO_DIALOG. The function VIEW_KUAGV is not a BAPI but it acted like one in that it required the PID to be cleared before calling the function.

What has happening here was that a purchase order was getting released, and somehow (due to a user exit) that set the PARAMETER ID to say batch mode had been invoked, and somehow that did not get cleared.

This is an argument for not using the "unreleased" standard functions in your site-customized programs (or even some of the released ones) as they may have such hidden dependencies upon the system state. A PARAMETER ID is a global variable in the truest sense—any program the user accesses during their session can set the value, so if this is used to control program flow there is no way of predicting how the function will behave at any given instant.

The obvious moral is that we need to write applications that have no such "hidden" dependencies, and ideally as few obvious ones as possible. Otherwise, if you transplant your program into a different environment, even if it worked perfectly in the source system, it is likely to do all sorts of strange things in the target system.

Put another way, the more dependencies a program has, the less portable it is.

What Can Be Done About Fixing That Problem?

To recap, in this example, a complicated existing system of site-customized programs has been built in the traditional monolithic style, and they need to be copied into another country's SAP system as-is. Time is so tight, as it always is, that totally redesigning a system that took ten years to build is not really an option.

Here is the process I followed when I had to deal with this exact situation. It can be summarized as follows:

- Breaking Dependencies in General — What is a dependency and why do you need to break it?

- Breaking Dependencies via Packages — What is a "package" in ABAP and how can it help?

- Breaking Dependencies via Interfaces — What is an "interface" in ABAP and how can it help?

- Not Breaking the System in the Process — By changing everything slowly but surely

Breaking Dependencies in General

Since it is not possible to redesign everything, the next best thing is to remove as many dependencies as possible and put new or changed code into new classes, but usually this is just scratching the tip of the iceberg.

As an example dependency, one thing that occurred to me as I drew Figure 1-5, where the core process was inside an ellipse, was that by *UK Terminology* I don't just mean using SY-LANGU when outputting messages and the like to the user interface. It has become very clear to me while working for my company around the world that even when two countries speak English they use different terms to say the same thing. As might be imagined, some of the worst differences are between the United Kingdom and the United States—"two countries separated by a common language," as they say.

For example, in the United Kingdom we might say "truck and trailer" or "dustbin," in Australia "truck and dog" or "garbage bin," and in the United States "truck and pup" or "trash can." The underlying physical nature of those objects is identical in all countries, and so the computer system should think of them in the same way, but when a computer is trying to talk to humans it needs to consider which country they live in.

The point I am trying to make is that all the custom programs that need to be ported are *crawling* with dependencies. Happily, as a first step, it is possible to remove a lot of those dependencies whilst staying 100 percent procedural.

This is in fact what I did. I made minor changes to all our custom programs in preparation for transplanting them to different countries. Dependencies—or, more accurately, assumptions—turned out to be all over our custom programs like a rash. I went through them all with a fine-toothed comb and extracted as many as I could find. You start off with the obvious ones like hard-coded language and currency, then hard-coded organizational units, and work your way up to hard-coded "magic numbers" (e.g., IF X = 53, where you have no idea what 53 means) and customizing values (e.g., material group 0010 means eggs in one country, but 0010 means bacon in another).

I got as far as moving a fair few of the business rules (large chunks of conditional logic) to site-customized tables. There is even a dedicated standard SAP Tool, BRF Plus, for abstracting complicated business rules from the main program, but at the time it was not yet available in my system.

I was also under the *mistaken* impression that you could not abstract everything (abstracting something = removing a dependency) as then there would be no program left. Earlier, you heard about the idea of a seamless connection between the description of the business process and the actual code in the program, and during the course of this book you will see that the more abstractions you have the closer this exotic concept gets to becoming a reality.

I did manage to migrate a grand total of one application into a fully OO design, and didn't people back home (i.e., from the country where the source system was) squawk about that! They had no idea what I was doing and thought I was a madman. It worked like a charm though. I did the redesign before I went overseas, and when the time came to adapt the application for another country (i.e., install the application in the target SAP system) I created a subclass into which I put all the changed bits, and that was like falling off a log, everything that was promised.

Then after I left, the programmers in the new country looked at this strange OO thing, decided they didn't like it, and got rid of it and created a procedural replacement, but that is probably because it was my first attempt at OO and I did not do it well enough.

Nonetheless, the point is that I was able to (fairly painlessly) migrate a very large number of applications from one system to another by removing as many dependencies as I could. However, the end code in the source and target systems was still nowhere near the ideal state mentioned in all the academic articles. Is that ideal state an impossible target?

After a while, the next country rollout will start in the target system where the migrated code just arrived, and chances are that it will involve copying programs into new versions (i.e., one new version per country) and changing each country-specific program individually, so they gradually diverge over time. In other words, things are just going to get worse and worse, with more and more dependencies added—just what I wanted to avoid. The obvious conclusion is that it is too late, and there is no way back. Fair enough, but let's just say, for argument's sake, that we do not want this to happen; instead, we want to somehow improve our code over time. That's not easy.

I noticed the other day that a 14-year-old won some sort of huge medical prize for inventing a new way to scan for cancer. Why did he discover this and not some adult? You could say it is because he is a prodigy, and he probably is, but more than that, when you are young you don't yet know what is not possible. You haven't yet had time to have lots of people say to you, "You can't do this, you can't do that, so don't even bother."

So, I might think such a task (fixing an entire system to make it optimal) is impossible, but what if I play a mental game and pretend all the practical (and, more important, political) problems do not exist; how would I go about totally redesigning the system, for the better, whilst causing no business disruption at all? "That's impossible!" Hang on, we are not allowed to say that in this game.

What do we have already? We have a high-level diagram of the business process, which is broken down into many small Visio diagrams (or whatever) showing all the sub-processes. Many people sweated blood and tears creating them during the early part of the huge ERP implementation project.

That is what a "waterfall" project is all about: having a big bunch of deliverables at the end of each stage that are supposed to form the starting point of the next stage, and maybe they do. I notice the academic articles were writing off waterfall projects as early as 1999 or maybe before, but waterfall projects are still as popular as hot cakes as far as I can see. Just for the record, the agile method (breaking a project into multiple short iterations, each delivering a small number of working changes) seems clearly better to me than waterfall (everything at once after two years), but when I attended a technology focus group in Australia (where people from lots of companies come together) some years back and the facilitator mentioned the agile methodology, I was the only one in the room who knew what he was talking about.

Anyway, we have this high-level business process diagram. Because it is high level and (if done well, which it was) is not related to any specific software system (because it was created before SAP was even selected to be the ERP system) it is a representation of the real world. As such, it does not vary very much over time and corresponds to the central part of the UML models we discussed earlier; i.e., the part "inside the ellipse" that does not relate to nitty gritty implementation details.

This can conceivably be converted into the actual UML diagram equivalent with all the abstractions around the outside of the ellipse that will "plug in" the country-specific implementations to the core system.

This begs the question—how exactly do you tell your ABAP system what lives inside and outside of the "ellipse"?

Breaking Dependencies via Packages

This is an aspect of code quality that will come as quite a surprise to many ABAP programmers.

In other languages, such as Java, the package concept is vitally important. The equivalent concept in ABAP does not appear to be important at all, and thus gets ignored all too often.

Back in the year 2000, clients on SAP projects had no idea of the purpose of packages in SAP. The consultants didn't either, and I am not even sure SAP did. The consultants at the start of the project would try to jam custom objects into arbitrary packages like "ZSD" or "ZMM," but that made no sense at all in an integrated system given that so few things are actually used by only one module. When the consultants hired at my site finally left, we naturally thought that, since packages had no purpose or meaning, we should put all new objects in one big package called ZENGENERIC. I did that for years. Oh dear.

In SAP it is possible to toggle all sorts of settings in a package to control what objects in that package can be used by other packages—but only if certain system settings are active, which they usually are not. After all, there is no apparent benefit in doing so.

How it works is thus: in languages like Java the packages live in different files, whereas in ABAP every single thing lives in the one database so you can access every single thing at once. In Java you have to specify what packages an application is dependent upon, and each of those packages will say what packages they need in turn, so all these dependencies get loaded at compile time. ABAP does not work like that at all, so why bother, apart from maybe classifying your code as an academic exercise?

Here are some reasons why it is important.

If you work at an independent software company that makes add-ons that you sell to SAP customers, none of this will be news to you. You have your own namespace and your own package hierarchy consisting of mostly objects in your own namespace, and you cannot refer to any objects in a standard SAP package unless you are 100 percent certain that object will exist in every system in which your software is to be installed.

If you program using the ABAP development tools (ADT, a.k.a. ABAP in Eclipse), when you first installed it you may have been puzzled as to why one of the first things it asked you was what your favorite packages were. That is because finding what you want to edit in Eclipse is generally done by navigating through a package hierarchy, as that is how other languages do it.

Nowadays, we have abapGit, which is used to transport open source ABAP software between systems, or possibly your own site-customized software between different SAP systems in your own environment. To use this properly—with all the advantages of Git as a source control system—you have to, in effect, pretend you are in a Java system and start compartmentalizing your code properly and declaring dependencies. As an example, if my open source ABAP project that I want to share with the world depends on another ABAP open source project, I can declare that dependency in my source code, and abapGit will download the dependent project (i.e., packages) before it downloads my open source project. None of that would be possible without the proper usage of packages.

It is more than possible to build your elegant hierarchy of packages, and the abstract or empty concrete classes within them, without touching anything at all in the working system. You can play around with the design until the result is a thing of exquisite beauty like the Sistine Chapel. Enjoy it while it lasts, because as soon as a battle plan comes into contact with the enemy it goes all over the place.

The next task is reclassifying all the existing objects, which will be labeled as an utter waste of time (where does that add business value, etc.?), but as I said, we ignore all obstacles for now. If a custom object is only used in one package of your wonderful design then the reclassification is easy. If a program or function or even class is so monolithic that you find yourself stuck as to choosing one of several places it could go, that is a clue it is doing too much and should be redesigned, so leave it where it is for now.

Breaking Dependencies via Interfaces

If the whole point of OO programming is to break dependencies by moving the implementation details (code) of specific countries outside the "ellipse," then how would we do that in ABAP?

At first glance, it would seem that subclasses are the way to go; i.e., a UK-specific subclass for breaking up rocks that inherits from the generic superclass for breaking up rocks.

What I am trying to avoid is every country having its own program to handle each area of the business. Even if you were using country-specific subclasses you could still end up with one program per country that calls its own subclass. This would seem to rather defeat the whole point of the exercise, and the academics would say this violates the DRY (Don't Repeat Yourself) principle.

When I suggested on the SAP Community website to use subclasses I was quickly informed that inheritance is over-rated and that *interfaces* are the way to go. It took a long time to finally get my head around the purpose of an interface as it was such an alien concept to my procedural mind, but it turns out this is the 100 percent most important concept in OO programming, and ultimately it is the key to writing better programs.

What Is an Interface in OO Terms?

It is unfortunate that the term *interface* has so many meanings in the IT world. In ABAP you create a global interface using transaction SE24, and it starts with the letters ZIF_, but the concept is universal across programming languages. Coming from a procedural background, at first glance the following is going to make no sense at all.

When you write a FORM routine you have the signature at the top of the routine and then the code in the body of the routine, and you most likely have some global variables knocking about. That is business as usual.

When creating a class in ABAP, you have attributes (which look a bit like global variables) and methods with signatures (which look a bit like FORM routines), and the main difference is that for routines you have "definitions" that say what the method names and signatures are, and "implementations" that contain the code for those methods.

When creating an interface in ABAP you just do the definition part—you list a bunch of attributes and then a list of methods with signatures, but with no code behind this at all. What? Why would you do such a crazy thing? This is a question I often ask candidates at job interviews.

Let me put it like this: Let us just say I am going for interviews at various circuses for the job of a clown. At each interview I am giving the ringmaster my CV (resume), which lists some personal details, qualifications, and relevant job experience. In effect, I am declaring that this is my name and age, I have a red nose, and these are the clown-type things I can do; e.g., throw custard pies, get shot out of a cannon, and so forth.

Now, let us pretend that everybody is 100 percent truthful on their CV and can do all that they claim perfectly, and the ringmaster ends up with ten seemingly identical candidates, all with the same set of skills on their CV. In such a case it does not matter to the ringmaster *which* clown he hires, as long as that clown can do what is required, and they all can.

In ABAP terms, if I define a clown interface, then the name and age of the candidate are attributes, and the methods are various clown-type activities that can be performed. I do not need to specify what the name and age actually are, or how the various activities get performed—after all, every clown does their act a bit differently.

When an ABAP class "implements" an interface, it is declaring to the outside world what it wants the world to know about it (name, age, etc.) and what it can do (clown-type activities, for example). This could be a main class or a subclass. It doesn't matter. All that matters is that the class declares the interface and by doing that is in effect making a contract with the outside world that it can do all the things claimed by the interfaces it implements.

Unlike humans, ABAP routines cannot lie on their CV, and, in fact, we use the "design by contract" principle to ensure that each routine (method) does what it claims to do.

Then, in the core circus program, there is an internal table of clowns, each one typed not to a specific class (person or type of clown) but rather to the clown interface. At runtime (show time) each clown is filled dynamically; it does not matter to the calling program which exact clown is going to do the work, only that the clown can in fact do the work.

Thus, we can improve the internal working of a clown so that they do a better job (have bigger feet) or fix bugs in a clown's behavior (like their not being funny) or introduce a new type of clown, and the calling program does not have to change at all.

Moreover, if you were a circus clown at night and a Formula One racing driver in the day, then the class that represents you would implement two interfaces—the clown interface, which only the circus cares about as it requests clown-related behaviors, and the racing driver interface, which only the racetrack cares about as it requests racing driver–related behaviors.

How SAP Uses Interfaces to Manage User Exits

The BAdi/Enhancement framework is how SAP itself manages user exits that vary based on country or any other criteria for such things as industry solutions. If it's good enough for them, then it's good enough for me. The first time I applied an example on the internet to use on something I was doing in real life I was amazed at how many steps there were, but, looking back, that is clearly designed to isolate the core program from any harm that fiddling about with an individual implementation could cause.

Once you have designed your program to use interface reference variables that are dynamically filled with concrete classes at runtime, then you have the ability to use the "open/closed principle" of OO programming, which initially seems like Black Magic. The idea is to not change the source code of an existing program yet have it do new things anyway. Via this principle, the core program remains totally unchanged and you can plug in new countries and keep the country-specific logic isolated.

Open/Closed Principle   This concept will be cropping up all through this book. It's not really magic. One example would be if you have one class per country that implements the same interface, you can add a new class for a new country without changing any existing code. The calling program is "open" in that it can call the new class but "closed" in that it does not have to be changed in order to do so.

Not Breaking the System

If you changed every single line of code in the system, you would no doubt end up breaking everything, but that is not what I am advocating. Instead, the idea is to improve things during the normal course of your work—bug fixes and enhancements.

In Scotland there is a concept called Painting the Forth Bridge. In Sydney, Australia, it is Painting the Harbor Bridge, but the principal is identical—you paint the bridge from one end to the other, and when you finish it is already time to begin again where you started.

Any software system is like that. When my father asked me what it was I did for a living, I tried to explain, and he said, "That is not very safe—what happens when all the users are happy?" Well, you would think that the Garden of Eden was a well-designed system, but the users weren't entirely happy there either. Even back then people wanted the latest Apple product (I'm sure that joke has been made a million times).

So, I am willing to go out on a limb and say that, at least based on my experience, in a five-year period:

- You will need to change every part of your custom code because users and analysts will want changes and improvements.

- The bits that you didn't change in that period didn't need to be changed, because no one was using them.

That is the "everybody is always unhappy with everything" theory. It does not bother me; it means I always have a challenge. What this *also* means is that over a long-term period you do have an opportunity to refactor bits of (or eventually all of) the current code whilst making changes and improvements.

In this ideal, perfect world, the Big Ball of Mud system gradually makes more and more calls to your new, elegantly structured set of classes. The latter is called an Island of Happiness, and you will hear more about this in Chapter 2.

Again, this is all about breaking dependencies, thus making things more portable. This may all seem very abstract, but I would make the following points:

- You have to make the changes/improvements anyway; i.e., any code that is actually used will need to be changed pretty much all the time.

- Any change you make in an ECC 6.0 system or later should really have unit tests created to make the program stronger and regression proof, and to test properly you often need a bit of a redesign anyway.

- Now that I am getting my head around OO design, I can actually see how it does make programs more reusable, less prone to break unexpectedly, and better able to respond to the ever-changing requirements. I find myself unable to express this properly and more worried, as I said before, that many people at SAP who say "do this OO thing because I say so" can't explain it either. It does not mean they are wrong. Many famous authors *can* explain it, but I can only say I am able to understand it myself if I can give examples in ABAP that are clearly useful.

What if a country-specific SAP system has to merge the local development system with the global one? Naturally, we want to have the custom programs survive intact in that new environment. To be honest, it is the customizing that is generally going to be the most difficult aspect of such a merger, but, according to all the theories, a Big Ball Of Mud set of programs would have great difficulty making such a jump, but a well-organized system would have no problems whatsoever.

So, is it possible to make such a dramatic transformation—i.e., big ball of mud to a system full of well-organized, portable, high-quality code? You'd hope so, wouldn't you? Happily, that is what this book is all about.

My Journey to OO Happiness

I'd like to start this section with a reflection on the nature of a lot of the articles about OO programming I've read. If I can use a beer analogy, it is as if I had been drinking in the same pub for years, let's call it the Procedural Arms, and then I heard about a wonderful new pub called the Hero of OO.

What is so good about this new pub? I don't know, so I ask an OO expert who frequently drinks beers there.

Back comes the answer: "To get there you leave the current rubbish pub, turn left, go up George Street till you come to the Argyle Cut, go left again, under the tunnel, turn right at the end, and at the end of Lower Fort Street is the new, better, pub."

I don't know if you've noticed, but that did not actually answer my question. The reply told me *how* to get there, and that the destination was good, but not *what* was good about the destination. The OO articles I read were all like that; it's good because it's good, and here is how you write the code technically.

That is why I started my own investigations and so, as you may have gathered from the title, this section is a little story about how I became convinced that OO really was as good as it was painted. First, I will talk about the theory—some great books I read on the subject—and then I will move on to the reality: my actual OO coding experience, starting with getting everything wrong and after a long, hard struggle getting to a point where I finally know what I am doing.

OO Happiness: The Theory

As a bit of background, although I have been programming since the age of 14, it was only ever a hobby. My degree is in economics, and for the first seven years of my career I was an accountant. I did not start programming as a full-time profession until I was working in Israel in 1999.

As such, I never had the formal education in computer science that someone who pursued a degree in that subject would have received. I learned all about programming via trial and error. It was only after programming in ABAP for *13 years* that I had the bright idea to go and look at the most famous books on the subject of OO programming and compare what they had to say (the abstract concepts) with my actual experience (what I do at work every day) and see if the former could help me improve the latter. That worked like a charm, so much so that I would encourage you to follow a similar path.

I have no commercial interest in any of the books mentioned in this section. Some other books I looked at (not mentioned here) were written when I was two years old. In that year (1970), Doctor Who (as portrayed by Jon Pertwee) said the following:

> *"I am not wild about computers, but they are a tool, and if you have a tool it is stupid to ignore its warnings."*
>
> —*Doctor Who*, "Inferno," 1970

The Clean Coder

I bought *The Clean Coder* by mistake. I had no idea author Robert C. Martin had written two books with virtually the exact same title, so I ordered the wrong one and only realized my mistake when it showed up.

I was trying to buy *Clean Code* as opposed to *The Clean Coder*. The first is about improving the code itself, while the second is about improving the professional skills of the person who writes the code; i.e., people like *me*. That wasn't what I wanted; I am a computer programmer, so I don't care about *people*, let alone myself. I only care about *machines*.

Nonetheless I am glad I made that mistake. Whilst I was reading this book it occurred to me that ordering the wrong book by mistake was in some sense serendipitous—a happy accident.

You might think such a book has nothing at all to do with code quality, but if you think about it, if you can in some way improve the quality of the person writing the code then that benefit will pass itself on to the code itself.

Here are some of the other things I found interesting in this book, in case you want to have a look for yourself:

- He gave a list of technical terms that all programmers should know; e.g., *Parnas table*, *conascence*, *tramp data*, etc. I didn't know any of them, but I looked them up quickly.

- An explanation was given for why Yoda said, "Do, or do not. There is no try." When I first heard that in the film all those years ago I thought it was nonsense. Now I have heard a cast-iron reason as to why saying "I will try" to whoever is asking you to meet that impossible deadline is really silly.

There are also strategies for telling the powers that be when something is impossible in the desired time frame, naturally something they don't want to hear; tips on doing time estimates (something I am hopeless at); how to avoid meetings if at all possible; how to deal with other people (urrggh); and generally how to deal with the difficult parts of your programming job (or seemingly not) directly related to the writing of the code itself.

One really useful programming trick this book pointed me at was the Pomodoro Technique. Pomodoro means "tomato," so I ordered a wind-up tomato online; it is like an egg timer.

The idea is you need a device that can time 25 minutes and then make a noise at the end of it. My mobile phone could do that, but it does not look *remotely* like a tomato.

The logic is that people keep breaking off from whatever they are working on to look at emails or go for a coffee or look up the news on the internet or whatever. You are supposed to pick something to work on uninterrupted for 25 minutes, set your tomato for this time period, switch off your email, and off you go. Instantly, your desk phone and mobile phone will start to ring non-stop, and everyone in the office, and even from the bus queue outside, will come to you one after the other, forming a huge line, all insisting they have a problem that you need to fix this very instant or the universe will come to an end.

I once got the programming team T-shirts that said, "Let me drop everything and work on your problem," as that is what people expect, but in the tomato game what you are supposed to do is fob off the people with problems, saying you'll get back to them when the tomato stops, and make a list of everyone you need to see/call back/etc.

Then, when the tomato makes a noise, you have to stop work on whatever it is you aimed for—instantly (that is if you got around to starting)—and then go and see everyone that bothered you straight away. This is supposed to make you more productive, and I have found it actually does work. Apparently, some people measure their success by how many tomatoes they do each week. One thing is for sure—one of my colleagues was really puzzled when he found a comment in my code saying how many tomatoes it took to get that routine working.

The really strange thing is that, amazingly, there is a whole website about this. You can download a 45-page book telling you how best to use your new wind-up tomato and pay 875 euros for a training course on this subject, and you can even take exams and become a "Master of the Tomato."

Clean Code

A very common way of viewing the software world is with the "change as little as possible to reduce your chances of breaking something" attitude, on the reasonable grounds that breaking things can get you sacked. The exact opposite opinion is mentioned in the foreword to *Clean Code*, where Fred Brooks is quoted as saying all major chunks of software should be rewritten from scratch every seven years. Then the foreword postulates that this should be decreased to every seven hours. That's going a bit far, even for me.

The point is that right from the foreword to the very last page, this was a (software) world-changing book. Author Robert C. Martin (known as "Uncle Bob") has acquired something of a cult following as a result, and naturally a lot of people also vehemently disagree.

I don't want to go into too much detail about the book here, because I want you to read it for yourself, but suffice it to say the basic premise is that a lot of code "smells." It smells disgusting; it makes you sick. I saw a piece of ABAP code just half an hour ago that made me feel that way. The *Clean Code* book is about how to remove that horrible smell.

Later on when you get to the heady heights of Chapter 3, you will see that SAP has released an open source website based on the principles in the *Clean Code* book, converted to ABAP, and even put out a set of automated checks you can apply to your code.

Head-First Design Patterns

This book is all based in Java, and once again the similarity between Java and what you can do in the latest releases of ABAP is so strong that the languages might as well be identical.

This book explains, using really frivolous yet technically valid examples, not only *how* to program using OO principles, but also, and a million times more important, *why* they are good; i.e., what practical benefit you get by writing programs this way, especially in the face of the ever-present monster coming over the hill—CHANGE.

I once had someone tell me that the sole purpose of OO programming was lowering costs. Can this be true? I am beginning to think that yes it is.

The "head first" part of the title relates to a psychological approach to designing textbooks that is supposed to get information into your brain faster than the traditional, long-winded textbooks we are all familiar with. It uses cartoons, humor, games, and redundancy (telling you the same thing several times using different formats), and all sorts of non-traditional methods. I think it works a treat.

I proceeded as follows.

First, I read the book one chapter at a time. Each covers a different design pattern (a set way to solve a common programming problem) and has an example program in Java.

My idea was that for each design pattern (with the example in Java) I would try to find a way to use that in an ABAP context. This shows the practicality and power of design patterns—they're proven solutions to common development design problems that are *not language specific*. That means I can share ideas with Java/C++ programmers without needing to know their language.

Next, it is all very well to read a chapter and *think* you have understood it, but if you really want to be sure you have gotten the message, then you need to try writing the same example program in a different language. I rewrote in ABAP the example Java program presented in the chapter.

Next, I tried explaining the concept I thought I now understood from each chapter to someone else; i.e., I would write a blog on the SAP Community website. If you can't explain something to anyone else, it is likely you don't understand it yourself. Conversely, if you can make jokes about the subject it is a clue that you do understand it. The good thing about blogs is that if you don't understand the concepts, the blog will be full of errors and the readers will correct you in the comments.

Even more important, I did not just try to make a carbon copy of the example; I tried to see if I could improve it. Since the examples in that book are intentionally pared down to concentrate on just one aspect and not over-complicate and confuse the reader, they (the example programs) naturally are going to have room for improvement. Then, in the blog comments people would be able to tell me if they were really improvements or not.

In my opinion at least, that whole exercise worked so well in regard to ramming a new concept into my mind, that I would encourage every single ABAP programmer to do the exact same thing I just described, if not with the *Head-First* book then with a similar one.

More on Design Patterns

The funny thing is that design patterns aren't really supposed to have their code reused. The idea is as follows:

> *"You can use this solution a million times over, without ever doing it the same way twice."*
>
> —Christopher Alexander

A pattern is supposed to be a guide to how to solve a problem as opposed to a fixed, reusable template.

In the same way that, when doing a math exam, you can get every single question wrong but still pass with an A, when describing a book about patterns, the author said:

> *"The true value of this book lies not in the actual steps to achieve a particular pattern but in understanding the thought processes that lead to those steps."*
>
> —Joshua Kerievsky, *Refactoring to Patterns* (http://industriallogic. com/xp/refactoring/)

Nonetheless, the opposite argument is that the only reason design patterns exist is because of gaps in the programming language. Over time, several people have made a huge effort to introduce built-in support in various programming languages for the major design patterns.

If I were to take ABAP as an example, it is clear that several design patterns have been "baked into" the ABAP language:

- Observer Pattern — In the examples (Java) I have seen, it seems quite an effort to set up the observer pattern, but ABAP has the EVENTS keyword for classes and the SET HANDLER FOR command to let classes observe changes to other classes, so the language seems to do the hard parts for you.

- Model View Controller (MVC) — SAP has always made a big thing about this, and the pattern is in fact mandatory in Web Dynpro, and so UI5 enforces it by having the model in ABAP, the controller in JavaScript, and the view in XML.

- Prototype — This is all about cloning an instance of an object. In SAP this seems to be embedded at the kernel level à la SYSTEM-CALL OBJMGR CLONE ME TO result.

- Proxy — I was reading the *Head-First Design Patterns* chapter on proxy patterns, and it was describing the incredibly complicated Java things you need to do to get remote proxies working so that remote systems can talk to each other. My eyes glazed over, and I thought this has no relevance to me. Then the lightbulb went on, and I thought, "Hang on—I did the same thing in SAP this very day." That is what transaction SPROXY (which lets SAP talk to PI and vice versa) is all about—built-in support for a complicated design pattern.

OO Happiness: The Reality

You can read all the articles and books in the world and become convinced that OO is the most fantastic thing in the universe, but there is only one way to become truly convinced: Start using the concepts you have discovered in your day-to-day programming work and see whether they actually make a difference. In this section, you will hear about various programming forays I have made over the years, and how they went.

Writing an Interactive Executable Report in OO

Back in 2006, I had read none of the OO books or articles I talk about in this chapter, but I was keenly interested in the topic. When the opportunity came along to write the next big application, I thought, *"OK, I will do this in a 100 percent OO manner."*

In real life that is impossible; ABAP just doesn't work that way. You always need some sort of procedural entry point. As an example, you can define an OO transaction whereby instead of calling a screen in a module pool or an executable program you can call a public method of a global class. *"Wonderful,"* you might think—so why do you never see this being used? That strategy was really only ever intended for use with persistent objects, and they never took off either. So, you never see an OO transaction code in real life.

Instead, you end up with a standard executable program where the start-of-selection classic ABAP event block calls a "main" method of a class to start everything going. Even back in 2006, I knew this was the way forward, so I had a "small" procedural program of 797 lines that dealt with the SELECTION-SCREEN and assorted PBO/PAI modules, but all the meaningful code was a separate INCLUDE full of classes and methods that was 10,607 lines long.

This was a program where you had a grid of sales orders at the bottom of the screen, and you dragged them up a tree full of trucks at the top of the screen, thus filling up the trucks with order items until each truck was full. The technical specification was written by the manager on the back of a napkin whilst we were at a restaurant.

I had never done a "drag and drop" program before and so used example SAP program BCALV_DND_01 as a starting point. The good news is, everything worked perfectly, and I was very happy with the result, and so were the business users.

However, looking back at the program 14 years later, I can see that it was not an OO program at all; there was virtually zero separation of concerns. There was a grand total of one local class filled with methods that contained the code that normally would have been in FORM routines. It handled data retrieval, business logic, and "view" tasks like dealing with ALV containers, all in the same class. That's not an OO program—that's a procedural program pretending to be an OO program.

I did have some global classes for data retrieval from objects like vendors, customers, and materials, but they were just function modules, like READ_MARA_SINGLE, wrapped in a global class.

Writing a DYNPRO Program in OO

Fast forward to February 2010, when I had to copy over a procedural DYNPRO module pool to maintain a business object from one country's SAP system to another, and I was told this would eventually be used in dozens of different countries. By that point I had a much better grasp of the idea of the separation of concerns, and specifically the Model-View-Controller pattern.

I created a specific database-access class and a dedicated business-logic class, which formed the model—they even had country-specific subclasses. I had no idea what interfaces were at that point, so I did not use them. I can look back on this without cringing nearly as much as I do when I look back on the fake OO program mentioned earlier.

However, when I look at the main DYNPRO program, I am puzzled to see I had three includes called Model, View, and Controller. Inside the Model were FORM routines that were called before an instance of the model class had been created; nowadays I know those would be static methods of the model class. Even better, I see that at some point in the last ten years someone decided that the Model include would be just the place to put FORM routines dealing with a DYNPRO table control—oh dear, those are "view" functions.

The View include had routines all based on DYNPRO-specific technology—e.g., LOOP AT SCREEN and MESSAGE statements—but there was some business logic in there too, and a few database reads.

The Controller include was almost right as well. All the PBO and PAI modules were directed here, and either a POPUP screen of some sort was called, or a CALL TRANSACTION, or a method of the business-logic class. At the very least, the model class was isolated from the DYNPRO screen. There was also some database access happening.

Once again, this fulfilled the business function it was intended for; it was very easy to create a subclass for a new country that did the business logic differently, but it still was not a real OO program. Taking FORM routines and putting them in different includes based on whether you think that FORM routine does a model, view, or controller type of function is still procedural programming by any other name.

Experiment

Moving along to January 2014, there was a huge debate occurring online in the SAP community about when (if ever) you should program in OO as opposed to sticking with procedural programming. The main argument presented against OO was that in any example program where a procedural program is translated into an OO equivalent, the program gets longer and more complicated as it gets "better."

The problem with making a fair comparison between a procedural program and an OO version that does the same thing is this: If you do a really complicated example, lots of people will get washed away by the complexity of it or get bogged down by the sheer amount of code, and ignore the point you are trying to make.

On the B side, the simpler the example, the more striking will be the percentage difference between the lines of OO code needed to do something and the procedural equivalent. For a small program the procedural version will be a lot shorter. As the complexity increases, the sizes will slowly equalize.

Around 2014 in my day job I was busy writing the most complicated application I had ever written in my life; it was also by far the biggest in terms of lines of code. I started off with a framework that was a lot bigger than a procedural version would be, but after four years of my providing new features it ended up smaller than it would have been had I written it procedurally.

However, that is neither here nor there. In a lot of senses it does not matter at all how many lines of code there are in a program; as you will see in the "Clarity" section, shorter is not always better.

What is vitally important is how easy the program is to understand and hence to change. Put another way, the acid test for a program is how it stands up to the non-stop stream of user requests that are bound to arrive.

I was nice and happy with that gigantic OO framework I had created, but naturally I had no procedural equivalent to compare it to, so I had no idea if it would have been easier to change had I written it procedurally.

I wanted to make such a comparison, so I did an experiment where I picked one of the programs from the *Head-First Design Patterns* book that was in Java and translated that program into ABAP—twice. The first time, I did it with all classes and methods; the second time, with all FORM routines. When doing such experiments it is easy to bias the result by writing one program deliberately worse than the other, so I made a huge effort to write both versions to the highest quality I could. I even put unit tests in the procedural version as well as in the OO version.

This program was not the incredibly simple example always given—i.e., read some data from the database and then call up an ALV—but rather a bunch of complex conditional logic: how a vending machine behaves when you put money into it and ask for a product. Even so, the procedural version still came out with fewer lines of code and looking more straightforward at first glance.

Next came the crucial test: I invented two new business requirements, and then went about changing both versions of the program to accommodate those new requests, to determine which one took the longest to change.

After I made one change to both programs, what was the verdict? It was certainly faster to change (enhance) the procedural version. However, the OO version seemed to lend itself better to reading more like natural language (which is one of the main aims of the game), and the error handling (using exception classes rather than SY-SUBRC), which some would describe as more cumbersome, did tend to convey a clearer idea of what actually went wrong.

When I was halfway through making the second change, it was already obvious I would need less code to achieve the same thing in the procedural version. The question I asked myself was this: Is it just because I don't yet know enough about OO to implement the OO change in a more efficient way?

Looking back, that was true to an extent, but doing things correctly in OO does seem to need a lot more code; e.g., an interface for the public methods of every class, plus agonizing over what to put in which class so as to not break the separation of concerns.

Also, part of my perceived problem was that I used customized global classes in the OO version, whereas the procedural version was all in one program. Had I been more familiar with them, I could have used all local classes, and things would have gone ten times faster; i.e., I could have auto-generated the definitions and implementations of methods.

The final result was that changing the procedural version took a lot less contemplation than doing so for the OO equivalent, and a lot less time making the changes. The procedural program throws all the rules found in books like *Clean Code* right into the dustbin. It has global variables all over the place, breaks the "open/closed" principle, etc.

I'm not much for rules, as assorted German managers would attest, but they are there for a reason, and when I am reading books like *Clean Code* all those rules make perfect sense. The question is, can they survive in the real world?

The aim of the game was to test the theory that OO programs give you the advantage by taking less time to change than procedural ones. My experiment seemed to prove the exact opposite. To be honest, that was not what I was expecting. At that point, I was not feeling much OO happiness.

It would have been easy at that point to fall into despair. It occurred to me, however, that even if it were true that OO did not help for small programs, I could not totally write it off until I had repeated the experiment on a truly gigantic scale. No small program ever stays small; any program in use gets bigger and bigger and more complex forever.

For such an experiment to be meaningful, it would have to be an enormous procedural program actually used—in fact, it would have to be business critical. I would have to be allowed to build a totally new version in OO, which would take ages and cost a lot. You would have to have one hell of a business case to get something like that authorized, so surely the whole idea was just a pipe dream?

Rewriting a Huge, Business-Critical Program in OO

Ever since 2009, I had being trying to convince the powers that be that the best way to write gigantic programs intended for use by dozens of different countries was to use a dedicated subclass for each country so a change to the business logic in Mongolia could not break the business logic in Peru. Everyone always nodded sagely and probably thought to themselves, "What is that idiot on about?" so nothing ever came of my crazy idea.

There was a problem building up over time, however. The analogy I would use is that you are driving a fast car in a straight line across a huge desert. In a thousand miles the desert abruptly ends in a cliff with a huge drop. You will not get to that cliff for a long time, but when you do you will be in trouble.

In programming terms, this translates to the following: Given a procedural program (without tests), when only one country is using it, making a change cannot affect any other country. When two countries are using it, and one wants a change, that change has (say) a 5 percent chance of breaking something for the other country, and then you have doubled the number of change requests. With each additional country, you increase the chance of any given change breaking something in one of the other countries, and as the number of change requests increases, you either start giving each country fewer changes than they were used to getting or have to employ more people (which does not usually work too well). Eventually, you end up with a flood of change requests, and each change is pretty much guaranteed to break *something* for one or more countries.

One day in 2018, a new CIO took over global IT and realized the problem—we were only up to five countries and already the cracks were starting to show—and suddenly my crackpot ideas were crackpot no longer. I will always recall the following exchange a manager had with one of my programming colleagues:

> *Manager: Do you think this "separation of concerns" thing will make it easier or harder to add the twenty-fifth country when the day comes?*

> *Programmer: It will make it—possible.*

Before I knew it, a project was under way to rewrite the two largest, most business-critical programs in a "perfect" OO manner following all of the textbook rules and using unit tests! Even better, I was on the team. It was wonderful.

How often does such a chance come along? It was a once-in-a-lifetime opportunity. Everything was done by the book, a proper implementation of the Model-View-Controller pattern this time, and 100 percent future proof; i.e., the new design can be used with the new ABAP Restful Application Programming Model (RAP), and we can swap out the SAP GUI for UI5 at the drop of a hat.

We even used the same terminology as the latest SAP technologies, such as the Business Object Processing Framework and its successor in the RAP:

> Derivations — For when the value of one field is changed based on the value of another

> Validations — For checking data integrity

> Actions — The artist formerly known as "user commands"

It took an entire year for two people to rewrite enough of the previous program for the new version to go live in a pilot country, but it worked a treat. We knew it would—*it had **automated** unit tests.*

After that point, each new requested change had to be made in both programs—the old procedural version still active in production and the pilot OO version. This is an ongoing process until such time as all countries are migrated onto the new version. So now for each change I can see what needs to be done in OO world to enable the change and what needs to be done in procedural world to enable that same change.

Is it easier in OO world? Yes. No ifs, no buts; just *yes*. It's far more obvious what part of the program does what, and thus it is ten million times easier to zero in on what part of the program needs to be changed. And because the OO version has automated unit tests and the procedural one does not, the risk of any given change is far less. Plus, country-specific subclasses remove the risk of a change to one country breaking another country. I made what I consider a radical change just this very day, and I was not worried at all, as running the unit tests proved to me I had not broken anything.

This was proof positive of my theory that OO makes programs easier to maintain, but rewriting a gigantic program for a year is not something everybody can do; in fact, I would imagine it is incredibly rare. So what can you do?

Slowly Transforming a Huge, Business-Critical Program to OO

Once again, I can talk from experience here, not just theory. We have more than one SAP system, and, as I am reminded every so often, one of them deals with just one country, and the other one deals with multiple countries. Naturally, the rewrite occurred in the "big" SAP system, and you cannot just transplant that into the "small" SAP system, as it is just too different.

The "small" SAP system has its own version of the huge program, and since we are only talking about one country, the business case to rewrite the whole thing (which would probably take another year) is just not there, because the underlying problem (multiple countries) just does not exist.

Thus I am in a situation to which hopefully you can relate: I want to convert a program to be all OO but cannot do it all at once. The idea is to change it slowly over time, making it more OO with every change request, in a risk-free manner.

The idea—and I got this from an open SAP course (Writing Testable Code for ABAP)—is to create an "Island of Happiness," which is a set of classes that will contain any new or changed business logic and have unit tests. These new classes will be called from the main program, which is not a new concept at all; you are used to adding new functionality to existing programs by adding a function module.

The "Island of Happiness" gets its name because every change is done in a test-driven-development fashion (which you will read about in the next chapter) and has a load of quality checks done after every small change (the entire purpose of this book).

With every change request, more and more code gets moved out of the main program (the continent) and onto the Island, such that eventually the Island will be bigger than the continent and the entire population will be in a state of happiness. I am doing this in real life, and it works fantastically.

That's what I am working on at the moment, and it is the current step in my journey to OO happiness. After all this real-life experience, I can safely make a little list of the real benefits of OO programming.

OO Benefits: The Reality

The benefits of anything at all, not just software, are often split into two categories: hard benefits, which are more to do with the way the physical world is and are almost impossible to dispute, and soft benefits, which are more to do with the way the human brain works and hence may "seem" right but are easier to dispute if you don't like whatever new thing is being proposed.

In this case, the "new thing" being proposed in the ABAP world is OO programming (it's not new at all, of course; it's 20 years old, but many programmers and managers still consider it new), so you will hear about the disputable soft benefits first, then the hard ones.

Soft Benefits

In this section, the benefits are people's opinions rather than anything that you can point at and say, "Look—there it is!" Nonetheless, at the very minimum you need to hear these arguments as to why OO is good, if only to disagree with them. I will start with the most abstract proposed benefit and work backward.

Design Thinking

If you read any SAP press releases in the last few years, you'd have noticed they were all regarding the concept of "design thinking," which means different things to different people, but basically means designing your program to reflect how the end users think and act (which is why I made such a big deal about OO's being able to reflect the business process at the start of this chapter). Note we are not talking about the detailed internal workings of an application here, rather an overarching design that somehow reflects the real world.

Many people have said that OO leads to design thinking, and that challenging a design helps make it better. That concept does not really arise in procedural programming—there is (generally) a set way to do things as opposed to having to come up with a UML design about how various classes with single responsibilities interact with each other. The flip side, of course, is that this gives you far greater scope to totally stuff things up if you come up with a terrible OO design, which a lot of people do (including me) when they start, and this can give OO a really bad reputation.

Once you do have the freedom to truly "design" your programs rather than following a set pattern, it is a great feeling. It has been said that what's great about OO is that because it is a concept and not language specific you could easily talk over the design with a Java (or any other OO language) developer. There are a lot more of them out there than ABAP programmers, and all of them would be really puzzled if you started talking about FORM routines and internal tables, but not if you mentioned the Model-View-Controller (MVC) pattern.

In fact, some years back my boss heard me talking about the MVC to another ABAP programmer and said, "Why are you talking about MVC? That's just for web developers!" The world has moved on—ABAP is no longer a weirdo proprietary language no one else understands. Nowadays (since the year 2000, amazingly), we can do what the "cool kids" do, which may or may not be good, but at least we have the choice.

Can this soft benefit be measured? No, not at all!

Ease of Maintenance

When reading the heated debate online on the SCN platform between the "Team Procedural" and "Team OO" ways of programming ABAP, I came across a really interesting observation.

One of the commentators had just finished reading the book
Practical Object-Oriented Design in Ruby: An Agile Primer by Sandi Metz.

In that book, apparently the author stresses that the benefits of OO (and specifically correct OO design) come down to one thing only: *it has to lower costs.* Every other benefit it may or may not have is entirely secondary to that core goal. It could of course be argued that increasing profit and/or market share is equally important, but that was not what that book was on about.

In regard to lowering costs, as far as I can see, that is all about the 90 percent of the software cycle that involves maintenance; i.e., the more difficult (hence longer) it is to change a program to do something new, the more it costs, and thus the entire OO versus procedural argument stands or falls on how easy it is to change existing programs.

Now, OO proponents always say that OO is easier to change, and I have found this to be the case, but it is not something you can scientifically prove.

ABAP programming guru Matthew Billingham, who works for Xiting AG, Switzerland, has this to say on the matter:

> *"Yes, OO is better when it comes to maintenance. But not if the maintainer is lacking OO skills. Now, some companies have taken as a corollary of this that it's better not to program in OO. Of course, you and I know the correct corollary is: 'Only employ developers who know/are capable of learning OO techniques,' then the benefit of OO will be reaped."*
>
> —Matthew Billingham

Note that he did not say, "Don't employ people who don't know OO"; rather, "People who are capable of learning OO," which is every ABAP programmer, unless they have a pathological hatred of the very idea of OO.

Can this soft benefit be measured? At first glance, a manager would say, "Yes, that is easy; let us just see how many more change requests we can pump through each month with the same number of developers now that we have moved to OO." I would say that yes, that metric would prove itself over the long term, but might also prove the death of the whole initiative due to, in the first few months, things appearing to be worse because (a) some developers are still struggling with this weird "new" concept and (b) Sods Law says the very first month you start doing this the change requests will magically become ten times more complicated than anything that went before, and OO will get the blame.

No One Goes Back

Here is one good way to judge if something is better than a similar thing: If you change your behavior and start doing the new thing, do you switch back the next week in disgust, or keep using the new thing forever?

An analogy here would be the ABAP debugger. When the "new" version came out many years ago I had already been using the old one for so long that I did not like the look of the new one, but I forced myself to use it anyway (there was a setting you could make to keep using the old one). Now I look back on the old one with horror. Going back even further, I did not want to use Excel instead of Lotus 123. So many people felt that way that Microsoft made sure all the Lotus commands worked in Excel. I used the Lotus commands for a year at least . . . but now I do not.

You might say we are not talking about the same thing—Lotus 123 and Excel were designed to do the same task and the difference was technical, and the difference between procedural and OO is more of a mindset. But nonetheless, we are talking about forcing yourself to do something new and seeing if you like it.

A better analogy might be an electric car. A lot of people are horrified at the very thought of driving one, let alone owning one—until the point they first drive one, and then they become a convert on the spot.

Going back to ABAP, programming guru Matthew Billingham phrases it thus:

> *"The only way you'll find out how absolutely incredible programming in OO is—you have to do it. No-one I've met who's made the conversion has ever regretted it. Just like no-one who was forced to learn piano as a kid, regrets it as an adult.*
>
> *So there's a challenge: name one development that it would be best to write procedurally."*
>
> —Matthew Billingham, comment to SAP Community Blog

As it turned out, no one could (properly) rise to that challenge. The only counter-arguments were (a) no one ever said that procedural was *better* than OO and (b) the program will never be changed, so it does not matter how hard/easy it is to change it.

Can this soft benefit be measured? In theory, yes. I suppose you could do a study and ask how many ABAP programmers who had moved to OO had become converted and how many had decided the whole thing was a colossal waste of time. I don't think anyone has actually ever done this. The question is, would the result of such a study mean anything? Everyone used to think the world was flat, and now most people don't (apart from the guy who used to live in the apartment below me in 2018), so the number of people who think something is true doesn't necessarily make it true; you need more scientific evidence, which is why we now move on to the next section.

Hard Benefits

Now we are talking about the technical way the system works, and there is no gray area here. The ABAP compiler treats FORM routines one way and METHODS another, and that is just the way it is. Denying that is like saying the sun does not come up every morning, or toast lands buttered side up when you drop it.

In the rest of the book the recommendations for improving code quality relate equally to procedural and OO programming, but are admittedly biased toward OO. In this section, you will hear assorted technical benefits of OO—avoidance of syntax errors, parameter handling, promoting reuse, and the ability to make code testable.

Avoidance of Syntax Errors

It is an easy mistake to make to think that a class is just like a function group and all the methods are just like function modules. At first glance it seems that way, and indeed many people (including some from within SAP) have designed classes in that exact way.

The problem is that a syntax error in any one function module of a function group kills the whole group. A syntax error in a subclass only affects that class. Thus, if you break a subclass that deals specifically with giraffes, it will not affect the subclass that deals with warthogs or indeed the parent class that deals with savanna animals generally.

Parameter Handling

At first glance, it might seem like a tiny thing, but the way parameters (also known as the "signature" of a routine) are handled is very different in the OO world than in the FORM routine world.

IMPORTING

First, in OO you cannot change an IMPORTING parameter. In a FORM routine you can declare a parameter as USING, which is supposed to mean you don't change it, and then you can change it anyway. So the caller of a FORM routine might reasonably expect the value(s) of a USING parameter not to be changed and then be unpleasantly surprised when they are. In other words, code should not only do what it claims to be doing but also be *forced* to do what it claims to be doing.

EXPORTING

Next, we turn to EXPORTING parameters. In a FORM routine you don't really know if a CHANGING parameter is actually a value calculated within the routine, or an existing value that needs to be changed, which is what the name suggests. Nine times out of ten it is the former.

In both FORM routines and methods you need to explicitly clear parameters calculated within the routine—i.e., EXPORTING parameters—but at least in a method such parameters are identified as what they are; they do what they say on the tin.

TABLES

This was the only way to pass an entire internal table in and out of a FORM routine. There is no equivalent in OO because internal tables are treated no differently than elementary fields and structures when they are used as parameter values.

RETURNING

The last type of parameter that is specific to the OO method is the RETURNING parameter, which does not have an equivalent in a FORM routine. If you declare such a parameter you are saying this routine has one result and one only, and that is the result it RETURNS; i.e., the code is supposed to read like plain English. A functional method with a RETURNING parameter looks just like plain English when it is called.

Such RETURNING parameters clear themselves automatically, which is one up on an EXPORTING parameter and 100 percent better than a CHANGING parameter in a FORM routine, which is supposed to return a single result. Using such a construct also makes the calling code a lot shorter and clearer, as shown in Listing 1-1, which shows both the procedural and OO ways of doing the same thing.

Listing 1-1. How RETURNING Parameters Make Code Shorter

```
FORM l01_01_elephant_fun.

  DATA: elephant_number TYPE i VALUE '1',
        trunk_size      TYPE i.

  PERFORM derive_trunk_size USING    elephant_number
                            CHANGING trunk_size.

ENDFORM.
 METHOD l01_01_elephant_fun.

   DATA(elephant) = NEW lcl_elephant( ).
```

```
    DATA(trunk_size) =
    elephant->derive_trunk_size( id_elephant_number ).

  ENDMETHOD.
```

OPTIONAL

OO has optional importing parameters (and in OO exporting parameters are always optional). Hoo-ah! Such an idea is unheard of in FORM routines—the caller has to send (USING) and receive (CHANGING) every single parameter in the signature.

So, how was this handled before the evil OO nonsense came along? Let us say there was a FORM routine with two CHANGING parameters, but the routine at hand only needed one. You could have two almost identical FORM routines with different signatures, which would be bad, because duplicate code is bad.

You could do what I used to do and pass in dummy values to the parameters you do not need, usually the CHANGING parameters. That is like in some standard SAP function modules where the TABLES parameter is compulsory, so you have to declare a table, and then include it in the function module call, even if you do not care at all about the contents. However you solve the problem, it is not as elegant as the OO equivalent.

NAMES

This subject will be revisited in both the "Clarity" and "Stability" chapters, but to summarize, an OO method with more than one importing parameter insists you specify which parameter you are passing what value to, as shown in Listing 1-2, which compares procedural and OO code.

Listing 1-2. Caller Being Forced to Specify Parameter Names

```
FORM lo1_02_circus_runaway.

  DATA: elephant_name TYPE string VALUE 'Nelly',
        circus_name   TYPE string VALUE 'Horrible Circus',
        run_away_flag TYPE abap_bool.

  PERFORM derive_run_away USING    elephant_name
                                   circus_name
                          CHANGING run_away_flag.
```

```
ENDFORM.  METHOD lo1_02_circus_runaway.

   DATA: elephant_name TYPE string VALUE 'Nelly',
         circus_name   TYPE string VALUE 'Horrible Circus'.

   DATA(elephant) = NEW lcl_elephant( ).

   DATA(run_away_flag) = elephant->derive_run_away(
     id_elephant_name = elephant_name
     id_circus_name   = circus_name ).

ENDMETHOD.
```

The OO equivalent might seem longer, but it forces you to get the order of the parameters right, because if you don't it looks wrong. In the procedural equivalent, you could much more easily put the circus name first and not get a warning if both variables were strings, and then *The Circus would run away from Nelly the Elephant*, which would be totally wrong.

TYPES

FORM routines can have untyped parameters. Therefore, the caller can pass in the totally wrong type of value (e.g., "BANANA" to an integer variable). The static syntax check cannot work out this is wrong, as you have not given it enough clues to work, as shown in Listing 1-3.

Listing 1-3. Incorrect Value Being Passed into a FORM Routine

```
FORM i_want_an_integer USING id_integer.
....
ENDFORM.

PERFORM i_want_an_integer USING 'BANANA'.
```

If you make sure each parameter in a FORM routine has a TYPE (e.g., TYPE I in the preceding example), then the problem is almost solved, unless you have two parameters in a row with the same type, in which case the caller could send them the wrong way.

FORMULAS

You can pass in formulas as arguments using OO programming, as shown in Listing 1-4, but you cannot do the same with FORM routines.

Listing 1-4. Passing Formulas into Methods

```
ME->GET_DRUNK(
IN_PUB      = ME->FAVORITE_PUB_OF( SY-UNAME )
BY_DRINKING = ME->FAVORITE_DRINK_OF( SY-UNAME ).
```

When calling an equivalent FORM routine, you'd have to move the returned values for calls to methods favorite_pub_of and favorite_drink_of to helper variables before using them in the signature of the called routine, making the program longer than it needs to be and just that little bit more difficult to understand.

Reuse

The book by Igor Barbaric called *Design Patterns in Object Oriented ABAP* is what got me looking into OO in the first place. He said that the first time he did a major application in an OO fashion he ended up with a whole bunch of components that could be reused in subsequent projects.

You could do that with INCLUDES, but that is a nightmare the instant an INCLUDE is used by more than one program. You cannot have a proper syntax check on an INCLUDE that is used by multiple programs, and that brings you the risk of short dumps in production. The extended syntax check warns you against having an INCLUDE that is used by more than one program. It doesn't help that this was common practice in older SAP code.

Function modules are supposed to be reusable and are procedural. You find functions like READ_TEXT or POPUP_TO_CONFIRM all over custom programs. OO does not have a monopoly in this area.

There is nothing inherent to OO that makes the code more reusable, but what I would say is that since good OO *design* in general, and unit testing in particular, forces you into the separation of concerns, where different things are in their own classes, it soon becomes apparent that some classes are clearly specific to the application at hand whereas others are far more generic—hence, reusable.

The point is that after a procedural program has been written, you are far less likely to have created reusable components therein, because you were not wearing the "separation of concerns" straitjacket whilst you were writing it.

Making Code Testable

You can have automated unit tests in procedural programs (though you have to use a test class), but it is ten billion times harder to write testable procedural code than it is to write testable OO code. This is because you can have test double classes in OO, and there is no similar concept in procedural programming.

If something is really incredibly difficult to do, and you don't feel you really need to do it, then you won't do it; that is just human nature. That's a huge shame, because adding tests is something you really need to do, as will become clear in Chapter 2.

I have seen the situation where there are two huge programs, one with automated tests, one without. The Monday after each quarterly release, the programmer looking after the "testless" program would have a bus queue of business analysts stretching all the way down the corridor waiting to come to him with bugs the users discovered in production, whilst the programmer with the program stuffed with tests could have taken that day off, if so desired, and spent it floating around in the swimming pool drinking cocktails, as there was nothing to be fixed.

Conclusion

The ability to use OO programming in the ABAP language has been around since the year 2000, but to this day very few ABAP programmers make use of it, and I think that's a crying shame.

In this chapter, you have heard about why OO never took off in the ABAP world and then why that is a pity; i.e., the benefits of OO programming.

You heard about the general theory of why OO can help in SAP projects, with the example of an SAP global rollout. Then, I related my personal journey of OO discovery that led me to believe that OO is in fact superior to procedural programming. The chapter ended with a little list of the OO benefits I have found in real life.

The central premise of this book is that in order to force yourself to make your programs the highest quality they can be, you need to write them using the test-driven development methodology, and if that is easier using OO programming (and it is), then that is reason enough to make the switch to OO, even if it has no other advantages over procedural programming at all (though it does).

That brings us nicely along to the subject of the second chapter, which is all about why test-driven development (TDD) is vital to ensuring code quality.

Recommended Reading

These have been arranged roughly in the order I read the various articles and books, over a period of many years.

Articles

A description of the generally chaotic state of most software systems:

http://www.laputan.org/mud/mud.html#BigBallOfMud

An explanation of the "design by contract" concept for coding routines:

http://se.ethz.ch/~meyer/publications/computer/contract.pdf

"Heuristics and Coffee": An example of OO design that abstracts the "What" from the "How":

https://flylib.com/books/en/4.444.1.119/1/

Books

A description of the "Business Object Notation" method of describing OO programs:

http://www.bon-method.com/book_print_a4.pdf

A description of the "Unified Modeling Language" method of describing OO programs:

http://cgi.di.uoa.gr/~halatsis/Books_EDY/Book-Eng-01%20-%20Uml%20
Distilled%20-%20Fowler.pdf

In regard to programming in Java:

https://www.goodreads.com/book/show/71672.Thinking_in_Java

An exploration of what it takes to be the best programmer you can possibly be:
The Clean Coder, Robert C. Martin (Pearson Education, 2011)

https://www.amazon.com.au/Clean-Coder-Conduct-Professional-Programmers/
dp/0137081073

An exploration of what it takes to write the best code you possibly can:

Clean Code: A Handbook of Agile Software Craftsmanship, Robert C. Martin (Prentice Hall, 2008)

```
https://www.amazon.com.au/Clean-Code-Handbook-Software-Craftsmanship/
dp/0132350882
```

A fun way of learning what designs patterns are, with examples in Java:

Head-First Design Patterns, Freeman et al. (O'Reilly, 2004)

```
https://www.amazon.com.au/Head-First-Design-Patterns-Brain-Friendly-ebook/
dp/B00AA36RZY
```

A look at those same design patterns, this time through the lens of ABAP:

Object-Oriented Design with ABAP, James E. McDonough (APRESS, 2017)

```
https://www.apress.com/gp/book/9781484228371
```

CHAPTER 2

Why Test-Driven Development Is a Must for Code Quality

Recently, Amazon claimed that it puts a new change into its production system every 1.59 seconds with no risk at all. How can this possibly be true? It's all to do with test-driven development (hereafter TDD).

A small fraction of ABAP programmers currently make use of object-oriented (OO) programming, and only a small fraction of that fraction has even heard of TDD, let alone used it. This chapter explains the very real benefit this approach can bring to the quality of your code, and how it could be viewed as being more about code quality than testing.

Ultimately, the logic is thus—if you want your code to be of the highest quality possible, you need to force yourself into a situation where you are constantly made to improve the quality of your code—and using TDD will get you there. This chapter explains why this is the case.

First, you will hear about the theory of TDD, what problem it was created to solve, and how it is supposed to go about solving that problem. Next, that theory will meet reality and you will read about my personal experiences programming using TDD. Lastly, you will learn about why TDD has never really taken off—the common arguments made against the whole idea and why those arguments are all wrong.

TDD Theory

In this section, we start with a discussion about the fragile nature of code and why most ABAP code currently being written is "legacy code," which is a bad thing. Then, we move on to the solution—automated regression tests—which also serve as the enabler

55

© Paul David Hardy 2021
P. D. Hardy, *Improving the Quality of ABAP Code*, https://doi.org/10.1007/978-1-4842-6711-0_2

for TDD. Next, we discuss why most current code simply cannot have automated tests without major changes. Lastly, I will talk about the TDD development cycle for both writing new programs and changing existing ones.

Fragile Code

In the 2004 science fiction movie *The Butterfly Effect*, the main character keeps traveling back in time to change something in the past with the aim of making the present better. Every time he attempts a "fix" in the past, back in the present the intended problem is fixed but an even worse problem has been caused. He travels back to fix that new problem, and he does, but the result is that things in the present end up even worse than before.

In many ways programming is like that. You have a request to fix a bug, and manage to fix it, but you break two unrelated things in the process. Then you fix them, and unwittingly break four seemingly unrelated things, and so on, a never-ending, vicious spiral of destruction.

The Butterfly Effect could not be a better analogy. The original definition of the term talked about a butterfly flapping its wings on one side of the world and thus causing a tornado on the other side. That is what happens with programs—you change some code to do with lightbulb manufacturing in Poland, and it breaks something to do with concrete production in Morocco, and the link between the two is impossible to understand.

This was the story of my life for as long as I care to remember, and of the lives of all my colleagues. It was always a sleepless night before the changes to a business-critical program went up to production.

Does it always have to be this way? Is there a way out? Happily, yes, there is, and that's how Amazon and the other "giants" manage to change their production systems multiple times every second.

In the "Recommended Reading" section at the end of this chapter is the book *Anti-Fragile* by Nassim Nicholas Taleb. That is not about software at all but rather things that get stronger when exposed to stress; e.g., biological organisms and political organizations that are being oppressed.

He makes the following definitions:

- Something is *fragile* if in the worst case it gets worse, and in the best case it stays the same.

- Something is *robust* if in the worst case it stays the same, and in the best case it stays the same.

- Something is *anti-fragile* if in the worst case it stays the same, and in the best case it gets better.

In our case, the "stress" is the need to make an ever-increasing number of changes to our programs, and we are talking about the existing code here. Traditionally, the best we could hope for was the first "fragile" state; if our changes didn't break anything, we were happy. We could never even reach the "robust" state.

The good news is that amazing as it may seem, the "anti-fragile" state of affairs is possible. We can actually get to a stage where every change to our code makes things better, not worse. What is holding us back?

Legacy Code

What is holding us back is that traditionally in the ABAP world we write what is called legacy code. That statement may come as a surprise to most SAP programmers and be met by instant denial, but that is because the term *legacy code*, like many IT terms, means different things to different people. Ask ten different programmers what that term means, and you will get ten different answers back. Let us look at some possible definitions of the term *legacy* and how it might indicate *bad* source code that makes our programs fragile:

- Legacy in the sense of being something that you are remembered for. A lot of really rich people want to in some sense live on beyond their lifetime by leaving a "legacy"; e.g., Elon Musk most likely wants to be remembered for moving the world onto electric cars. In the same way, a programmer might think his code is so good it will go down in history. If the code is in fact that good, then that cannot be what we are talking about here.

- Legacy in the sense of an inheritance or a bequest. This is code that you have inherited from a former system, the ERP system you had before your current SAP ERP system, called the Legacy System in IT terms. In most cases, such a Legacy System was not an SAP system at all, so you could not have inherited the code, so that is not what we are talking about either.

- Legacy in the sense of code written in a programming style that is deemed obsolete. This is stretching the dictionary definition of the word *legacy*, but some people think that procedural code is "legacy" and OO code is "modern." As it turns out, programs written in either style can be legacy code according to what I consider the proper definition, which we are now coming to.

For some time now in the IT world the accepted definition comes from American author and IT expert Michael Feathers, who defined *legacy code* as "code without tests." He means automated unit tests, and here is the exact quote:

> *"Code without tests is bad code. It doesn't matter how well written it is; it doesn't matter how pretty or object-oriented or well-encapsulated it is. With tests, we can change the behaviour of our code quickly and verifiably. Without them, we really don't know if our code is getting better or worse."*

> —Michael Feathers, *Working Effectively with Legacy Code*

As you can see by that definition, if a procedural program has unit tests and an OO one does not, then it is the OO program that is legacy code. That is why SAP did not restrict the ABAP Unit framework to just classes and methods. My very first use of ABAP Unit was to add tests to an existing procedural program, and the benefit was enormous; more on this later.

Here is another quote from Feathers about tests, just to ram home the point:

> *"Most of the fear involved in making changes to large code bases is fear of introducing subtle bugs; fear of changing things inadvertently. With tests, you can make things better with impunity. To me, the difference is so critical, it overwhelms any other distinction."*

> —Michael Feathers, *Working Effectively with Legacy Code*

To summarize:

- The problem statement is: 99 percent of development work is changing existing programs, and the biggest problem with changing existing programs is breaking something unrelated to the change. Even worse, with every such change the program becomes more fragile.

- The question is: How can we stop programs from being "fragile"?

- The answer is: Automated regression testing.

Automated Regression Tests

The point of automated regression tests is instant feedback. The idea is that if you change a piece of code to solve a problem, you want to know instantly if that change has broken anything else at all in the program.

There are in fact many types of automated tests you can do, but here we are talking about unit tests—testing one or more grouped routines that deal with business logic; i.e., not an end-to-end test involving the user interface and interfaces to external systems and so on.

Although ABAP has been around since the 1980s (when it stood for Allgemeiner Berichts-Aufbereitungs-Prozessor, German for "Generic Report Preparation Processor"), in some ways it is still the "new kid on the block" compared to other popular programming languages like Java. As such, SAP has been quite smart in that if there was a huge problem with the language then they went looking to see if other languages had already solved that problem, and if they had then SAP adopted the same solution; i.e., do not reinvent the wheel.

The generic term for an automated unit test framework is *xUNIT*. This gets implemented differently in each language (e.g., JUNIT in Java, QUNIT in JavaScript), but the basic principle is always the same.

SAP's tool that implements the xUNIT concept for low-level automated regression tests is called ABAP Unit. It has been a built-in part of the standard ABAP system for a long time now.

There are three areas to note:

1. The test code calls various routines in the code under test—the real code that runs in production. The test code lives with your real code and is transported alongside it, but does not execute in production.

2. The tests should run so fast that you do them after every single code change, just like the syntax check. This way, you know the exact instant your code change has broken something seemingly unrelated (instant feedback). If an automated test run took half an hour, then you might do it once a day overnight, but certainly not many times a day.

3. The test code is an executable specification, which should be readable by a business analyst. It is a list of things IT (the program) is supposed to do, and then proves the program actually does them (living documentation). That should, in theory, promote closer understanding between programmers and the business users who state the requirements.

This is lovely, but there is a problem—you cannot write automated tests for 99 percent of your existing code because of something called *dependencies*.

Dependencies and How to Break Them

In other words, existing code has to be adjusted to enable testing, and that is a lot of work.

Your current code base is most likely filled with dependencies—calls to external things like the database. This prevents you from automatically testing the business logic, because if the code being tested actually calls the database then you need proper data in the database (not very likely in development), and if the code being tested actually asks the user questions then you need a real user, and so on.

So, you have to replace each dependency with a specialized class—this follows the "single responsibility" principle; i.e., a class should have one job only. The single responsibility will be reading the database or talking to the user or calling a specific external system or some other dependency.

Then, in the production code, instead of writing a SELECT statement or doing an AUTHORITY-CHECK or making an actual call to an external system via PI/PO, you make a call to a method of the specialized class, which then performs that task. Initially, that would seem to make no difference. If you were to debug you would see the same lines of code being executed in the same order; there are just more method calls. The crucial thing is these specialized "helper" classes can be replaced by test doubles during a unit test run.

PI/PO

SAPs middleware product—known variously as XI, PI, and PO over time—uses the "proxy" design pattern where a call to an external system is wrapped in a class, and the calling code thinks it is just calling a regular method from within the same SAP system as it is running.

In earlier versions of SAP those proxy methods were static. You did not need to create an instance of the class; you just did a static method call. Then one day, after an upgrade, all your proxy code suddenly got syntax errors, as now the methods were no longer static; you had to create an instance first, and then call the method using the newly created instance.

I imagine many developers all around the world were cursing the fact they had to rewrite loads of code just to get rid of the syntax errors, for no apparent benefit whatsoever. I fell into that basket. Then one day the reason suddenly hit me—SAP made that change so that the proxy classes could be replaced by test doubles. You cannot do that for classes that are 100 percent static.

Moreover, redesigning programs this way (having specialized classes with a single responsibility like reading the database) makes the programs better anyway—more solid and easier to debug.

Later in this chapter when you learn about the TDD workflow, you will see that you only create such specialized classes the exact instant you first need them. The very first database read you need to do in a new program, for example, or for existing code, where you need to redesign whatever routine it is you want to change to use such specialized classes.

In a nutshell, it is the act of breaking all the dependencies that is what makes the code "testable," and thus is the bedrock on which TDD rests.

The TDD Development Cycle: RED/GREEN/BLUE

TDD is seen as a "radical new idea," and established ABAP developers will most likely hate the concept when it is first explained to them.

Earlier, we talked about automated regression tests' being the solution to the problems with fragile code. Here, I would like to stress that TDD and automated unit testing are two different things, although closely linked. Test-driven development is a programming methodology that relies on having an automated unit testing framework in place. You can have automated unit tests and never touch TDD with a ten-foot bargepole. I would say that programming using TDD forces you to create automated tests *properly*.

The concept of test-driven development was first written about in recent times in 2003 by American software engineer Kent Beck, though he only claimed to have "rediscovered" the concept. The first recorded usage in computer software was in 1944 in the United States by a group of female programmers called the Top Secret Rosies, as they developed unit tests to make sure rockets landed in the correct place (i.e., on top of the enemy).

TDD is what makes ABAP programmers (though not those in other languages) scream and run for cover. This is because you do everything backward. You start with a desired result (the most important thing your program does not yet do) and then write a test without actually writing the production code.

Naturally, the test will fail because there is no production code. At this point, you have completed the RED phase. It is called the RED phase because the automated testing framework shows the failing test with a red light icon.

You then write the minimum amount of production code needed to get that test to pass. Once that happens you have completed the GREEN phase. The logic is the same as for the RED phase: this time you get a green light when the automated test runs.

Once it does pass, you can mess around making the code better (i.e., increasing the quality without changing the behavior, a concept known as refactoring), and you will know if you break anything, as the test will start to fail again. This is the BLUE phase and is in fact the primary focus of this book. Chapters 3 to 6 could be seen as an exploration of the various things you improve during the BLUE phase.

Automated regression tests are fantastic, but strangely enough many people say that TDD is not about *testing* so much and is more concerned with forcing the design of the code to be better: more decoupled, more generic, more SOLID.

What does SOLID Mean?

In this context SOLID does not just mean good, or strong and robust. It is an acronym of five OO principles you will find explained in the works of authors like Robert Martin. It stands for:

Single-Responsibility Principle — Classes do one thing and one thing only.

Open–Closed Principle — Black magic whereby you can make code behave differently without changing it (amazingly, this is possible). What this really means is that components are closed for modification but open for extension.

Liskov Substitution Principle — Where you can switch the class that does the work and the calling program will not notice.

Interface Segregation Principle — The "contracts" that say what a class can do should not be too complicated.

Dependency Inversion Principle — Classes should not depend on actual other classes but rather on the *idea* behind those other classes.

Many times in the past I have wondered if I was the first (and only) ABAP programmer to ever do TDD in real life. The good news is that this approach is now being adopted in SAP standard code—tests are even getting added to incredibly old programs like the standard SAP sales order entry program SAPMV45A—and hopefully is catching on in the Z code written by SAP customers.

My Journey to TDD Happiness

This section will deal with the reality of using TDD based on my experiences, and the sub-sections will mirror that journey. I first started playing around with tests in ABAP as far back as 2012, but up until 2018 I was doing what most ABAP programmers do when they start to experiment with automated unit testing—adding unit tests after the event. Then I moved on to adding tests before writing the actual code (the core idea of TDD). Now, I actually have come up with a proper process for TDD that I use, which will be explained here. Lastly, I will explain with examples why this can actually give you a huge benefit in terms of code quality.

Testing After the Event

Once, I was writing a procedural program to look at customer open items and make a proposal of how to clear them (a souped-up version of the standard SAP F-32 transaction that clears open items and is a bit on the user-unfriendly side, in my opinion).

In an ideal world, you would send your customer an invoice and they would pay the exact amount (on time). In such a situation, it would be really easy to clear customer open items—you would just look for an invoice for $100 and an offsetting payment of $100 and clear the two off against each other. In some industries it probably works like that, but in other industries customers usually pay late, or instead of paying off individual invoices pay a certain amount each month, or week, or use any of a million different possible payment patterns, and no two customers are the same in this regard. This makes the job of an accounts receivable clerk a nightmare, as it is not that easy to match the payments against the invoices.

After a while though, the clerks learn to spot certain patterns and develop strategies to come up with proposals of what items to clear against each other. These strategies had been written down as a specification, and I had to code them in ABAP. Nowadays, SAP has developed machine learning algorithms to try to solve that exact same problem, but when I was writing this program such things were still a pipe dream (though even at the time it did occur to me this was a use case for AI).

As is sadly the case with many specifications that programmers get, the requirements were very vague and kept changing, but nonetheless I had enough to go on to enable me to write a working prototype. Like all new programs, it was full of bugs, and since what I was dealing with was almost 100 percent business logic, evaluating the contents of internal tables and the like, I thought this would be a job for unit tests.

I started by creating some test data manually in the development system, running the program manually, and discovering that the rules I thought I had programmed properly didn't seem to be followed at all. The important thing was that I knew what the result should be.

That was important because then I could write a unit test where I hard coded the test data values that were not working, hard coded what I wanted the result to be, and then messed around with the relevant code until such time as the test passed. I then repeated the process until I had nailed down every one of the requirements I had been given, and that seemed wonderful to me. I knew for a fact everything worked perfectly, so what could possibly go wrong?

What went wrong was that after the program was in production the "most important" requirement suddenly arrived out of the blue. That requirement had never been mentioned to me on paper or otherwise because it was "so obvious," and I suppose in the mind of the requesting manager it was. But I have never been that good at telepathy, which is a pity as it seems to be an ability that programmers are often in desperate need of.

So now I had three problems:

1. The "most important" requirement was not catered for at all *BUT* now I knew what it was.

2. All the other requirements changed subtly once some end users "tested in production," *BUT* I had been shown screenshots of what was currently happening (i.e., what had been asked for in the first place) and what they actually wanted to happen.

3. There were some actual bona fide bugs in my code that sprung up despite all my wonderful unit tests, *BUT* once again I had screenshots from production showing the errors.

The important thing to note here is that previously I was making up the test data (which caused my program to fail) based on what I thought might happen in production, and now I had some data that was actually generated in production (which caused my program to fail). The more realistic the data you have to work with is, the better your tests are going to be because no matter how you try you can't guess what is going to happen in real life.

For each of these three problems encountered in production I created one or more new unit tests, or adapted an existing one, but this time the hard-coded input data was copied from production. I am not talking about somehow migrating the data to development; I am just talking about cutting and pasting the values, but the point is the tests were as realistic as they could be.

The end result looked like Listing 2-1, which is the list of test methods inside a local test class.

Listing 2-1. Test Methods for a Procedural Program

```
METHODS : setup,
          given_company_code IMPORTING id_bukrs TYPE ekko-bukrs,
          class_invariant,
          "IT SHOULD.....
          determine_customising_values   FOR TESTING,
          clear_one_payment_vs_all_items FOR TESTING,
          clear_2_plus_pmnts_vs_all_itms FOR TESTING,
          clear_all_if_balance_is_zero   FOR TESTING,
          clear_invoice_noted_in_payment FOR TESTING,
          clear_one_payment_vs_one_month FOR TESTING,
          clear_all_payments_vs_1_month  FOR TESTING,
          clear_2_plus_pmnts_vs_1_month  FOR TESTING,
          group_things_correctly         FOR TESTING,
          clear_cash_sales_by_allocation FOR TESTING,
          handle_tolerances_correctly    FOR TESTING,
          handle_customer_invoices       FOR TESTING,
          not_clear_single_documents     FOR TESTING,
          not_group_when_no_bank_payment FOR TESTING,
          not_group_reversed_invoices    FOR TESTING,
          work_for_all_company_codes     FOR TESTING.
```

Each automated test method calls one or more PERFORM statements. That might seem strange, as the entire unit test framework is OO based, but whereas global classes cannot do a PERFORM (you get a syntax error), local classes can call any FORM routine in the program, which is great for unit tests. Global variables actually help here, because if you have a FORM routine dealing solely with global variables with no USING or CHANGING parameters (which is usually seen as a very bad thing), in your test you can set up the state of the global variables you want before calling the routine to be tested, and then easily evaluate the changed state of the global variables afterward to see if they are correct. Don't tell anyone I said this, but in some ways that is easier than unit testing OO methods, where you sometimes need to set the value of private attributes.

Testing after the event could be called the "test last" approach; i.e., you do the test after writing the code. Most people would call this the "normal" or "classic" way of testing code.

That is how I started out, but in subsequent developments I started to try out the opposite, "test first," approach.

Testing Before the Event

Once, a business analyst came to me and told me she was getting bored with her job and was thinking about a career change. She asked me if I thought she would be happier as a computer programmer (presumably because I seemed to be happy all the time at work, which for some reason does not seem to be the case for everybody in the world).

I said there was a really easy "acid test" that could answer that question for her. I went to the cabinet and pulled out the document that described how to design the recipe for concrete. Now you might think concrete is all the same—it all looks the same, after all, gray and boring—but in fact no two construction jobs ever use concrete with the exact same mix of ingredients. It varies depending on if it's a bridge, or a sidewalk, or a tower block, how fast it has to set, and so on. It's like the beer in Germany: by the German purity law there can only be four ingredients in beer, one of which is water. Yet there are thousands, if not tens of thousands, of varieties of German beer, all tasting different.

In the same vein, the manual about how to design concrete correctly for any given purpose was the thickness of a telephone directory and was largely filled with quadratic equations and the like. So I said to the analyst, "Have a quick look through this—if the prospect of turning the contents of this document into a computer program fills you with joy, sets your heart racing with excitement, then programming is for you!"

After about five minutes of looking through that document, she decided that being a business analyst maybe was not so bad after all.

Now, I had picked that document as a realistic example, as I knew one of my colleagues in Germany was in fact converting it to ABAP as I spoke.

Little did I know that a few years later I would be tasked with the exact same exercise, this time in Australia, with just as complex—but totally different—logic. As I predicted, I was incredibly happy to be given that assignment. It was the most complicated set of applications I had ever had to develop in my life, and the project took *four years*.

It was not only the most difficult program I had ever had to write, but also, relevant to this chapter, the riskiest program I had ever had to write with the worst possible real-world consequences if I stuffed up. If I got this wrong, the building or bridge would fall down.

As an example, I live near Sydney Olympic Park, and on Christmas Eve 2018 the gigantic Opal Tower (an apartment block) literally started cracking up, and all the residents had to be evacuated in case the whole building collapsed—not a nice Christmas present for them. Luckily, it was not due to concrete my program had designed, but that is the sort of possibility that absolutely has to be removed, because we are talking about people's homes and possibly even their lives. It is not just an elaborate computer game.

So, in effect, I was being asked to code something for four years and not make any mistakes along the way. I don't know about you, but I cannot even get through a single day without making at least one mistake. For example, this morning I tried to switch the fan on in the bathroom and switched the light off by mistake, and it was still dark so I could not find the switch to turn the light back on. That does not bode well for my chances of success.

Nonetheless, this story has a happy ending. The project was a gigantic success, shortlisted for an Australian innovation award, and there were no failures at all that were not of a trivial nature.

The question becomes, how did I go about this? How did I eliminate the risk?

I'll start by talking about the business requirements. First of all, there was a technical expert. He had been designing concrete for 30 years, if not longer, and what he did not know about concrete design was not worth knowing. He knew that eventually he would have to retire, and it would be criminal if that expert knowledge was lost forever. I am sure in the future you will be able to just stick something in your ear and magically download the entire contents of your brain to a computer, but we are not quite there yet, so turning that knowledge into a computer program was the way to go.

He started with a VISIO diagram of the process, with about 30 boxes; the first box captured the customer requirements, the last box delivered the finished product. Computer programmers love flow diagrams like this.

Even better, that technical expert was also really good at Excel macros, and so the high-level process flow was backed up by a 43 MB spreadsheet where you put the inputs on the first sheet, pressed a button, let the macros run using reams of configuration data from the other sheets, and BINGO—out came the correct result.

All I had to do was convert the code in the macros into ABAP. How often do you get such a detailed specification? What could possibly go wrong? Well, lots of things, as might be imagined.

Luckily, I could rest assured that the spreadsheet was correct, as that was based upon real life. As long as my program could produce the exact same output, I would be OK.

This is an obvious use case for TDD. I built the program from the ground up by writing unit tests for all the steps (squares) in the VISIO diagram, as for each square I knew the expected inputs and outputs.

That worked like a dream. I could make sure each square worked perfectly for a range of possible input values before moving on to the next square. An important point to note is that I could do all this without even having created the database tables to store the configuration details, as I was using a test double to read the database. I wrote internal tables based on what I thought the database tables might look like. Naturally, my initial guess was totally wrong, so by the time I actually did create the database tables my internal tables in the test double had gone through many iterations. This is a lot easier than creating the database tables up front and having to constantly add and remove columns and regenerate them.

That went very well, and everything was done in SE80. However, as time went by I learned that if you really want to do TDD efficiently, then you need to be programming in ABAP in Eclipse.

TDD Workflow in Eclipse

What is meant by "workflow" in this context is not SAP Business Workflow but rather the steps you take when creating new code in a TDD manner. The following examples are based on what I have been doing recently when creating new programs and improving old ones.

The process is ten times easier in ABAP in Eclipse (official name ADT) than in SE80. In fact, it is such hard work in SE80 that this is probably why a lot of people give up the first week (or day) they start trying to use TDD in ABAP. It is easier in Eclipse due to the auto-generation of method definitions/implementation. In procedural code you are used to writing a call to a FORM routine that does not yet exist, double-clicking on the name of the new routine, and having the system tell you that the routine does not exist and ask if you would like to create it. You say yes, and the definition of the FORM routine together with the signature is created for you.

Now, in SE80 this works pretty much the same for global methods, but not for local methods, and 99.9 percent of test classes are composed entirely of local methods. In SE80 if you double-click on a call to a local method that does not yet exist, nothing happens at all.

Conversely, in ABAP in Eclipse if you code a call to a local method that does not exist you start off by getting a little red light to the left of the code and a message saying that the method does not exist. The difference is that you can put your cursor on the new method name and press CTRL + F1, and up comes the "Quick Assist" menu. In the menu, you have an option to create the new method, and if you choose that then skeletons of both the method definition and its implementation are automatically generated. Moreover, if at the time you coded the call to the non-existent method you passed variables in or out, then the system will look at those variables and automatically create a method signature with the correct variable types. This is better than when a FORM routine is automatically generated, as though that also creates a signature, the parameters in the signature are untyped.

I would be remiss if I did not mention at this point that there is a standard mechanism in ABAP for generating test classes and test methods. The idea is that you write all your production code, and when you are finished you press a magic button and a skeleton test class is generated for the real class with skeleton test methods for each of the actual methods.

That sounds wonderful at first glance, but if you think about things that approach completely and utterly misses the point. It is in fact the reverse of test-driven development because in TDD you create the tests before the production code. Moreover, having the test methods mirror the structure of the production methods is bad as well—the test methods should be based on the nature of the business requirements, not on how you have decided to code those business requirements. This is because you need to be able to refactor—i.e., change and restructure—your code (e.g., delete and add methods) without breaking all the tests.

Creating Test Doubles

With TDD the main difference in the way you write the program's code is what you do when you come across a dependency—a database SELECT or a POPUP_TO_CONFIRM; i.e. something that if coded directly would render the code untestable.

Let us say your production code needs to read the database. You would need a database dependency (helper) class whose single responsibility would be to handle every single database read in your application. At the point you need to create such a class you will only have one method you want to create—to wrap whatever database SELECT you need. Since the whole point of helper classes is that they get called by other classes, that method needs to be public, and good OO design states that all public methods and attributes of a class should be defined via an "interface" in the SE24 sense of the term, although of course that interface could also be local.

Nowadays, you get a warning in the code inspector if you don't follow the rule about defining all public methods via an interface, but I never advocate doing something just for the sake of doing it. In this case, following that rule gives you an added bonus that will enable you to use the ABAP "test double framework" to automatically generate your test doubles for you. That framework only works on global interfaces, not class definitions.

You can think of an interface in terms of a "contract" between the calling code and the code that actually performs the work. The calling code knows what it wants and is presented by the called code with what it has to supply in return. In real life, an analogy might be going to a mortgage broker to arrange your mortgage. You say what you can afford, and it doesn't really matter which financial institution provides the mortgage provided they give you what you want and don't ask for anything too ridiculous in return. In real life, you end up knowing which company actually gives you the mortgage, but in the computer world the calling code does not know who is doing the work on the other end of the contract (interface), and it doesn't care.

You create the interface ZIF_DATABASE_READER with the one method you need, and then a class that implements that interface, let's call it ZCL_DATABASE_READER for now. In real life, both the interface and the real class would have an application-specific name. You would not want one database reader class for the whole system.

A crucial aspect that will ensure your code is always testable is that when you create such a global dependency class you need to set its attributes such that it has PRIVATE instantiation. That way, the calling code cannot get an instance by saying something like DATABASE_READER = NEW ZCL_DATABASE_READER( ).

Using the NEW statement inside a class method creates what is called an internal dependency, and makes it impossible to test the code. You need to set things up so that the only way the calling code can get an instance of the dependency method is via a special factory class using code like the following:

```
DATABASE_READER = DEPENDENCY_FACTORY->GET_DATABASE_READER( ).
```

For this to happen, you of course need to define the factory class. Your application could have quite a few dependencies, each requiring a helper class, and it would be silly to have a separate factory class for each one, so you create one factory class for each application. As a spoiler, all the factory classes' methods are going to be public, so you create an interface ZIF_DEPENDENCY_FACTORY first. The next question is, what goes in that interface?

First, since the factory class itself is going to have private instantiation, you need a static factory method in the interface. If I wrote code like

```
DATA(DEPENDENCY_FACTORY) = ZCL_DEPENDENCY_FACTORY=>FACTORY( ).
```

someone would shout at me, "I heard you the first time!" To avoid such "stuttering" I like to call the static factory method GET_INSTANCE. That method has a single RETURNING parameter typed with reference to ZIF_DEPENDENCY_FACTORY or whatever you want to call the interface. In actual fact, the real name should have some sort of reference to the application at hand, as you will end up with different factories for different applications.

Next, define an instance method to return in an instance of your helper class. This will be called something like GET_DATABASE_READER and again have a single RETURNING parameter, which will be typed with reference to the *interface* of your database reader class.

You are done with the ZIF_DEPENDENCY_FACTORY interface for now, so create a global class definition for the dependency factory class that implements the interface that you just created. For now, just create an implementation with one blank line for the single method in the class.

Now that you have a factory class defined, you need to change the definition of the helper class ZCL_DATABASE_READER such that it is "friends" with ZCL_DEPENDENCY_FACTORY. What do we mean by "friends" here? We are not talking about the TV series. Instead, when a helper class states that the factory class is a "friend" (in ADT you declare this in a code-based manner, in SE80 in a form-based manner) it means that the friend (factory class) can access all the helper classes' private attributes and methods. In our case, this means that the factory class can create new instances of the helper class; in fact, you have set things up so that this is the only way new instances of the helper class can possibly be created.

Only after this "friends" step has been performed can you begin coding the dependency factory class. Navigate to the "Aliases" tab and give the components inherited from the interface the exact same name as they have in the interface and set the visibility to "public." That just makes the calling code a lot shorter.

Next come the attributes. The factory class is going to be a "singleton" (only one instance ever exists) and thus it has a MO_FACTORY private static attribute typed with reference to the class. The GET_INSTANCE method follows the singleton pattern where the first time it is called a new instance is created and stored, and in subsequent calls the stored instance is used, and thus the code looks like Listing 2-2.

Listing 2-2. Factory Method for a Factory Class

```
METHOD zif_dependency_factory~get_instance.

  IF mo_factory IS NOT BOUND.
    CREATE OBJECT mo_factory TYPE zcl_dependency_factory.
  ENDIF.

  ro_factory = mo_factory.

ENDMETHOD.
```

Then, you need a private instance attribute for the database reader class, say MO_DATABASE_READER, typed to the interface used by that class; i.e., ZIF_DATABASE_READER. That is going to be a singleton as well. The factory interface now defines the interface method GET_DATABASE_READER, and this is implemented by the factory class. Once again, the singleton pattern is used, leading to the code in Listing 2-3.

Listing 2-3. Factory Method of Factory Class That Returns an Instance of a Helper Class

```
METHOD get_database_reader.

IF mo_database_reader IS NOT BOUND.
  CREATE OBJECT mo_database_reader TYPE zcl_database_reader.
ENDIF.

ro_database_reader = mo_database_reader.

ENDMETHOD.
```

At this point, the factory class is at a stage where it can be called by the production code that you are writing a test for. If you just left it there though you would not have gained anything; as things stand, the real class will always be returned and thus the real database read.

Now is the time to flip the record over and play the B side, which in this case is what is called an injector class, which is only ever used when running unit tests. This is going to be like when cuckoos go into other birds' nests when they are not looking and swap the eggs with cuckoo eggs. The other bird doesn't notice the difference and raises the cuckoo chick as its own. In this case, we are going to be replacing the "egg," which is the real database-reading class, with a test double for the purposes of automated unit testing.

73

The injector class is going to have all its methods as public, so once again you start with an interface, say ZIF_DEPENDENCY_INJECTOR, though as I mentioned earlier the real name will have something to do with the application being tested.

For now the interface will have one method called INJECT_DATABASE_READER with one IMPORTING parameter typed with reference to ZIF_DATABASE_READER. It's as simple as that; you are done with the interface.

Now create class ZCL_DEPENDENCY_INJECTOR, but the most important thing to note here is that when the little box appears asking you for the name of the new class make sure to click the radio button to make this a test class. It isn't really, as it will not contain any tests itself, but setting that flag means that instances of the class cannot be created in production. Considering what this injector class is going to do, it could wreak havoc in the live system, so making sure no instances can be created there is quite important. Set it as final with public instantiation—the opposite of the settings I make for most classes, as we are in the anti-matter world of unit tests, where everything is back to front and inside out.

Go to the "Aliases" tab and set the alias name of the one interface method to the same name as in the interface, enter a blank implementation in the INJECT_DATABASE_READER method for now, and activate the class.

Hooray! Now that the injector class exists, it is time to go back to the ZCL_DEPENDENCY_FACTORY class. There, you will add ZCL_DEPENDENCY_INJECTOR as a friend; i.e., in class ZCL_DEPENDENCY_FACTORY the declaration GLOBAL FRIENDS ZCL_DEPENDENCY_INJECTOR will be added. This is needed because the injector class is going to grossly violate the privacy of the factory class, which is not how friends are supposed to behave in real life, but that is how they carry on in the software world.

With that change made you can go back to the ZCL_DEPENDENCY_INJECTOR and start coding. First up, it needs a private attribute that is called MO_FACTORY and typed to ZCL_DEPENDENCY_FACTORY—not the interface this time but the class itself, as you need to access its private attributes.

Next, the injector class needs a constructor with no parameters. In the constructor the MO_ FACTORY is going to be filled with a brand new, squeaky clean instance of the factory class. Normally that would be impossible, as the factory class is a singleton—you always get the same instance back. In the injector's constructor, however, because it is a so-called friend of the factory class it can wipe out the private attribute in the factory used to store the singleton instance, in effect stopping it from being a singleton. The code to do this is shown in Listing 2-4.

Listing 2-4. Constructor of the Injector Class

```
METHOD constructor.

  CLEAR zcl_dependency_factory=>mo_factory.

  mo_factory = zcl_dependency_factory=>get_instance( ).

ENDMETHOD.
```

Why are we inflicting such a cruel and unusual punishment upon the poor old factory class? It is all to do with the concept of "test isolation"—when we run a large number of automated unit tests it is vital to the future of the universe that the result of one test cannot be influenced by anything that went on in a previous test. Each one should stand on its own. SAP claims this is enforced because the tests run in a random order each time. I don't actually think they do, but you have to *pretend* that they do.

The factory class could be stuffed with test doubles that have had all sorts of weird data put into them during the last test. Since we want to make sure none of that is carried over to the next test, the safest way is to "nuke" the factory and force it to be rebuilt from scratch.

Speaking of stuffing the factory with test doubles, it is time to code the INJECT_ DATABASE_READER method. This is very simple—the injector class just overwrites a private variable in the factory with whatever has been passed into the injection method, as shown in Listing 2-5.

Listing 2-5. Injector Method of Class ZCL_DEPENDENCY_INJECTOR

```
METHOD zif_dependency_injector~inject_database_reader.

  mo_factory->mo_database_reader = io_database_reader.

ENDMETHOD.
```

All the pieces of the dependency-breaking jigsaw are now in place. In the global class that is going to be tested (the CUT) in the local test class section (in ADT that appears as a tab at the bottom of the screen, in SE24 you navigate using the menu *Goto* ➤ *Local Definitions/Implementations* ➤ *Local Test Classes*) for each external dependency class, you need to create a local test double—a class that looks like the original (i.e., it has the same interface) but does not really interact with the database or external system or whatever. It just sends back fake hard-coded data.

You put the definition and implementation of any test double classes at the start of the "local test class" section in SE24, and as shown in Listing 2-6 that does not look very impressive.

Listing 2-6. Local Test Double Definition and Implementation

```
CLASS ltd_pers_layer DEFINITION FINAL.

  PUBLIC SECTION.

    INTERFACES zif_database_reader.

ENDCLASS.

CLASS ltd_pers_layer IMPLEMENTATION.

ENDCLASS.
```

Before every unit test is run, the SETUP method, if defined, is automatically called. You code that method yourself, and in that method first create instances of however many test doubles there are, and then inject them all into the factory.

Lastly, you create a new instance of the global class being tested (Class Under Test, or CUT). You do that last in case the CUT uses any helper variables in its CONSTRUCTOR method. It should not if it is well designed, but better safe than sorry. The end result is shown in Listing 2-7.

Listing 2-7. Test Class SETUP Method That Uses Injection

```
METHOD setup.

  "Prepare Test Doubles
  mo_mock_pers_layer = NEW ltd_pers_layer( ).

  DATA(lo_injector) = NEW zcl_dependency_injector( ).

  lo_injector->inject_database_reader( mo_mock_pers_layer ).

  "Create New Instance of Class Under Test (CUT)
  "for every test method
  CREATE OBJECT mo_cut.

ENDMETHOD.
```

We have now ridden the train all the way to the end of the dependency injection line. Now, when the code being tested runs for real the actual classes that read the database or whatever are returned by the factory. During the automated test run the test double gets returned instead.

The routine being tested will never know the difference; it always thinks it is running in productive mode.

The Unspeakable Evil that is the TEST-SEAM

I cannot stress enough how important it is that production code not know when it is being tested. You could have production code full of constructs like IF UNIT_TEST_ RUNNG = ABAP_TRUE THEN do something different. That's not a good test at all, but it is worse than that—you have probably heard of the scandal where Volkswagen set their software such that when the car was driving down a real road it did one thing (released a huge amount of emissions) but when in a laboratory being tested it did something totally different (released a small amount of emissions). They got found out and had to pay huge fines, and change their very business model, but the point is if the software had no way of knowing it was being tested they could not have come up with such a scam. They would have had to come up with a different scam.

In the SAP world, the equivalent mechanism is called a TEST-SEAM. You take a section of production code and add BEGIN TEST-SEAM XYZ above it and add END TEST-SEAM below it.

Then in the test method for each such "seam" you write some replacement code wrapped by putting BEGIN TEST-INJECTION XYZ above it and END TEST-INJECTION below it.

There is no logical reason to do this. In such a case, the production code knows it can be tested, and there is just as much effort and risk—if not more—in changing production code to use a TEST-SEAM as opposed to replacing whatever dependency it is you want to mock with a call to a specialized class.

More important, you can put TEST-SEAMS around chunks of business logic and have them behave differently during a test than they would during productive use. That would be just like the Volkswagen example and defeat the whole purpose of unit testing.

Creating a New Test Method

Your starting point is the big list of user requirements you have in the functional specifications. Sometimes you don't get much of a functional specification or it is very vague. In that case, you guess what is required and then your starting point is the bug list of user requirements you *think* are needed.

At the very highest level these requirements are what are known as "user stories"—a piece of software would not be much use if it did not benefit a human in some way or another, and a "user story" nails down what the benefit is exactly.

Such "stories" take the "AS A / I NEED / SO THAT I" format as in "**As an** order taker **I need** to see the customer address properly formatted **so that I** can make sure the product is delivered to the right place."

These are very high-level requirements, and OO programs are full of tiny methods that work together in order to fulfill such high-level requirements. Therefore, you usually do not create a single test for the whole of the high-level requirement, but for several lower-level requirements that enable that high-level requirement.

Imagine your requirement is, "As a thirsty person I need to have a drink so that I am no longer thirsty." You can break that down as follows:

- To have a drink I need (a) a beer and (b) a glass to hold that beer.

- To get the beer I need (a) a pub and (b) a barman and (c) money.

- To get money I need (a) a bank card and (b) my PIN number and (c) an ATM.

In our world each "requirement" could be a method. As can be seen, each requirement has one or more lower-level requirements (lower-level methods called by the higher-level method), and each of those lower-level requirements can have one or more lower-level requirements and so on. Where do you stop?

You could take the approach of testing every single method, no matter how small. That would work OK, but you would have in some senses painted yourself into a corner. Every time you decided to change the structure of your class and remove or add a method you would have to remove or add a test. This is why most experts recommend you do not test private methods; instead, what you should be writing tests for are the lowest-level requirements that have public methods. If that test passes OK you can be confident all the low-level private methods that combine to make that public method work are correct, and, more important, you can tinker with the internal implementation (how many private methods you have and how they work together) without having to constantly rewrite the tests.

Put another way, the tests should mirror the business requirements (the WHAT) as opposed to mirroring the methods (the HOW).

When you have done such an analysis of the business requirements and have come up with a list of things to write tests for (and hence the production code to make those tests pass and thus fulfill the business requirements), you may end up with a list of ten requirements, or a hundred, and now you are paralyzed as you don't know which one to do first.

You could be on a programming team that uses some form of "agile" methodology (whereby you release a small number of features to the end users on a regular basis) or one that uses a "waterfall" methodology (where you get every single feature working and then release the finished product to the end users). Most large SAP implementations use the latter approach, certainly all the ones I have ever been on did, but the former approach (common in the web world) is slowly taking hold in the ABAP world.

If you are using the waterfall methodology, imagine you are using the agile methodology. If you are actually using the agile methodology, you don't need to imagine anything. In an agile project the myriad user stories (features, if you like) are split into small groups that form a minor release (a so-called sprint), and in any given sprint you are working on a small number of requirements that could be described as "the most important things the program needs to do which it does not yet do." Who decides what is most important? If you work for an independent software company it is the paying company, if you work for a commercial organization or the government it is your internal customers, if you are on a waterfall project and have just been told to get everything working at once then you have to make a best guess.

You may have heard of the term *minimum viable product*—a piece of software that does the absolute bare minimum it needs to do without one single "nice to have" (and most software ends up being 95 percent composed of "nice to have" features). Then the game becomes to identify the "must haves" and start with them.

Now you can actually start writing some code. "Hooray!" you say. "At long last!" Not so fast—to start off with, we are just talking about a list of comments. Now stop crying and listen: test methods always follow a certain format. In the method definitions the SETUP method goes first to create a new instance of the class under test for each test method and create test doubles.

After that, you make a list of the specifications/requirements/features, whatever you want to call them, the things you have decided need tests, and try to rank them in order of importance.

Start by describing what IT is—that is a description of the application (or part of the application) that you are going to be testing. Then you list (as comments) all the various things IT should do. If you are only adding five new behaviors in this release, then just list those; by the time you have gotten those working it is more than possible all the other requirements will have changed.

In this example, you have been told that the most vital thing in the universe is that once the customer has been chosen on the main screen the customer group displays correctly (it doesn't matter why that is important; yours is not to reason why, as they say). The next most important thing is that the address then comes up in a highly specific format to make 100 percent sure the invoice doesn't get delivered to the wrong place, which is what used to happen all the time in the old system. The next most important thing is "such and such" and so on.

You start by writing—in the test class, in the private section—code like that in Listing 2-8.

Listing 2-8. Comments Indicating What Test Methods Will Be Created

```
CLASS ltc_model DEFINITION FOR TESTING
    RISK LEVEL HARMLESS
    DURATION SHORT
    FINAL.

  PUBLIC SECTION.

  PRIVATE SECTION.
    "What class are we testing? (Class Under Test = CUT)
    DATA: mo_cut TYPE REF TO zcl_octopus_model.
    "Test Doubles
    "Global Variables for Test Methods

  METHODS:
    setup.
    "IT (SCREEN) SHOULD.....
    "<------------30--------------->
    "Fill the customer group on the sales data subscreen
    "Format the customer name and address properly
```

```
    "Only show delivery address belonging to the customer
    "Format the delivery address properly
    "Etc..

ENDCLASS.
```

At this stage, you only have the SETUP method defined, as well as a list of comments that are saying what functionality IT needs to do that IT does not yet do.

You may have noticed the dots (periods) after the comment IT SHOULD and wondered why they are there. Am I going dotty? There are not an arbitrary number of dots, as it turns out. The letters forming IT SHOULD, including the space between IT and SHOULD, plus the dots add up to exactly 30 characters, which is the maximum length for a method name in ABAP.

In other languages method names can be as long as you want, and hence as descriptive as you want. In ABAP we are limited to 30 characters, and hence usually have to use abbreviations, often to the point where the method name becomes cryptic.

Naturally, the comment can be as long as you so desire and span several lines (though it really should fit on one line), but the method name has to be such that it is not longer than the last dot in the IT SHOULD comment; if it is, you will get a syntax error. The point is that the business analyst should be able to have a look at this section of the code and recognize it as being a 100 percent match for the functional specification they wrote.

The definition of the test method has no parameters, as that would make it read less like plain English; you don't say things like EXPORTING or RETURNING when you are writing in natural language what something should do.

Put another way, test methods are "executable specifications"—they say what the program should do and prove that it does (or does not) in fact do what it is supposed to do. At the moment, the program is not doing a whole lot, as we have not written any code yet. Happily, now you can start. Underneath the comment write the name of the first test method followed by the addition FOR TESTING, as in

```
"Format the customer name and address properly
Format_customer_name_address FOR TESTING
```

The FOR TESTING at the end means that the test method will be automatically called every time the developer is in any part of the program and takes the menu path *Execute ➤ Unit Tests*. The addition also means the method not only cannot be called in a productive system, but will not even compile in a productive system—it is like the code is not there. This way the test code is inextricably linked with the production code and can never be separated, but cannot do any harm in production or even slow the compilation of the program down.

There will be a little red X to the left of the new method name to indicate it does not yet exist. In SE80 you would have to manually create the implementation; in ABAP in Eclipse all you need to do is press CTRL + F1 and ask for any empty implementation to be created automatically. Thus far, that has only saved you a minute or so versus SE80, but just wait—the time savings are all going to mount up.

So, now you have the definition that you just manually created and the blank implementation that was automatically created. After this, things should move very quickly.

Coding the Test Method

The test method itself should not have any actual statements within it, but rather be a call to at least three other "semantic" methods. This is based on a principle called behavior-driven development, coined by Dan North, where a test has the following three stages:

- The GIVEN stage, where the data needed to run the test is prepared

- The WHEN stage, which actually calls the routine that is being tested

- The THEN stage, which validates whether the result of the test is correct or not

Once again, this code is going to look like plain English, and a casual reader (like a business analyst) could look at the method calls in the test method and understand what is being tested. This should look like a written test script for use in manual testing, where first it tells you what inputs are required, then what transaction to call using those inputs, and lastly what the outcome should be. Turning a test script into a test method should be as easy as falling off a log.

A test script for manual testing might look like the one in Table 2-1.

Table 2-1. *Test Script for Manual Testing*

Step	Trans. Code	Instruction/ Input X-Reference	Expected Results/ Output X-Reference
1.	ZVA01	Enter a customer of account group NORMAL	The customer group field on the screen should show the value NORMAL
2.			

The code for the corresponding test method will look something like Listing 2-9.

Listing 2-9. An Example Test Method

```
METHOD derive_customer_group.

  given_account_group( for_customer = normal_customer
                       is_group     = normal ).

  given_customer_number( normal_customer  ).

  when_screen_is_shown(  ).

  then_cust_account_group_is( normal ).

ENDMETHOD.
```

Note how you can use parameters to get around the 30-character limit on method names. You still cannot have the method name as long as you want, but this trick can make the code read a bit more like plain English, avoiding the need for abbreviations.

At this point, none of the three "semantic" methods actually exist, so they all have the little red cross error message to their left with a message in each case stating that they do not exist. For all three methods you press CTRL + F1 to invoke the "Quick Fix" menu and auto-create the definition and implementation for each method.

Coding the THEN Method

In the THEN method, you evaluate the results of the test. It may seem strange to code this first, but remember in TDD we are doing everything backward from the traditional ABAP way of doing things.

In ABAP UNIT, as indeed in every sort of xUnit framework, you use an ASSERTION class to evaluate the test result. In ABAP that class is CL_ABAP_UNIT_ASSERT, which has a whole bunch of methods to check if two values are equal, or if something is blank (initial), and so on. You can even code custom assertions if you have some very strange and specific logic.

The vast bulk of the time you will be using the ASSERT_EQUALS method, where you compare the data in the class under test after the test has been run with what you expect the result to be. This method has lots of optional parameters, but the important ones are as follows:

> MSG = The message that appears during the automated unit test run if this test fails

> EXP = What you expect the result to be if the test succeeds

> ACT = What the actual result was

As with any method call, you can put the parameters in any order you feel like—a reasonable guess would be to put them in the order in which they occur in the signature; i.e., ACT first, EXP second, and then MSG at the end. However, if you code the method call in ABAP in Eclipse using auto-code completion it arranges the parameters in what might be called the order in which a human brain would process them; i.e., the order I have listed them in. The result can be seen in Listing 2-10.

Listing 2-10. An Example THEN Method

```
METHOD then_cust_account_group_is.

  cl_abap_unit_assert=>assert_equals(
  msg = 'Customer Account Group not Set Properly'
  exp = normal
  act = mo_cut->customer_account_group ).

ENDMETHOD.
```

As an aside, CUT stands for "Class Under Test"—you are testing a method of that class. You will hear more about this when you get to the WHEN method.

The next step is also going to seem strange. At this point, you run the automated unit tests. Choose the menu option *Local Test Classes* ➤ *Execute* ➤ *Unit Tests.* The test will fail. Of course it will fail, as the only thing you have coded thus far is the test for the correct result, and that cannot possibly pass until you have written the actual production code, and that will not happen until you write the WHEN method. Nonetheless, running the test at this point and seeing it fail means the RED phase has started.

If you do not start off with a failing unit test then you cannot possibly know that any production code you write actually does what it is supposed to do. If the test passes before you write the real code, and still passes afterward, then you have not proved anything.

Coding the GIVEN Method

This method "sets the scene" for the test; i.e., it sets up the input data that is going to be passed into the routine to be tested. There are two types of such data for which you can set the values here:

- Member variables of the test class, elementary data types, or structures—basically anything that the routine being tested takes in as an input parameter. You could of course hard code those values in the main test method, but then it would not look so much like plain English.

- The values inside test doubles (fake database access classes and the like). Instances of the test doubles are created during the SETUP method of the automated test run just before each test method is run, and these values are going to be retrieved during the execution of the routine being tested. How? This is because the production code will not create helper classes directly, but rather will do so via a factory method, and the SETUP method will ensure that during the code a test double is used in the production code rather than the real class, and that test double will use the hard-coded values set here.

Listing 2-11 shows an example of the first type—setting up member variables to be passed into the routine being tested. In the following example we set up a situation in which two items already exist in a sales order with the plant entered, and now the user has changed the plant.

Listing 2-11. An Example GIVEN Method

```
METHOD given_two_order_items_entered.

  mt_all_items = VALUE #(
  ( posnr = '000010' werks='1234' )
  ( posnr = '000020' werks='4321' ) ).

  ms_current_item = VALUE #( posnr = '000010' werks='9999' ).

ENDMETHOD.
```

Later in the WHEN method, both MT_ALL_ITEMS and MS_CURRENT_ITEM will be passed into the method being tested as IMPORTING parameters.

When it comes to the second type, filling a test double with data that will then be used by the method being tested, at this point we encounter a bit of circular logic, what could be called a catch-22. You are trying to put values into test doubles that are going to get called during the method that is going to be tested—but you have not written that method yet, so how do you know what test doubles are needed?

The answer is that if you know for a fact that your routine is going to be reading the database, or asking the user something, or some other dependency, then you can prepare the fake response data right away. Otherwise, this is going to be an interactive process. You start by setting any input parameters here, and then you are finished with the WHEN method.

Thereafter, when writing the productive code, if you find your test failing because a dependency was not faked, then you can come back to the GIVEN method to pass the desired values into that dependency.

For the sake of argument, say you know for a fact the routine to be tested is going to query the database to get the customer group for a customer. Your fake database access class does not actually read the database; it reads an internal table. If that table is in the public section of the test double then great, you can directly set the values here. Alternatively, you can make things more explicit by adding a special method to set the desired values in the test double class. You don't even have to navigate to the test double class—just code a method call to the method that will update the values in the test double (a method that does not yet exist).

You auto-generate the GIVEN method(s) in the test method, and the system is clever enough to look at constants like NORMAL_CUSTOMER, which is typed as KUNAG (customer), and automatically type the IMPORTING parameter in the generated method correctly, so the definition looks like Listing 2-12.

Listing 2-12. Definition of a GIVEN Method

```
given_account_group    IMPORTING for_customer TYPE kunag
                                  is_group     TYPE ktokd,
```

Then you code the implementation as per Listing 2-13.

Listing 2-13. Implementation of a GIVEN Method

```
METHOD given_account_group.

  mo_mock_pers_layer->set_account_group(
    id_customer = for_customer
    id_group    = is_group ).

ENDMETHOD.
```

Inside this GIVEN method, some of the parameter names look a bit odd because of the way they need to read in the main test method, but I am sure you get the idea. What you are trying to do is pass in some hard-coded values to a test double of the persistency (database) layer. Then, when the routine being tested goes to read the database, what actually will be returned are these hard-coded values.

It is highly likely at this stage that the SET_ACCOUNT_GROUP method of the persistency-layer test double does not yet exist, nor does the test double class itself, because you haven't needed it yet and you are only supposed to create things as and when you need them to prevent filling the system with useless nonsense you once thought you might need. Earlier in this chapter, you saw the procedure to create a test double class; here is the point you actually do this.

The fact that the test double class has no SET_ACCOUNT_GROUP method yet is no problem at all—simply put your cursor on the method call and then use a quick fix to auto-generate the SET_ACCOUNT_GROUP method definition (which will have importing parameters typed as KUNAG and KTOKD) and implementation. Once the skeleton implementation has been generated, put your cursor on the new method name and use the forward navigation feature (which is F3 in Eclipse as opposed to just double-clicking like you do in ABAP) to get to the method implementation in the test double, where you can code how a private internal table inside the test double definition is to be updated, as shown in Listing 2-14.

Listing 2-14. Method to Inject Data into a Test Double

```
METHOD set_account_group.

  READ TABLE mt_kna1 ASSIGNING FIELD-SYMBOL(<ls_kna1>)
  WITH TABLE KEY kunnr = id_customer.

  IF sy-subrc EQ 0.
```

```
      <ls_kna1>-ktokd = id_group.
   ELSE.
     INSERT VALUE #(
     kunnr = id_customer
     ktokd = id_group ) INTO TABLE mt_kna1.
   ENDIF.

  ENDMETHOD.
```

The internal table definition (MT_KNA1) does not yet exist, so you auto-generate that by using a quick fix as well. We are only creating methods and attributes at the exact instant we first need them, which is the reverse of the usual process of making a detailed list of methods and attributes you think you are going to need and then creating them all up front, and then weeks or months later realizing you don't need three-quarters of them and deleting the un-needed ones (or worse still, leaving them there).

Coding the WHEN Method

In the WHEN method, you call the routine in the "class under test" (CUT) that is going to be tested. An instance of the CUT is created in the SETUP method that runs before each test class is executed. An example implementation is shown in Listing 2-15.

Listing 2-15. Example WHEN Method

```
METHOD when_screen_is_shown.

  mo_cut->process_main_screen( ).

ENDMETHOD.
```

The method PROCESS_MAIN_SCREEN does not yet exist. I imagine by this stage you are thinking "I know—I will just auto-generate it via the 'Quick Fix' mechanism like I did for all the other methods in the test class!" How right you are. You are now finished generating all the various methods. In Eclipse, as you have seen, this takes no time at all; in SE80 it would have taken a lot longer. Everything created thus far can only execute in development, but now you can commence what you have always considered your "proper" job; i.e., writing the code that will execute in production.

Writing the Production Code

The TDD theory says that you should write the minimum possible code to get the test working as fast as you can—cut corners, cut and paste code; the code you write can be as poor quality and inefficient as you want as long as it works. That is what people tend to do more often than not, so no change here. The difference is that this time we are going to clean it up later, as opposed to the normal practice of making some vague commitment to do so whilst knowing in your heart of hearts that it's not going to happen. The IT saying for this is "Later = Never," which is why TDD forces you to do it (improve the code quality) right away as opposed to some nebulous unspecified time in the future.

There is no need to teach my grandmother to suck eggs here—you all know how to write code! Here, you will just see how production code should use the dependency factory.

In this case, the production code could look like Listing 2-16.

Listing 2-16. The Actual Production Code

```
METHOD process_main_screen.

    DATA(lo_factory) = zcl_dependency_factory=>get_instance( ).

    DATA(lo_pers_layer) = lo_factory->get_database_reader( ).

    customer_account_group =
    lo_pers_layer->derive_customer_details( customer_number )-ktokd.

ENDMETHOD.
```

When the method in the CUT runs for real, the actual database will be read. When the unit test runs, the test double will bring back a hard-coded value instead. At this point in SE24 when you take the menu path *Method* ➤ *Execute* ➤ *Unit Tests* all the unit tests will run (there is only one at the moment) and pass.

Once you have written enough (testable) code to make the test pass, the GREEN phase is complete. To be 100 percent accurate, you have reached that phase when you have written enough code to make the current test pass, and every other previous unit test for the class under test still passes as well. Put another way, if you get the current test to pass but break something else you have not finished—you are still in the RED phase.

The Simplest Thing That Will Work

If you follow the letter of the law then you have to write the least amount of code in the fastest possible time to get the current test to pass. In this case, the expected result is that the customer account group has the value represented by the constant NORMAL.

So the simplest, fastest way to get the test to pass would be to code the production method as follows:

```
RD_CUSTOMER_GROUP = NORMAL
```

That is really simple and gets the test passing within seconds. Technically, that means the GREEN phase is complete. However, that is of course a ridiculous thing to do. Nonetheless, that is the way many leading programming experts—like Robert Martin—present the first iteration of a production method created via TDD to their students. It's not because it is a good thing to do—of course it is not—but it demonstrates a different principle entirely.

The first test would pass, but as soon as you added another test—where you are expecting the result SPECIAL, for example—the second test would fail, as the result is currently hard coded. Thus, you are forced to do things properly and make a call to the database, and that has to be done via a specialized persistency-layer class that can be mocked. The more different tests are added with different values, the more the production code has to change to accommodate all the different possibilities. Robert Martin describes this process thus:

"As the tests become more specific, the code becomes more generic."

This is called the inventor's paradox—solving a general problem is easier than solving a specific problem.

The BLUE Phase

Here is another quote, this time from American software guru Kent Beck:

"First make it work, then make it good, then make it fast."

The RED phase is all about defining what is required and proving your program does not currently fulfil that requirement. The GREEN phase is all about changing your program until you have proved it can in fact now satisfy the requirement. The BLUE phase is about something that is generally totally ignored once something is working—ensuring that all your code is the best quality it can possibly be.

That is the whole focus of this book. Increasing the quality of your code is something you should do anyway, but following a TDD methodology forces the issue.

This phase is not even that difficult, especially as you have only just added a few lines of code. Apart from looking at the new code and thinking about it, now is the time to run the extended program check and code inspector and see what they have to say about your new code. Ideally, you want to end the BLUE phase with a clean slate from both checks—either because you have fixed the errors they highlighted or because you have flagged those errors as false positives.

When it comes to a false positive, always put a comment saying why it is a false positive. If you cannot come up with such a comment then it is not a false positive—it is a real error you should do something about.

Does This Actually Give You a Benefit?

As you can see, the whole TDD approach adds what seems like a bucketload of extra work every time you want to add or change code. The obvious question is, is it worth it? Do you get some sort of concrete benefit as a result that outweighs that extra work? Or is this just some sort of ivory-tower theory that falls to bits the instant you try to apply it in the real world?

I was lucky enough to be allowed to follow this approach where I work, so my TDD story is real. How did it go for me?

We had a gigantic, monolithic, procedural, business-critical DYNPRO program, and the goal was to rewrite it in an OO manner using TDD. At first glance that does not seem like writing a "new" program, but for all intents and purposes it was: the structure of an application written in OO is totally different, and in this case the business requirements could not be defined more clearly. It had to do exactly what the old program did, and that behavior was defined in the existing code.

So I went through the existing code and analyzed it to see what each screen did—the various "things" the screen did as defined in its PBO and PAI modules. Each screen became a test class where "IT" was the screen, and in that test class for each "thing" the screen did a unit test was written, and then the production code, in the manner described earlier in this chapter.

From a Gut Feeling . . .

How did I find the TDD process the first time I did it for real? There is no point in lying—this is *agony* at the start. The analogy would be if I were somehow forced to speak only in German for the rest of my life (my native language is English, but I lived in Germany for many years). Even after all this time I still find speaking in German incredibly difficult, but if I had to do that all day every day eventually it would become easier, and probably a lot sooner than I might initially think.

All the textbooks say the RED-GREEN-BLUE TDD cycle should take minutes. How long did the very first such cycle I did in real life take? Two days. Oh dear. No wonder so many people give up.

However, just like speaking a foreign language—or doing any difficult new thing—the more you do it the easier it becomes, and after a relatively short amount of time I find I can now go through the cycle in minutes, just as it was advertised.

Even though the idea is to only build the code you need based on tests, when I started trying to use TDD, I could not stop myself doing things the way I had always done them, and so I built a skeleton architecture—classes and what have you—up front based on how I thought things should work.

Once I started writing the tests and trying to get them to work, it became instantly apparent my initial design was full of holes like Swiss cheese. I have found that development via TDD forces design change, which is a good thing as it makes the resulting application SOLID. Going back to Michael Feathers, he said in a blog that unit testing forces the programs to be more modular, and "*with modularity, comes quality.*"

I have found that you can literally feel the program getting better after each forced change—and that is a wonderful feeling. This feeling is of course a soft benefit, and here is another one: Once you get the hang of it, the whole TDD cycle becomes great fun. Programmers generally think programming is fun rather than a chore, and here is another way to have more fun than usual during your workday. Of course, that is not a benefit you can take to management as a reason to move to TDD.

. . . to a Concrete Example

Let us move from talking about the "warm glowing feeling" that doing TDD gives you to a really specific example. This is taken from real life.

We have two different programs being developed in tandem; both wrap the sales order-entry process. One is written using procedures and changed in a traditional way, while one is written in OO and changed using TDD. Conventional wisdom would say it is faster to change the procedural one because you just have to add the new code and don't have the extra overhead of writing a test first.

Our example business requirement has to do with payment terms. In standard SAP you can have header-level payment terms that apply to the whole sales document, or individual sales document items can have their own payment terms if they so desire. This information is stored in table VBKD.

Both existing programs had the rule that when creating a sales order with reference to a contract, the payment terms should be taken from the contract header, and the payment terms on the contract-item level should be ignored. One fine day, one country said, "No, we have all different payment terms on all our contract items, they need to be copied to the sales order at item level." Fine, no problem. We can create a customizing setting that controls which countries are going to use that new rule.

In the procedural program, there are already two conditional branches with identical blocks of code. The programmer simply adds a new branch and cuts and pastes the exact same block of code into that new branch, as in Listing 2-17, which shows the pasted code between the IF and the ELSE.

Listing 2-17. Cutting and Pasting Code into a New Branch

```
* Payment terms copy from contract item into SO item
      IF gcv_it_zterm_not_from_ref IS INITIAL.
        IF NOT lw_cvbkd IS INITIAL.
          MOVE lw_cvbkd TO lw_vbkdvb.
          lw_vbkdvb-posnr = t_vbap-posnr.
          lw_vbkdvb-bstkd = t_vbap-bstkd.
        ELSE.
          MOVE-CORRESPONDING vbkd TO lw_vbkdvb.
          lw_vbkdvb-posnr = t_vbap-posnr.
          lw_vbkdvb-bstkd = t_vbap-bstkd.
        ENDIF.
      ELSE.
```

There are 11 extra lines of code (most of which are duplicate code), but adding the new branch and cutting and pasting the code takes no time at all, and everything works fine.

Meanwhile, in the TDD world, we write a unit test first. If you take all the method definitions and implementations, even though each method is really tiny, that is still more than 11 lines of code, maybe double that or even more, and of course it takes longer than simply pressing CTRL + C and then CTRL + V. Then the new code is added into the corresponding OO method, which is written using the techniques described in this book and so has no duplicate code. All that is needed in the production code is to add an extra branch, which sets a flag as opposed to containing a load of duplicate code, as shown in Listing 2-18.

Listing 2-18. Alternative to Cutting and Pasting

```
ELSEIF mo_gc->item_pterm_not_from_refdoc EQ abap_false.
  "Payment terms copy from contract item into SO item
  lf_use_header = abap_false.
ELSEIF ls_ref_doc_business_item-vsart IS INITIAL.
```

You will learn about this sort of technique in the "Clarity" chapter, but in essence the conditional branches set a flag, and based on the flag certain code is called, rather than having that same code in every branch that is TRUE or FALSE. Only two lines have been added to the production code. In both the procedural and OO programs, the new change works just fine.

On the surface, the non-TDD program wins, as the change is made faster and provides exactly the same benefit. However, the procedural program has just become a lot longer, and hence more difficult to understand, and the longer and more difficult to understand a routine is, the higher the risk is of its breaking when you make yet another change to it in the future. More important, if you make a change to the procedural program in a year's time, and that new change works but breaks the change to do with copying from contract items, you will not know, as typically only the latest change is tested. In the TDD version, however, because of the unit test, if a new future change breaks the item-copying logic you will know instantly.

Both programs have become stronger in the sense that they can now do an additional business requirement. However, this change has made the procedural program more likely to break something in the future—not only the feature just added, but possibly any other logic in the changed routine. In the TDD version, however, the increase in risk is zero, as every bit of logic in that routine, including the new bit, is covered by a test. In addition, sometimes the process of adding a test in advance forces you to change the design of the existing code for the better—making it more generic, or more stable, or some other really good change.

On balance, the TDD program has become stronger, and the procedural one has become weaker, as a result of this change. Moreover, this process will continue with every future business requirement; in other words, programs without tests "rot" over time, becoming worse with every change, whereas programs written via TDD become better with every change.

Some Unit Tests Might Seem Pointless . . .

Hopefully at your organization there is some sort of peer review process where before your code changes are released to test one of your colleagues has to look over the code—the so-called Four Eyes principle. Some programmers resent this and feel the whole process is a statement by management questioning their ability, but in actual fact not only does such an activity act as an implicit knowledge transfer between more experienced programmers and less experienced ones, but much more importantly it covers your back in that someone is checking for obvious mistakes—and *everyone* makes obvious mistakes from time to time. You're lying to yourself if you think you don't.

The peer-review process was aimed at production code, but there is no logical reason not to have your test code reviewed as well. When and if this happens, you are quite likely to get a comment saying a particular unit test seems to be pointless at best, ridiculous at worst.

Once, when I was writing about unit tests on the internet, I gave an example of a test that proved that an initial screen filled various fields correctly using parameter IDs. Someone on the internet said that was crazy, as getting a value from a PID always works, and what sort of a lunatic test was that? On the face of it, they were correct; doing such a thing seems a colossal waste of time and energy right up until the point where, five years later, someone has an idea that there is a far better way of getting the values than using PIDs and changes the code and breaks everything, and you don't know anything has broken because there is no test.

Here come two more such examples.

It's Too Short to Test

Many years back now, someone working on the open source project ABAP2XLSX (which creates Excel spreadsheets based on ABAP code) decided that adding unit tests was a really good thing. The class in question was ZCL_EXCEL_COMMON, and if that is available in your system I would advocate having a look just to see some examples of sensible unit tests. The unit tests all work now, but when they were new I was adding those new unit tests manually into the class in my system as I did not want to copy the latest version of the entire class automatically, as it would overwrite some other changes I had made.

There was one test where a zero value was being passed in and the expected result was a date with an initial value; i.e., "00000000." There were only two or three lines in the method being tested, and those three lines looked simple and obvious. Yet the test failed. I was really puzzled. I cannot remember what the problem was now, but I clearly remember sitting and looking at the three lines of code for an hour wondering how on Earth this could possibly not be working, until eventually a flash of light went through my brain and I had an "Of course!" moment. The moral of the story is that no matter how trivial and obvious a piece of code is, and no matter how short it is, it can still go wrong, so test it. It is so very tempting to look at a two-line routine and decide it is silly to waste time writing a test for it, only to find you look a hundred times sillier when it goes to production and suddenly stops working for no apparent reason.

It's Too Simple to Test

The following example is a unit test I wrote myself just this year, and after I had written it and looked back at it I started wondering if I had lost the plot and should get down to the brain doctor ASAP. In this case, the business process was that if the shipping conditions were a certain value then the sales order was "linked," and the end user could press a button and, if the shipping conditions were currently linked, the value would be changed to "unlinked."

The test method looks as shown in Listing 2-19.

Listing 2-19. Example Test Method

```
METHOD break_link_on_request.

* Given a Certain Shipping Condition
    mo_cut->ms_header_data-vsbed = mc_linked.

* When the order taker presses the BREAK_LINK_BUTTON
    mo_cut->action_break_st_link( ).

* Then the link is Broken
```

```
cl_abap_unit_assert=>assert_equals(
msg = 'Link has not been Broken'
exp = mc_unlinked
act = mo_cut->ms_header_data-vsbed ).
```

```
ENDMETHOD.
```

So far, it's not so unreasonable as you might think. However, looking at the initial version of the production code in Listing 2-20, you might change your mind in a hurry.

Listing 2-20. Method Being Tested

```
METHOD action_break_st_link.
* Preconditions
    CHECK ms_header_data-vsbed EQ mc_linked.

    ms_header_data-vsbed = mc_unlinked.


ENDMETHOD.
```

In effect I am supplying both of the values to a CHECK statement and then testing that it works, and then checking whether assigning a constant to a variable works. Well, of course both of those things are going to work. Calling that test the work of a madman would be a valid criticism—provided the code being tested stays the same forevermore. As it turned out, within days of writing the test the business requests started coming in to make the logic behind pressing that button more "flexible" (read: complicated). Before you could say "Jack Robinson" there was half a ton of new conditional logic in the former two-line method, plus loops and calls to the database.

At that point, having a unit test for this method no longer seemed quite so daft.

. . . but They Are Not!

You may have worked in an environment where every day when you log on you get a "tip of the day" or a "message of the day." A long time ago, Excel used to do so every time you opened it up. Most of the messages were sensible tips, but occasionally you would get a humorous one like, "Don't Run with Scissors."

A colleague of mine worked for a company that ran SAP and was "big into" unit testing, and as such whenever an employee logged on to development they would get such a message. It was the opposite of Excel in that 95 percent of the messages were jokes, but one that stuck in his mind was, "Unit tests make you think." I would phrase it slightly differently: "Unit Tests Make You *Think Twice.*" In his example, he changed some existing code based on a problem situation that had been reported. His fix solved the problem at hand, but when the unit tests ran he found he had broken something else. He was forced to think about why, and after a while realized he had assumed that "such and such" condition was always true, but sometimes in rare cases it was not.

Whenever you find an implicit (unstated) assumption in your code it is a really good thing to document that assumption—in the worst case as a comment, in the best case in the code itself; i.e., by an ASSERT statement followed by some conditional logic (you can set those so they never actually cause short dumps, but simply make it crystal clear what your assumptions are).

Message in a Model

I had been cutting corners and writing lots of methods in a non-TDD manner, so I decided to clean up the barn, as it were, and write the missing unit tests until I had gotten my test coverage back to where I was happy.

At one point after adding a new test, I executed the automated test run, and to my horror a screen popped up—during the test run—asking me for input. That is an absolute no-no, a clear sign of a dependency (in this case, a dependency on the UI and a user being on the other side of it) that has not been mocked. It turned out my model class (which was supposed to be 100 percent business logic) had a method that was trying to directly ask the user a question and wait for a response. That call was quite well hidden, which is why I had not spotted it, but the very fact of writing a test exposed a design flaw in my application—the responsibilities of the various classes had not been 100 percent separated. Put another way, the more unit tests you write, the more you are forced to improve your application's design.

You Can't Get There from Here

When you run the automated unit test you in fact have two options: "Run Unit Tests" and "Run Unit Tests with Coverage." The latter looks at which lines of the production code in the methods in the class being tested are actually executed and then gives you a report showing the percentage of lines covered; i.e., if you have a class with ten million methods and you only have a unit test for one of those methods, the percentage coverage is going to be very low. To help guide you when you drill into the coverage analysis, the lines of production code that were executed are colored green, and those not executed are colored red. In real life it is probably not feasible to get 100 percent test coverage, at least for existing programs where you are adding tests after the event, but it is something to strive for, even if you never get there.

One fine day, I was trying to get 100 percent test coverage in a particular method by writing various tests until every IF branch and CASE option had been fully covered. There was one line of code that stubbornly refused to go green no matter how many tests I wrote, meaning it was never executed by any test. After looking at the code in Listing 2-21, I suddenly realized the problem—can you spot it?

Listing 2-21. Flawed Conditional Logic

```
IF md_crud_mode <> zif_sd_sofe_const=>create_mode.
  IF cs_item_details-sign <> zif_sd_sofe_const=>sign_insert.
    RETURN.
  ENDIF.
ELSEIF md_crud_mode = zif_sd_sofe_const=>display_mode.
  RETURN.
ENDIF.
```

It's very simple: If the value of MD_CRUD_MODE is in fact DISPLAY_MODE, then the very first condition in the IF statement will be true; i.e., the ELSEIF condition will never be reached. Thus, the code is silly; the second condition needs to go first, as shown in Listing 2-22.

Listing 2-22. Corrected Conditional Logic

```
IF md_crud_mode EQ zif_sd_sofe_const=>display_mode.
  RETURN.
ELSEIF md_crud_mode <> zif_sd_sofe_const=>create_mode.
  IF cs_item_details-sign <> zif_sd_sofe_const=>sign_insert.
    RETURN.
  ENDIF.
ENDIF.
```

If I had not been so obsessed with writing unit tests I would never have noticed the problem; no static code check was going to warn me about it.

Simpler but Wrong

I had copied some code from one program to another, and because the original code seemed to take ten times as many lines of conditional logic than was needed to achieve the desired result, I decided to simplify it. Of course, I got something wrong, but it didn't look wrong to me—it looked a lot better. In the traditional way of doing things, I would have initially felt really pleased with myself for improving the code, and then looked like an idiot when it went into production.

Luckily, I wrote a unit test based on what the original program did. That failed, thus highlighting to me the mistake I had made whilst simplifying the logic. I ended up with much simpler code—that actually worked! The moral of the story is that simplifying incredibly convoluted code is good, provided you have a safety net.

Why TDD Has Never Taken Off

Thus far, you have heard about *why* you should do unit testing/TDD and my experiences in *how* I have been doing it. However, as mentioned earlier, the unit test framework in general, and TDD in particular, does not appear to be used very much. Part of this is that people just don't know it exists, but there are also some commonly used arguments against using it. Let us look at the most common of those arguments in order to refute them.

In this section, we will start with the argument that the organization already has an automated testing solution so there is no need for TDD. Next up will be the argument that because a given program is too complicated or too simple there is no need for TDD. Lastly, we will deal with the most dangerous argument of all—the idea that the TDD approach vastly increases development costs.

I Already Have an Automated Testing Framework

This was the very first argument I encountered from management types. Lots of companies have invested in tools like HPQC (HP Quality Center) or use the standard SAP ECATT (Extended Computer Aided Test Tool), where you store all your test scripts in such a tool and then every so often run loads of automated tests to verify if everything is still working. At first glance, this sounds exactly like running automated unit tests. The quite reasonable argument is, if I have already spent a load of money on an HPQC license, why in the world should the development team spend even one second on this TDD nonsense if all it achieves is the exact same thing we already do?

That sounds like quite a compelling argument. However, as it turns out, unit testing and HPQC (or equivalent) are not actually in competition with each other. I would describe them as complementary—having one is good, having both is even better, but if you do have both they do not tread on each other's toes. You can see the differences in Table 2-2.

Table 2-2. *ABAP Unit vs HPQC*

	ABAP Unit	HPQC
Where is the test written?	Inside Program	Separate System
Where does the test run?	Development	Pre-Production
How many programs are tested?	One	Hundreds
When does the test run?	After Every Change	Once a Week
How long does the test take?	Seconds	24 Hours
Who analyses errors?	Developer	BSA
What is the test scope?	Small Parts of Program	End to End Transaction
What is tested:-		
- Business logic	Yes	Yes
- Database Access	No	Yes
- UI	No	Yes
- Authority Checks	No	Yes
- External Interfaces	No	Yes

By the way, what I mean by BSA in the preceding table is the business analyst. As can be seen, the answers to the various questions are different in all but one case, so the two tools have very different purposes.

My Program Is Too Complicated for TDD

This argument is that it is impossible to add unit tests to complicated existing programs, as in, "That TDD nonsense is all very well when creating new OO programs, but my program has ten billion lines of procedural code and so TDD cannot help here, so I should be exempt from using it."

It is true that you cannot rewrite such a monster just to add tests. It would take forever, thus costing loads of money, and in the absolute best case it would give you no perceived business benefit at all, as the behavior would be exactly the same as before. Further, because nothing in this world is ever anywhere close to perfect, you would be bound to make mistakes, and thus the huge exercise would most likely increase the number of bugs. So, the business case would sound like, "I want you to spend a ton of money, and a year's development effort, and in the best case you will notice no change at all but most likely you will be worse off at the end of the process," and I think you can guess what managers would say to that.

So, a major rewrite is out of the question. But that does not mean TDD does not have a part to play in improving such monolithic programs. Imagine your program as a grid such as that in Figure 2-1, where each square represents one of the hundreds of functions the program carries out.

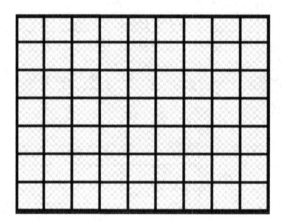

Figure 2-1. *Lots of functions in a program*

The next time a business requirement comes in to change the behavior of one of the squares, or to add a new square, you could do a lot worse than to try to make that change via TDD. You write a test for the new behavior, it fails (RED phase), you change the production code, the test passes (GREEN phase), and then you refactor the changed code (BLUE phase). You don't change anything outside of the routine you are working on. Think about it—you could get into a lot of trouble if you changed something outside of the area you need to change and broke something else as a result, but you cannot possibly get into trouble for changing the area you are *supposed* to be changing, even if you do break it.

At the end of the change, you have a grand total of one automated unit test, one tiny square in a huge grid. About 0.01 percent of the program is now covered by tests. You know that your current change works perfectly, because it has a test, but you have no idea if you have broken anything in the other 99.99 percent of the program that does not have tests. Let it go at that; do not bother refactoring anything else.

When the next change to the program comes along, the next month or the next week, to a totally different part of the program, repeat the procedure. Then you have two tests, you know the latest change works, and furthermore you know the second change has not broken the first. At this point, you have 0.05 percent (say) of the program under test. You still can't tell if your new change has broken anything in the remaining 99.95 percent of the program, but you are still fractionally better off than you were before you started with TDD. Without TDD you still would not know if your new change had broken the last change or not.

With every such change, the amount of the program under test slowly but surely increases, and the chances that a new change will break something existing very slowly decreases.

If you rigidly enforce this then after a while you will benefit from a facet of human behavior that was famously noted by Roman courtier Gaius Petronius Arbiter, who was fashion advisor to Emperor Nero. Petronius said, *"No one is ever satisfied with anything,"* which 2000 years later translates to, "If a part of a program is being used by a human, sooner rather than later they will want it changed." Therefore, after a five-year period, every single part of the program that is in use will have been subject to a change request, and thus if you make every such change using TDD, every part of the program that is actually used will have a unit test of some sort, and the bits that are not used will not, but who cares? They are not used. This is very simplistic, but that is the general idea. Put another way: a *revolutionary* development approach—TDD—is applied to a legacy program in an *evolutionary* manner.

My Program Is Too Simple for TDD

The next argument against TDD and unit testing is the opposite of the previous: instead of asking for an exemption because the program is too complex, some programmers will ask for an exemption because their program is too simple.

They would say something like, "Look, I am sure that TDD nonsense is OK for complex programs, but all that my program does is a database SELECT followed by calling the ALV to display the data thus retrieved. The program is only 20 lines long, for goodness sake! Surely I should be exempt?"

That argument sounds right, does it not? It sounds even more right if you consider this: in unit tests for such a program you would mock out both the database access (the SELECT) and displaying the data (the ALV). Unit tests only test the business logic, and there is none in this program, so what exactly is it we are testing? Nothing, obviously.

However, that argument only holds so long as one basic assumption holds true. It is an assumption many programmers keep making, and it goes like this: "This program will stay the same forever and no one will ever ask for any changes or improvements." The programmer might then point to the functional specification, which says this is a one-off report designed to fulfill a specific business problem we have at the moment; after three months it will never be used again. After over 20 years of programming I can say with 100 percent certainty that this assumption is "fake news."

One example of something that gets more complicated over time is a frog. It starts off as an egg, an incredibly small sphere. However, before you know it, it has turned into a tadpole, which is a lot more complicated than the egg was but in turn nowhere near as complicated as the frog it is going to grow into. Lastly, that frog might become a TV and movie star and have to sing and dance and ride a bicycle, all requirements you would have never imagined when looking at the egg.

The program that does one call to the database and then one call to the ALV is the egg in this analogy. However, in my experience no program that actually gets used stays this simple.

It will expand over time. At first, the changes will be simple, like adding a few more fields or selection criteria. Then you might be asked for some calculated fields. Next, the end users will ask if some fields can be editable, and you need to add a Save button to update the database with those changed values. Now you have one button with one function, how about some other buttons to do a variety of tasks based upon the data on the screen?

In addition, my experience has been that the "one off" programs stay around forever, and often end up being business critical. So you keep adding more and more functionality and before you know it there are five thousand lines of business logic. Since the business logic is what you have to test, and it is pretty much inevitable it will arrive sooner or later, why not have a unit test framework built into the program right from the start? How I do it is to have a template report program, complete with a unit test section.

There may not be any tests at the start, but as soon as the business logic arrives, you can dive right in with TDD. If you have such a template, you have not even increased the development time for the initial "egg"-type programs.

It gets better: You don't even have to create such a template yourself. I have written a generic one for pretty much any type of report where the output is in the form of an ALV report, and that is available as part of the source code for this book at `http://www.apress.com/source-code`. You are bound to want to change it or, even more likely, totally rewrite it, but it gives you a starting point.

TDD Is Far Too Expensive

With the previous logic you may well have convinced the developers that maybe we will give this TDD thing a whirl, but if management gets a whiff that you are doing this strange new thing they will shut down the initiative without a second thought because of one supposedly "killer" argument.

This argument is that it takes twice as long to write a program with unit tests. What is more, this argument is *true*—there is no sugar coating it. Possibly it will take even more time.

I went looking for an example that would seem to support this argument in some test code I had recently written. It did not take long to find.

I was testing a method that was 46 lines of code long. It was full of conditional logic—CASE and IF statements all over the place—and I wanted to give it 100 percent test coverage; i.e., test every possible outcome.

This involved writing eight different unit tests, which added up to 183 lines of code. In total that is 229 lines of code versus 46 if I had not bothered with the tests; i.e., five times more code than is "actually needed."

When managers hear that they will be horrified because that implies you will be half (or less, as in this case) as productive. Even if it were "just" twice the code, it either takes you twice as long to write the same program (double the cost) or they need to employ two people to do the same thing as before (double the cost plus training costs; plus adding extra people rarely speeds up development).

If you are asked, "Can we live without this TDD thing?" the answer is yes, of course we can, we have been living without it since time immemorial. Then you will have management saying, "Don't do something we don't *need* to do," as in this rebuttal I saw on the internet from when a programmer advocated refactoring code to increase the quality and adding tests:

> *"Anonymous said . . . one of the sure signs of a programmer . . . not a mention of costs and time to completion. When you hire a painter to redo the kid's bedrooms, you don't expect them to 'refactor' a hole in the back wall 'to make it easier to repaint the rooms when they are teenagers.' "*

At first glance, the whole concept seems like madness, so why would any halfway sane manager give the go-ahead for such a thing?

TDD Reduces Development Costs

When countering such arguments, you need to fight fire with fire. Since the argument is that doing TDD will double the cost of development, you need to show that it will in fact lower the cost of development. If you can convince a CFO of that (and most IT departments report in to finance for historical reasons) then suddenly you are laughing.

Where I work it was the CIO I had to convince, as he reports directly to the CEO. I managed to convince him that TDD was a really good thing, and he concentrates on results just as much as any other CIO, if not more. What did he see that other CIOs who say "no" out of hand could not? The answer is, I showed him the diagram in Figure 2-2.

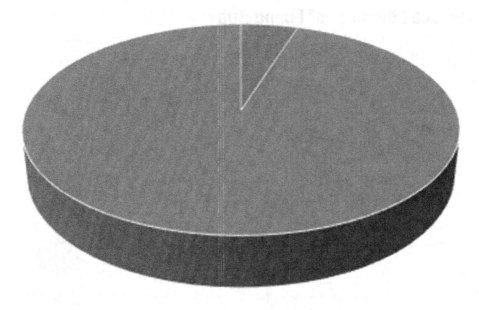

Software Life Cycle

■ Development   ■ Maintenance

Figure 2-2. *Software lifecycle*

Like all of my examples, this is not even made up—it is straight from real life. The first version of a certain business-critical program was written in about two months just prior to go-live in the year 2000. That is what I define as the "development" phase in the software lifecycle. After go-live, of course, many bugs were found that needed to be corrected, but even once the program was stable, because it was so important and impacted so many people, there were many requests for changes and enhancements—at least one, sometimes as many as ten at a time, every month, every single month, for the next *20 years*. It has not stopped now, and it never will. This is what I call the "maintenance" part of the software lifecycle.

Furthermore, the development phase of the program will become a smaller and smaller piece of the pie as the years go by. TDD is intended to make the development phase fast, risk-free, and thus cheap. So, from a financial point of view, the question becomes, over a 20-year period does doubling the cost of the development (5 percent) phase get offset by reducing the cost of the maintenance phase (95 percent) to next to nothing? Obviously it does, and it does not even take 20 years. TDD starts paying for itself almost at once.

That is one financial argument to use on your CFO. Here comes another.

TDD Reduces the Cost of Fixing Bugs

Have a look at the bar chart in Figure 2-3.

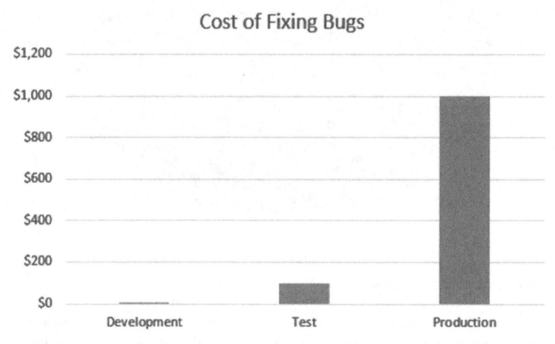

Figure 2-3. *The cost of fixing bugs*

There has been an enormous amount of study done on the so-called software bug cost curve, but if you think about it the logic is self-evident. If a developer finds a bug whilst writing the code, it takes seconds to fix and thus costs almost nothing. If it is found in a test then the tester has to explain to the developer what is wrong, and then the fix gets transported back to testing. It may still not work, and this cycle may go around three or four times, so fixing that bug may cost ten to a hundred times more than if it had been found in development initially. If a bug is discovered by an end user in production then there is probably some sort of business impact—often financial—and then the end user has to explain what is wrong to first-level support, who have to explain it to the business analyst, who then has to explain it to the developer, possibly losing information at each step due to the "telephone" effect. The bug-fixing cycle is much longer and more drawn out, including scheduling when the fix goes to production. That fix might break something else, so the cost of fixing a bug found in production is between a thousand and ten thousand times more than if it had been found in development.

TDD Reduces the Financial Risk of Failure

The preceding two money-based arguments would convince any accountant, let alone the CFO to whom IT usually reports. Money talks, after all. But how many people can think in the long term or even in the medium term? Sadly, many commercial organizations are focused solely on the next quarter, and if someone doesn't hit the target for the next quarter (say a piece of ABAP software going live) they get sacked. In that case, for a manager, allowing TDD (for the first time) would be like cutting your own throat, so they have the biggest incentive in the world to cut corners, which is why it happens all the time. Do I have a magic bullet solution for this? No, I do not. Obviously people are going to look after their own best interests. All I can demonstrate is that TDD serves the best interests of the organization as a whole after an initial shock, but that argument may fall on deaf ears.

If the argument about saving money over the long term is no good because I (manager) am going to get sacked in the short term, let us turn the whole argument around. The manager is quite rightly concerned with not getting sacked in the next quarter because something that was scheduled has not gone live. That is all to do with new software—but is that the only reason you can get sacked?

To use another analogy, why in the world do you pay house insurance, or car insurance, or health insurance? In any given month, it is not very likely that your house will burn down and/or you will crash your car and/or get a serious illness. You would be a lot better off if you did not pay out any of that insurance money.

That logic holds true until the instant something bad happens. If you have no insurance on your house and it burns down, the cost of building a new house dwarfs what the insurance cost would have been, and so in the event of a disaster you are much, much worse off. You might say, "That is obvious, that is the reason I pay insurance!"

Do you recall that quote earlier about programmers' being idiots because they want to fix the hole in the wall whilst painting the room? It could be argued that repairing the hole in the wall now might stop the house from falling down in a few years, and that cost savings will offset the current cost of hole-repairing by a factor of a thousand.

The question is, "If that logic makes sense in your personal life, why not in your professional (programming) life?"

Let me put it this way—choosing to not write a test is, in effect, a bet that the extra monetary cost of writing the test (i.e., doubling the development time, hence cost) is more than the monetary damage you will inflict on yourself and your organization (lost business, fines, and so on) if the functionality fails, multiplied by the percentage chance of that failure. To write that as an equation, we get:

```
SAVING = 10,000 USD - (1,000,000 USD * (XYZ / 100)).
```

The XYZ is the percentage chance of the software's failing after making a change. I put it to you, ladies and gentlemen of the jury, that this figure is an unknown quantity. However, in the example, if the percentage chance of failure goes above 1 percent then chances are that making the change will leave you worse off financially.

That is the point of TDD—to reduce this variable. It could be said that every time you make a change to a program you are gambling (because there is a chance the change will break something), but with TDD you give yourself much better odds.

Naturally, I made up the $10,000 development cost and $1 million failure figure; for your industry you have to start with thinking about what the worst possible thing that can happen is if the software goes wrong (and in the pharmaceutical or airline industries, that could be horribly bad, but if you think you are off the hook because you are not in those industries, note that every single industry and government relies more and more on software every single day).

Conclusion

In conclusion, TDD (enabled by ABAP Unit) is designed to increase program quality, which is the reason this chapter lives in this book.

It is a lot of extra work—for a lot of payback. I liken TDD to climbing a mountain: It is a huge effort to get to the summit, but once you are there you are sitting on top of the world.

The end result of the whole process is programs that are highly unlikely to break when changed. But if they do break you will know instantly in development as opposed to finding out when something goes wrong for an end user in production.

In some senses everything that comes after this chapter is part of the BLUE phase of test-driven development, so you needed to know what that term means before moving on to the next chapters. You can do the BLUE phase even if you have vowed never to do TDD in your life.

Recommended Reading

Definition of the Term "Anti-Fragile":

https://fs.blog/2014/04/antifragile-a-definition/

Key Points from Michael Feathers' book *Working with Legacy Code*:

https://understandlegacycode.com/blog/key-points-of-working-effectively-with-legacy-code/

How to Structure Unit Tests:

http://dannorth.net/introducing-bdd

CHAPTER 3

Clarity: The First Pillar of Code Quality

In this chapter (and the next two), you will encounter some theoretical concepts about a specific area of code quality, and then see the practical benefit of following that theory based upon a large number of real-world examples.

This area of code quality is the concept of clarity, which many programmers attach zero importance to, not realizing they are shooting themselves in the foot. Here, you will learn why this is vital to both ensuring the program can be easily changed in the future and highlighting the problems dealt with in the next two chapters; i.e., stability and performance.

Clarity means different things to different people, but in a nutshell the general problem is this: Your job is to fix or enhance something in an existing program, but when you have a quick look at the existing code you find that you have no idea how in the world that code works. It just *does* work—seemingly by black magic.

This is what I mean by clarity, or the lack thereof. Deciphering code often makes up 75 percent to 95 percent or more of the effort expended changing a program—you spend two days wading through a swamp of code until you blindly stumble across where the problem is, and then it takes ten seconds to fix it. Next year when you need to change the same area, there is no way on Earth you will be able to find it again.

The previous chapter talked about test-driven development. When you have a lack of clarity, it is very difficult to add or change code using the TDD method. This is because it is almost impossible to pin down what parts of the program to test, as you just cannot figure out what part of the program does what.

A lot of procedural programmers argue that it is object-oriented (OO) code that causes this lack of clarity in the first place. Earlier in the book, I mentioned this quote by an SAP instructor: *"The trouble with OO code is that you cannot tell what the code does*

113

© Paul David Hardy 2021
P. D. Hardy, *Improving the Quality of ABAP Code*, https://doi.org/10.1007/978-1-4842-6711-0_3

by looking at it." I have concluded that this is not true at all. Over the years, I have seen plenty of OO code where indeed you cannot tell what in the world it is supposed to do, but I have also seen lots of procedural code like that.

In either case, there is no reason *at all* why you cannot always write code, OO or procedural, that is instantly readable by the reader. I think in the preceding OO quote the instructor was alluding to the use of inheritance and interfaces and their obscuring what actual class was doing the work—but that should not matter. I would say that well-written code always tells you what is happening. The exact mechanics of *how* the work gets done obviously need to be correct as well, but without the *what* someone reading the code is sunk. One example of clarity is when the program is what Robert C. Martin calls a "screamer," as in, it is screamingly obvious what it does.

Another example of clarity in programs is what is known as "literate programming"—a concept invented by Donald Knuth (`http://www.literateprogramming.com/knuthweb.pdf`). While Knuth talks more about the new tool he invented to implement the idea than the idea itself, nonetheless the concept is clear enough—programs should be able to be read by humans as well as by the compiler.

Yet another related principle is called "make wrong code look wrong": `http://www.joelonsoftware.com/articles/Wrong.html`.

The idea is that if your code is clear, then mistakes stand out in letters of fire ten thousand miles high, but if it stays a muddled mess, then the errors can happily hide in plain sight where no one can ever find them.

Thankfully, there is a straightforward methodology to untangling the big ball of wool of a program until you get to the point where you have half an idea how it works. Even better, this can be done in a slow, risk-free manner.

As you recall, we ended the previous chapter talking about the BLUE phase of test-driven development; that is, after you have gotten a piece of functionality working, you need to mercilessly refactor it at once to ensure it is of the highest quality possible. How to spot what is wrong and how to make it better is the focus of this and the next two chapters.

Thus, we start this chapter with a discussion of the BLUE (refactoring) stage of the TDD cycle, which comprises refactoring the code using both automated and manual checks. Then, we can move on to clarity-specific topics, starting with code complexity in general. Next come sections about specific areas that make code difficult to understand—the naming of various elements in the program, how comments can help (or make things worse), and lastly documentation within the SAP system (which is not the same as comments).

Refactoring: Automated and Manual Checks

Let's discuss a typical situation where you have just changed or added some code. The code works, and now you are going to ensure that that code is good as well, something that traditionally has never happened, which is why programs rot over time, even if remaining functionally correct.

You can utilize the following process even if there are no automated unit tests, but the wonderful benefit of tests is that if you make any of the improvements suggested in this or subsequent chapters then you will know instantly if such tinkering has broken anything. If it has, then back out the change and *try again*. Don't give up. You can have functionally correct and high-quality code at the same time, even if you don't see it much in real life.

If you are changing existing code, you may find at this stage that you have changed every single line of the original routine until possibly not even one letter of the original code remains. Indeed, someone somewhere once said, "*Some days I wonder if I've written or deleted more lines of code since I started as an ABAPer,*" and that is in fact a good thing. If you are deleting more lines than you add and the program ends up both shorter and more coherent, then that is a wonderful result.

The BLUE phase comprises both automated and manual checks.

Automated Checks

The first step in checking the code quality is to step through the various automated static code checks available within the ABAP environment: syntax check, extended program check, and the code inspector. We will look at each one in turn. It is also possible to run a remote check from another system, so you will also read about why you might want to do that. Lastly, you will hear about a way to try to force the issue when it comes to getting people to run such checks.

Syntax Check

I would say that when I am programming away in SE80 I press the Syntax Check button (CTRL + F3) about a billion times a day—pretty much after every line of code I change. Naturally, the syntax check also gets run when you press the Activate button.

This is all obvious, you might say—you have to fix the syntax errors, and so everyone does that—to which I would reply that if that is the case then why do programmers cavalierly ignore the yellow warnings that appear at the bottom of the screen when the syntax check is run? I have seen this time and time again.

A yellow warning is not a syntax error and will not stop the code from compiling, but such warnings are clearly important to SAP; otherwise, they would have downgraded the severity of these messages.

An example of such a warning is "USE PARAMETERS: not PARAMETER:" in SELECTION-SCREENS. It is easy to ignore that one as being far too trivial to be concerned with—why bother adding the letter *S*—a total waste of time, surely? I can think of two reasons—one trivial, one serious.

The trivial reason is just to stop the annoying warning message from popping up all the time. If it is such an inconsequential change then *why not* make it, just to make the pain go away?

The more serious reason is that SAP (probably) does not make those warnings appear just to annoy you. In this example, they are sending a clear signal that leaving out the letter *S* will not cause a syntax error now, but in a higher version of ABAP it could. So why not fix the problem now, every time you come across it, rather than having to make seven hundred such changes all at once at upgrade time?

Extended Program Check

The extended program check is invoked by the ABAP Editor menu option *Program* ➤ *Check* ➤ *Extended Program Check* or CTRL + F4. Its original purpose was to do static checks for functional correctness, though many checks cover other areas.

Often when I look at code in production I can see BREAK BLOGGSJ and BREAK DANCER and so on—those would cause a red error in the extended program check. A developer-specific break-point in production code will not cause any harm at all, but leaving such a break-point could be described as sloppy–it is somewhat like the developer in question sending a clear signal that they have not run the extended program check before releasing the transport.

History shows that when writing programs in the traditional way, people would, if they could be bothered, run the extended program check right at the end of program development, just before transporting it to test, and if there were lots of findings they would say, "Oh, I don't have time to address these now; this has to be in the test system in 15 minutes."

There is an obvious way around this problem—to run the extended program check after every change. Hence, during the BLUE phase you should always run it, and as you have only changed one small routine, the number of findings should be very small and easily fixed within a minute (or flagged as a false positive). Once again, it is better to do this frequently than to get to the stage where there are so many warnings you take one look at the huge list and say, "I am not going there!"

Before I started with unit tests I was reckless enough that I would go into a big program, make one small change, run the extended program check, and clean up every single error and warning. Sometimes that *would* cause problems, and some of my colleagues would have a go at me for doing something (cleaning up the code) that was not needed.

As an example, back in about 2003 I came across the following line of code:

```
READ TABLE GT_SOMETHING.
```

Amazingly, that actually compiled with no errors. It filled a work area (also called GT_SOMETHING) and somehow was always picking the correct line of the internal table. The extended program check told me that was not a good line of code and that the addition USING KEY should be added. So I did just that—and of course, because of Sods Law, the code stopped working. Luckily, where I work people are more concerned with fixing problems than ten-hour meetings deciding who to point the finger at, so I was able to work out that I was reading the table with the wrong key and fixed the issue.

The end result was that the program worked exactly as before—so some would ask, what was the point of the exercise? I would say that before, the program was working by accident, and afterward, it was working deliberately, and, moreover, you could now see what it was supposed to be doing. If something is working by accident it is incredibly fragile, and in this case you also had no idea what was happening; i.e., what line was being read.

Anyway, I had gotten things to the stage where there were no warnings or errors at all in this beast of a program, and then I left to go and work in another country for a few years. When I came back, I had to make a change to that same big program. When I left, the extended program check had zero findings. When I came back, it looked like Figure 3-1.

SLIN Overview

Display Results   Display All Results   Display Single Test

Check for Program	Error	Warnings	Messages
Test Environment	0	0	0
PERFORM/FORM Interfaces	0	16	19
CALL FUNCTION/METHOD Interfaces	48	0	0
External Program Interfaces	0	0	0
Authorizations	0	0	0
GUI Status and TITLEBAR	0	0	0
SET/GET Parameter IDs	0	0	0
MESSAGE Statements	9	2	0
Character Strings	30	40	5
Show CURR/QUAN Fields	1	2	0
Field Attributes	0	515	880
Superfluous Statements	0	6	146
Syntax Check Warnings	1	142	0
Check on Load Sizes	0	0	0
Internationalization	0	0	0
Problematic Statements	0	4	15
Structure Enhancements	21	26	0
Hidden Errors and Warnings	14	58	4

Figure 3-1. *Extended program check with lots of warnings*

Is this a blistering attack on my colleagues and indeed programmers in general? Yes! Actually, no, not really. Everyone is under such enormous pressure to do so much as fast as they possibly can. How could they possibly spend two days fixing hundreds of extended program check errors? Obviously they cannot, which is why so many people do not bother even running the check. This is why in the BLUE phase you fix every such problem the instant it arises. After all, it is easier to get rid of one wasp in your house than to wait until they have built a hive in your attic, and your basement, and your garage, at which point *you* are the one who has to leave.

One final point here is that I have often been told that some of the checks are meaningless. An example would be that you get a red error if you write some text for a message or something directly in your program that does not reference a text symbol. The reason that comes up as a red error is that if someone logs on in a different language they cannot see whatever text it is.

If you have an SAP system that is only used in one country then you might think, "Why bother—the process of assigning every piece of text to a field symbol takes forever and is really boring (SAP really ought to have an automated tool for this) and all for what?" It does indeed seem pointless right up until the day your company is taken over by a multinational, and then you have to go through that horrible exercise of assigning text symbols not just for one program, but for *thousands*.

Code Inspector

As with the extended program check, running the code inspector (known as SCI) involves the programmer making a slight effort. You have to choose the menu option *Program* ➤ *Check* ➤ *Code Inspector*. I am old enough to remember when SCI first came out. I thought it was a wonderful improvement, but I get the feeling that, both back then and now, not everyone is as wonderfully enthusiastic about this as I am. The original purpose of this tool was to focus on performance-related problems, though as time has gone by performance is now just one category of the available checks.

Traditionally, running the code inspector was only done (if at all) 30 seconds before the deadline to release the transport. All the arguments made about the extended program check in the previous section apply here as well.

Just to *really* confuse matters, the extended program check has a radio button titled "Run ATC-Relevant Checks," which, if selected, runs all the extended program checks plus 20 code inspector checks. That is sort of an "All Dog + Half Cat" check.

Code Inspector versus ATC

It is easy to get really confused when you hear people talking about code inspector checks and also ATC (ABAP Test Cockpit) checks. In fact, they are one and the same thing. When you do an "ATC Check" on your code it is almost the same as doing a code inspector check. The subtle difference is that when you are inside a program and run the code inspector it will use the DEFAULT variant to decide what checks to apply, and in an ATC check you can specify a different variant.

Transaction SCI is what controls the configuration of the code inspector. The important thing to note is that there is a very large number of checks available, and most of them are not active by default. You have to decide with your team which checks actually add meaningful value and activate them in the global default code inspector variant. You could have different sets of checks for every different developer, but that would be crazy; one person who changed the code would not get a warning, and the next person who changed it would—on the same piece of code!

As before, the idea is that during the BLUE phase you always run the code inspector after every change and fix things as you go so as to prevent a gigantic buildup.

The obvious question is this: Why in the world are there two different mechanisms to run automated static checks on ABAP code? It could be described like a pyramid—the standard syntax check stops a small amount of vital problems, the extended program check warns against a much larger range of serious problems, and the code inspector warns against a very large amount of "less vital" problems. I don't quite see it like that, however. As far as I am concerned, a lot of the standard checks in the code inspector count as "vital" to me.

There does seem to be somewhat of an overlap between the scope of the extended program check and the code inspector, but the main difference is that the latter is very concerned with performance. We will return to this in Chapter 5.

Speaking of other chapters, Chapter 2 was all about automated tests, and SCI also can run ABAP unit tests on whatever program is being analyzed by selecting the "Dynamic Tests" checkbox in the Check Variant block.

The most interesting thing about the code inspector is that you can add your own custom checks to it; you will be walked through the process of doing so in Chapter 10. Moreover, if you think those extra checks you have invented could be useful to the ABAP world in general, you can put them on a GitHub repository, and all SAP customers can download them using abapGit.

The future of downloading open source ABAP code—and indeed of the standard SAP Change and Transport System (CTS)—revolves around an open source project called abapGit invented by Lars Hvam Petersen. You can read the documentation at `https://docs.abapgit.org/`. This is based upon Git and GitHub, which are tools that programmers in other languages use to store versions of their code.

Thus far, there have been two main sets of extra code inspector checks made available on GitHub, and I would recommend downloading them both—after all, it is free. The relevance to this chapter is that both of them are concerned with code clarity. The two sets of checks in question are ABAP Open Checks and Code Pal.

ABAP Open Checks

The ABAP Open Checks were written by the same gentleman who invented abapGit. You can download them at `https://github.com/larshp/abapOpenChecks`.

The idea was to concentrate on the look and feel of the code (how easy it is to read) rather than on functional correctness, which was the focus of the extended program check, or on performance, which was the original focus of the code inspector.

As with all code inspector checks, you get a little blue "information" icon against each problem found, which in this case uses a hyperlink to take you to an explanation of why the problem at hand makes the code less clear than it could be.

Code Pal

The SAP world has changed dramatically over the last few years. Traditionally, SAP liked all its software to be proprietary. Nowadays, it as a company has embraced the open source movement. Now, community-led projects sometimes get officially endorsed by SAP. One such example is abapGit, which even got a huge mention in the keynote speech at SAP TechEd in 2017.

In the same way, Code Pal is an open source project on GitHub that adds extra code inspector checks to do with clarity, and can be found at `https://github.com/SAP/code-pal-for-abap`.

Its aim is exactly the same as that of ABAP Open Checks, but the difference is that (a) it is mostly run from inside SAP and (b) it is based on the "clean code" principles laid out in the book of the same name by Robert C. Martin. Not all such principles can be automatically checked by a static code inspection, so a little later in the section about manual code checks you will be referred to the "Clean ABAP" guidelines website.

Remote ATC Checks

Thus far in the BLUE phase, you have checked your code using the extended program check and then the code inspector (with assorted add-ons). If you wanted to go really bonkers (and I do), you could complete the phase by doing some remote ATC checks from a 7.52+ system to see if your code would work in an S/4HANA system or even ABAP in the Cloud. Chapters 8 and 9 deal with these topics, respectively.

Continuous Integration

In other programming languages, such as Java, the term *continuous integration* refers to the fact that each developer writes the code on their local machine and then at intervals (the shorter the better) merges that code into a central development system.

In a traditional ABAP context, that term has to mean something different because all developers work directly in the central development system as opposed to on their local machines.

The aim of the approach in both cases, however, is clear: to spot errors as early as possible in the development cycle. This is called "shifting left," as a bug caught in development is a hundred times cheaper to fix than a bug caught in a quality check, and ten thousand times cheaper to fix than a bug caught in production by an end user.

It occurred to ABAP developer Andreas Gautsch that ABAP in Eclipse (known as ADT) does a continual syntax check every time you add even a single letter of code, whereas in SE80 you have to press a button to trigger the syntax check. That doesn't seem like such a huge deal, but when I thought about it I realized I pressed that button hundreds of times a day.

So he thought, why not extend that concept to the other checks that ABAP developers are supposed to do (but often do not) after changing a line of code, for which they need to press a button or choose a menu option; i.e., running the ATC checks or running the unit tests.

So, he created a plug-in for ABAP in Eclipse called ABAP Continuous Integration (`https://marketplace.eclipse.org/user/agautsch/listings`), which is available on the Eclipse Marketplace for free. If you install that and configure it then you can set your development environment up so that every single time you activate your code changes the following happens:

- The Pretty Printer runs (a very underrated aspect of code clarity).

- The ATC (code inspector) checks run and tell you any warnings/errors.

- The unit tests for the code being changed all run and tell you of any failures.

None of these are things you could not do manually, but all of them are things that many developers do not bother to do at all for various reasons. If the idea is to "shift left" so that bugs are caught earlier, then how much more "left" can you get than every single time you activate your code changes?

Pretty Printer

Many times, I have seen code that clearly has never had the "Pretty Printer" run over it in its life. You can spot this a mile off because of the mixture of upper- and lowercase for keywords. I would say that if a programmer doesn't care enough to take the one second to format their code, then they don't care about *anything* and you should treat their code with deep distrust.

Manual Checks

The automated static code checks just described are all well and good, and indeed a must as far as I am concerned, but, amazing as it may seem, computers cannot do everything automatically—sometimes you have to think for yourself!

Here, we will look at some resources available on the internet and how to use them, combined with your own common sense, to create a personalized checklist for doing manual checks on the code you have just changed.

Clean ABAP

This is an open source project initiated from within SAP. It is a "style guide" that gives a large number of recommendations on how to write your code in a "clean" manner and is loosely based on the book *Clean Code* by Robert C. Martin. Many ABAP programmers unfortunately ignored everything in that book once they realized all the examples were in Java and C++.

You can access the style guide here: `https://github.com/SAP/styleguides/blob/master/clean-abap/CleanABAP.md`.

It is a very long document, and there is no point in my repeating it here, but I am going to stress one important point, which goes like this:

> *"Since its publication, Clean ABAP has become a reference guide for many of SAP's in-house development teams, including the several hundred coders that work on S/4HANA."*

If it's good enough for SAP, it's good enough for me. I would encourage you to get every single developer on your team to read this in full. You are not going to agree with every single point (rule) made—in fact, you may vehemently disagree with some

(I know I do)—but it's not that difficult to get everyone on the team to agree to a large subset of the recommendations and attempt to adhere to them in their day-to-day programming.

A summary of these can be added to the personalized checklist that is discussed at the end of this section.

ABAP Gore

You may have heard of the term *anti-pattern*, which is where you are presented with examples of how *not* to do something. Many other programming languages have specialized websites stuffed full of such examples, and SAP guru Jelena Perfiljeva created a similar one for ABAP programmers and invited people to post examples of strange or bad code they've come across in their day-to-day job.

You can see the list here (there were so many submissions it had to be split into two):

```
https://answers.sap.com/articles/491054/share-your-abap-gore.html
https://answers.sap.com/articles/12984186/share-your-abap-gore-part-2.html
```

I encourage everyone to have a look. It is very funny. You will see some contributions from me in there—a lot of those will also crop up in this book with a more detailed explanation. I am not using any of the other examples though, so please take note of them!

Creating a Personalized Checklist

What you see on the Clean ABAP and ABAP Gore sites can give you a really good starting point for compiling an organization-specific checklist of what to look for in code that won't be automatically picked up on by static code-checking tools like the code inspector.

So, in the BLUE phase, you would first run the static checks on new or changed code and follow up with a manual inspection looking for the things on your checklist.

As an example, here is a list I made for myself 14 years ago. As you can see, I remind myself to run the static checks and also to perform some manual checks (some of which have since been included in the code inspector).

```
******************************************************************
*** Program Finalization Checklist—January 2006
******************************************************************
*The Steps of Finalizing a Program
*Make it conform to the template
*Activate Unicode Checks
*Naming for Global Variables
*Remove hard coding—put values as constants if unavoidable
*Make sure every database SELECT uses an index—and state which index is
going to be used in a comment just before the SELECT statement
*SQL Trace to check for identical selects
*Check all internal tables to see if they should be hash table
*Check for un-nested loops—they cause a geometric progression
*Make sure all remaining searches on internal tables use binary searches
*Make sure all exceptions are handled or noted if they don't matter
*Check to see if field symbols could replace header lines
*Add user documentation including recovery procedure
*Extended syntax check
*Code Inspector
*Make sure internal tables are freed when certain they are no longer needed
```

That brings us to the end of the general process of seeing what is wrong with the code. Now, we move on to the specific problem area dealt with in this chapter, namely clarity, and the first aspect of that we deal with is code complexity.

Code Complexity

In the *Clean Code* book by "Uncle Bob," which is pretty much constantly referenced in this book, the observation is made that programmers are authors, insomuch as after you write something (code), at some stage in the future someone else (maybe even yourself) will come back and look at it to make a change or just to understand what on Earth is going on.

He did some sort of screen capture of a programmer (himself) at work and found that 90 percent of his time was spent paging up or down within the same code block trying to get an overview of what was happening. The logical conclusion some people reached when reading that was to have each routine be no bigger than one page so there would be no need to page up and down and—presto—you can program ten times faster! Hooray! Hang out the flags!

Did you know, amazing as it may seem, there are some people who, when confronted with that argument, express doubts? Who would have thought?

Leaving paging up and down aside, there is no doubt that trying to maintain over-complicated code is agony, and so we must always be on the lookout for ways to reduce such complexity.

In this section, we look at the following four common things that cause code to be far more complicated than necessary:

- Huge routines

- Confusing code

- Duplicate code

- Dreaded global variables

Huge Routines

Going straight back to paging up and down, one of the ABAP programming guidelines in the SAP Press book of the same name does in fact advocate having every subroutine be no bigger than one page. Like all guidelines, that is most likely something to be aimed for rather than something that is actually possible as a matter of course.

Going back to 1981 when I first started programming, I had to make the program as terse as I possibly could, as the machine I used only had 1K of memory to work with. Clearly, your first experience with something sticks with you for the rest of your life, as 35 years on I still cannot stand to have extra lines when they can be avoided.

For example, I cannot stop myself from changing Listing 3-1 into Listing 3-2.

Listing 3-1. Lots of Nested IF Statements

```
LOOP AT INTERNAL_TABLE.
  IF SOMETHING.
    GET_SOME_DATA USING INTERNAL_TABLE.
    IF SOMETHING_ELSE.
      GET_SOME_MORE_DATA USING INTERNAL_TABLE.
```

```
    IF SOMETHING_ELSE_YET_AGAIN.
      DO_SOMETHING.
    ENDIF.
  ENDIF.
 ENDIF.
ENDLOOP.
```

Listing 3-2. No IF Statements at All

```
LOOP AT INTERNAL_TABLE WHERE SOMETHING = TRUE.
  GET_SOME_DATA USING INTERNAL_TABLE.
  CHECK SOMETHING_ELSE = TRUE.
  GET_SOME_MORE_DATA USING INTERNAL_TABLE.
  CHECK SOMETHING_ELSE_YET_AGAIN = TRUE.
  DO_SOMETHING.
ENDLOOP.
```

The two routines are functionally identical; it is just that the second one has fewer lines, so if having to page up and down less is important, and I actually tend to think it is, then you have enabled the casual viewer to see more of the routine on one screen.

And yet the *SAP Clean Code guidelines on GitHub* say not to use CHECK statements inside loops. This is a case of swings and roundabouts—using an IF statement inside a loop instead of a CHECK statement makes the code longer . . . but does it make it clearer?

In the preceding example, you will notice I reduced the number of IF/ENDIF constructs. The programming term for having deeply nested control blocks (IF, CASE, and so on) is *cyclomatic complexity*.

In the ABAP programming guidelines book, one of the rules is to restrict control blocks like IF statements to a nesting level of five. This is very sensible advice—I have seen, time and again, enormous IF statement blocks, deeply nested so that when you do a "Pretty Print" the part in the middle gets indented all the way to the far right of the screen.

In such situations, I have an unbearable urge to encapsulate the sections between IF and ENDIF into their own routines. This can change things that are literally impossible to understand into the blindingly obvious.

Listing 3-3 is an example that makes me want to cry due to the IF statements' being so deeply nested. Before my starting work on that code there were not even any comments after each ENDIF. I added the comments as a first step to simplifying the code; i.e., you need to understand it before you change it.

Listing 3-3. Deeply Nested IF Statements

```
              ENDIF. "We have a production order number
            ENDIF. "Reason code 01–never batched or 09 batched
          ENDIF. "Have we been able to block it?
        ENDIF. "Workflow OK
      ENDIF. "Is the order locked?
    ENDIF. "Workflow OK
" for stock transport orders we simply delete the delivery
ELSE.         "non sales order
```

After I finally understood the exact nature and purpose of a 20-deep nested IF structure, I could reduce the central routine to about a dozen lines, as shown in Listing 3-4.

Listing 3-4. End Result After Half a Million IF/ENDIF Constructs Removed

```
      CASE g_deltype.
        WHEN c_deltype_create.
          PERFORM create_delivery.

        WHEN c_deltype_delete.
          PERFORM delete_delivery.

        WHEN OTHERS.
          PERFORM error_handling USING 'IDOC_TRANSACTION_UNKNOWN'.

      ENDCASE."What type of transaction–create or delete?
```

Listing 3-4 used to be more than one thousand (honestly) lines of code. I got heartily sick of pressing the "page down" key dozens of times to try to find the part that dealt with deletion. Afterward, I could find that part straight away and then drill into the routine, and for each level down I went, there was only one IF or CASE construct, thus making the code incredibly easy to follow.

Confusing Code

There is some code that you can spend half an hour just staring at trying to work out what it does, and the longer you look the more your brain hurts and the more you curse the original author (especially if that author was your younger self).

In this section, you will see eight techniques for confusing a reader of the code so much that it makes them wish they had taken up horse whispering as a profession rather than programming.

Double Negatives

A famous example of a double negative is a condition like IF LF_NO_ERRORS NE ABAP_ FALSE, which makes one's head spin. To take it to the next level, a real-life example is shown in Listing 3-5; it is something I submitted to ABAP Gore because it took me so long to understand what was happening it was not funny.

Listing 3-5. Confusing Code

```
    MOVE TBL_VBFA-POSNV TO R_DELIVERIES-LOW.
    MOVE 'EQ' TO R_DELIVERIES-OPTION.
    MOVE 'E' TO R_DELIVERIES-SIGN.
    APPEND R_DELIVERIES.

ENDLOOP.

IF R_DELIVERIES IS INITIAL.
ELSE.
   CHECK TBL_ZSD04-POSNR IN R_DELIVERIES.
ENDIF.
```

The code is horrific. As far as I can see, the CHECK statement is evaluating a double negative, so if the value being checked (ZSD04-POSNR) is IN the range, then in fact it is *not* excluded (because the sign is E for *exclude*), and so the result of the CHECK statement is TRUE.

That is bad enough in and of itself, but what if the evaluation were a thousand lines away from the routines that filled the range? It is just not in human nature to expect a selection range to *exclude* things. The *SAP Clean Code guidelines on GitHub* recommend always trying to use positive checks—i.e., IS SOMETHING rather than IS NOT SOMETHING—because the former is far easier for a human to understand.

It Gets Worse

In addition, in Listing 3-5 the R_DELIVERIES table actually contains sales orders, thus confusing things even more. In one program, I even saw an internal table called TBL_LIKP that contained the contents of table VBAK. There is no way anyone reading the code for the first time would be expecting that.

As you will see when we get to the "naming" section, the (not so radical) idea is to try to name tables and so on so as to give the reader a clue as to what might be inside the internal table and not deliberately mislead them as in the preceding examples. In this case, the aim is to avoid names that would exacerbate double-negative statements.

Text Symbols

When you have text in a program it is important to assign each text to a text symbol, so the texts can be translated into other languages, and so someone logging on in a different language can still see and understand the texts. A good example of when this *doesn't* happen is when an end user gets a short dump whilst logged on in English and the standard SAP message about the dump comes up in German.

However, some programmers think that because you have to refer to a text symbol by its number when defining a SELECTION-SCREEN as in

```
SELECTION-SCREEN BEGIN OF BLOCK blk2 WITH FRAME TITLE TEXT-001.
```

that you have to *always* refer to it by its number. This can lead to code like that shown in Listing 3-6.

Listing 3-6. Bad Usage of Text Symbols

```
**Start RT13270
  PERFORM check_for_cash_sale_ma USING     vbkd-bzirk
                                           vbak-auart
                                           vbak-vkgrp
                              CHANGING lf_cash_sale.
**End RT13270
```

```
*  IF sy-subrc NE 0.
  IF ( lf_cash_sale NE 'X' )."RT13270
* cash sales not on
    FORMAT COLOR COL_BACKGROUND INTENSIFIED OFF.
    WRITE: / icon_message_error AS ICON, gcv_error_line  .
    SKIP.
    SKIP.
    FORMAT COLOR COL_NEGATIVE  .
    WRITE:/2   TEXT-116 .
    WRITE:/2   TEXT-117 .
    SKIP.
    FORMAT COLOR COL_KEY .
    WRITE:/2   TEXT-118 .
    WRITE:/2   TEXT-119 .
    SKIP.
    SKIP.
    FORMAT COLOR COL_NEGATIVE INTENSIFIED ON INVERSE.
    WRITE:/2   TEXT-120 .
    WRITE:/2   TEXT-121 .
```

If someone were trying to read the preceding code they would have no clue what was going on, as numbers like 116 and 117 mean nothing at all. You can double-click on the text symbol number and see what it means, but it is far easier if the actual text is in the program itself alongside its text symbol number, as in Listing 3-7.

Listing 3-7. Good Usage of Text Symbols

```
PERFORM check_for_cash_sale_ma USING      vbkd-bzirk
                                          vbak-auart
                                          vbak-vkgrp
                            CHANGING lf_cash_sale.

IF lf_cash_sale NE 'X'.
  "Cash sales not on
  FORMAT COLOR COL_BACKGROUND INTENSIFIED OFF.
  WRITE: / icon_message_error AS ICON, gcv_error_line.
  SKIP.
```

```
    SKIP.
    FORMAT COLOR COL_NEGATIVE.
    WRITE:/2
'1. Orders must not be delivered unless pricing is OK.'(116).
    WRITE:/2
'   Please check details and adjust if necessary.'(117).
    SKIP.
    FORMAT COLOR COL_KEY.
    WRITE:/2
'2. Have you obtained authorisation and entered details on'(118).
    WRITE:/2
'   to the Order?'(119).
    SKIP.
    SKIP.
    FORMAT COLOR COL_NEGATIVE INTENSIFIED ON INVERSE.
    WRITE:/2
'If you have problems with the above please contact your'(120).
    WRITE:/2
'coordinator or responsible manager immediately.'(121).
```

Pointless Variables

The extended program check will warn you against using variables that are never used at all. They just clutter up the program, distracting you from code that is actually used. Even worse are variables that get a value set but are never evaluated; this is bad because it looks to the reader of the program that the variable has a useful purpose—otherwise, why pass a value into it?—when that is not the case.

So when you see either, delete them. That said, as with every rule there are some exceptions; e.g., splitting a string into two and discarding the second half. Yet that second half needs a variable to be written to. In such a case, you add the pragma ##NEEDED after the data declaration to exempt the variable from the extended syntax check.

Contradictory Instructions

Sometimes SAP lets you do strange things without any sort of error whatsoever. In Listing 3-8, we can see an instruction to the program to do two contradictory things at the same time.

Listing 3-8. Contradictory Instructions

```
READ TABLE int_weigh INTO ls_weigh
WITH KEY werks            = <ls_wgh_bridge>-werks
         network_address = <ls_wgh_bridge>-network_address
         scenario        = gc_scn_read "Weigh Scale scenario
         TRANSPORTING NO FIELDS.
```

You would initially think that work area LS_WEIGH is getting filled with the vales of a row of INT_WEIGH. It is only at second glance that you notice the TRANSPORTING NO FIELDS, which means *do not* fill the work area with anything.

If the reader missed the second bit they might proceed on the basis that LS_WEIGH had values after the READ statement, inviting disaster. The extended syntax check will warn you if there are no reads on LS_WEIGH, but if it was actually read you would get no warning from the syntax check and whatever was reading it would just get blank values.

This example is purely an existence check—does the row exist? It could be replaced by the ABAP construct LINE_EXISTS, and that way it is not only shorter but far clearer.

END-OF-SELECTION

Like many other people, when I started ABAP programming many years ago I looked at the programs that were already in the system and coded mine the same way, thinking it must be right.

For years and years, when I was still doing procedural programming, I would structure my ALV reports by having routines that got the data listed after START-OF-SELECTION and routines that manipulated and displayed the data listed after END-OF-SELECTION. That made semantic sense, and that is what everyone else was doing, so I did not give it a second thought.

It was only after about ten years that someone told me that END-OF-SELECTION had no purpose at all unless you were using a logical database. I am only 52; I am far too young to have ever used a logical database in an ABAP program. The concept was obsolete before I even started programming, so of course I had no idea what one was.

The only reason the routines listed after END-OF-SELECTION are executed is because the compiler does not even "see" the END-OF-SELECTION and thus thinks all the routines follow START-OF-SELECTION.

I have not used the END-OF-SELECTION statement since—one more useless statement gone to make the problem ever so slightly shorter and easier to understand.

DATA Declarations

In recent years, the ABAP language has been enhanced with some new "functional" constructs copied straight from other languages. For example, you can use the LET statement to declare a so-called short-lived variable within a loop. The trouble is that the variable is not short-lived—it can be used outside the loop as well. A programmer coming from another language would see code that looked seemingly identical to what they were used to, but that actually behaved in a different way.

Such programmers who migrate from other languages to ABAP would also draw the wrong conclusion if they saw something like the code in Listing 3-9.

Listing 3-9. Misleading Data Declarations

```
LOOP AT ITAB.
  DATA: something TYPE string.
ENDLOOP.
IF SOMETHING.
  DATA(LD_SOMETHING) = ABAP_TRUE.
ENDIF.
```

In other languages, the "something" variable would be local to the LOOP and thus would be initialized on every loop pass. In the same way, the variable between the IF/ENDIF could not be used outside that construct.

That's not the way it works in ABAP. It does not matter to the compiler where you put the DATA: something—it treats it as if it were at the top of the routine. In that case, the variable can be used anywhere in the routine.

For the inline declaration inside the IF/ENDIF block, the variable cannot be used before it is first declared, but can be used at any point afterward, not just inside the IF block. That is why the ABAP guidelines warn against doing an inline declaration inside a branch of a conditional statement, instead telling you to put the declaration at the top of the routine to make obvious its scope.

Unrelated Tasks

One of the core principles of OO programming is the Single Responsibility Principle—a component should do one thing and one thing only.

For example, last week I had to make a fix that involved changing the logic for how a certain value was calculated—logic that had been wrong for 17 years. I noticed the routine I was fixing did two totally unrelated things. It calculated the value, and then it went off and looped through the output table, turning certain lines green based on logic totally unrelated to the value that had just been calculated.

I could guess how that situation had arisen. Often when someone is asked to add a piece of logic they just put it wherever they feel like, often at the end of a routine that does something totally unrelated to the new change. Is it really that difficult to create a new routine? Clearly some people think so.

In this case, since there was no logical relationship between these two tasks, I split them into two routines, each with a name saying what that routine did. If a routine does two totally unrelated things, then whatever name you call it will be wrong.

The acid test is this: If someone asks you what task your routine performs, and your answer includes the word *AND*, then the routine is doing two different things and should be split.

Not Being Able to Locate a Routine

On July 17, 2020, I had to make a change to a program I knew really well, one to which I had made literally hundreds of changes over the years. It still took me over ten minutes to find the code I wanted. It was so frustrating. I knew what I was looking for but still could not find it. So, if it is that difficult for someone who is intimately familiar with the program, who has literally 20 years' experience with that program, how much harder is it going to be for someone who just joined the company yesterday?

How do things get to that stage? How can a routine hide itself so well you cannot find it when you want to fix or enhance it?

I love to use analogies to explain things, so I will use the example of when I had been translating some "pseudo-code" written by someone from the business who must have been familiar with BASIC. I saw GOTO statements scattered here and there. I used to write in BASIC myself back in 1981, and I can see the argument that the statement GOTO 210 is not very meaningful to anyone reading the code.

If we are trying to write a program that is easy to understand, then it could be said that understanding the flow is important—vital in fact.

Maybe here is where your bog-standard procedural program calling an ALV shines; it is crystal clear in what order each procedure is called. A programmer could go bananas if the evil plan was to confuse anyone looking at the code by jumping around illogically within procedures (e.g., one procedure calls another as the last statement). However, those I have seen are fairly easy to follow—just a list of procedures after START-OF-SELECTION, which, if well named, describe the tasks being carried out by the program. If they were *really* well named, it would be obvious if they were in the wrong order; e.g., if DISPLAY ALV were before DATA_SELECTION you would suspect something was amiss.

Once you bring DYNPRO screens into the equation, all bets are off. On a screen, after user input, the system processes the AT EXIT-COMMAND or ON-USER_COMMAND. That is easy to follow and understand, but to make things even more fun, the EVENT AT-USER_COMMAND is also triggered, so, in some programs I have seen, half of the user command processing was handled by a module in the PAI section, and the other half in the EVENT block responding to AT-USER_COMMAND.

Why does this cause me grief? What happens is that about once a year—just long enough for me to have forgotten everything—I need to change a certain routine. I know for a fact that the routine gets triggered when the user presses the XYZ button. It should be easy to find each time—in theory. Let us go on a Sherlock Holmes–type investigation to try to find the routine in question.

In this program, there are 32 different screens, all of which are pop-up boxes firing from user commands from the main ALV screen. It's a very old program—from 1999 originally—and uses a lot of old-fashioned technology like using WRITE statements on those pop-up screens.

This is an ALV program using the REUSE_ALV_LIST_DISPLAY function module, no less—all user commands flow through the user-command routine specified when invoking the function, which, luckily, the original programmer called USER_COMMAND. If they had really hated the world they could have called the user command routine BANANA or something and then no one would ever be able to find it.

So far so good. It is the work of seconds to locate the USER_COMMAND routine and drill into it, and a few seconds after that I have found the correct branch of the CASE IF_UCOMM structure that processes the XYZ button.

At this point my heart already begins to sink. There are about 30 branches, and all of them have one line of code under them calling a routine—except the one I am interested in. That one used to have a one-line procedure call under the CASE option, but no longer. It has clearly changed since last year, and the more I look at the changes the more I want to cry.

The code I found is shown in Listing 3-10.

Listing 3-10. USER_COMMAND Code with Assorted Flaws

```
* Weigh Banana Delivery
WHEN '&WEIGH'.
"check for apple deliveries
PERFORM check_apple_deliveries.
IF gf_not_apple_plant EQ abap_false.
  IF ( gd_total_deliveries GE gd_quota_deliveries )
  AND gf_hour_restricted = abap_true.
    lv_msg = TEXT-431.
    REPLACE '&1' IN lv_msg WITH gd_time_remaining.
    MESSAGE lv_msg TYPE 'I'.
*   MESSAGE 'Cannot ticket this delivery. No of ticketed
*   deliveries reached for current hour.
*   Reprocess this delivery in the next &1 Min.'(431)
*   TYPE 'I' .
  ELSEIF ( gd_day_total_deliveries GE gd_day_quota_deliveries )
  AND gf_day_restricted = abap_true.
    lv_msg = TEXT-531.
    MESSAGE lv_msg TYPE 'I'.
*   MESSAGE Cannot ticket this delivery.
*   The max no of ticketed deliveries for today has been reached.
*   TYPE 'I' .
  ELSE.
    PERFORM weigh_banana_delivery USING if_ucomm.
  ENDIF.
ELSE.
  PERFORM weigh_banana_delivery USING if_ucomm.
ENDIF.
```

There are several things in Listing 3-10 that make me unhappy; here they come in no particular order:

- When one needs to add a big bunch of conditional logic, it is best not to pollute the highest-level routine by directly adding the complicated IF structure. A much better way would be to create a new routine to wrap the original WEIGH_BANANA_DELIVERY routine. That way, the USER_COMMAND routine would stay simple instead of gradually getting longer and harder to understand over time.

- I am not a huge fan of having "anonymous" messages shown to the user. When you use the statement MESSAGE ... TYPE 'I' there is no number, so when the user complains about getting a message and you manage to replicate it, you cannot do a where-used search for the message number to find what part of the program generates that message.

- The programmer must have worked out that just having a text symbol number was meaningless, but instead of writing "This is the Text(531)" they decided to leave the description of the text symbol in the form of commented-out code. The point is that the contents of the text symbol could change but the comment would not, making things even more confusing than before.

- The programmer has decided to try to line up the comments with the code by putting an asterisk at the start of the comment line and then manually inserting space until the comment looks like it is lined up. It is far better to use the double quote symbol before a comment, as then it automatically follows the code it is commenting in the event more conditional logic is added and the "Pretty Printer" changes the indentation of the code.

In any event, once I get over that shock, it is time to resume the hunt for the routine I want to change. I drill into the routine called by the USER_COMMAND routine and then sink down a few more levels, as that routine calls more routines. Eventually, I get to the stage where the command CALL SCREEN 0100 is invoked.

I drill into that screen and call up the graphical screen painter. There is nothing there. I look at one of the PBO modules and see it invokes the command SUPPRESS DIALOG and then does a load of WRITE statements to fill up the screen with options for the user to choose from, complete with a check box at the front of each option.

The end user then clicks on a check box and presses Enter, and then normally you would expect the PAI processing to occur—but no. Because of the SUPPRESS DIALOG there is no PAI processing as such; even if it looks like there is in the flow logic, that is just a red herring. Instead, in such a case the event AT USER-COMMAND is raised.

So, I navigate there and see a CASE statement based on the value of SY-DYNNR. There is a CASE branch for screen 0100, and that calls a FORM routine that then starts reading what's on the screen using SY-LISEL until it finds a ticked checkbox.

The next FORM routine is the one I want. All the code in this case uses archaic concepts, and the program flow jumps around like a raving lunatic, making it almost impossible to follow. Since I am not allowed to change any of this, I put comments at every stage trying to explain the program flow, but even those are not enough to help me the next time this horrible task comes around.

If you are lucky you will never come across such things—screens with SUPPRESS DIALOG that use WRITE statements; the more modern way of doing things is to have an ALV grid on the screen instead.

With the ALV, things are not that straightforward either. With the old-fashioned function module version of the ALV, you passed in the name of a FORM routine that would be dynamically called when the user performed an action.

The OO class-based versions, CL_GUI_ALV_GRID and CL_SALV_TABLE, work off "events." These really confuse procedural programmers. The concept is quite simple, however; it is all to do with the separation of concerns. ALV technology is used in the view, and its single responsibility is to show the user the data. If the user wants to do something related to that data, such as drill down into a sales order, then that is outside the view's job description, so it raises an event to say the user clicked on column A in row 3, and its job is done.

Thus, the layer that invokes the view (known as the controller in the MVC pattern) needs to "register" for such events; i.e., say that it is interested in the fact the user might double-click on a cell, and here is the method in the controller that will deal with that event, as in Listing 3-11.

Listing 3-11. Registering Event Handlers Using the SET HANDLER Statement

```
alv_events = alv_grid->get_event( ).

SET HANDLER handle_link_click   FOR alv_events.

SET HANDLER handle_user_command FOR alv_events.
```

Model-View-Controller

This is the most famous programming design pattern in the world, and it describes how you split up an interactive program into three areas: the model (which handles the business logic), the view (which handles the user interface display), and the controller (which handles interactions between the two).

What's all this got to do with clarity? As you have seen, in ABAP there are assorted different technologies for handling user commands depending on how old the program is. How can someone coming in to maintain a program they have never seen before know exactly what sort of UI technology is being used? The answer is, it should not matter. They should not have to go on a wild goose hunt all over the program to see if it is an ALV or some more archaic technology. Nor should they have to, after discovering the technology in use, follow a trail of breadcrumbs from routine to routine to find where the user command is handled, hitting dead ends whenever an event is raised.

In my example, I would *start* in a routine called USER_COMMAND and then go on a wild journey of discovery, and I would forget the route by the time I had to follow that path again in six months' time.

It's your job as a programmer to ensure that whoever comes back to maintain your program—and that might be your future self—can go straight to a routine called something obvious, and have it not matter how the program flow gets there as long as it does.

What I have been doing recently is calling such routines, be they methods or FORM routines, ACTION_SAVE or ACTION_DRILL_DOWN or ACTION_GOODS_ISSUE. The word *ACTION* at the front is SAP speak for "user command." That terminology is used in standard SAP frameworks like the Business Object Processing Framework (BOPF) and the ABAP RESTful Application Programming Model (RAP). If you think your team will never ever get used to such a radical change in terminology, you could call the routines USER_COMMAND_SAVE, etc., but the point is you can then easily find the routine at once every time rather than having to worry about how that routine gets called.

Duplicate Code

It could be argued that one of the most dangerous tools in a programmer's arsenal is CTRL + C followed by CTRL + V. This is because when a programmer has to add a new block of code they often look for a similar block of code and then cut and paste it into the new place, changing (or forgetting to change) something to adapt that code to the new location. This is so easy and so fast it happens all the time. The end result is the same 30 lines of conditional logic repeated 54 times throughout the same program, each with minor changes.

Once upon a time, I came across such a chunk of code that appeared all throughout a big, complex program, subtly different each time. On each occasion, it popped up a dialog box, seemingly the same dialog box.

I knew that duplicate code was bad and did not want to make the same change in four different places, possibly missing one.

The obvious solution was to move the code into its own subroutine so the program would become shorter, and future changes would be in one place only.

The problem was each block of code was in a routine with a strange name and full of obscurely named variables, so I had no idea what was actually intended; i.e., what the code was actually doing. I was trying to find out which, if any, of the four slightly different blocks of seemingly identical code was correct. My gut feel was that three of them were wrong.

Luckily for me, sitting opposite me at that exact instant was a guy who had been with the company for 40 years. Not everybody has that luxury. Anyway, it was all obvious to him; he rattled off the four occasions when that box should pop up and why.

I added this information as comments at the start of the new (common) subroutine; i.e., *why* this was happening, and what was going on in the real world outside of SAP that made this behavior desirable in certain circumstances.

Armed with this knowledge, I could now see which of the four blocks of existing code was correct—*none of them*. They had all started the same with one condition only, and over the years the other three conditions had been added to one or more of the blocks of code, whichever blocks the programmer came across, always missing at least one.

In this case, I had a business expert to help, but even if I had picked one of the four blocks at random and redirected the other three calls to that, at least the behavior would have become consistent. As it was, the user was getting different results depending on what order they pressed the buttons on the screen, and that would have confused the living daylights out of them.

In the ABAP Open Checks that can be run from the code inspector, identical code blocks are highlighted, letting you zero in on situations like the one just described.

Global Variables

At first glance, it might appear that the use of global variables has nothing at all to do with clarity, so in this section you will first look at the arguments as to why they are bad, then move on to what you can do about the problems they cause, and end by looking at the distinction between global variables in a procedural program and member variables in an OO program (which can appear to be the same thing).

Why Are Global Variables Bad?

All OO people will tell you that global variables are the work of the devil and you should get rid of them at all costs. Even the standard code inspector will give you a warning for each and every global variable, saying don't declare anything globally, as will the extended program check in ATC mode.

On the other hand, one of my colleagues tells me he once had a job interview with two interviewers, and they told him one of them was strongly for global variables, and one was strongly against. Why would anyone say they were a *good* thing?

Let's try to be objective for a second and have a look at the pros and cons of global variables.

Pros—at least what people would *say* are the advantages:

- It's easy, and so you write your program a lot faster.

- SELECTION-SCREENS and DYNPROS are designed to work with global variables, so why fight the way SAP is supposed to behave?

- You don't end up with routines with gigantic signatures that could be deemed confusing.

- We've always done it this way, so it must be good (a very common argument in both business and IT).

- There's no need to replicate the definition of the same local variable in multiple subroutines, as you just declare it once globally.

Cons:

- It makes unit testing a lot more difficult, as you cannot guarantee the order in which unit tests are run, and so you have to make sure all global variables are set to the "right" values at the start of each test method.

- Without the variables being changed actually being in the signature, you can end up with badly named methods that change *something*, but you don't know what just by looking at the routine name.

- Any routine can change a global variable, so if you pinpoint the source of an error and debug at that point you can see that the global variable has the wrong value but not which of the million possible places set that wrong value.

- When adding new code or changing existing code, it is not evident whether it is safe to use the value of a global variable or whether it is safe to change its value.

This book argues that having unit tests is the most important thing in the universe, and, if you believe that, then it would point you toward avoiding things like global variables that make such tests more difficult to implement.

In addition, I would say that global variables are clarity killers based on the last three arguments in the "Cons" section. The idea would be to try to reduce them to the bare minimum. If you can get rid of all of them, fantastic, but that is not always feasible.

The standard SAP example I would give is SELECTION-SCREENS: Do you really have to go to the trouble of moving all the global variables into a data object that is then used inside local classes and then pretend the global variables (for such are selection options) do not exist?

In such a case, your local classes would be referring to selections via something like LCL_SELECTION->S_VBELN, when they could equally refer directly to S_VBELN as it is a global variable. The only time I do such a thing is if my program is split into includes, because in that case when you are changing an include you keep getting an (incorrect) syntax error saying that S_VBELN does not exist, although you can still activate the program with no problem.

What Can You Do About Global Variables?

With newly written OO programs, it is easy to avoid creating global variables, but in real life most of our work revolves around maintaining huge, business-critical procedural programs.

In such programs, written many years ago and vital to the day-to-day business, there are so many global variables that trying to get rid of them wholesale is not only difficult but incredibly risky, so generally you have to live with them. The biggest risk you have is getting rid of a global variable only to find it's used on a screen—the syntax check doesn't always warn you about that.

In the next example, we have a bunch of routines, all of which change the values of some global variables. In Listing 3-12, you will see that you cannot tell what the routine changes, or even be 100 percent sure what the routine does.

Listing 3-12. Routines That Change Global Variables

```
PERFORM get_weigh_user_selections.
PERFORM check_weigh_user_selection.
PERFORM check_load_user_selection.
PERFORM get_ale_info.
PERFORM populate_weighbridge_info.
PERFORM send_weighbridge_idoc.
```

The first step is to change the names of the routines so they describe what they do; that goes some way to defeating the enemy (incomprehension), but only so far.

In Listing 3-12, the names of the three routines, starting with getting ALE information and ending with sending an IDOC, made sense when the program actually used to send an IDOC, but in fact the program was changed from sending an IDOC to using PI years ago, so after that change the routine names made no sense at all. This is an example of routine names "rotting" when all someone does is change the code to fix the current problem at hand and does not look at the surrounding code.

A common solution is to add a comment above each routine with a strange name, thus explaining what the routine actually does:

```
" comment explaining subroutine get_weigh_user_selections goes here
PERFORM get_weigh_user_selections.
" comment explaining subroutine check_weigh_user_selection goes here
PERFORM check_weigh_user_selection.
```

```
" comment explaining subroutine check_load_user_selection. goes here
PERFORM check_load_user_selection.
" comment explaining subroutine get_ale_info goes here
PERFORM get_ale_info.
" comment explaining subroutine populate_weighbridge_info goes here
PERFORM populate_weighbridge_info.
" comment explaining subroutine send_weighbridge_idoc goes here
PERFORM send_weighbridge_idoc.
```

That is indeed an improvement, but how much better would it be to actually change the name of the routine to reflect what it does? Then you would not need a comment and it would be easier to find in the SE80 overview of routines.

The next step is to change the signatures of the routines so when you look at them you see what is getting changed. You do this by replacing every single reference to a global variable inside a routine with a reference to either an IMPORTING or EXPORTING parameter (USING and CHANGING in procedural world); the result is shown in Listing 3-13.

Listing 3-13. Routines with Added Signatures

```
"Build table saying what the user has selected
PERFORM get_weigh_user_selections CHANGING int_row_mark[].

"Check that table and error if selections are wrong, if not
"then return the selected entries
PERFORM check_weigh_user_selection
USING     int_row_mark[]
CHANGING w_id_sel_row      "Selected Weighbridge
         w_equip_sel_row  "Selected Equipment
         gf_splitload.

"Check user selection for the loading points (obsolete)
PERFORM check_load_user_selection.

PERFORM   populate_weighbridge_info
USING     w_equip_sel_row
CHANGING gs_being_weighed
         int_notpick_delivery.
```

```
PERFORM connect_to_weighbridge USING    w_id_sel_row
                               CHANGING g_weighbridge_wt
                                        g_weigh_failed.
```

Now we have a better idea of what the subroutine is expecting as input and what data it returns. It also highlights the horribly inconsistent naming conventions used for the global variables—an example of making bad code look bad.

Having no references to global variables within the individual routines makes them more capable of being reused, and at the very minimum it will be a lot more obvious if they are being called in the wrong order.

In addition, if you find that replacing all the references to global variables with parameters means you end up with a routine with 54 parameters, then an OO person would say if your method has such an enormous signature it is most likely doing too much.

Adding such signatures paves the way for the eventual retirement of the global variables in question. At this point the global variable is still mentioned when the routine is called, but that variable has gone one level up the call stack.

Let's say the next time you make such a change you replace all the references to global variables with references to parameters in the routine that calls the string of routines in the preceding examples. The global variables will have gone one level up the call stack again.

If you keep doing that, eventually you find they do not need to be global variables at all—they can be local variables at a high level of the call stack.

Global Variables Versus Member Variables

I find getting your head around some of the ABAP programming "guidelines" from official or unofficial sources makes your head spin like an owl. For example, everyone says, "Global variables are bad—they are the spawn of the devil." The argument seems sound, so off I go, trying to get rid of them.

In the other corner, you have the guideline: Don't put very many parameters in your methods, and you want to have "high cohesion," which means that the member variables you declare in your class get used in as many methods of the class as possible.

I used to think that was a direct contradiction in terms, until I belatedly realized—many years on—that the private member variables in the class definition are not global variables in the procedural sense; i.e., anything anywhere in the program can change the value. I thought a member variable was global because it (a) was not declared locally within a method and (b) was not in the signature of the method—because that is the way it works in procedural programming.

The more you get into this, the more you realize that forms are not like methods at all, in the same way classes are not like function modules. That takes a big mindset change. I take comfort in the fact that it took the programmers at SAP a long time to make the same jump, as evidenced by all the standard SAP function modules wrapped in static classes—what did that achieve?

For test classes, let alone productive classes, having the private member variables used by all the methods certainly makes the code read a lot more like plain English.

Naming

It has been said there are only two really difficult problems when it comes to programming: caching, naming things, and off-by-one errors.

In this section, you will see examples of how not to name things, and, more important, suggestions on the correct way to do so. To me the rule is simple—if naming something a certain way looks like plain English then it is a good thing; otherwise, it is a bad thing.

First, we cover names for "things with fluid values"—subroutines (METHODS or FORM), the parameters (signatures) of those subroutines, and the variables that the subroutines manipulate.

Next comes "things with static values"—so-called magic numbers, other forms of hard-coded values, and constants.

Last is a discussion of the often chaotic way DDIC objects are named, and naming can really help (or make impossible) easy reuse of code between applications.

Method/Routine Naming

One thing I complain about, over and over again, to anyone who will listen, is having variable and routine names that don't mean anything, often in the form of numbers; e.g., routine GX09876. You may think no one would call a routine that, so I'll leave it to you: Did I make that example up or is it a real one I actually saw?

This is one area where I have changed my behavior since my 1981 programming days. In the days of the ZX81, variables were called "X" or some other one-letter value, so you had no idea what they represented.

Oddly enough, to this day, in a lot of the Java examples on OO programming I see on the internet or in books, many of the variable names seem to follow the same convention, and so does some of the ABAP help you get when you press F1 whilst highlighting a keyword.

I will give some examples that actually happened to me—all of which drove me up the wall.

Misleading Names

One of the monolithic programs I am always changing (a tiny bit at a time) is crammed with global variables like a turkey full of stuffing, and one day I wanted to find where some global data got set.

It took me ages to find that exact point in the code because there are about a hundred routines where data of different sorts gets set, and they are evenly split between routines with the following prefixes: GET_, SET_, INIT_, POPULATE_, DETERMINE_, and about six others. I have to search through five different areas of the subroutine list to find what I want.

I imagine some people (especially OO fanatics) would be horrified by using a routine named GET_ to actually set the value of something!

I also had to struggle for days to determine how something worked. I got it down to two routines that were named as follows:

```
GET_DELETE_USER_SELECTION
CHECK_DELETE_USER_SELECTION
```

This was all about deleting various things the user had chosen; so far so good. However, the routine starting with GET_ performs assorted checks on what the user has selected, and the routine starting with CHECK_ actually does the deletions. Eventually, I found another routine starting with DETERMINE_ that actually asks the user what they want to delete.

As might be imagined, the way forward is that whenever you encounter routines with misleading names, do a little bit of renaming such that afterward, when the next programmer comes along looking to make a change, it is actually possible to guess what each routine does by looking at its name.

If you were to follow the naming conventions used by standard SAP frameworks like the BOPF and the RAP, you would name routines where a value is calculated or read from the database with the prefix DERIVE and routines that check data for correctness with the prefix VALIDATE.

Totally Incorrect Names

In this example from real life, there was a bug reported on a pop-up screen in a program. I recreated the error, put my cursor on a field on the screen to get the technical information, and thus discovered the screen with the problem had the number 0220. I then went to the main program and went hunting for the routine that called up that screen.

Eventually, I found it, and it looked like Listing 3-14.

Listing 3-14. Badly Named Routine

```
*&-------------------------------------------------------------------*
*&      Form   DISPLAY_SCREEN_0219
*&-------------------------------------------------------------------*
*       text
*-------------------------------------------------------------------*
FORM display_screen_0219.
* Sort items by delivery time
  SORT t_link BY zzlatestload_tm.
* Set the LINK POSNR equal to the record with earliest delivery
  READ TABLE t_link INDEX 1.
* move t_link-posnr to zzlinkposnr.
  MOVE t_link-zzlatestload_tm TO zzlatestload_tm.

  CALL SCREEN 220 STARTING AT  4  3
                  ENDING AT   80 6.

ENDFORM.                    " DISPLAY_SCREEN_0219
```

How in the world did it come about that a routine called DISPLAY_SCREEN_0219 called Screen 0220? I looked around the program and found a screen called 0219 with the description "Not Used." So at one point DISPLAY_SCREEN_0219 did indeed call screen 0219, and then that screen was retired and brand-spanking-new screen 0220 was put in its place—and the programmer just could not be bothered to update the routine name. That is like shooting yourself in the foot. I bet if that very same programmer came back a year later looking for where screen 0220 was called they would not be able to find it, just as I could not.

The moral of the story is that when you make a change to a routine such that it changes the fundamental nature of what that routine does, then, in order to make the world a better place, you need to rename the routine so it describes what it now does. Some people balk at that because the routine is called in 54 million places and thus you have to make lots of changes. I say it's worth it. In procedural you can do a "find and replace," and in the OO world using ABAP in Eclipse it is even easier—there is a "Quick Fix" for renaming methods that even looks for usage of that method in other programs.

Sloppy Naming

Here, the problem was that the users were having problems selecting more than one SB at once. It does not matter what an SB is; it could stand for "Straight Banana." It does not matter. What does matter is that I knew for a fact that there was a routine dealing with multiple SB selection, but I just could not find it using the "find and replace" method. I tend to use that technique first when searching for things in programs with ten billion routines, as it is easier and faster than scrolling down an incredibly long list.

The "find and replace" totally failed to find the routine though I knew it was there. I thought I was going mad, because I had written that routine myself and no one had touched the program since. I had to resort to scrolling down the huge list, and I did indeed find the routine—at which point I thought I was going even more insane. Why did the "find" not work?

Can you spot why not from looking at Listing 3-15?

Listing 3-15. Sloppily Named Routine

```
FORM check_for_mutiple_sb_selection
  USING    put_selected_rows   TYPE g_tt_selected_row
  CHANGING pcd_sb_row          TYPE numo3.
```

That's right—it's because I was looking for the word *multiple* and the routine contained the word *mutiple* (sic) instead. The programmer was being sloppy, misspelled a word, and did not notice—and even worse, that programmer was me!

This is the sort of trivial mistake that does not seem to matter at first glance but can cause frustration later. The best way to avoid such problems is to have a peer-review process where hopefully a second set of eyes spots things like this.

Parameter Naming

In Chapter 1, there was a discussion about why using OO programming helped code quality. There are two concrete aspects of methods as opposed to the messier FORM routines, which can clearly help in the area of code clarity: first, just like with function modules, the caller has to pass values in to named parameters, and, second, the concept of a functional method.

Named Parameters

It has been said that one reason to use methods is that the parameters are named; i.e., the caller has to pass a value to a name (keyword parameters) rather than just listing the values that will be passed without any sort of context (positional parameters)—as demonstrated in Listing 3-16.

Listing 3-16. Parameters in Methods Are Named

```
PERFORM fill_gas_tank USING gasoline
                             lighted_cigarette.

fill_gas_tank(
put_in_gas_tank    = gasoline
abort_process_when = lighted_cigarette ).
```

Let us say the two variables in Listing 3-16 are both strings. In the OO method call, if you got the order of what you were passing in incorrect, it would be obvious in the calling program because the instruction PUT_IN_GAS_TANK = LIGHTED_CIGARETTE just looks bad.

However, in the procedural call, you could get the two variables the wrong way around in the caller, the syntax check would not warn you as both variables are strings, and you would not be able to tell exactly what was receiving the variable the caller was sending because the parameters are not named.

Thus, you would blow up your car, and yourself, and maybe even the gas station, and the fire would spread to the nuclear power station next door to the gas station, which would then explode, killing millions of people—all because FORM routines don't have named parameters.

That is a bit of a drastic example; however, I have seen cases where a programmer switches the order of the parameters in a FORM routine, changes some places where that routine is called to reflect that change, but forgets to change other places the routine is called, and as a result all sorts of strange things start to happen.

Now, amazing as it may seem, some people may think my example with the lighted cigarette is silly, so here is another, again something I see all the time. Have a look at Listing 3-17.

Listing 3-17. Passing Values to Cryptic Parameters

```
PERFORM calculate_the_interest USING abap_true
                                      abap_false
                                      abap_true.
```

Anyone looking at Listing 3-17 would have absolutely no idea what effect the TRUE and FALSE flags would have on the routine being called. At the very minimum the programmers should add comments to say what those flags mean, but most people do not bother. With methods, you are forced to say what the values being passed in mean, as in Listing 3-18.

Listing 3-18. Passing Values to Named Parameters

```
calculate_the_interest(
preferred_customer = abap_true
show_log           = abap_false
store_log          = abap_true ).
```

Boolean Types

It would be far better in Listing 3-18 if we could just write TRUE or FALSE rather than having the ABAP prefix. On the need for a true Boolean TRUE/FALSE variable in a programming language, opinion is divided. Every single other programming language ever invented says YES; ABAP says NO.

Functional Methods

A functional method is a method that has a single RETURNING parameter. There are many functional methods built into the ABAP language, such as LINES( ) to return the number of lines in an internal table.

When using a functional method, you don't need to specify the RETURNING parameter in the calling program, because the method name should (if named correctly) make it obvious what is going on. Moreover, if that RETURNING parameter is of type ABAP_BOOL, then you do not have to write IF IS_A_CASH_SALE(ORDER_NUMBER) = ABAP_TRUE. You can shorten it to IF IS_A_CASH_SALE(ORDER_NUMBER).

That reads a bit more like plain English, even if it makes you sound a bit like Yoda. Let's take another example. You could write a method call like this:

```
IF SHALL_WE( THE_CAR_IN_FRONT->UP_TO_CATCH( ) ).
```

That's an exact word-for-word translation of the equivalent German phrase, but does it read well to an English speaker? I would say yes, I have no problem at all with that. In fact, I have never had any problem with the word order being different when learning German.

Some internet articles on ABAP programming have gone as far as to say that *all* methods should be functional methods. I don't think that proposed rule is all that practical in real life. I would say you can strike a happy medium and try to use them as much as possible in an effort to increase the clarity of the code, but don't go crazy trying to fit a square peg into a round hole.

One common argument against always using functional methods is that lots of methods return multiple EXPORTING parameters. An OO person would argue right back that if your method has many such parameters then it is clearly doing more than one thing and so is a bad method, shame on it.

In one example I devised, I had a method that took a few input parameters and then came back with the values for a fourth-order polynomial. It was clearly doing only one thing and thus following the OO rules.

However, a fourth-order polynomial contains, shockingly, four values. I was passing these back as four export parameters. The answer I got back was that the method wasn't returning four values; it was returning one value that happened to be a 4-tuple. Thus, returning those values in a structure is the way forward.

The modified rule would be, if the various EXPORTING parameters in a method obviously belong together (e.g., various fields from a sales order item), then using a functional method and putting the results in a structure is the way to go; if the EXPORTING parameters seem unrelated to each other (an order number and the current temperature in Death Valley, for example), then keep them as EXPORTING parameters and reconsider whether the method is doing more than one thing.

Some people say they cannot use a functional method, because they have two EXPORTING parameters, one of which is a return code. In such a case, I would say using exception classes instead of a return code will make the code a lot clearer.

Variable Naming

Having covered method and parameter naming, we move on to a discussion on what to name variables. There are two strands to this: one incredibly contentious, the other rather less so. First, we will look at the contentious argument that makes people's blood boil (whichever side of the fence they sit on)—whether or not to use prefixes. Then, we will examine the non-contentious one—the idea that good variable naming makes code self-documenting.

Lastly, we will consider whether to use German acronyms when naming variables (which we all have done for a very long time).

Hungarian Notation

Hungarian notation is a term that means slightly different things to different people, but in general you can define it as adding prefixes to a variable name in order to classify it in some way; e.g., you could say G_BANANA_COUNT to say variable BANANA_COUNT is global, or LT_DELIVERIES to say the variable DELIVERIES is both local and an internal table.

Why is that concept called Hungarian, you might ask. It all started many years ago when a programmer at Microsoft (who was born in Hungary) wrote an article about variable naming. He wrote a short introduction, starting with the benefits of using prefixes, and then spent the bulk of the article explaining why they were not a good idea. However, nobody ever read past the introduction, and so they got totally the wrong end of the stick, and before you knew it prefixes were the Microsoft naming standard and all programmers everywhere were using them.

That was a long time ago and has caused a great number of very emotional debates on the subject in the intervening period.

SAP itself sends out mixed messages. The official position (as in the official programming guidelines) is to not use prefixes, but if you look at standard SAP code you will see that code from 20-plus years ago either has no prefixes or a seemingly random naming convention, but code from a year ago seems to have a uniform convention with all variables having prefixes. Even all the examples in the ABAP RESTFul programming model use prefixes.

Prefixes in an OO Context

In an OO context, some people have pointed out the anomaly that comes with giving a prefix to global variables, when you do not do the same thing to methods. The example is that when you call a method you write something like this:

```
BANANA->PEEL( ).
```

Nobody would ever consider putting a prefix in front of a method name; e.g., call a method G_PEEL. That would be silly. So, if you had a read-only instance attribute of the BANANA class, why should you write the following:

```
BANANA->G_CURVINESS
```

To be consistent, you would have to write BANANA->CURVINESS.

In an OO context, if you want to say a variable is available all throughout the class (i.e., a member variable), then you can write ME->SIZE for an instance attribute and ME=>SIZE for a static attribute, and in both cases you do not need a prefix.

Random Naming Conventions

Even if everyone thought that prefixes were a good thing, the problem is that no two ABAP programmers in the world could agree on what those prefixes should be. For example, should a global variable that is an integer be prefixed with GV_ or with GD_ (for elementary data element) or GI_ or any of a million other options? The only thing you can be sure of is that no two organizations name things the same way, and there is no global set of conventions (that anyone actually follows). There is a recommended naming convention in the official ABAP programming guidelines—they say "we do not want you to use prefixes but if you insist, use these"—but I am not sure this recommendation ever caught on.

As a result, if you started a job at a new company and went looking at the code, you would not be sure what the prefixes meant. For example, say you found a variable called GL_VKORG. What is the scope of that? Is it global? Is it local? You would have to go hunting for the declaration, which would totally defeat the point.

If your organization does like using prefixes, then it is vital that all the programmers use them in the same way. This can in fact be checked using the code inspector, which you can configure to check for your specific rules, but I wonder how many people actually use that capability?

Misleading Names

You may able to use the code inspector to see if something is a local variable and thus check the prefix, but it cannot check for stupidity. Thus, you can call a local variable that is an integer LT_SALES_ORDERS with no problem whatsoever.

In fact, the code inspector check on naming is rarely used, and so you get misleading names like LV_ORDER, which is in fact a global variable. Also, people can declare what they *think* is a local variable inside a PBO module and call it LV_ORDER, but all variables in PBO modules are in fact global. In the examples just cited, the prefixes do more harm than good as they are sending out false information to the programmer making a change, and that might cause them to make an error based on a false assumption.

As another example, once there was a very strange piece of code I had to change that exported some data to a Z table, and then the first Z program submitted a second Z program, which read back that exact same data from that Z table and printed it out. That was the entire purpose of that Z table.

That did not seem very sensible to me, so I made a change to call a function module instead, passing the function the data that was formerly stored in a Z table via an IMPORT parameter. The function module had the same code as the Z program that used to be called via a SUBMIT. I thought I was being really clever, but in fact I broke the program.

It took a lot of looking, but I discovered the culprit was a control variable called L_CNT. I had presumed that because it started with L it was a local variable, and indeed it was declared at the start of a subroutine, but on closer inspection it was declared thus:

```
STATICS: L_CNT.
```

So, it was a global variable. That was fine when the code was called via SUBMIT, as it was always initial, but that did not work so well during repeated calls to a function module. Upon even further investigation, I discovered that the reason the variable was declared as a STATIC and named starting with a L was because the whole section of code had been cut and pasted from the internet as example code of how to print a SMARTFORM with multiple copies in the same spool.

My advice would be never to use STATICS at all, as they are as obsolete as the dinosaurs, and if you come across a variable where you find the name misrepresents the scope either get rid of the prefix altogether (*no* information is better than *misleading* information) or change it so it correctly reflects the variable's scope. Or maybe, just maybe, never cut and paste code that you do not understand into your system.

Very Old Programs

Once, I was maintaining a very old program (more than 15 years old), and the way it worked was to put an ALV grid on screen 0100, and then you would select one or more records and choose a menu command or icon, and 99 percent of the time another screen would pop up asking you something else related to what you were about to do. Screens need a global variable for the OK_CODE, so in this program such a variable had indeed been declared, called OK_CODE. That variable was used in every screen.

I am sure you can see the problem coming, especially if you call three different screens one after the other, or call one screen from another screen. At any given point, how can you be sure which screen's OK_CODE you are evaluating in the code?

At least with a function module you are isolated from such things; you can control what gets passed backward and forward via the signature, which is why SAP recommends wrapping function modules around screens.

Going back to the program at hand, just to make things even more funny, in the USER_COMMAND after the main screen, the OK_CODE was stored for posterity in another global variable called SAVE_OK. This was done, I presume, because the programmer knew that OK_CODE would change after the next screen got called.

Then, we had the following in the USER_COMMAND:

```
PERFORM call_up_xyz_screen USING SAVE_OK.
```

This, in the FORM definition, becomes the following:

```
FORM call_up_xyz_screen USING ok_code.
```

Lovely. A parameter with the same name as one global variable, which actually refers to a different global variable. When the screen gets called, the global OK_CODE changes, but the OK_CODE parameter variable within the subroutine does not.

In fact, after the screen is called (which sets the global OK_CODE), the calling subroutine cannot tell what the global OK_CODE has been changed to, as that value is masked by the local (parameter) variable with the same name.

Even worse, inside one such routine was a local variable also called OK_CODE, which masked both the global variable called OK_CODE and the USING parameter called OK_CODE.

The whole thing was a complete mess. It is very difficult to unscramble such eggs without breaking the program, but what I could do was add prefixes such that the global variable was GD_OK_CODE, the parameter was PUD_OK_CODE, and the local variable was LD_OK_CODE. At least that way I knew if I was coming or going.

This is why, to all the people who say calling variables PUD_OK_CODE or GD_OK_CODE or LD_OK_CODE is pointless, it could be said that in the OO world they are most likely 100 percent correct, but what about "legacy" programs like this that have to be maintained?

The conclusion would be that prefixes have their place in old procedural programs to avoid "shadowing" and in signatures (usually), but not in local variables.

Inline Declarations

What some ABAP programmers had started to do was this: instead of declaring the local variables at the start of the routine, they declared the variable just before it was used. That made it obvious it was local and thus it did not need a prefix to indicate that fact.

That was good, but then with the 7.40 release of ABAP SAP came up with the concept of inline declarations, where you do not even need a data declaration at all; you just declare the variable at the point it is first used, as in Listing 3-19.

Listing 3-19. Inline Declarations

```
LOOP AT sales_order_list INTO DATA(sales_order_data).
DATA(current_row_number) = SY-TABIX
```

It is obvious such variables are local, so there is no need at all for a prefix to indicate the scope.

Self-Documenting

Self-documenting means that when you see the name of anything in a program it is so obvious what the purpose of that thing is that you do not have to go wandering off looking for a thousand-page instruction manual to work out its purpose.

If you find that you need to put a comment after a variable name to say what that variable represents, or to put a prefix at the start to say it's an integer or a structure or whatever, then it could be said that the name is not self-documenting in the slightest, which is why you are adding those extras to help people understand the variable's purpose.

And for every person who diligently adds such comments or prefixes, there are ten programmers who do not.

Let's say I need to define a structure with names and types, as shown in Listing 3-20.

Listing 3-20. Silly Structure Definition

```
DATA: BEGIN OF g_typ_data,
        xyz123   TYPE i,
        string   TYPE string,
        value_1  TYPE p DECIMALS 3,
        text_1   TYPE c,
        "same length & type as EKPO-BSTAE
        "but no semantic similarity
        tax_code TYPE ekpo-bstae,
      END OF g_typ_data.
```

Anyone trying to understand the purpose of that structure would be out of luck. You may say no one would do something so silly. I didn't believe it either, until I started looking at some of my own programs, and indeed some standard SAP ones.

It's easy to understand that, as opposed to variable names like STRING or XYZ123, if you call a variable a name that actually describes what sort of data it contains and what it is used for—e.g., ERROR_MESSAGE as opposed to STRING, or HEIGHT as opposed to XYZ123—then the code becomes self-documenting to a much greater extent.

Naturally, you must pick a name that the next programmer who looks at the code will find meaningful; a wrong name choice can do more harm than a bland name like VALUE. With a name like VALUE the programmer has to work out what the variable contains. If the variable has a misleading name, the programmer will make an incorrect assumption.

As an example of this, I offer the time when, whilst debugging a problem, I found a variable with the name COMBINED_WEIGHT, which gave me a false idea of what it might represent. After a lot of searching I found that this global variable was only filled if a user had been given a pop-up and manually entered the weight. So I changed the variable name to MANUALLY_ENTERED_WEIGHT. After a good old find/replace on that variable the code made a lot more sense in certain places and made no sense at all in others. This is an example of "making bad code look bad." Once everything was obvious, I could then zero in on the bits that made no sense, and before too long my problem was solved.

In regard to indicating the nature of the variable, rather than adding a T prefix for "table" or an S prefix for "structure," the idea is that simply by differentiating between "customer" and "customers" you should know if it's a table or a single object. A variable called `customer` could be an object, and you need to be really clear, so one naming convention could be as follows:

> `Customer` — object representing a customer, contains KNA1, KNB1, and so on
>
> `Customer_list` — internal table full of customer objects
>
> `Customer_header_list` — internal table full of KNA1 data
>
> `Customer_header_data` — structure full of KNA1 data
>
> `Customer_number` — KNA1-KUNNR

It does not really matter what the convention is, as long as it is (a) consistent and (b) blindingly obvious to the reader what the variable represents. There is an easy way to check that—show the code to a non-programmer and ask them to guess what the variable names mean. The results of that test often have you rushing back to the drawing board in a big hurry.

German Acronyms

As you find out on your first day of dealing with SAP, all the database tables and field names therein are based on German abbreviations; e.g., KUNNR for customer, or VBAK for "Sales Order Header," where the K at the end of VBAK stands for the German word KOPF; i.e., "Head."

In recent years, most large German multinational companies have adopted English as their official corporate language, and SAP is no exception. Hence, the SAP recommendation is to put all the comments in your ABAP code in English. That, of course, goes along with the fact that all the ABAP keywords are in English; i.e., READ TABLE instead of TABELLE LESEN. In older SAP programs like SAPMV45A (Sales Document maintenance program) the subroutine (FORM routine) names do indeed start with LESEN, but in recent standard SAP codes the subroutines are (a) more likely to be methods than FORM routines and (b) more likely to start with READ rather than LESEN. Function modules generally have English names as well—especially BAPIs.

So, you end up with the following:

- Comments in English

- ABAP keywords in English

- Standard fields in German; e.g., `TABLES: LIKP,VBAK,VBRK`.

- Custom fields most likely in English; e.g., `VBAK-ZZMY_CUSTOM_THING`

- Variables in a mixture of German and English

Let's talk about the last one—variable names. Do you call a local variable to store a sales order number `VBELN` or `SALES_ORDER_NUMBER`? Do you call a parameter that imports such a value `ID_VBELN` or `ID_SALES_ORDER_NUMBER`? I have found that roughly half the programmers do the former, roughly half do the latter, and some use their own esoteric, incomprehensible naming convention. Some programmers veer between all three behaviors depending on what hour of the day it is. Over time, different programmers make changes to the same program, and don't stick to whatever naming convention was used before, instead using their own naming convention without renaming existing variables.

As a result, you end up with bizarre constructs like Listing 3-21.

Listing 3-21. Inconsistent Parameter Naming

```
METHOD do_something IMPORTING
id_vkorg                 TYPE vkorg
                                    id_distribution_channel TYPE vtweg
                                    id_p3                   TYPE spart.
```

It goes without saying that naming anything `P3` is just crazy, as it completely obscures the meaning of whatever it is the variable is supposed to represent. I would say at the very minimum you must agree with your team to be consistent; i.e., either values like `VKORG` all the time or values like `SALES_ORGANIZATION` all the time.

Some people say that values like `VBELN` and `VKORG` are so well known that naming variables after them has no adverse effect on the clarity of the code. Whilst I would agree that those values are very well known, there are some database tables that are very rarely used, and some that have very obscure field names. For example, you may be able to instinctively know what `VBAK-VBELN` means, but can you tell me off the top of your head what field `KNMT- J_1BTXSDC` means? (It's the SD tax code in the Customer Material Info Record table, you will be happy to know). In such a case, maybe calling the variable `TAX_CODE` would give the casual reader more of a clue as to what is going on in the code.

I would advocate using English names for the variables; it might make the code slightly longer, but then you would have uniformity in language between the keywords, the comments, the variables, and the routine names. It's always a good thing when your code reads as much like plain English as possible.

Normally, if you have an internal table that you are going to fill with a subset of rows from a database table, you would name all the fields in the internal table the same as the database fields so you can use the INTO CORRESPONDING FIELDS OF clause when you write your database SELECT statement. The resulting code would look something like Listing 3-22.

Listing 3-22. Normal-Looking SELECT Statement

```
* VBAK/VBAP—Use Primary Key
    SELECT vbak~vbeln vbak~kunnr
           vbap~posnr vbap~matnr vbap~zzfirstload_tm vbap~werks
           vbap~zzoverride_dist  vbap~zzshort_dist   vbap~zzdistz
      FROM vbak
      INNER JOIN vbap
      ON vbak~vbeln EQ vbap~vbeln
      INTO CORRESPONDING FIELDS OF TABLE rt_sales_orders
      FOR ALL ENTRIES IN sales_item_key
      WHERE vbap~vbeln EQ sales_item_key-vbeln
      AND   vbap~posnr EQ sales_item_key-posnr.
```

Listing 3-22 shows the usual mix of standard fields with German names and custom fields with English names. When you append standard SAP tables it is mandatory to start your custom field name with ZZ, but when you come to use that name later on in your program it does not feel very natural; e.g., ZZDISTANCE is not really an exact match for the English word DISTANCE.

One approach I have seen a few programmers take is to rename all the fields in the internal table such that they have English names—e.g., SALES_ORDER_NUMBER TYPE VBELN—and then use the facility in a SQL query that lets you write something like VBELN AS SALES_ORDER_NUMBER, which changes the SELECT statement to that seen in Listing 3-23.

Listing 3-23. A SELECT which converts German abbreviations into English names

```
* VBAK/VBAP-Use Primary Key
    SELECT vbak~vbeln          AS sales_order_number
           vbak~kunnr          AS customer_number
           vbap~posnr          AS sales_order_item
           vbap~matnr          AS material_number
           vbap~zzfirstload_tm AS first_load_time
           vbap~werks          AS supplying_plant
           vbap~zzoverride_dist AS over_dride_distance
           vbap~zzshort_dist   AS short_distance
           vbap~zzdistz        AS distance
      FROM vbak
      INNER JOIN vbap
      ON vbak~vbeln EQ vbap~vbeln
      INTO CORRESPONDING FIELDS OF TABLE rt_sales_orders
      FOR ALL ENTRIES IN lt_sales_item_key
      WHERE vbap~vbeln EQ lt_sales_item_key-vbeln
      AND   vbap~posnr EQ lt_sales_item_key-posnr.
```

This approach makes the SELECT statement a lot longer, but as this statement is (hopefully) hidden away inside a method in a specialized database access class that will not pollute the important bit of the code—i.e., the business logic—that important part will now be easier to read.

Magic Numbers

One thing I mention again and again in my blogs is the so-called magic numbers that pop up in programs. If we are talking about how to make things less confusing for the reader, and at the same time easier to change as business requirements change, then I am going to have do the broken-record thing and bring this up again (I wonder if anyone below a certain age has the slightest idea what the term *broken record* originally referred to?).

As an example, the other day, in a specification I was given that had *tons* of business logic within it, I was supposed to multiply the result by 1.645. Easy enough to do, but I thought to myself, what is so wonderful about that number and, more to the point, can it change?

A quick hunt all around the internet came back with the answer that 1.645 was the "famous" such and such's constant, which he had come up with via an exhaustive series of scientific experiments proving that the result is wrong unless you multiply it by this number. All well and good. So, if it is a scientific constant, like pi, it can't change, can it? A-ha! Every country has a different interpretation of this result, so this "constant" has different values in calculations done, for example, in India and in Australia.

If it had been a universal constant then I would have declared it as a constant with the correct scientific name, and probably given a little explanation of what this was all about as a comment. In this case, it varies from country to country, so the value needs to be read out of some sort of customizing table, but it still needs a meaningful name for the variable.

Hard Coding

Hard coding anything is bad. There is never any excuse for it—it's just laziness. There is always a way to avoid it.

Time and again I have seen hard-coded values used to determine the associated processing, such as doing one thing when the sales order item category is "Y096" and another thing when the sales organization is "BYZ2." Those codes are meaningless— no one reading the program would have a clue what they meant unless there was a comment, and, as we will see a bit later, such comments often end up causing more harm than good.

There are multiple ways around this problem.

- Many times things like the language are hard coded—you should use SY-LANGU instead.

- Text values in your code are hard coded until you assign them a text element, and then they can be varied by the log-on language. It's the same deal for messages (SE91).

- Currencies or units of measure are often hard coded; these can be replaced by database table fields like WAERS for the currency or VRKME for the sales unit of measure.

- Some values vary by country or business line. Instead of a huge, convoluted conditional structure crammed with hard-coded values, this situation is crying out for a configuration table where the result is read based on whatever it is that varies and is placed in a variable with a meaningful name; e.g., Y096 becomes FREE_OF_CHARGE or BYZ2 becomes Outer Mongolia.

- Values that are the same for everybody should be replaced by constants.

Constants

Constants are ten billion times better than putting hard-coded values all over the program—when they are used correctly. However, as you will see, when *not* used correctly they can cause more harm than good.

Redundant Constants

I could not begin any discussion of constants without relating the habit some consultants used to have, circa 2000: If they were going to add ten to a value (say to determine the next line item of a sales order) they would declare a global constant called C_010. What value does that add?

Then, of course, five years down the track, the value we want to add changes to five—then we think, "Good job, this is a constant, we only need to make the change in one place," and thus you end up with a constant called C_010 that has a value of five.

In such cases, get rid of the redundant constants or see if you can dynamically read the database to get the value. In this example, the value of ten was coming from database field TVAK-INCPO to see what value the system proposed for a new sales order line item.

Meaningless Constants

The other thing that makes me bang my head on the desk is that when confronted with an obscure code that SAP uses to denote a piece of equipment flagged for deletion—a meaningless value like ISRU—instead of declaring a constant called C_FLAGGED_FOR_ DELETION, "they" decided to call the constant C_ISRU. Well, thanks for that, everything is much clearer now. Of course, one day SAP might decide to change the deletion code to JKML, and then you'd end up with a with a meaningless name pointing to a different meaningless value; i.e., C_ISRU VALUE 'JKML'.

Let us look at some actual code examples I have found where this sort of thing occurs.

One thing to note about Listing 3-24 is that "Picking Status" in SAP is represented by database field VBUP-KOSTA.

Listing 3-24. Bad Constant Names #1

```
CONSTANTS: c_pick_status_1    TYPE c VALUE 'A',
           c_pick_status_2    TYPE c VALUE 'B',
           c_picking_complete TYPE c VALUE 'C'.

"LFSTA = Delivery Status of Sales Document
CHECK ght_vbup-lfsta = c_pick_status_1 OR
      ght_vbup-lfsta = c_pick_status_2 OR
      "LFGSA = Overall Delivery Status for all items
      ght_vbup-lfgsa = c_pick_status_1 OR
      ght_vbup-lfgsa = c_pick_status_2.
```

Calling a constant C_PICK_STATUS_1 (which has the value A) is somewhat different to calling it C_PICK_STATUS_A. In fact, it is worse. At least when it has the A in its name you might guess it's related to the value A in the database, but when it is called 1 you have no idea at all what is going on. In both cases, you have no idea that it means the delivery has not been picked yet.

Also note the picking status constant is being compared to the delivery status field. The value is the same (A, B, or C), but the semantic meaning is totally different.

Another example can be seen in Listing 3-25. Here, we have a large number of constants where, for example, constant MC_QF04 has the value QF04. I cannot see the difference between Listing 3-25 and actually hard coding the meaningless values.

Listing 3-25. Bad Constant Names #2

```
zif_sd_tdy_controller~mo_model→zif_sd_tdy_quickfilter_model~set(
  id_filter = zif_sd_tdy_quickfilter_model=>mc_qf04
  id_value  = |{ lv_toggle }| ).
zif_sd_tdy_controller~mo_model→zif_sd_tdy_quickfilter_model~set(
  id_filter = zif_sd_tdy_quickfilter_model=>mc_qf08
  id_value  = |{ lv_toggle }| ).
zif_sd_tdy_controller~mo_model→zif_sd_tdy_quickfilter_model~set(
  id_filter = zif_sd_tdy_quickfilter_model=>mc_qf09
  id_value  = |{ lv_toggle }| ).
```

```
zif_sd_tdy_controller~mo_model->zif_sd_tdy_quickfilter_model~set(
  id_filter = zif_sd_tdy_quickfilter_model=>mc_qf10
  id_value  = |{ lv_toggle }| ).
zif_sd_tdy_controller~mo_model->zif_sd_tdy_quickfilter_model~set(
  id_filter = zif_sd_tdy_quickfilter_model=>mc_qf07
  id_value  = |{ abap_true }| ).
```

The moral is clear—a constant has to be an English name describing something and not a secret code.

How Not to Use Constants

In Listing 3-26, the programmer is trying to declare some constants to represent values of icons that will be displayed on some sort of ALV grid.

Listing 3-26. Using Constants for Icons

```
*****************************************************************
*** Constants (GC_)
*****************************************************************
DATA:
gc_icon_green_light    TYPE icon-name VALUE 'ICON_GREEN_LIGHT',
gc_icon_yellow_light   TYPE icon-name VALUE 'ICON_YELLOW_LIGHT',
gc_confirm_stock_take  TYPE i VALUE 300,
gc_enter_stock_values01 TYPE i VALUE 400.
```

The first mistake is that the programmer (which was me ten years ago, by the way) should have used CONSTANTS as opposed to DATA—that saves memory, because a constant lives in a special area of memory that is shared between all running instances of the program, whereas a variable declared via a DATA declaration is replicated in memory by each running instance. Moreover a "constant" declared via a DATA statement is not a constant at all; the program can change the value at any time. Accordingly, do not use a DATA statement to define a constant.

Furthermore, there was no reason to declare constants for icons at all. You can just use ICON_GREEN_LIGHT directly in your program (it is part of a TYPE-POOL, and those can be accessed by any program).

ABAP Data Dictionary Object Naming

As you have seen, giving meaningless or misleading names to methods or variables can really make life difficult for the next programmer who needs to change an individual program. However, if you make a similar mistake with a DDIC object—a table name, or a structure or similar—you can make life difficult for all the programmers in the system at once. Moreover, you can rename a program variable with no ill effects, but trying to rename a DDIC table once it is filled with data is more trouble than it is worth; a mistake here is a mistake forever.

Let us look at various possible DDIC objects and how to name them correctly.

Tables

Most standard SAP table names are very short—e.g., VBAK or T001W—which I presume was a limitation that existed 30 years ago. Even now, you can only have 16 characters for a table name, which means 99 percent of the time you have to use abbreviations.

Given the very short amount of space you have to work with, the question immediately arises—can you afford to waste even a single letter?

The reason this comes up so often is that some organizations have a naming policy that insists that you add SD or MM right after the Z at the start of the table name. I would argue that, due to the highly integrated nature of SAP, is it highly unlikely any Z table will be used by just a single module, making that rule silly.

Even if that table was just used by, say, the CO module, if you could give the table a good enough name it would make its purpose obvious. Also, humans do not think in terms of obscure SAP modules. CO stands for "Controlling," but that is called "Management Accounting" in the United Kingdom.

One thing you should definitely *not* do is name tables as shown in Listing 3-27.

Listing 3-27. Bad Choice of DDC Table Name

```
IF r_deliveries IS INITIAL.
ELSE.
  CHECK  zsd04-posnr IN r_deliveries.
ENDIF.
```

In this case, the programmer decided to number the Z tables and called them ZSD01, ZSD02, ZSD03, and so on. If you call a database table ZSD04 and give the matching internal table the same name, how can anyone guess what that table is for, except that it might be something to do with SD, but maybe not, because you are seeing it referenced in MM and FI type programs as well.

A lot of programmers like to stick a T at the front of the table name as well to indicate that this is a table as opposed to a structure. Thus, you end up with a prefix like ZTSD_; i.e., five characters gone before you can start adding anything meaningful. Combine that with the fact that if you want to associate a text table with the main table you have to leave two blank spaces at the end of the table name so that the text table can have the same name but end with _T. With the big prefix, that leaves only nine characters to express the meaningful part of the table name! Oh, dear!

Structure names can be longer than table names, so one way to make it obvious something is a structure rather than a table is to make sure all your structures have names longer than 16 characters and always refer to the singular, as tables refer to the plural; e.g., ZMOUSERACE_ITEM_DATA for the structure and ZMICERACEITEMS for the table. In the same way, table types can have long names and should always refer to the plural.

Transaction Codes

A transaction code can be 20 characters long, so you could give it a meaningful name if you wanted to, but most users want a really short name as they like typing it in the command box rather than choosing it from a menu.

Back in the year 2000, I had to create a large number of Z reports and, as I had no idea what I was doing, in my infinite wisdom, I used the exact same naming convention I warned against just now: I called the SD reports ZS01, ZS02, ZS03, etc., and then someone had to create a help card to say what they all meant. When, 12 years later, I had a second crack of the whip in another SAP system, I used abbreviations instead.

The strangest transaction codes I have seen in SAP are the standard ones in FI transactions; e.g., asset accounting. One example that springs to mind is standard SAP transaction S_ALR_87012026. That calls up a report showing you depreciation for the current year. I would imagine most people would not consider the name of that transaction to be snappy and self-explanatory.

In summary, nowadays I consider naming transaction codes using meaningful abbreviations; e.g., ZSOL for "Sales Order List" and ZIVL for "Invoice List" rather than ZS11. If I had a custom fixed-asset deprecation report, I would call it ZFADP as opposed to a meaningless eight-digit number.

Another top tip is that when you create a parameter transaction to maintain a Z table via SM30, call the transaction code the same thing as the table name, thus avoiding years of questions from business analysts such as, "What is the transaction to maintain table ZBOING?" In the table maintenance generator, I call the function group the same name as well; thus, when maintaining a table, there are three tightly linked objects all with the same name: the table being maintained, the transaction to maintain it, and the function group that enables that maintenance.

Structures

In the previous section, I suggested making structure names longer than table names and making the name always refer to the singular. Here, I would just like to give an example of an anti-pattern I saw from the year 1999. Back then, SAP experts were in short supply, and a lot of consultants found themselves bouncing from company to company, often working for two or more companies each week.

It was easy for them to get confused, and so some decided that in order to remind themselves which SAP system they were working with the obvious solution was to include the name of the current customer in the DDIC name.

So if a consultant found themselves working for the ACME company every Wednesday, and the first structure they had to create was to store inventory data, rather than call the structure something like ZINVENTORY_DETAILS they called it ZACMESTRUCT1. They could look at the that name and know (a) it was created for the ACME company, (b) it was a structure, and (c) it was the first one they had created for that customer. Wonderful for the consultant, not so much for the customer.

I did not make that up—I saw that time and again back in 1999 and presumed that practice had died off over the years. Until I saw it again last week—in 2020. A new consultant had created a structure, and the first eight or so characters were prefixes— one of which was a two-letter abbreviation of the company name.

I put it to you, ladies and gentlemen of the jury, that most clients know the name of their own company, thus rendering the addition of that company name to Z structure names redundant. Moreover, in the preceding example, the ACME company changed its name round about 2003, thus making the structure name that contained the word *ACME* even more ridiculous than it already was.

Indexes

With a Z table index you only have two characters to play with, one of which is a Z, so the concept of having a meaningful name is out the window here. What you need to do is give the most meaningful name you can in the short description.

What *not* to do is shown in Figure 3-2.

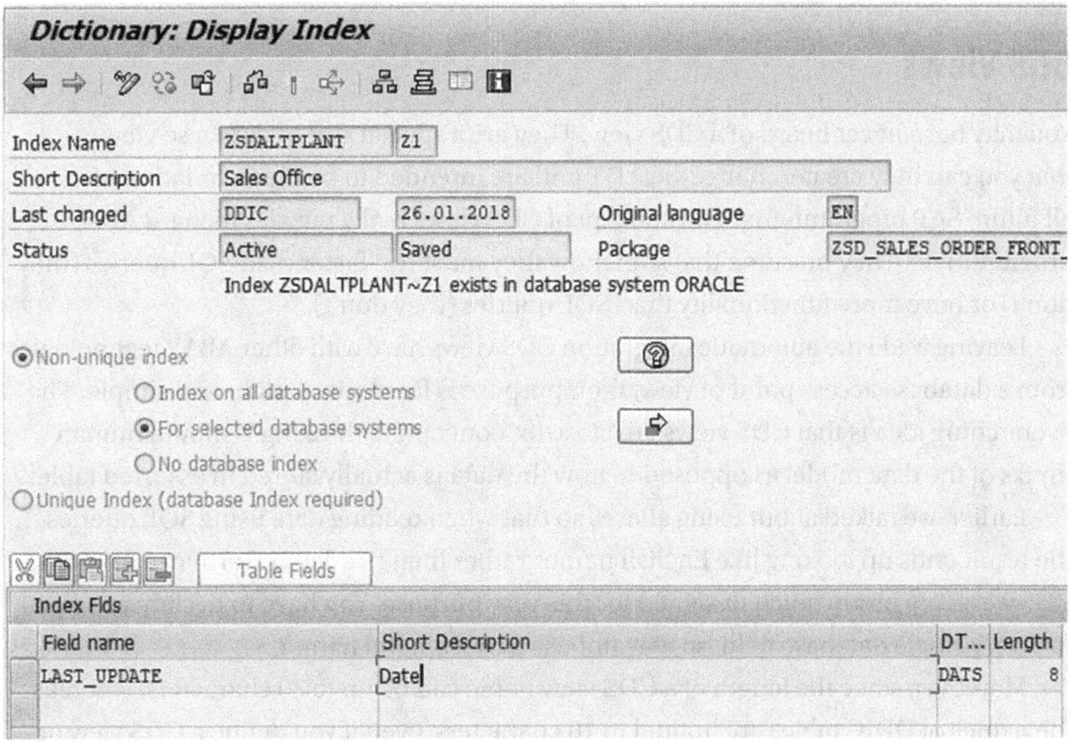

Figure 3-2. *Index with sub-optimal short description*

Some people list the field names in the short description of the index, which is a bit redundant. Describing the business purpose of the index in the description is the way forward. If you don't know what that purpose is, why are you creating the index in the first place?

Program Names

You can have 30 characters in the name of an executable program or a module pool, so it is relatively easy to give such a program a meaningful name. One trick I like is to keep transaction codes short and, for an executable program like an ALV report, start the program name with the transaction code; e.g., for a fixed-asset depreciation report, ZFADP_SOMETHING.

Why would I do such a strange thing? For the sole reason that when the help desk or BASIS contacts me and tells me something has gone out of control in the production system I can look at transaction SM66 and, just by looking at the start of the program name, I can know what transaction the culprit is.

CDS Views

You may have never heard of a CDS view. They are a special sort of database view that you can only create/change via ADT and are intended to be the foundation of all future SAP programming. The concept of CDS views really puzzles diehard ABAP programmers. They presume that somehow they must run faster than SQL queries (they don't) or have more functionality than SQL queries (they don't).

Leaving aside the automatic integration CDS views have with other ABAP technologies from a database access point of view, their purpose is for clarity—plain and simple. The overarching idea is that CDS views are close to "conceptual thinking"—how a human thinks of the data model as opposed to how the data is actually stored in assorted tables.

Earlier, we talked about using aliases so that when reading data using SQL queries the result ends up looking like English names rather than five-letter German acronyms. CDS views are pretty much designed for this very purpose. You have to declare an alias for every single database field, so why not use a meaningful name?

Moreover, since the length of a CDS view name can be up to 30 characters, whereas the names of DDIC tables are limited to 16 characters, even if you define a CDS view on just one table you can give that view a far longer and hence more meaningful name (the underlying DDIC view still has to have a short name, but the calling program can use the full-length CDS view name).

This means if you do all your SELECTS on custom CDS views (including those that wrap standard SAP tables), you could potentially have an entire Z program with *no German acronyms at all*. I have never written such a program, I have to admit, since I am so used to VBELN and the like, but not only is such a thing possible, it's actually incredibly easy.

How Correct Naming Enables Reuse

If anyone were to ask you why you create function modules and global classes rather than have everything local within the program at hand, you would most likely argue that those global objects are "standalone" to such an extent they can be reused by multiple programs, and that every time you create such a reusable object it makes your future life, and those of your colleagues, easier.

Naturally, if, instead of writing something from scratch, I can find an existing artifact that does the exact thing I currently I want, then I can and will reuse it.

The standard SAP code base is so gigantic that if you have a programming problem to solve, it is almost certain someone has been there and done that and gotten the T-shirt; i.e., there is a standard class/method/function module that already does what you want.

The problem is finding it.

There are more function modules in the standard SAP system than there are stars in the sky, and more recently a lot of classes/methods as well, though it will take time for the latter to catch up numerically due to the vast period of time when OO things were not available in ABAP.

It is my horrible suspicion that hundreds, if not thousands, of ABAP programmers spend their day writing functions that are exact copies of things that already exist in the standard system, or creating user exits that achieve functionality that either exists in enhancement pack business functions that have not been activated in their system, or can be achieved by customizing.

Even worse, I think the same thing happens within SAP itself. When I have searched for standard function modules to achieve XYZ I usually get either no results or six functions doing exactly the same thing.

In the book *Thinking in Java* by Bruce Eckel, he says that if you did not know the name of a method in the Java GUI "swing" framework, you could guess what it was called because the naming conventions were so strongly followed. That does not seem to be case in SAP; if anything, there is an utter lack of naming conventions in standard SAP repository objects.

Even the BAPI naming is all over the place. One of the four principles for BAPIs was supposed to be its consistent naming, along with meaningful documentation, he he he. But you end up with BAPI names containing various naming conventions—e.g., for creating a new business object of some sort you have CREATE or CREATEFROMDATA or sometimes even stranger names that are impossible to guess.

With other standard functions, even if the function at hand is the sort of thing that is reusable in many contexts, the SAP programmer names it after the project they are currently working on, so you get class names like JAPANESE_MICE_RACING_MATHS_ FUNCTIONS that contain many useful mathematical functions that could be used in many applications that are unrelated to mice, or racing, or Japan.

I don't like to call a function module or class with a name like that, as it would confuse any casual reader of the code.

Very often, we create our own function module or class, and then later on we might accidentally stumble on an identical one in standard SAP and wish we had known that it was there before we started reinventing the wheel.

Once, whilst I was transitioning code in an Excel macro into ABAP, what I found in the spreadsheet was the Excel function MAX. I thought there must be one in standard SAP that did the same thing—as indeed there is—but at the time I couldn't find it for love nor money. A load of Google searching did not help. I searched for function modules and found BELGIAN_TRUFFLE_GROWERS_MAX_VALUE, which was almost OK but had a few odd mandatory import parameters.

In the end, I wrote my own method to do this, and then every so often I did another Google search using different parameters—the term *BUILT IN FUNCTION* did not help much, for example—and in the end I discovered the standard function is NMAX. There was no way to guess this.

The point is that the only way you are ever going to achieve one of the Holy Grails of software development—creating reusable code—is by naming things properly.

Comments

Many people misunderstand the purpose of comments. It has been said that the acid test for whether you've written good code is when your code needs no comments at all because it is so obvious what is going on.

Comments do have a place in the grand scheme of things, but they are intended to say *why* you are doing something as opposed to *how* (which the code itself explains anyway).

Why, Not How

It is important to say *why* you changed something, especially if you are doing something odd to avoid a specific problem; otherwise, some well-meaning person in the future will say "that's odd" and change it right back again.

Once upon a time, I changed a line of code that said

```
M_FLAG = 'X'. "Ticket 530333
```

to

```
M_FLAG = 'X'. "M_FLAG means such and such, as we set it here because of
such and such etc.
```

I once did some counterintuitive logic in a complex database SELECT to avoid the wrong index's being chosen, and years later, from the safety of another country, when I looked at my code in the system I used to work in, I found a consultant had changed things back and written:

```
* Above Code is very strange - cannot be understood without any background
* and functional specification. Therefore trial and error to solve customer
* problem (cannot exclude any side effects):
```

He was right about the side effects. Since he was an advocate of leaving dead code in the program, I could clearly see the problem I had tried to avoid in the first place coming back, and then the consultant made about 15 different (to be precise—17) attempts to solve it before deciding it was impossible.

What I should have done is write a big comment above my SELECT statement explaining why I was doing something that appeared to make no sense, which was to avoid a specific problem, and that way the next programmer who came along would not have assumed the code was wrong and "fixed" it, thus bringing back the original problem.

Quotation Marks Versus Asterisks

There are two ways to add comments. You can put an asterisk at the start of a line above whatever code you want to say something about, and then write the comment, or instead put a quotation mark above the first character of the code you are commenting on.

Sometimes a programmer will combine the two approaches and start the line with an asterisk and then manually insert spaces to make the start of the comment line up with the statement below it.

The three approaches are shown in Listing 3-28.

Listing 3-28. Three Ways of Commenting

```
* Fill the calculated fields
    zif_sd_tdy_model~fill_calculated_fields( ).
    "Fill the calculated fields
    zif_sd_tdy_model~fill_calculated_fields( ).
*   Fill the calculated fields
    zif_sd_tdy_model~fill_calculated_fields( ).
```

The ideal approach is to use quotation marks if you are saying something meaningful about the actual statement under the comment, as opposed to just describing why a routine is there in the first place.

The reason for this is that the indentation could change—i.e., if a new IF or CASE statement is added (or removed) above the code that has been commented, then when the "Pretty Printer" is run the code will most likely jump a few places to the right (or left) to maintain indentation with the reformatted lines.

If the comment is on a line starting with an asterisk, it will stay put, whereas a comment starting with a quotation mark will magically follow the code it is above and jump the same number of spaces to the right (or left). Thus, if someone spent a huge amount of effort manually lining up their comments by putting spaces after the asterisk all that effort will have been wasted.

Meaningless Comments

The most common thing you see in code is comments that exactly mirror the code below them, word for word. This could be above a variable, or a routine name, as in Listing 3-29.

Listing 3-29. Meaningless Comments

```
* Fill the calculated fields
    zif_sd_tdy_model~fill_calculated_fields( ).
```

```
* Apply quick filters
    zif_sd_tdy_quickfilter_model~apply( ).

* Apply fuzzy search
    zif_sd_tdy_model~apply_fuzzysearch( ).
* populate the old material number
      PERFORM populate_old_material_number.

* populate the material description
      PERFORM populate_material_description.

* populate the plant and vendor descriptions.
      PERFORM populate_plant_vendor_descr.

* populate the tare weights
      PERFORM populate_tare_weights.
```

A suggested approach is as follows:

- If the comment is exactly the same as the code below it, get rid of the comment.

- The worst possible thing to do would be to mirror a routine with a meaningless name by adding a comment with the same meaningless name about it; e.g., if the routine name is XY76, don't comment it with "Call Routine XY76."

- Instead, if the routine (or whatever) name has no meaning, change the routine name to be meaningful rather than writing a comment above it explaining what the routine does.

As an example of a comment that is being used to explain a cryptic name, take a look at Listing 3-30.

Listing 3-30. Abbreviated Name

```
      CASE fcode.
* FCODE is set from Initial screen in Module MODIFY_SCREEN_100.
      WHEN c_txn_crt.
        " Create
        MOVE c_txn_crt TO t_exclude-fcode. APPEND t_exclude.
```

In this code, the programmer did not think it was clear the CRT meant CREATE and so wrote a comment to try to make it clear. A far better approach would be to change the constant name to C_TRANSACTION_CREATE. If you have the space (i.e., the full name is less than 30 characters) then there is no reason at all to use abbreviations in the names of anything, and, as a bonus, it reads like English.

Incorrect Comments

Often, the code that the comment refers to changes, but the comment does not, making the comment a big fat lie, so in that sense the fewer comments the better to avoid this situation. Listing 3-31 demonstrates this perfectly.

Listing 3-31. Incorrect Comments

```
WHEN 218 OR 221 OR 222 OR 225 OR 229 OR 230 OR 231 OR 500.
* In response to action on Screen 218, 221, 222 & 225
        CASE sy-ucomm.
          WHEN 'CONT'.
            LEAVE TO SCREEN 0.
        ENDCASE.

    WHEN 220.
* In response to action on Screen 218
        CASE sy-ucomm.
          WHEN 'CONT'.
            LEAVE TO SCREEN 0.
        ENDCASE.
```

At one point, the comments in Listing 3-31 might have been correct, but over time the code has changed, and the comments have not. This is bad because the human brain finds itself drawn to looking at the comments before looking at the code because the comments are in English. In the worst case, it could lead to someone's blindly believing what the comments say without looking at the code, then proceeding on that (incorrect) basis.

If you see a comment that is a lie, get rid of it at once. As mentioned earlier, no information is better than false information.

Reference Numbers in Comments

When we talked about naming earlier, the concept of magic numbers came up, where a value like 23 is used in conditional logic or a calculation and the reader has no idea what it means. You can have magic numbers in comments also; in this case it is a number, usually quite long, that is a reference to some sort of change request in an external help-desk system. Some years later, a programmer comes along, looks at that big number, and finds it means nothing at all to them.

SAP itself started this nonsense with the way they comment SAP Support Note. They make changes where a line of code is commented out with a comment with a big reference number after it, and a new line is inserted with a comment with a big number after it, and we gullible programmers look at this and think since SAP does this it must be good and so do the same ourselves, as shown in Listing 3-32.

Listing 3-32. A Change in the Style of an OSS Note

```
* IF SOMETHING THEN DO_SOMETHING    "Remove - Ticket 765438765
IF SOMETHING OR SOMETHING ELSE THEN DO SOMETHING "Replace - Ticket 765438765
```

In Listing 3-32, a line of dead code has arrived to turn the routine into a bloated corpse and spread Bubonic plague around the program, but the worst thing is the huge reference number.

This trick of putting ten-digit numbers as comments happens often, and whoever makes this change usually is pleased as punch and says, "Look, I have given a reference number so if someone really wants to know why that change was made then they can go off and look it up".

True enough, unless of course the comments were written by consultants on the implementation project who are referring to *their* help-desk system in *their* company, which you as a customer could never access anyway, and they have been gone ten years (that was an actual example from real life).

Leaving aside how easy or difficult it is to wade through the change request system to find details of the magic number you have encountered in the code, I can think of two better ways to achieve the same thing straight off:

1. If it is that important that someone looking at the code should know why it changed, then, in my lunatic world at least, maybe you could *tell them*. Right there and then. Maybe, and I could be

the fool here, you should not drop obscure hints in a secret code to make them think they are in a Dan Brown novel, but instead write a comment saying why you changed it.

2.   Even better, if the code itself has variables with meaningful names and what have you, then by using the version management comparison, hopefully, it is obvious at first glance why the code changed. That only works if the code you removed had meaningful names as well; otherwise, you do need a comment.

Listings 3-33 and 3-34 show an example of changing a magic number into an explanation, which I actually did in real life.

Listing 3-33. Before Transforming Magic Number Comments

```
*{RT19027+
    WHEN 'RMRP'.
       l_object_type = 'BUS2081'.
       CONCATENATE <wa_pca>-refdocnr <wa_pca>-refryear
       INTO l_object_id.
*}
```

Listing 3-34. After Transforming Magic Number Comments

```
    WHEN 'RMRP'.
 "Invoice from PO that uses "global payments" process
 "this process was only introduced in 2012 and involves paying from one
 company code and charging another
       ld_object_type = 'BUS2081'.
       CONCATENATE <wa_pca>-refdocnr <wa_pca>-refryear
       INTO ld_object_id.
```

Comments Going for a Walk

At first glance, you would think that a comment could not go for a walk—it would just stay where you put it. But no. In fact, comments can "move whilst standing still," and here comes an example.

I had written a comment above a line of code as a warning. This code is inside an implementation of a standard SAP BAdi, as shown in Listing 3-35.

Listing 3-35. Helpful Comment

```
"I have discovered if you call SET_DATA more than one time in this user
"exit then you lose some of the changes e.g. it blanks out the quantity
IF lf_change_needed = abap_true.
   im_item->set_data( ls_item ).
ENDIF.
```

I thought that was a useful warning—it did not say *what* the code was doing but highlighted a problem to be avoided.

Then the next programmer came along a few months later and needed to insert a big chunk of code. He decided the best place for the new code would be between the comment and the IF/ENDIF statement. It was a big, long section of code, so the poor old comment was moved up well away from the command it related to, so it no longer made much sense and just seemed like a random musing.

Even worse, I have often seen code deleted, and the comment remain. In that case, it is not the comment that has gone for a walk, but the code (it walked right out of the program) leaving behind a comment that now makes no sense at all.

In these situations the answer is clear—if the comment has gone for a walk, bring it back home to just above the code it was supposed to be commenting. If it is the code that has gone for a walk, then delete the now useless comment.

Commented-Out Code

One of my favorite examples of rotting code is the ever popular commenting-out of the code you have just replaced. The first time, this makes perfect sense. You might think, "When someone sees this, they will get a clear picture of the before and after," usually without any explanation of *why* the code was replaced. In this section, I note some of the things I have noticed about commented-out code.

It Makes the Program Harder to Follow

In no time at all, you get a huge sea of blocks of commented-out code with little islands of live code in the middle feeling really lonely, looking around and wondering where all their friends are. I have seen this again and again. There is no way this makes things easier to understand! You have to page up and down like a lunatic looking for the small portion of code that is still live in order to get a grip on what is going on.

When I first saw this I presumed the programmers had no idea there was a version management system for ABAP programs, which gives you a complete history of changes. As time goes on, I am forced to conclude people do this because "we've always done it this way."

It Causes Short Dumps

How can commenting-out code possibly cause a short dump? It's easier than you might think. Have a look at Listing 3-36, where someone commented out what they thought was useless code.

Listing 3-36. Bad Example of Commenting Out

```
DELETE lt_csm_list WHERE uname IS INITIAL.

CHECK lt_csm_list[] IS NOT INITIAL.

"Now we will sned an email to each CSM with just their orders
*  LOOP AT lt_csm_list ASSIGNING <ls_csm_list>.
*    lt_csm_out[] = lt_csm_report[].
   * DELETE lt_csm_out WHERE pernr NE <ls_csm_list>-pernr_in_so.
   * CHECK lt_csm_out[] IS NOT INITIAL.
   * ld_report_name = 'ZXYZ Sales Order List'(085).

   PERFORM send_email USING <ls_csm_list>-uname
                            ld_report_name
                            lt_csm_out[].
*  ENDLOOP."List of CSM's
```

In Listing 3-36, the most important problem is that the <LS_CSM_LIST> FIELD-SYMBOL is not assigned, which would cause a short dump. Plus, the LT_CSM_OUT table would always be blank.

In such cases, the vast amount of commented-out code surrounding the problematic code masks the problem. If the commented-out code were not there, the problem would be that much more obvious.

As an aside, I also cannot stand spelling mistakes in comments—such as SNED (sic) in Listing 3-36—and will always correct them.

It Doesn't Always Work

One of my colleagues decided to change a commented-out section of native SQL commands (i.e., where you access the database directly instead of using the normal SELECT) from having an asterisk at the start to having the quotation mark at the start. Little did we realize that when you comment out such open SQL commands with a quotation mark you are not commenting it out at all; it tries to execute. Who would have thought? He was trying to make the code clearer and—oh dear!

It Should Be *Deleted*

Therefore, the conclusion is clear—do not comment out code. Instead, *delete it*. If you want it back at some point in the future, it will still be there in the version management history.

Documentation

Here is a radical idea—when you have custom DDIC objects like data elements and tables and, indeed, classes and programs, why not use the standard SAP facility to add some sort of documentation to them?

Otherwise, whilst you are still at the same organization where you created the (say) table, you will keep getting the question, "What is this Z table for?" and after you have left nobody will know.

The fact that SAP itself rarely fills in the documentation for standard data elements and tables should not be taken as a good example.

At the point you are creating such things, you know for a fact what their purpose is. Even the next day, that knowledge might become blurry, and three months later when you look back you may wonder, "Why did I create that?" It's best to strike whilst the iron is hot and make some notes—right inside the SAP system—as to why whatever it is you have created exists. Your colleagues—and your future self—will thank you later.

Taking executable programs as a specific example of this, many years ago I had to create a large number of ALV reports. These were all executable programs for which you can add online documentation, and that documentation will be available to the end user via a big blue "I" icon on the report selection screen. Just in case you are unfamiliar with this documentation facility, select from the menu *Goto* ➤ *Documentation* while editing a program in the ABAP editor (SE38). It also is available on the initial ABAP editor selection screen where you are provided with the choices for Source code, Variants, Attributes, *Documentation*, and Text elements.

It would appear this documentation is end user–facing, but in reality in can be just as helpful to the programmers.

Here is an example of some documentation I wrote for an ALV report. The "Short Text" and "Title" parts are generated automatically, while the other sections I created myself as a series of questions. If I could not answer any of those questions that implied I did not understand the purpose of the program I was writing.

Short Text

Report: List of Deliveries

Title

ZXXX: List of Deliveries

What is the Business Need?

To have a real-time view of activity at the plants.

What question am I asking by running this report?

What has been delivered out of each plant?

How do I measure this?

Quantity delivered, split by material, truck, customer, etc.

Is there a standard SAP report that does something similar?

The standard SAP delivery monitor – Transaction VL06

So why do we have a custom report?

We have our own delivery monitor for processing deliveries. ZXXX is not designed to be interactive, but to fulfill a purely reporting function. As always the selection criteria and information displayed in the standard SAP report does not exactly match the company's needs.

Performance Hints

The two vital fields are plant and delivery date, which is why they are both compulsory. For large selections this report will only let you run it in the background.

Recovery Procedure

This is just a report and can be canceled with no ill effects.

The "Performance Hints" are designed to guide the end user to supply fields upon which there is a database index, and the "Recovery Procedure" is aimed at IT support.

Conclusion

This chapter is the first of three that deal with different aspects of the BLUE phase of test-driven development, where you improve the quality of the code without changing its behavior. We started with a discussion of the steps involved in such refactoring.

Then, the focus changed to the core topic of this chapter: code clarity. Various aspects of this topic were covered: complex code, badly named code, redundant or misleading comments, and (the lack of) documentation in custom DDIC objects.

Recommended Reading

"Literate Programming" by Donald Knuth:

http://www.literateprogramming.com/knuthweb.pdf

"Making Bad Code look Bad":

http://www.joelonsoftware.com/articles/Wrong.html

Clean ABAP Guidelines:

https://github.com/SAP/styleguides/blob/master/clean-abap/CleanABAP.md

ABAP Gore:

https://answers.sap.com/articles/491054/share-your-abap-gore.html
https://answers.sap.com/articles/12984186/share-your-abap-gore-part-2.html

CHAPTER 4

Stability: The Second Pillar of Code Quality

Now that you have gotten your code into a state where you can at least understand what it is supposed to be doing, you can move on to the next pillar of code quality. To recap: You are using the test-driven development (TDD) methodology and have gotten to the stage where the code appears to work (the unit test passes), and you are in the BLUE phase looking for potential problems. In this chapter, we are looking for stability problems.

Most programmers think stability is the only measure of code quality; i.e., that a program does what it is supposed to do 100 percent correctly, every time. Obviously, that is the most important measure (though not the only one).

Keyboard errors made by end users on the first day your application is live unfortunately have the horrible habit of making you realize that your program is not actually as stable as you thought it was. Many people would not use the term *stability* but rather *robustness*. That is why you have a section of tests in the code inspector called "Robust Programming."

According to the book *Anti-Fragile*, the definition of something (not necessarily a software program) that is "robust" when subjected to "stress" is:

"In the best case it stays the same, in the worst case it stays the same."

In this case, the "stress" is the software's actually being used by a human being. It should stay the same whatever the end user throws at it.

The definition of *staying the same* is the exact same definition we use when writing a unit test—for the exact same inputs the results should always be the same. You don't get that sort of predictable behavior from dealing with humans, but you expect it from nature (e.g., sun comes up every morning) and you expect it from machines (including computer software).

© Paul David Hardy 2021
P. D. Hardy, *Improving the Quality of ABAP Code*, https://doi.org/10.1007/978-1-4842-6711-0_4

Thus, the very first section in this chapter deals with the Principle of Least Astonishment, adhered to when a program behaves in a way that matches exactly what any sane human would expect.

Then, we move on to the Principal of Programming by Accident, which is when software seems to work correctly but it really should not, because the program is a house built on sand that will come crashing down sooner or later.

The next principle discussed is the Don't Repeat Yourself principle, applicable when code appearing to be the same occurs again and again throughout the program, but in fact is subtly different each time, leading to different results seemingly at random.

Any other potential causes of instability are lumped together in the following section as a sort of "mixed bag" of problems.

As might be imagined, we end with a discussion of the best way to handle any such instability problems you encounter—in a code-based way or in a human-based way.

Principle of Least Astonishment

It is all very well using dictionary definitions, but I always like to use real-life examples—preferably things that have actually happened to me—to explain concepts. This is what I am going to do to explain the Principle of Least Astonishment.

I had an online bank account with a bank in Australia. I actually had two accounts—the day-to-day account into which my salary went and a savings account. I used the day-to-day account to pay bills; indeed, I had been told by the bank it was impossible to pay bills out of the savings account.

One day, I got some sort of bill, and I had already set up the payment details for that supplier, so I had to pick the supplier name from a drop-down list. I did just that and entered the amount and the reference number, double checked everything on the screen, and pressed Submit.

I instantly got an error. Why? Because one field on the screen was the account number I wanted to pay from, and that value had defaulted to the savings account number. I did not notice, because it is very difficult for a human being to memorize ten-digit numbers and remember what they relate to. Now, since there were only two possible values that could go in that field (you can choose which via a drop-down), and one would 100 percent cause an error if used, I was *astonished* that it defaulted to the invalid value. It's like defaulting the month of the year to the value 13. Furthermore, I was *astonished* that if there was only one possible valid value, why have a drop-down at all?

It gets worse. Once I realized what had happened, I used the drop-down to select the valid account number. I checked the screen—no values had blanked out, and the amount and reference number were still there, so I pressed Submit again, and it went through this time.

What I had not noticed was that when I changed the account number, although the reference number and amount had not changed, one field had—who I was paying. That value had changed as a result of the program's looking at the list of my saved suppliers and picking *the first one in the list sorted alphabetically*. So I had paid someone at random, and not paid who I wanted to pay. I had to (a) try to get the money back from the company the bank had picked for me and (b) pay the real company again or get my electricity cut off.

That sort of behavior by an application—changing one vital field seemingly at random—is the antitheses of the textbook definition of the Principle of Least Astonishment. If the application does something so surprising you just cannot believe it, and anyone you tell cannot believe it either, then the application does not adhere to the principle.

Now, if I don't like that sort of thing's happening to me, then I would be the world's biggest hypocrite if I wrote software applications that did things that were equally astonishing. Rather, I should aim not to astonish people at all and have the application I have written do what any sane person would expect.

Here come some examples, and as usual the structure will be the example, followed by why it is bad, followed by what to do about it.

Enhancement Category

Part of the bread-and-butter work of a developer is creating custom tables and structures. Even after 20 years, what still catches me out is when I create a Z table or structure and activate it and get a warning like that shown in Figure 4-1.

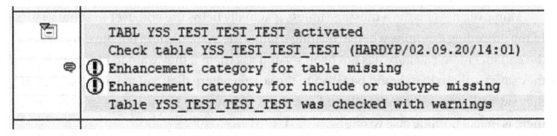

Figure 4-1. *Activation warning*

The reason it is so easy to forget the enhancement category for a table or a category is that SAP appears to have gone out of its way to hide the place you make that setting. You would logically expect that setting to be part of the technical settings. Instead, you are astonished to find the setting can only be made via the menu path *Extras ➤ Enhancement Category*. It gets stranger. When you follow that menu path you are astonished to find that you get the message shown in Figure 4-2.

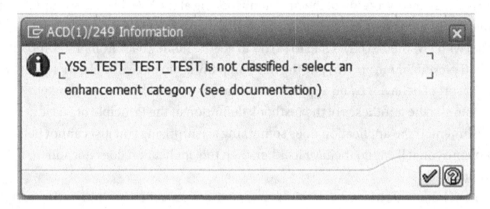

Figure 4-2. *Useless information method*

That is the textbook definition of a useless message. It never appears until you are trying to fix the problem it describes; hence, you already know there is a problem; hence, you don't need a message.

This is a UX (user experience) problem rather than a stability issue, but it demonstrates the Principle of Least Astonishment very well.

The answer here is that when coding something similar yourself you should avoid spreading related mandatory settings all over the place—some on the main screen, some on tabs, some on subscreens you manually call up by pressing a button, and some hidden amongst the three dozen available menu options. You would be surprised how often this happens.

Moreover, never issue a message unless it actually helps the end user in some way. In the preceding example, when activating a table, the system could tell the developer the enhancement category has not been set and ask them if they want to maintain it. If they say yes, then they should be taken to the screen where they can make the setting. If they say no then the activation should complete without any further messages (provided there is in fact nothing else wrong).

Material Substitution

In this example, there was a custom front end in which the end user entered sales order data, and then at the end the standard SAP BAPI (Business Application Programming Interface) was called to create a sales order.

In SAP there is the concept of material substitution—the end user enters one material number and then based upon configuration the system either changes that material number to another automatically or pops up a little box with a list of different materials and the user chooses one. The entered material ends up in field MATWA (Material Entered) and is used in MM areas like inventory management, and the substituted material ends up in field MATNR (Material Number) and is used in SD areas like pricing.

The custom application mirrored the standard SAP logic and popped up the box for the user to enter a substitute material from the list. At that point, the MATNR and MATWA values were in an internal table.

We had presumed that when passing in the MATNR and MATWA fields to the standard SAP BAPI it would populate the respective database fields for that order.

Instead, we were astonished to find that, instead, the standard SAP code looks at the MATNR value passed in, reads the list of possible substitute materials (that the end user would see in a pop-up box), and picks, seemingly at random, *the one with the lowest material number*, regardless of the actual MATWA value passed in.

There is nothing you can do about this; I only highlight this as an example that if you pass a specific value into a field in a standard SAP BAPI you might be astonished at what value actually ends up in the database. To be fair to SAP, this sort of situation is quite rare.

Data Declarations in Modules

This *is* a stability issue, one caused by the developer's making a seemingly logical assumption that is incorrect. Many times I have seen code like that shown in Listing 4-1.

Listing 4-1. Data Declaration in a Module

```
MODULE check_assignment INPUT.
DATA: LV_PROJECT_NUMBER TYPE KUNNR
```

The problem here is that data declarations in modules are global, whereas in a FORM routine they are local. Because a module *looks like* a FORM routine and you can put as much code inside a module as you want, a lot of people tend to treat them interchangeably. However, it is more than possible that the correct functioning of the code in the module depends on the variable being declared's having an initial value when the module in which it appears to be defined is called. If it does not, then the result will be different.

This is really dangerous in DYNPRO programming as screens can be called in any order, and by the time this module is called the user could have pressed 15 different buttons, and the result of this module call will depend on which of those 1,306,674,368,000 different possible paths the user has traversed. You would actually want the result to be the same whichever one of those multi-billion paths was traversed before the routine was called.

There is an easy solution to this problem. You get warned about such data declarations in the extended program check, but really there should never be any ABAP statements in a PBO (Process Before Output) or a PAI (Process After Input) module— just calls to FORM routines or (preferably) methods. This solves the "unexpected global variable" problem, and as an added bonus when you go looking for your code in the SE80 overview you don't have to guess whether it is in a module or a subroutine.

Hashed Tables

In this real-life example, I had created a table to store the attributes of screen fields— were they grayed out or invisible or mandatory and so on. This table was stored in the model and could be passed out to whatever UI technology the application decided to use.

Since I did not want a field to be both mandatory and invisible at the same time, I declared it as a HASHED table with a unique key of the screen name and the field name; that is, the table could only have one row with that unique combination of key fields.

The end users were complaining a certain field was not getting grayed out (sometimes at random) when it should have been. I looked at the code and was really puzzled. Under the required business conditions, the code was attempting to add a new row to the table.

Then of course I debugged it, and when the line was reached that tried to insert the new row nothing happened at all. The table remained the same size. After a while, I realized there was already a line with the same key in the table (sometimes, but not all of the time, hence the unstable behavior).

I had honestly expected a short dump in a situation like that, because my code was feeding the system conflicting instructions; i.e., you cannot have two lines with the same key, and I want two lines with the same key. A dump would have been far better than sweeping the problem under the carpet which was actually what was happening—that is why we have short dumps in the first place, to alert us to such problems.

The solution is clear—when adding a line to a hashed table you have to check if a line with the same key already exists and if so delete it before inserting the new one.

Incorrectly Typed RETURNING Parameter

This is another example of my making a stupid mistake in my code and being somewhat astonished I was not at least warned about it by the compiler.

The code in Listing 4-2 is all about BOMS (Bills of Materials), though that is not really relevant. The important thing is that at one point the code makes a check on structure ES_BOM_LINKS to see if it is initial or not.

Listing 4-2. Checking if ES_BOM_LINKS Is Initial

```
CLEAR: es_bom_links.

CHECK is_item_details-stlnr IS NOT INITIAL.

es_bom_links = mo_pers->derive_material_2_bom_link(
          id_matnr = is_item_details-matnr
          id_werks = is_item_details-werks
          id_stlan = id_bom_usage
          id_stlnr = is_item_details-stlnr ).

IF es_bom_links IS INITIAL.
  RETURN.
ENDIF.
```

Method DERIVE_MATERIAL_2_BOM_LINK did a database read on database table MAST, which failed. Since ES_BOM_LINKS was cleared before the method was called and since the database read inside the method failed, the RETURNING parameter should have remained initial, but when evaluated ES_BOM_LINKS was *not* initial. I just could not work out what was going on.

A second set of eyes always helps, and when my colleague debugged it he told me the reason was that element POSNR in ES_BOM_LINKS had somehow been set to SPACE as opposed to its real initial value of 000000.

The reason for this strange behavior—the mistake that I had made—was that the functional method had a RETURNING parameter typed as MAST.

That MAST structure was being passed into structure ES_BOM_LINKS, which was defined ever so slightly differently, as shown in Listing 4-3.

Listing 4-3. Structure of ES_BOM_LINKS

```
types:
    BEGIN OF m_typ_vmast.
      INCLUDE TYPE vmast.
  TYPES:   posnr    TYPE posnr_va.
  TYPES: END OF m_typ_vmast .
```

VMAST is the MAST structure plus a one-character change indicator on the end. The custom structure adds POSNR as an extra field on the end as well. If any of those extra fields were values or quantities, the Unicode check would have failed, but because the extra fields were all character fields they seem to have snuck past the automated checks.

As a result, when the MAST structure was returned it filled up the corresponding fields in the custom ES_BOM_LINKS structure OK, but then filled the change indicator and the POSNR with blank spaces. There was no warning at all about this in the extended program check or code inspector.

Therefore, during the BLUE phase when you are checking 100 percent new code for quality, it might be a good idea to manually check if the structure being filled and the structure being passed back have 100 percent the same type. One way around the problem is to use an inline declaration to declare the variable at the same time it is being filled, as in Listing 4-4. That way, you cannot possibly go wrong.

Listing 4-4. Corrected Code

```
DATA(ls_bom_links) = mo_pers->derive_material_2_bom_link(
            id_matnr = is_item_details-matnr
            id_werks = is_item_details-werks
            id_stlan = id_bom_usage
            id_stlnr = is_item_details-stlnr ).
MOVE-CORRESPONDING ls_bom_links to es_bom_links.
```

This is a fine example of when you think that there should be an automated static check for this sort of thing but there is not. In such cases, the correct behavior is to create such a test yourself and then share it with the world. In Chapter 10, you will do just that, albeit with a different example.

Programming by Accident

The best way to define the term *Programming by Accident* is to use an analogy. Let us say you are given a business requirement to implement and you accidentally make one or two really serious mistakes in your code, mistakes that could be described as "fatal errors." Furthermore, let us say you don't pick up on the mistakes yourself, because you don't use test-driven development and only did the most cursory (or no) manual tests yourself on the code you just wrote/changed. When you hand the code over to the business analysts and/or testers, saying, "This should work, please start testing," there are several things that could happen, as follows:

1. Because the code is riddled with errors the new functionality either does not work at all or does something totally different than what was documented in the requirement. The testers pick up on this straight away and report this fun fact back to you. You get all embarrassed and quickly fix things up so the code works like it should have in the first place. This time the testers are happy, green lights all around, the code goes to production, everyone is happy. That is how things *should* work in a sane world.

2. The next possibility is that despite all the glaring errors in the code, when the testers put it through its paces they find that it appears to work perfectly. This is not because they are not testing it properly— even when Jock McPedantic the Pedantic Scotsman tests the program and tries every single thing he can think of to try and break it (there are testers like this who take delight in telling you your code is not working; such people can be really annoying, but having them is in fact a blessing) he just cannot break the code. Everything seems to be working perfectly, all green lights, the code goes to production, it works perfectly there as well, everyone is happy. This situation should be impossible—there is no way in the world code filled with so many errors can possibly work at all, let alone perfectly—*and yet it does.*

3. The final possibility is that either due to your totally misinterpreting the requirement, or due to your making loads of errors, the code does something utterly different than what was stated in the requirement. It might do that different thing perfectly, but that different thing was *not* what was asked for. In this scenario, you don't notice, the analysts do not notice, the testers don't notice, all green lights, it goes to production, the end users don't notice either, everyone is happy. On the face of it, that is *insanity* and thus should never happen. It's like me going up to the bar and asking for a gin and tonic and being given a fire extinguisher instead and I say, "Thank you, that is just what I wanted."

The latter two situations are examples of Programming by Accident because, although the business is happy with the outcome, that outcome was achieved not because you did your job perfectly but rather by some sort of black magic.

Why is this bad? That's a good question—if everyone is happy with the result, then how can there possibly be a problem? The trouble is this—if something works perfectly *but you don't know why* then in five years' time when the code suddenly stops working in production out of the blue—despite having had no code changes applied for years—you will have no idea how to fix it. You'll do an analysis and say (and I have heard this in real life), "I can't see how that ever worked in the first place." That is cold comfort to the users who rely on the code.

What I tend to see is suddenly a batch job that has worked perfectly for years suddenly starts short-dumping in production. Whatever that job is doing is vital, so one or more programmers starts troubleshooting in a hurry. None of them can work out what is wrong, and then suddenly the dumps stop. The programmers are congratulated for having fixed the issue so quickly. An honest programmer would say, "But I did not do anything," while an unscrupulous one would take the credit—especially if it is coming up to bonus time. After a year, there have been no more dumps, but I am not reassured. The trouble is that a problem that fixes itself at random will one day come back at random.

So, what is bad about Programming by Accident is that it is like being stalked by an invisible maniac. No one can see him, no one even believes he exists, but you know he is there. One day he will explode with rage for no reason and stab you to death, and there is absolutely nothing you can do about it. Or is there?

Let us look at real-life examples of the two strange cases—wrong code that nonetheless works, and incorrect behavior being perceived as correct. We will look at what causes these situations (it is not actually black magic) and what you can do about them.

Wrong Code That Works

Listing 4-5 shows some code that I came across in a code review. Looking at the version management, I could see the code had been in production unchanged for over ten years with no one complaining. Indeed, this code was part of a business-critical batch job, so if it had not worked someone would have noticed. Have a look at Listing 4-5 and see if you can spot what is wrong with this picture.

Listing 4-5. Incorrect Code That Still Works

```
LOOP AT ITEMS_B.
  READ TABLE T_STOCK WITH KEY MATNR = ITEMS_B-MATERIAL.
  IF SY-SUBRC = 0.
    ITEMS_B-ENTRY_QNT = T_STOCK-STOCK.
    ITEMS_B-ENTRY_UOM = T_STOCK-MEINS.
    MODIFY ITEMS_B INDEX SY-TABIX.
  ENDIF.
ENDLOOP.
```

Can you spot what is wrong? The code is looping over internal table ITEMS_B, and when the MODIFY ITEMS_B statement is reached the intention is to change the current row in the loop. System variable SY-TABIX is used to specify which row is to be updated.

The problem is that although SY-TABIX gets set to the current row of the internal table at the start of each iteration of the loop, as soon as the READ TABLE T_STOCK command is executed the value of SY-TABIX changes to the value of whatever row of T_STOCK was found. Thus, by the time the MODIFY ITEMS_B command is reached, SY-TABIX is essentially a random number, and instead of the current row of ITEMS_B getting modified a random row was getting modified.

In theory, that should not have worked at all. However, in real life it always worked, not because of black magic but because tables T_STOCK and ITEMS_B always had the same number of rows and were sorted in the same order.

This is a fine example of Programming by Accident—something works, and it has worked perfectly for years, so no one ever gives it a second glance. However, what if one day a new programmer makes a change somewhere else ten routines earlier in the program, so the two internal tables are no longer equivalent? It would not even need a programming change. Maybe the data in the database tables changes, so in one of the two tables there are suddenly two records with the same material when there had only ever been one before?

If either happened—code change or data change—everything would come crashing down in flames.

For this specific example, there is a good way to fix the code, and an even better way.

The good way is that as a rule you should transfer the value of SY-TABIX to a variable as soon as you possibly can to avoid its getting overwritten. The logic inside a LOOP will just get more complex over time, and someone will stick in a read on an internal table or a call to a huge function module or some such that will overwrite SY-TABIX.

The even better solution would be to loop using a FIELD-SYMBOL as in LOOP AT ITEM_B ASSING FIELD-SYMBOL(<ITEMS_B>) and then you don't need to care about SY-TABIX at all because you do not need a MODIFY statement. As soon as a value is passed into <ITEMS_B>-ENTRY_QNT, the row of the internal table being looped over is automatically updated. Using a FIELD-SYMBOL in this case not only increases robustness/stability but also improves performance and uses less memory. The code inspector checks will prompt you to (a) not use internal table header lines as work areas and (b) to use FIELD-SYMBOLS when looping over internal tables.

Incorrect Behavior Being Viewed as Correct

In this example, the original business requirement was that if a sales order was "cash sales"—i.e., the customer had to pay on the spot—then in the application two menu options should be grayed out. The programmer was told the way to spot a "cash sales" order was to look at the payment terms (VBKD-ZTERM), and if the payment terms were set up such that the customer had zero days before they had to pay then this was a cash sale.

That payment term calculation is non-trivial, and so the programmer did the correct thing and encapsulated the logic in its own routine—you pass in the payment term, and the routine does the hard yards and calculates whether that payment term is cash sales or not and returns a TRUE/FALSE indicator of type ABAP_BOOL. The idea was that if the result was TRUE (which is the value X in ABAP_BOOL) then two user commands would be added to an exclusion table so they would not appear as icons at the top of the screen, and the entries would be grayed out in the menu.

Have a look at the code in Listing 4-6 and see if you can spot what is wrong.

Listing 4-6. Code That Incorrectly Checks for Cash Sales

```
PERFORM check_for_cash_sales USING    g_zterm
                             CHANGING lf_cash_sales.

IF vbkd-zterm EQ 'X'.
  MOVE 'CPYCRT' TO t_exclude-fcode.
   APPEND t_exclude.
  MOVE 'CPYCHG' TO t_exclude-fcode.
   APPEND t_exclude.
ENDIF.
```

The subtle clue is that the field VBKD-ZTERM is a four-character field. In theory, it could contain the value X, but in most of the systems I have seen all four characters are usually used.

I was alerted to the problem by the extended program check's telling me that the variable LF_CASH_SALES was set but never read. A little bit of debugging told me the global variable G_ZTERM and global field VBKD-ZTERM had the same value (which was always four characters long).

The mistake was obvious. The original programmer had wanted to evaluate the value of the one-character LF_CASH_SALES field to see if it was TRUE but by mistake was evaluating the four-character ZTERM field. Thus, the result of the IF statement could never be TRUE, and so for cash sales the functions were never excluded.

Since the error was so obvious, like the idiot that I am I decided to fix it as part of something else I was doing. Looking back, this should not have come as a surprise, but as soon as that fix went into production we got a ticket saying that the functions had vanished for cash sales orders, could it please be fixed?

As it turned out, the documentation was really good for the original change, and I was able to look it up. The original requirement from many years ago was very clear—those two functions should be grayed out for cash sales. Furthermore, I could see that the change had been signed off on by various people as working correctly even though it obviously never had.

There is a moral to this story. More than one programming guru has seen that once something is in production it becomes its own specification. In other words, if the business asks for A and you give them B, once B is in production and signed off on as working perfectly, then magically a George Orwell–type revision of history is done, and suddenly B is what they had asked for in the first place and anything else is an error. In other words, end users come to rely on "wrong" behavior, and if that behavior is ever corrected to what it should have been in the first place then the person making the fix is in trouble.

There is an even better example of this sort of thing that comes from Microsoft. In Excel, dates after February 28 in the year 1900 are actually one day out. Excel behaves as though the date February 29, 1900, existed, which it did not. That is an obvious bug.

Microsoft *intentionally* included this bug in Excel so that it would remain compatible with the spreadsheet program that had the majority market share at the time Excel was created, Lotus 1-2-3, which also had that bug. You would not think many people were doing spreadsheet work using dates from 1900, but they obviously were, and they had come to rely on the wrong behavior and would not migrate to Excel if it behaved differently; i.e., if they had fixed the bug.

The clear conclusion is that once some obvious bugs are in production the end users learn to not only expect them but also rely on them, and so that bug cannot be removed and must remain forever.

To a purist like me, this whole concept grates on the nerves. I don't think an entire software system should be expected to behave based on various accidental mistakes assorted programmers have made over the years. It should behave based on assorted behaviors that the business deliberately asked for. If the business changes its mind (by "the business" I could also mean a government agency; I am just talking about the organization that uses the SAP system), and they often do, that's fine.

In the cash sales case, when it became clear that no one had ever wanted those two functions to be grayed out, I just deleted all the code. That is far better than relying on code that tries to work but never does, especially if you in fact don't want it to work. The former code relied on a bug to do the right thing, and that is just plain wrong. It had to go.

I don't want to get into this situation in the first place. When a new requirement comes along, I want it to be impossible for something totally different than what was asked for to not only be coded but actually make it to production and become the de facto correct behavior.

If you have been following this book so far it will come as no shock that my proposed magic-bullet solution to this problem is test-driven development. The unit tests are based on the actual requirement you got and will not pass until the code fulfills that requirement.

It is more than possible—very likely, even—that what someone asks for turns out to not actually be what they want, but that is fine as well. Once a requirement change becomes clear, the next step is to change the test to reflect the new requirement (so that the test now fails) and then change the production code until the changed test passes.

The result of following the TDD approach here is that when the code does the correct thing is it always doing that correct thing deliberately rather than by accident.

Ever-Changing Requirements

Sometimes when I am giving a presentation about TDD someone in the audience complains that when they changed a program a load of the unit tests started failing, and so they had to change the test code, and therefore the whole idea of unit tests is a load of extra effort for no benefit. My answer is that whoever is saying that has the whole concept back to front—if some fundamental things that the program is doing have changed due to different requirements/assumptions or whatever, then the tests that say what it used to do are now out of date and thus need to be updated to say what it should be doing now. In fact, the tests should be changed *before* you change the real code, as only that way can be sure you have really done the new changes properly. As the tests are also a form of "living documentation," when the requirements change, if you use TDD you are literally forced to change the "documentation" in the code in order to get the change working. Thus, this form of documentation is always up to date, which is a big improvement over some sort of Word document in a cupboard.

Archaic ABAP Statements

A running theme throughout this book is that programmers are often too scared to change working code because they don't know what it does. As you have seen, the problem with code that you do not understand is that even if it works at the moment, you still have no idea if it will keep working, because you have no idea of what is making it work in the first place.

The strange code could be working as a result of something that happens in another part of the program, and since you do not know which part of the program contains the "secret sauce" that enables the program to work, you end up too scared to change any part of the program. It could even be working due to something that happens in *another* program, and since you don't know what other program is magically causing this one to work, you might be too scared to change anything anywhere.

Some of this mysterious code ends up in custom programs as a result of being cut and pasted into the Z program from a standard SAP program written 30 years ago. It is quite possible that two system upgrades later the standard SAP program will no longer use whatever outdated mechanism it did before, but of course the code copied to the Z program will stay the same.

Two examples of this follow, the second one particularly horrific.

Strange Data Declarations

One day while changing an old procedural program, I came across the strange code that can be seen in Listing 4-7.

Listing 4-7. The LOCAL Declaration

```
FORM kurgv_select .

  LOCAL: kurgv-kkber,
         kurgv-knkli,
         kurgv-klimk,
         kurgv-sauft,
         kurgv-skfor,
         kurgv-ssobl.
```

I had been programming in ABAP for 20 years at that point, and not only had I never used the LOCAL keyword, but I had never even seen it before.

I could guess what it meant, and of course you can look up the ABAP keyword documentation. It is the opposite of the equally strange STATIC. With STATIC you turn a local variable in a subroutine into a global variable; i.e., it keeps its value once the routine ends. LOCAL does the opposite—it creates an identically named copy of a global variable, and this becomes a local variable for the duration of the routine. The real global variable does not get changed. In the same way, if you were feeling particularly mad you could create a local variable in a FORM routine with the same name as a global variable, and that would have the same effect.

Luckily, none of this nonsense is allowed in methods. However, what could I do with the procedural code? I didn't want my custom programs working by using bizarre techniques like this. I could see how it had gotten into the code (20 years ago)—it had been copied from standard SAP program SAPMV45A, and a quick look showed that the equivalent FORM routine MV45AFOK_KURGV_SELECT_POSITION still had the LOCAL declaration at the start and had even added one more KUGRV declaration during the intervening 20 years.

I didn't want the global variable at all, but was removing it going to cause grief? Was that KURGV work area used on a screen somewhere? How did it get filled? Why was it important that only those certain fields were not changed? Halfway through both the standard routine and the copied custom one, a call was done to another subroutine that used the global KUGRV structure. What version did the called routine use—the global structure before the routine started or the one defined using LOCAL? After all, the routine that did the LOCAL declaration had not finished yet.

The whole thing was a nightmare. In the end, I disliked the idea of LOCAL so much I just deleted the whole LOCAL declaration and waited to see what would break. It turns out, nothing at all. I can only presume such a declaration is important in SAPMV45A, which crawls with global variables, many shared between different programs via the horrible SHARED PART mechanism (where you can make a variable global across totally different programs!).

The routine in the custom program was clearly just copied from the standard one without regard to which parts were actually needed in the custom one. There was no benefit in copying the LOCAL declaration across, and it could potentially even have had negative effects in the custom program.

The moral is very clear—don't cut and paste standard SAP code into your custom program if you have no idea what some parts of the code you are copying actually do.

Implicit Work Area

In this example, I had opened a help-desk ticket to solve a problem where every so often in production a deadlock was occurring caused by two programs' trying to update the same table entry at the same time. The BASIS department had identified that one of the programs was a standard SAP program being run in dialog and one was a custom program running in batch.

I did a quick bit of investigation on the custom program and found it had been written back in 2002 and had been running in production every night ever since. It had clearly being doing either (a) whatever it was supposed to or (b) nothing useful or meaningful for all that period; otherwise, we would have heard complaints. The deadlock problem only came up due to a sudden surge of work being done by end users at 2:00 in the morning when the batch job was running for a one-off business project.

I had a look at the custom code, and it was pretty horrific, as can be seen in Listing 4-8.

Listing 4-8. Horrible Code

```
tables: mbew.

select-options: sbwkey for mbew-bwkey, smatnr for mbew-matnr.
parameters: test default 'X', proto.

DATA: LT_MBEW LIKE MBEW OCCURS 0,
      LS_MBEW LIKE MBEW.

select * from mbew into table lt_mbew
where matnr in smatnr and bwkey in sbwkey
AND VPRSV = 'S' AND MLMAA = 'X'
.

write: / sy-dbcnt, ' entries from mbew selected!'.

loop at lt_mbew into ls_mbew.
  if test is initial.
    update ckmlcr
    set pvprs = ckmlcr~stprs
        SALKV = CKMLCR~SALK3
    where kalnr = ls_mbew-kaln1
    and   poper = ls_mbew-lfmon
    and   bdatj = ls_mbew-lfgja
    and   untper = space and vprsv = 'S'
    .
```

There are lots of things wrong with Listing 4-8, formatting and so on, and, most important, we should not be doing direct updates on standard SAP tables in Z programs. That is a first-degree felony. But leaving all that aside, I want to concentrate on the bit that baffled me.

Whenever I have updated a (Z) database table in ABAP in one of my programs, I have either passed in a variable of some sort or a constant to the field to be updated.

Here, we have SET PVPRS = CKMLCR-STPRS. The source field looks like it comes from a work area defined via a TABLES statement, but as you can see in Listing 4-8 there is no TABLES statement that defines a work area called CKMLCR. As a result, I honestly would have expected a syntax error.

The preceding code is apparently working by taking advantage of an obscure ABAP behavior that neither I nor any of my colleagues had ever come across. Clearly when you update CKMCLR (or any table), an implicit work area is created with the contents of the row being updated, and you can use that work area in the UPDATE statement—in this case, moving values in that database row from one field to another.

Programming that depends on "under the hood" ABAP behavior makes the code really difficult to understand and troubleshoot. That is why logical databases were so bad—they did everything seemingly by magic.

In this case, what I really wanted was not to update standard SAP tables at all, but since we had been doing it for almost 20 years with no ill effects, I was stuck. All I could do was add a call to the standard SAP ENQUEUE function to see if the table to be updated was currently locked.

What Do You Do?

The way out of the horrible situation you find yourself in when confronted with 30-year-old archaic ABAP statements is that hopefully you know what the custom code is trying to achieve and what the end result should be. Therefore, you can create a unit test that verifies that the behavior is currently happening. You see how I always keep coming back to TDD?

Then you can replace the old-fashioned code you do not understand at all with a mechanism that aims for the same result using a mechanism you *do* understand. When you get the test passing, you know you have not broken anything. Plus, if a new requirement comes along in this area you actually know how to change the code, and you have the bonus that your program is not working purely by black magic.

Don't Repeat Yourself

The phrase "Don't repeat yourself" in regard to software was coined in 1999 by Andy Hunt and Dave Thomas in their book, *The Pragmatic Programmer*, and is nowadays abbreviated as the DRY Principle.

I want to use my own analogy here to describe the problem. I am a stereotypical computer programmer, so I watch a lot of science fiction. A common plot device in such books and shows is to have one or more identical clones made of someone for whatever reason. Let us just say, for the sake of argument, my company thought I was a really good programmer and so they had nine identical clones made of myself.

At the start, all ten of us would not only look exactly the same but have the exact same memories and so would all act identically. However, from the very first second of existence all ten would have different memories going forward, starting from the simple fact of being in different physical locations. As time went on, this would make the behavior of all ten more and more divergent, but anyone encountering any of the ten would expect them to behave the same because they look the same. However, if you were to ask any of the ten the same question, you would most likely get a different answer.

What does this nonsense have to do with programming, you might ask? Well, you might not realize it, but you may already have been guilty of such a bizarre cloning experiment (or worse) in your own code.

At one point circa 1999, SAP actually encouraged you to do this—not clone human beings, but if you wanted to make a change to a standard SAP program, the official advice was to take a Z copy and then make your changes in the Z version.

Since that was the recommended SAP process, many organizations did just that—I know I did. I was just starting out in the ABAP world, and it made sense to me at the time. It turned out that it was the worst advice they could ever have given, and eventually SAP did a 180-degree pivot and said, "Now we recommend that if you want to make a change in one of our standard programs then do a modification" and even invented the enhancement framework to enable you to do that in a much easier manner than before.

Fast forward to 2020, and now the Open ABAP Checks in the code inspector warn you about duplicate code blocks. Why? You might well ask. Before going into why that is bad, let us look at why there are duplicate code blocks scattered all over your program like a rash in the first place.

Here comes one of the most common programming situations in the world. You have a new requirement given to you. Since the most important concept in programming is reuse rather than trying to reinvent the wheel, you see if anyone else has solved this problem before.

Often, you find that is indeed the case—you find some code one of your colleagues has written, or that maybe you yourself wrote some years back, or maybe even some standard SAP code, that solves either the exact problem at hand or one very similar. Sometimes that code is already in the same program you are changing but in a different routine.

You have two choices:

- You can extract the existing code you found into some sort of reusable function module or class method and then have the existing code call the new function/method and your new code call the new function/method as well. That seems like a lot of work. You have to create new ABAP artifacts and have to change existing code possibly in 20 places, and the whole idea is *too much effort*, and, moreover, changing existing code is risky.

- You can cut and paste the existing code you found into the area where you are making your new change, and then (maybe) make some minor changes to accommodate the new scenario. That takes ten seconds, and often you don't have to make any changes. That is so quick, it's so easy, and the existing code being copied *must surely* work, so there is no risk.

Put like that—time consuming, difficult, and risky versus quick, easy, and risk-free—is it any wonder that the second choice is made the bulk of the time? This can be split into two—time and difficulty go together, and riskiness sits on its own. Let's look at each in turn and then see if the argument really makes sense.

Dramatic Irony

Some say there is no such thing as a coincidence, but whilst I was in the middle of writing this section about the dangers of cutting and pasting, one of my colleagues emailed me to tell me I had made a mistake whilst cutting and pasting some of his code into my own method last month.

Time/Difficulty

There are two scenarios here: the first is that you are adding new code and need to decide whether to just do a cut and paste or instead create a new method; the second is that later, whilst reviewing existing code, you discover duplicate code all over the place and need to decide whether to just let it be or instead try to clean it up. In both scenarios, you have two options, and the first is the "easy" option and the second is the "difficult" option. Let us look at how difficult the second option is for each scenario.

Before the Event

Here, you are considering whether to just cut and paste a big chunk of code.

It is impossible to argue that creating something new to encapsulate the code is faster than just cutting and pasting code, because the latter takes just a few seconds, whereas you actually have to think about the former.

The consideration here is this: Does the extra time it takes you now to encapsulate the block of code outweigh the time saved later by reusing this encapsulated block of code when you find a need for this functionality in another program (and if you need it again once, then you are bound to need it again sometime down the track).

Encapsulating the code saves time because if you need to reuse the functionality you can just call the encapsulation block, and you know it works since it works somewhere else. More important, you avoid any negative consequences should the multiple versions of the same code in your system fall out of synch.

Most people come down on the side of taking the easy way out and doing a cut and paste. But just for argument's sake, say you did not—say you actually wanted to move the block of code into its own function or method—how difficult would that be?

To complicate matters, usually you are not just copying a huge block of code and leaving everything unchanged. Far more often you copy a hundred lines of code and then change (or forget to change) two or three values that are scattered evenly throughout that code. You end up with six blocks of code identical except for a few values that are different in each block.

The logical way forward is to have a new method that contains all the 99 percent of the code that does not change and have the 1 percent that does change—the varying values—passed into the method via parameters.

Now is the time to talk about ABAP in Eclipse (ADT) again. In that environment you can highlight an existing block of code and use the "Quick Fix" facility to extract it to its own method. The system is clever enough to analyze the block of code and see which existing variables need to become local variables and which need to become parameters.

Branch Manager

When the code inspector warns you about a huge nesting depth (nesting is when you have IF statements within other IF statements that are within CASE statements and so on), and any depth over five is considered bad, extracting a branch into its own method using the extraction technique is the way forward.

In conclusion: Creating a new method does take longer than just doing a cut and paste, but when using ADT it's not that much longer.

After the Event

Here you are in the BLUE phase and you have been notified by the Open ABAP Check in the code inspector that there are lots of identical blocks of code in the program you are fixing/improving.

Again, you have two choices—just sweep the problem under the carpet (which takes zero seconds) and move on, or actually do something about it; i.e., try to encapsulate the duplicate code in a new method, which takes some effort.

Hopefully, you would take the second choice because you know that the very existence of duplicate code is an affront to nature.

As you have just seen, if you develop using ADT, creating a new method to hold the code that is currently duplicated is actually no big deal. It reduces the time spent and difficulty of encapsulating repeated code somewhat, but although you have been told by the code inspector every place the repeated code currently lives in the program, you still have to manually navigate to each such piece of code and replace that with a call to the new method. So, of course you might forget to make the replacement in every single place.

The other problem is that the code inspector check for identical code only works within the single program being analyzed. Ideally, you'd want to see if that identical block is anywhere at all in all of your Z programs.

It would be the bee's knees if the two pieces of functionality used in this process—the check that identifies identical code blocks and the quick fix that extracts that identical code into a new method—could be combined. Then, after the new method was created, all the chunks of identical code could be automatically replaced with a call to that new method. Whilst I am daydreaming and asking for the moon on a stick, what would be even better is if such a "find and replace" mechanism worked across Z programs.

Hopefully one day there will be a facility added in ADT to let you do just that—in fact, if that sounds like a good thing, after reading Chapter 10 you may be motivated to invent such a tool yourself.

In that Utopian future, the time/difficulty problem of encapsulating duplicate code will just melt away, and there will be no excuse at all for taking the "cut and paste" option.

Riskiness

We have just discussed the extra effort involved in taking the "difficult" option instead of just cutting and pasting the code. There, the mathematical equation was "extra time taken to encapsulate a method minus theoretical time saved the next time you need this functionality." If that number is less than the time it takes to cut and paste, then you should really not take the "easy" option.

In fact, this equation can be expanded. You should also account for the hours of time spent debugging and correcting the huge problems that always come at you when you take the "quick and dirty" approach.

As Steve C. McConnell once said:

"The thing about quick and dirty, is that the dirty stays around long after the quick has gone."

To state this as a mathematical formula you would say:

Time spent (A) is equal to

Time it takes to encapsulate the block of code (B)

Minus time it takes to copy and paste the code (C)

Multiplied by number of times anticipated copy and paste would be required in the future (D)

Minus extra time anticipated to be spent debugging and correcting copy and pasted code (E)

In short:

$$A = (B - C) * D - E$$

A negative result for A would favor encapsulation, and once you take E (extra time for debugging and corrections), the result will always come out negative; i.e., in favor of encapsulation. This is because taking the quick and dirty approach is incredibly risky. In this section, you will see four real-world examples of why this is the case.

Surgeon Example

Let us just say you were really ill and needed multiple operations on different areas of your body. The surgeon would not do all the operations at once—that would probably kill you. Instead, they would do the different operations in stages, with big gaps in between to allow you to recover and make sure the last operation had not actually made things worse.

I am sure that you can see the same applies to altering programs. The more you change, the bigger the risk.

IT author Martin Fowler has coined the term *shotgun surgery*—when you have to make the exact same change in several dozen places because the code is identical in all those places. Let us just say for the sake of example that you have a whacking great CASE statement with 15 different branches, and you discover the logic is wrong in one of those branches, and thus needs to be fixed as a matter of urgency.

You identify the problem, and it is an easy fix. If that code were only in one place it would be no problem. But it is not just in one place. It is in ten different places in the program where the bug was reported, and moreover it is most likely in hundreds of places in Z programs all over the system as a result of people copying and pasting it over the years.

In this case, the analogy is the surgeon not only doing multiple operations on one patient at once but also simultaneously doing multiple operations on hundreds of different people all at the same time. Now that could be considered a bit on the risky side.

Hang on! I can hear you say, if that code being changed was only in one shared method, and one hundred programs called it, and you got the change wrong, would that not still stuff up all one hundred programs at once?

Indeed it would. However, if the fix made was wrong, then you would only need to correct that fix in one place.

The other scenario has the code in a hundred different places. To play it safe, you make your proposed fix in one place only and then ask the business to test the new code to see if it works. They say yes, this now works fine, and so you manually apply the fix to the other hundred identical blocks of code, scattered across many programs.

It is highly likely that whilst doing such a boring, labor-intensive task you would end up (a) forgetting some places where that change needed to be made and (b) accidentally making the fix slightly differently in some places.

Then, of course, the change goes into QA (hopefully not production), and the testers tell you, oh, actually, we got it wrong—it does not work at all, can you please fix it? Then you would have to repeat the whole process in a hundred different places again, forgetting different places this time. Things just get worse with each change.

What you would end up with would be a large number of slightly different sections of code all trying to do the exact same thing with varying degrees of success and giving different user experiences. I have even seen this within the same program—if you press the icon at the top of the screen, one screen pops up; if you choose the same option from the drop-down menu, a different-looking screen pops up, but both screens take the same input data and then try to do the same thing.

Drill-Down Example

One fine day, one of my colleagues was tasked with doing a final purge of all custom code that tried to call transaction ME23 as opposed to ME23N, on the grounds that technically transaction ME23 had been obsolete for a very long time.

He found such a reference in a program I was working on at the time and thus was locked to my transport request, and he said while I was doing my current changes could I also change the `CALL TRANSACTION` in a certain subroutine from ME23 to ME23N.

Naturally, I told him that it was no problem—after all, it was the work of seconds. After I told him I was done, he said, "Oh, I forgot, I also found it in the same program in subroutine XYZ as well." Off I went to that subroutine, and to my puzzlement I found it *exactly* the same as the first subroutine I had changed. Clearly, all of the code, dozens of lines, had been cut and pasted from one place to another, in the same program, resulting in two identical (large) subroutines concerned with drilling into assorted transactions. Presumably each one gets called half of the time by different areas of the program.

The obvious consequence is that those two routines will diverge over time. In this case, if my colleague had not told me about the second subroutine, then we would have ended up with a program that sometimes drilled into ME23N and other times into ME23, seemingly at random from the user's point of view.

The answer to this example is obvious—the subroutines were 100 percent identical, so delete one, then run the syntax check. The resulting errors would tell me where the deleted routine gets called, and so I would replace the call with one to the remaining subroutine.

As another risky duplicate code example, I got an email from a colleague once saying, "You recall when we improved the XYZ logic? It turns out we changed four programs where the logic was but missed program ABC, and the salesmen are up in arms as it is price rise time next week." If the code had been in just one place that literally could not have happened. Needless to say, it is in one place now.

Text Names Example

When I find myself solving the exact same problem twice in two different areas of the same program (or different programs), I find it physically impossible to just cut and paste the old code in.

The ultimate example is when you find yourself solving the same problem not just two or three times, but hundreds of times, in almost every program you encounter. If that solution suddenly needs changing, do you really want to change every single program in the system? Now *that* would be risky. You would lock hundreds of objects other developers need to change, and you are *bound* to miss some.

The example I would like to share is one where I find myself spending an inordinate amount of time getting the names of things, like sales organizations, divisions, vendors, materials, equipment types, etc. To make life fun, SAP has no consistency at all with names; some are in text tables; some are in a fixed-value list in a domain; some, like vendors, are in the main table. There are as many different ways to store the name as there are stars in the sky.

As the years go by, I find I memorize which tables to read for various data element text values, but I sometimes forget and have to go looking again, and it's not always obvious. In the spirit of doing a favor to not only my colleagues but also my future self, I thought I'd fix this once and for all.

I did a one-off exercise of building in a complex algorithm that did a runtime identification of the data element passed in and then searched for text tables, and then a domain value list to get the text name. If that did not work, I subclassed the complicated ones like vendors and materials—not that the calling program knows this. I won't go into detail on this now, but it is the principle of the thing.

Having completed and implemented this complex algorithm, I will never have to worry about going hunting for the correct text table again. That is my ultimate example of doing a bit of work up front for a large time savings later.

Payer Example

In this example, we have a new business requirement—to add a new selection criterion to a program that produces an ALV report on the "payer" partner function. That should (in theory) just be two lines of code that need to be changed—add a new SELECT-OPTION on the SELECTION-SCREEN and then change the SELECT statement that brings back the data to take account of the new filter criteria. In an OO program you might need to change a few more lines to get the selection criteria from Lands' End to John O'Groats (the two opposite ends of the United Kingdom, by the way) because selection criteria are global variables and have to be passed into the various classes somehow, but that is still not the end of the world.

In this particular example, we are dealing with a procedural program, so we should be finished in ten seconds flat. However, after those ten seconds of work, I run the report as a test and the change does not seem to work at all. How can that be? A simple change like this—what could go wrong?

The first thing I notice is that the name of the "payer" on the result screen is wrong. Since I am now selecting by "payer," that is somewhat worrying. The program has been getting the payer name since time immemorial; I have not changed what fields get read, or how they are assigned to the result table—only the filter in the database selection. How could that stuff things up?

The obvious test is to run the report in production and see if the payer name is correct. Well, it is not. This clearly has not been working, possibly since day one, and no one has noticed. Worse, the report was probably signed off on by the analysts and business as working correctly when it was first created.

So, my change in development has worked—now only records with the correct "payer" are returned from the database. It is just that the name is wrong in the result screen, just as it has always been wrong.

214

I could just let it go and say "all done," but as sure as eggs are eggs when someone tests this in development or QA they are going to tell me the payer name is wrong, and it must be my latest change that has "broken" the program, regardless of the fact it does not work—and has never worked—properly in production. Quite possibly the person who is moaning to you now about the "new" fault was the same person who signed of on the program many years earlier as working perfectly and OK to go to production.

This is actually good—you now have carte blanche to fix an existing bug because "your current change has broken it."

So, if the payer name is wrong, I have to find out where it is getting set—and this is easier said than done. Although just a report, this program has ballooned so much over the years that it has routines all over the place. There are various ways to pin this down— do a "find/replace" search in the ABAP editor or do an ST05 trace and look for reads on KNA1.

I find the problem code in the end—in a routine called GET TEXT DESCRIPTIONS, which gets the text names of a whole bunch of unrelated fields based on their key values. Here is the first problem—if it takes ages to find the place you need to make your change, then if you have to make another change in a year's time, it is going to take ages to find that code again, just as it took me ages to find in this example (which is as always a real-life example).

Having it take forever to find the routine you are looking for is a sign written in letters of fire a thousand miles high telling you to rename the routine—say, DERIVE PARTNER DESCRIPTIONS. If some of that routine has nothing *at all* to do with getting the partner descriptions, then it should be in its own routine, with a name describing what the code does more accurately. This is the Single Responsibility Principle once again—each routine should do one thing only.

If you keep making these sorts of changes, you will end up with more routines than before, but ones with better names so that in the future you can zoom in on the problem area more quickly. When I say "routines" I really mean "methods" as opposed to FORM routines, but as this is a procedural program I am sticking with routines, at least at the start.

Getting back to the problem at hand, after the agonizing process of finding the routine that sets the names, I finally found the code with the problem, as shown in Listing 4-9. Can you spot the mistake?

Listing 4-9. Incredibly Common Coding Mistake

```
"get bill-to and name.
SELECT kunnr
  INTO <gs_alv_output>-kunre
  FROM vbpa
  WHERE vbeln EQ <gs_alv_output>-vgbel
  AND   parvw EQ 'RE'.

"get payer and name.
SELECT kunnr
  INTO <gs_alv_output>-kunrg
  FROM vbpa
  WHERE vbeln EQ <gs_alv_output>-vgbel
  AND   parvw EQ 'RE'.
```

The example code in Listing 4-9 illustrates about ten billion zillion points, all at once.

Just to clarify what the abbreviations mean: in SAP terms the abbreviation *RE* means "bill-to" (who you send the invoice to) and *RG* means "payer" (who pays that invoice). The original programmer even built those abbreviations into the variable names; i.e., KUNRE and KUNRG.

The original problem must have arisen whilst doing the ever popular cut and paste. Clearly, the second SELECT statement was copied from the first, and the variable name was changed from KUNRE to KUNRG, but the value for the selection option on PARVW was not changed from RE to RG—hence the error.

This also fulfills the "make wrong code look wrong" principal—the names of the variables were such that they clearly indicated what they were looking for—i.e., RG instead of RE—but still no one noticed. An argument can be made for using constants, or some other way of arriving at the value RG and also renaming the target variable, as in Listing 4-10.

Listing 4-10. Wrong Code that Looks Wrong

```
"Get Payer and name.
SELECT kunnr
  INTO <gs_alv_output>-payer
  FROM vbpa
  WHERE vbeln EQ <gs_alv_output>-vgbel
  AND   parvw EQ gc_bill_to.
```

When you look at the code in Listing 4-10, it is a lot more obvious something is wrong. There are two lessons we can learn from this.

The first is to replace literals with meaningful names in order to highlight possible errors that can occur whilst cutting and pasting.

The second and more important lesson is not to cut and paste in the first place. As mentioned in the previous section, every time you feel like cutting and pasting, think to yourself, "Can I move this code into its own routine and then parameterize the differences?"

The obvious counter-argument runs along the lines of, "We are only talking about five lines of code here," so it seems like an enormous effort to create a new routine with just those five lines inside it. After all, nothing could possibly go wrong when copying those five lines of code!

Well, it can, and it did. So I would say every time you have the urge to do a cut and paste of some code, think to yourself, "Is this going to come back and bite someone in the future? More important, is it going to come back and bite *me*?"

Avoiding Repetition in OO Programming

In this section, you will hear about a trap it is easy to fall into when starting with OO programming, a trap I fell into myself, a problem whereby you feel the only way to do things "properly" is by having duplicate code in lots of classes.

When you start learning OO, the first thing that is explained to you is inheritance because that is an easy concept to understand. You are told, "Separate the things that change from the things that stay the same," and that makes perfect sense—all octopuses have eight legs, so any code dealing with eight-legged-type matters should be in the superclass, but only the Australian Golf Ball Octopus (which is the size of a golf ball) kills you when you pick one up from a pool on the beach (though you don't notice at the time that you have been injected with poison; you just die the next time you go to sleep), so code to do with poisoning should live in the AGBO subclass; all the other octopus-type behavior should be inherited.

Top Tip

If you are ever in Australia and on the beach and see something the size of a golf ball in a pool that is bright blue and yellow—*don't pick it up*.

So far so good. Then, as your knowledge of OO increases, you are (seemingly) told to avoid inheritance whenever you can; instead, you must define the behavior of classes, which do the same thing, via an interface.

These instructions at first glance appear to be totally contradictory. An interface has no code at all.

A common mistake is to give up on inheritance and create ten classes of octopus all implementing the octopus interface, all with the same code repeated in each class, with some bits changed due to the specific nature of the octopus at hand. This is the exact thing we have been trying to get away from.

We do want to have the object instance variables in our programs typed as interfaces rather than concrete classes so we can swap whatever we pass in with a totally different class if need be, with the program being none the wiser, and most importantly inject test doubles during unit tests.

But, on the other hand, interfaces don't have any code, so to avoid repetition where do we put the code that is always the same between the low-level subclasses?

Happily for us, we just have to look at a few examples of standard SAP classes like `CL_RECA_MESSAGE_LIST`, often touted as a fine example of an error-handling class. The `RE` in the name stands for "Real Estate," but nonetheless it looks like it was designed to be as generic and reusable as possible.

Based on the example of class `CL_RECA_MESSAGE_LIST`, the design should have an abstract interface like `ZIF_OCTOPUS` and then a base class that implements that interface and contains all the code that never changes. Sometimes that base class is defined as "abstract," which means you can never create instances, so you are forced to create subclasses, but that is not mandatory. Indeed, that design might result in your being forced to create a subclass identical in every way to the base class, which would be silly.

With this design we have the best of both worlds—the calling program only knows about the interface, so we can use test doubles at unit test time, and we have separated the things that change from the things that remain the same, as the base class has the code that does not vary (instead of that being duplicated across many subclasses) and the subclasses have the code that does vary; i.e., `ZCL_GIGANTIC_OCTOPUS` inherits from `ZCL_OCTOPUS_BASE`.

Then in the main program (the so-called client), instances of individual octopi are created using a factory method that works out the exact type of octopus to instantiate. Hopefully, you will use this technique in all your octopus-based coding going forward.

Other Common Causes of Instability

As much as I would like to have a ready-made programming principle into which every potential instability problem neatly fits, that is not actually the case, so here you will read about three disparate areas that can cause instability problems:

- Global variables

- Incorrect use of parameters

- Memory problems

Global Variables

The idea of global variables' being evil will crop up all over this book. In the context of stability, the argument goes that the more global variables you have in your program the more unstable it is.

As you will have come to expect by now, this is going to be demonstrated by various real-world examples.

Cannon Example

At one point in your life you may have been to the circus and seen someone getting shot out of a cannon. They are professionals and so know what they are doing, but I put it you, ladies and gentlemen of the jury, that in all other contexts, being shot out of a cannon is not the most reliable way to travel. You could, for example, build a big cannon in your garden and then put a big trampoline at your work site ten miles away and attempt to commute to work each morning by having an accomplice fire you out of the cannon in your garden.

If that worked it would be really cool, but to be honest the chances of its working are not actually that high. The longer the distance involved, the higher the risk of something going wrong—a gust of wind blowing you off course or colliding with a flock of birds or any one of a dozen other potential problems.

This possibly explains why very few people commute to work by being fired out of a cannon. It is an obviously silly thing to do—so why do we do the exact same thing in our code?

I see this sort of "cannon" situation at work when fixing or improving old programs, and when I do it makes me want to cry. This is because the change I have to make still involves using the cannon. These types of changes (fixes) work and take a very small amount of time, but are so fundamentally wrong it beggars belief.

"What sort of changes might those be?" I hear you ask. For example, after one change I made—that worked perfectly, by the way, and took no time at all—I commented my change thusly:

"I have just changed the above global variable in this subroutine, off it goes into the wild blue yonder, in many subroutines time it will get exported into a custom Z table, a table which exists for the sole purpose of storing data until this program SUBMITS another program to read back that same data from the Z table one second after it has been written."

This is all wrong on so many levels. It works *now* because none of the subroutines between where the value is written and where it is read change the global variable value, but what if one day someone makes a change to one of those many subroutines between my writing the value and its getting exported to the table? Or someone changes the program that gets submitted? There is so much scope for disaster in the future.

I have in effect put that global variable inside a cannon within the subroutine where I change its value, and then fired it off hoping it lands safely in the trampoline waiting for it in ten subroutines' time.

As doing a wholesale rewrite of the program is probably impractical, the solution is to somehow find a way to ensure the value of the variable does not change between where you "fire" it and where it needs to land. In other words, it needs to be "immutable" (i.e., once set it cannot be changed), which is the very opposite of the nature of global variables.

Amazing as it may seem to us ABAP people, in some "functional" programming languages you cannot change the value of any sort of variable once you have set it (so variables are only "variable" in that they can change once between an initial value and a fixed value), but ABAP does not work like that at all.

In fact, there is no way to make a variable 100 percent immutable in ABAP. A common approach to the problem is to define the variable as a read-only public variable of a class and then have a method that sets the value, but only if the variable is initial. That's not perfect at all, as any other method of that class could change the value at any time, but it is as close as you can get.

Half-Dog Half-Cat Example

In Listing 4-11, half the values used in the routine come in as parameters, and half the values rely on global variables' being set.

Listing 4-11. Half-Dog/Half-Cat Code

```
FORM calculate_deliveryflow  USING     pa_zzldspace  TYPE zzldspace
                                        pa_zzmaxload  TYPE zzmaxldsze
                             CHANGING   pa_zzdelflwhr TYPE zzdelflwhr.

  DATA: lv_load_size       TYPE zzmaxldsze.
  DATA: lv_load_space(3)   TYPE n.
  DATA: lv_capacity        TYPE zz_truck_cap.
  DATA: lv_flow            TYPE p DECIMALS 1.
  DATA: lv_load_space_c(5) TYPE c.

  SELECT SINGLE capacity INTO lv_capacity FROM  zsd_trucksize
        WHERE  truck_type      = vbap-zzvtype
        AND    capacity_uom    = vbap-meins
        AND    dispatch_group  = zt001w-bzirk.

  lv_load_size = lv_capacity.
  IF pa_zzmaxload LT lv_capacity.
    lv_load_size = pa_zzmaxload.
  ENDIF.
```

Listing 4-11 is bad for two reasons.

First, the signature of the routine is in effect lying about what it needs in order to do its job. It is quite possible someone making a change to another area of the program just looks at the signature and passes in the required values without realizing that some global variables need to be set as well.

The second related problem is that the routine will behave in an unstable manner; i.e., it will return different values given the same input parameters seemingly at random depending on at what point in the program it is called and the state of the global variables at that point.

Matters might be even worse—the signature of the routine might say it changes or exports only one value, but inside the routine the code might decide to change one or more global variables. This can cause what are called side effects—the programmer decides to make a call to the routine thinking it will only set/change one variable (the one mentioned in the signature), and instead at runtime they are astonished to find half the global variables in the program have been changed.

Side Effects

I mentioned functional programming earlier. In that programming paradigm, which is not supported by ABAP, a routine (function) is not allowed to have any side effects; i.e., it cannot change the value of any variables outside of its signature. This is different than both procedural programming in ABAP, where you can change global variables, and OO programming in ABAP, were you can change member variables that are also not in the signature. In both cases, in the ABAP world you have to think really hard as to whether changing such variables will destabilize the program.

Function Modules

Function modules are another fine example of this problem with global variables. Since their global data is shared between all function modules in a function pool, the result of calling a particular function module could be dependent on which other function modules of the same function group have been called before it.

With function modules, the solution is to only have one function module per function group (unless you are deliberately trying to share the global data) or to call a routine that clears out every single global variable as the first routine in the function module. Both solutions mean that calling one function module cannot possibly have an influence on a subsequent call to another function module.

Cross-Program Calls

Here, the term *cross program* does not mean the program is angry, but rather that it uses the construct PERFORM XYZ IN PROGRAM ABC IF FOUND. This is a really bad thing to do for two reasons, both of which are killers of program stability.

First, let us say the routine you want to call in the other program has four parameters. You can call it with three parameters in your program and will not get a syntax error. At runtime, however, you will get a dump. Moreover, if someone adds a new obligatory parameter in the remote program, then suddenly the calling programs will start dumping.

As if that isn't bad enough, I have seen cases where a program does such a cross-program call on standard SAP programs; e.g., a routine or two in SAPMV45A. Later, that program tries to call a standard SAP BAPI to create or change a sales order and it does not work at all, despite the fact that another Z program calls that BAPI with the exact same input parameters and succeeds. Why in the world is that?

There is no great mystery here. If in your custom program you do a cross-program call on a routine in SAPMV45A, then that whole standard SAP program is loaded into the memory of the current session along with all its global data. When the BAPI is called, that too tries to use the global memory of one or more standard SAP programs and gets into trouble. There is no great mystery here. The Z program that did not work did a cross-program call. The Z program that worked did not.

When I first had that BAPI problem I got around it by using the STARTING NEW SESSION addition in the function call, and that solved the issue, as in the new session all the global data was blank.

In any event, there is a simple answer to the problems caused by cross-program calls—don't do them ever under any circumstances. There are so many other options available to you.

If you feel the desperate urge to perform a cross-program call to a routine in a standard SAP program because you think it does what you want, think again. As you have seen, even cutting and pasting the SAP code into your program (which is better than a cross-program call) can cause all sorts of problems. Instead, work out what the standard SAP code does and code your own version.

There is even less reason to do a cross-program call to a routine in a Z program. Custom code can be encapsulated in function modules, or preferably methods of classes, and that (a) is really easy and (b) avoids all the terrifying stability problems caused by cross-program calls.

Table-Based Work Areas

A global structure declared via a TABLES statement with reference to a database table is a particularly horrible form of global variable. The very fact that such a variable has the same name as the table to which it refers makes the code look strange; e.g., SELECT SINGLE * FROM VBAK INTO VBAK WHERE VBELN = VBAK-VBELN. In that statement, one reference to VBAK is to the database table and the other is to a global structure, yet both have the exact same name.

In a lot of 20-year-old code, I have seen cases where the program starts off with a huge TABLES declaration listing all the database tables that may or may not get read at runtime, and then inside a routine instead of declaring a local variable for receiving the result of the database read, the global work area is used, as in Listing 4-12.

Listing 4-12. Bad and Good Ways to Read VBAK

```
SELECT SINGLE * FROM VBAK INTO VBAK WHERE VBELN = LD_CONTRACT.
SELECT SINGLE * FROM VBAK INTO LS_CONTRACT_HEADER
WHERE VBELN = LD_CONTRACT.
```

There are assorted problems with the first approach in Listing 4-12:

- As you have seen, the more global variables you have, the more unstable the program becomes. You could have one routine relying on a VBAK work area and being set in one routine and read unchanged in another, and yet it might be changed by any routine in the program.

- It's a waste of memory. Tables like VBAK or VBAP have hundreds of fields. It's far better to define your own structure to hold only the fields you need and then only fill them during the routine where the data is actually needed.

- From a semantic point of view, you cannot tell what the work area is being used for—it is just a German abbreviation. In the preceding example, you could have a program where sometimes VBAK refers to sales order data and sometimes refers to contract data.

To be fair to all the programmers who got into this habit 20 years ago, they were just copying what SAP did in the standard code at the time. Then, as new people came along, they just copied what had gone before. However, slowly but surely, this practice has been dying out. You even get a warning about it in the code inspector checks that says the TABLES statement is obsolete. It is not allowed at all in ABAP in the Cloud.

The one thing that has kept the TABLES statement alive in ABAP code is the perception that you need it in executable programs in order to use SELECT-OPTIONS in SELECTION-SCREENS. You can define a parameter by directly typing it into a data element, but it seems as though you can only type a SELECT-OPTION by using a TABLES statement first, as in Listing 4-13.

Listing 4-13. Using TABLES for SELECT-OPTIONS

```
TABLES: VBAK.
SELECT-OPTIONS: S_VBELN FOR VBAK-VBELN.
```

The bad news is that you do a need a global structure in order to get SELECT-OPTIONS to work. The good news is that you do not have to use TABLES.

Let us just say that an ALV report reads from ten different tables, and as such requires optional selections from certain fields in those tables. I have seen such selection screens seemingly go on forever. The traditional way would be to declare a TABLES definition for each database table, and then declare each SELECT-OPTION with reference to the database table.

As we have seen, this means you end up with a bucket load of global structures that are hopefully always empty but nonetheless consume memory.

What you can do instead is declare your own global structure that just contains the fields you would need as selection options on your selection screen, and then have the SELECT-OPTIONS refer to that global structure, as in Listing 4-14.

Listing 4-14. Using a Global Structure as Opposed to a TABLES Declaration

```
DATA: BEGIN OF GS_SELECTIONS,
                VBELN TYPE VBAK-VBELN,
                WERKS TYPE VBAP-WERKS,
            END OF GS_SELECTIONS.
SELECT-OPTIONS: S_VBELN FOR GS_SELECTIONS-VBELN,
                S_WERKS FOR GS_SELECTIONS-WERKS.
```

This way, you only have a small global structure as opposed to many large ones. Furthermore, as your executable program ideally would be just calling the "main" method of a class and passing in all the values from the selection screen, that global structure will never be used for storing or retrieving values.

Parameters

While talking about global variables earlier, the concept of "side effects" was mentioned—you call a routine expecting it will do "what it says on the tin" and then are astonished when that routine changes the value of something completely unrelated.

Here, we talk about several aspects of parameters—those that are imported, those that are exported, how you define both sorts, and just how many you should have.

Importing Parameters

In FORM routines you have the concept of USING and CHANGING parameters. The idea is that the USING parameters are the inputs and the CHANGING parameters are the outputs. However, the compiler does not enforce this at all. Thus, you could have a FORM routine where you input the month number (say, 1) through a USING parameter and get the name of the month back through a CHANGING parameter. The last thing you would expect is that the variable holding the month number you passed in would get changed to 2 by calling that routine.

You would hope no one would program something so strange, but I have seen many similar (though not so obvious) cases over the years. It must be really common, as there is an extended program check error you get if it sees the code in a program changing a USING parameter.

In OO there is no such problem—there is no USING parameter and you cannot change an IMPORTING parameter; if you try to do so in the code then you get a syntax error.

Exporting Parameters

In FORM routines the equivalent of an EXPORTING parameter is the CHANGING parameter, but it is not really an EXPORTING parameter at all. As its name implies, its purpose is to enable changes to the value of the variable being passed in. However, 95 percent of the time in procedural programs it is being used as an EXPORTING parameter simply because there is no other choice.

Let us say you have a FORM routine where you pass in the type of a shape-shifting lizard person and expect to get the name of that type back as a text description, as in Listing 4-15.

Listing 4-15. Getting the Name of a Shape-Shifting Lizard Person Type

```
PERFORM GET_LIZARD_TYPE_NAME
USING LD_LIZARD_NUMBER
                        CHANGING LD_LIZARD_TYPE_NAME.
```

The problem is that if there is already a value in the LD_LIZARD_TYPE_NAME and an incorrect value is passed in, the text name will not be automatically cleared—it will retain the same value it had before. You have to remember to clear the "changing" parameter right at the start of the FORM routine if you want it to function as an "exporting" parameter.

Many people forget to do this, and hence calling programs proceed on the assumption that the value has been changed or even check to see if it is blank and presume if it is not blank then the value was changed correctly. In both cases, the program is then working under false assumptions and can behave in an unpredictable/ unstable manner.

In the OO world, matters are much improved. The first benefit compared to FORM routines is that EXPORTING parameters and CHANGING parameters have different names, and thus you can clearly indicate if you are actually trying to change a value or to drive a totally new value.

You still have to manually clear the EXPORTING parameters at the start of the method, but in OO code you are given a warning by the code inspector if you do not do this.

With an OO RETURNING parameter, things are even better. The variable in the RETURNING parameter is automatically cleared when the method is called without your having to do anything. A value is only returned if it is set somewhere in the method and no EXCEPTIONS are raised; i.e., if the method concludes successfully.

Fully Typed Parameters

One difference between ABAP and some languages is that in ABAP variables are strongly typed; i.e., a variable is either an integer or a string or whatever, and usually has a fixed length. That is in contrast to some languages where a variable takes on the type of whatever value is passed into it; e.g., JavaScript

However, in FORM routines there is no requirement for parameters to be typed at all— you can write something like Listing 4-16.

Listing 4-16. Untyped Parameters

```
FORM GET_LIZARD_TYPE_NAME
USING    PUD_LIZARD_TYPE                CHANGING
PCD_LIZARD_TYPE_NAME.
```

The extended syntax check will warn you about such untyped parameters—i.e., it will tell you to add the type definition—but in my opinion the warning does not make it clear enough just how dangerous untyped parameters are.

If a parameter does not have a type, the syntax check has no way of statically checking whether the variables being passed in or out are of the correct type. If they are typed and you try to pass a number into a string (for example), you get a syntax error.

Sometimes there are five or six USING parameters, and since FORM routine parameters are not named it is really easy to put the parameters in the wrong order in the calling routine. If those parameters are untyped, then you won't get a syntax error in such a situation, but *hopefully* when the code runs you get a dump.

I say *hopefully* because at least then you would know you have a problem. Far, far worse would be if there were not a dump and the program continued. That could happen if two variables of the same type are passed into the routine in the wrong order, or because the ABAP language always tries its best to convert variables of different types and might succeed; e.g., pass a time or date into a numeric field or vice versa. If any of that happened, then heaven only knows how the program would behave.

In the OO world, none of these problems can arise. It is mandatory to type parameters, and if you are programming in Eclipse the type can often be auto-generated when creating the definition. In addition, the fact the parameters have names means the caller sees the names of the parameters to which they are passing values, which eliminates the possibility of passing values to the parameters in the wrong order.

All in all, using methods as opposed to FORM routines vastly reduces the risk of unexpected behavior due to incorrect parameter usage.

Big Trouble with Big Signatures

Code inspector checks like the ones from the SAP Code Pal, which are more to do with how easy the code is to understand than with possible incorrect behavior, give warnings and errors if a signature is too big—especially if has more than two EXPORTING parameters.

Amazingly, the number of parameters can also have unexpected effects upon the correct functioning of the program, which is what this section is all about.

To recap, if you have a routine that takes in about ten values and returns about five values, then you have two choices—pass everything in and out via parameters (the "signature") or use global variables (in procedural programs) or member variables (in OO programs). Since global variables are unequivocally bad, we will discuss the use of parameters here.

Often when I read the reams of material available about how to write object-orientated programming, I find seemingly contradictory instructions. Whilst that is frustrating on the face of it, the good thing is it forces you to think about both ways to do something and make up your own mind. It is better to have two options than to have no clue at all what to do.

The first OO recommendation you get is to conform to the idea of "high cohesion," which says that if a variable gets used in most if not all the methods of a class, then you should make it a "member" variable (which looks like a global variable but only exists within one instance of a class) as opposed to constantly passing it backward and forward in the signatures of all the methods. This would make the signature simpler.

That argument goes on to say that if there are no member variables at all within an instance method—just local variables and parameters—and nothing at all changes apart from the exporting parameters (there are no "side effects" in IT terms), then it might as well be a static method.

When I started off with OO, I wrote code that had lots of values going into and out of methods. My gut feeling was to stick with a big signature and have no member variables in the method. My rationale was that this made it obvious exactly what a given method needed to do its work, and what values it derived or changed. It is possible this attitude came from years of procedural programming, but someone who had come from a functional programming background would have felt the same way as in most of those languages you are forbidden to cause side effects.

So I was a bit worried I was going against official OO recommendations and not being "cohesive." However, there is a saying in some places in the world that if you don't like the weather just wait a few hours until it changes. It seems to be like that with the OO books I read; if I decide to do something, then sooner or later I will come across an argument that justifies my opinion.

The counter-argument to "cohesion" talks about the idea of "temporal coupling." This is when the correct outcome of a program depends on the routines' being called in a specific order. Traditional procedural programs are just like that—if you call the FORM routine that displays the ALV before the FORM routine that fills up the global table to be displayed, things will not work too well.

Temporal coupling is deemed to be a bad thing in OO programs because if you change the order in which methods are called then the program behavior changes unexpectedly in a way that is difficult to debug. In OO programs, methods are not always called in the static "one after the other" sequence that you get with procedural programs, which is partly why procedural programmers hate the idea so much.

At one point in the past, I found myself writing an application in an OO fashion, all to do with variant configuration. I had a series of methods corresponding to Visio squares on a flow chart I was given. The point of a flow chart with lots of YES/NO branches is that you can get to the same square via several different routes, rather like a "Choose Your Own Adventure" book. Moreover, it is highly likely that the flow chart itself will change over time, and then the squares will 100 percent get called in a different order.

They say that a lot of the art of programming is making a guess as to what may change in the future so you can prepare for it, and to my mind the order of the squares in the flow chart's changing was a virtual certainty. A similar flow diagram for a previous project changed 27 times before everyone was happy with it.

Therefore, if one of my "squares" could be called effectively at random, then it absolutely could not depend on anything that had been called before—in the same way unit tests cannot rely on the results of previous tests, as they are deliberately called at random. It had to be "side effect"–free, which meant just looking at what had been passed in and returning a result based solely on that.

The conclusion here is that you have to make a guess as to whether your routines will need rearranging in the future. If the application is simple and linear, like a report that reads data and then displays it, then probably the "high cohesion" approach is best, and you don't need big signatures. If the application is like my Visio one and the routines will be called in an unpredictable order, then the "non-temporal coupling" approach is best, and the routines should have no side effects; otherwise, the program could have all sorts of unexpected behavior, seemingly at random.

Memory Problems

I was going to put this section earlier in the chapter, but I forgot, because I have a memory problem.

Often in this chapter we have talked about problems that occur seemingly at random. There is nothing worse than getting a help-desk ticket saying that an application dumps for different people once a week right out of the blue, and it does not matter what the end user is doing at the time. Furthermore, the problem cannot be replicated. Even if you happen to be lucky enough to be standing right behind an end user when the dump happens, and then go back to your computer and do the exact same thing, it likely works fine for you.

It is rather like going back to 1995, when Excel used to crash at random for no reason, or to this very day when your program editing session in the SAP GUI got the fatal message "error in parser thread" for no reason, which forced you to kill all your SAP sessions via the task manager.

I don't know what caused Excel to keep crashing all those years ago, and I don't know what caused the "parser thread" thing (I wish I did), but I do know one possible cause of "out of the blue" dumps.

Sometimes if you look at the dump you will see a description along the lines of "unable to extend internal table XYZ" or some such—there are many variations, but all are to do with the user session's running out of memory. This usually happens when the user runs a report requesting a ridiculous amount of data; e.g., all general ledger postings for the past 30 years.

Sometimes, however, when you look at the dump it seems to have occurred just after a SELECT SINGLE on the customer master table with a specified customer; i.e., just one row was returned. What could be happening here is the dreaded "memory leak."

With most applications the user does not actually stay in them for all that long. They run a report and then do something with the result or create a sales order or some such. After they are done, they get out of the transaction and start doing something else. Even if someone only does one transaction all day long—e.g., creating sales orders— the system resets everything after the order is created, so the next order is created in a brand-new transaction, even if the user thinks they have never left the sales order creation screen.

However, there are some transactions (often custom) in which the user stays all day. CIC0 is a fine example, if a bit outdated. This is where a call center agent stays in the CIC0 transaction all day taking phone calls from customers. Though CIC0 a standard transaction itself, it spends 99 percent of its time calling assorted custom code based on configuration settings, with no two companies ever being the same.

Another example is a 100 percent custom interactive report that lets you do things with the retrieved data, so a user can stay in that report all day, refreshing it every so often, and call assorted functions to manipulate the displayed data.

In both cases—transactions like CIC0 that call Z code and 100 percent custom interactive reports—the user can get an "out of memory" dump irrespective of what they are doing at the time, but rather based on how long they have been in the transaction.

There are several possibilities, as follows:

- A database SELECT appends rows to an internal table rather than just replacing everything. If this is called repeatedly during a refresh of the data, that internal table just gets bigger and bigger (usually with duplicate rows) over time, until it exceeds the memory limit.

- An internal table gets identical rows added to it again and again. The example I have seen is the "exclude table" you fill to suppress icons before calling an ALV report. The same values (icons to exclude) got added to the table every time the user pressed the Refresh button. It took a long time, but eventually all those duplicate entries made the table exceed the memory limit.

- There is an "internal buffer" table that remembers the values of previous queries—e.g., the name of a customer or material—to prevent multiple identical SELECTS on the database. This is wonderful in a report where the same values are going to pop up multiple times, but if the user is in the transaction all day, then eventually so many results are "remembered" that the table exceeds the memory limit.

Happily, there are solutions for each case, as follows:

- If you are appending rows to an internal table, then it stands to reason you are amalgamating the results of several different queries on the same table. If this is happening during a data refresh, you have to make sure the very first such SELECT blanks out the table. That first SELECT should not be using APPEND anyway, but in any event it should clear the table first. Note that even if the first read actually does use SELECT INTO and somehow fails, the table will not be cleared, so explicitly clear the table if SY-SUBRC is not zero.

- When adding rows to a table that would duplicate existing rows, either blank out the table before starting or, if that would make no sense, check if the entry already exists before adding it again.

- In regard to internal buffer tables, you might note that in standard SAP buffering function modules there is a "maximum buffer size" variable, and if the size of the buffer table goes above that value then the whole table is wiped out and starts again. That is a wonderful idea—sadly some standard SAP modules set that maximum size at five records, which is a touch on the low side, but I would advise one to adopt the same approach and have a somewhat higher maximum value.

Unhappy Medium

You can get the situation where the user asks for a large amount of data and the report just manages to get all of that data before timing out. The user will be presented with an ALV grid with thousands of rows and the really obscure message, "Memory Full. Leave the transaction before taking a break." What that means is that the report has consumed so much memory it is causing the system as a whole grief and the system desperately wants the user to back out of the transaction and release all that memory. Thus, if the report finishes 30 seconds before lunch hour, the message suggests the user leave the transaction before going to lunch. However, I have seen people interpret the message the opposite way and think the computer is telling them to take a break, which they then do, and go off and have a cup of coffee or something. In any event, in your custom programs you can do something to help avoid this situation—if you have global (or member) internal tables that get merged into one main result table, then FREE them the instant you think they will never be needed again. A CLEAR or REFRESH on an internal table will not release the memory, but a FREE will. As someone on the internet observed, one programmer once called an internal table WILLY just so they could write FREE WILLY when the table was no longer needed.

Dealing with Instability: Using Code

Here, I would like to make a distinction between "correctness" and "stability."

Correct = Returning the correct result for a set of inputs

Stability = Always returning the *same* result for the same set of inputs

Thus, a stable program could always return the wrong result, and an unstable program could return the correct result 90 percent of the time, with the wrong result appearing seemingly at random. Obviously, you want both correctness and stability.

It is easy to think that your code is "correct" if it appears to return the correct result, and so you think your job is done. Then as soon as the code hits production, nothing works at all, and you are really puzzled. It is a common situation that when an end user reports a problem to someone in IT, the response is, "Well, it worked for me!"

The problem is that the developer is given the test script, which more often than not just contains the "happy path"—you are given the situation where the end user enters all the values perfectly and get the expected result when they do that.

However, no battle plan survives contact with the enemy, and a real person using the functionality is not reading from a test script, and so they either put in what they think are the right values or make all sorts of mistakes. If the code cannot handle either situation and falls over in a heap—or, worse, appears to work but in fact comes back with an incorrect result—then it is not stable.

In the TDD cycle (I always come back to this subject) you initially just write the absolute bare minimum of code to get the functionality working with the "happy path" data inputs. The bare minimum by definition does not include error handling or any of the other stability issues described in this chapter.

Then, in the BLUE phase, you run the static checks on the new code, and in both the extended program check and the code inspector there are bucket loads of checks dealing with "robust programming"; i.e., error handling (or the lack thereof).

Those automated checks will prompt you to add more code to address any of those issues that have been highlighted; e.g., you might get a warning that you have not dealt with SY-SUBRC's not being zero after a database read. This will most likely cause you to add extra branches into the production code; e.g., an IF/ENDIF construct to deal with the possible error situation highlighted. Those branches will cause the code coverage to fall below 100 percent, and to get that back up again you will have to add more tests with different inputs. Those new "non–happy path" tests might fail, meaning you have to change the production code again, and when they pass and you've run the static checks again they might highlight yet more stability issues, causing you to add extra branches, and the process repeats.

That might sound like a never-ending nightmare, but if you follow this process then in theory you get to a stage where every possible strange thing the user might do or mistake they might make is handled. At that point, the code has become stable.

In this section we examine the various mechanisms that you add during this process in order to get to that Utopian stable situation. You will read about how to handle problems that you pretty much know will happen, problems you think are likely to happen, things that really shouldn't happen but just possibly might, and things that should never happen under any circumstances.

Problems That Virtually Always Happen

Once upon a time, I was investigating a short dump that cropped up in production, seemingly randomly, about once a week. The dump was caused by an "overflow"—it turned out a user exit was trying to move the value of a quantity field into a numeric field with a length of 1. Therefore, any value of 10 or above caused a dump. The easiest fix would be to increase the length of the target field to the same as the source field, but I always like to understand the business process first. It transpires this was a user exit called whilst creating a sales order, and the user exit only fired when a particular material was entered. In such cases, the end user was supposed to enter a constant quantity of 1 because the material represented a service it was physically impossible to do more than once per customer.

Currently, they could enter any quantity they wanted, hence the dump. I talked this over with the responsible programmer, and we agreed it would be far better that if the end user entered anything other than 1 for this material, rather than the application dumping, they got an error message explaining why they had to enter 1 in this case. Ideally, we would have defaulted the value to 1 and grayed it out, but that was in the "too hard" basket based on time pressure so an error message was the best we could do.

The programmer went to his boss to explain the proposed change, and ten seconds later I was called into the manager's office to explain the problem in as much detail as I could. The manager summed it up thus: "What you are telling me is that the users are supposed to enter a value of 1 in such situations, and in fact the training documentation tells them to do this?"

I said yes, that was the case, and he told us not to make any changes because "this is not a programming problem. This is an end user problem. They are making mistakes. Tell them not to!"

Well, I *could* tell the entire human race to stop making mistakes all the time, but I am not sure how far that would get me. I would be amazed if there was anybody on the planet who did not make at least one mistake every day, possibly every hour, varying from minor things like trying to open a door with "pull" written on it by pushing it, all the way up to accidentally shooting down passenger jets.

Given that, you have to live with it—that's just the way the world is. So the users are going to put in incorrect values, no matter how much you tell them not to, and this sort of "non-happy path" behavior, if left untreated, could cause your program to behave in all sorts of unexpected ways.

You have no doubt heard the phrase "prevention is better than cure." The best way to prevent unstable program behavior caused by dodgy input values is to make sure those dodgy values don't reach the program in the first place.

For an interactive application, the obvious way to handle this is at the UI level. If a field is vital for the program to work, make it mandatory; if the value needs to be a date, don't make the field free text; don't allow a date of birth that is in the future, and so on. That is, try to make a big list of all the incorrect things someone might do whilst entering data and try to programmatically safeguard against them all.

There is even a special term for this—*gorilla testing*—which is where someone tries to enter the stupidest values they can think of onto a screen to see what happens.

Negative Consequences

In the SAP GUI, when you "paint" a screen the default setting for quantities is to not allow negative numbers. After all, you cannot have minus ten bunches of bananas loaded onto a truck, so that seems to make sense. The trouble starts when some sort of calculated figure comes up with a negative value (e.g., total truck capacity) and tries to output that value to the screen. The result is a short dump. In the short term, you need to either modify the screen definition so the field accepts negative values (looking wrong is better than dumping) or programmatically ensure the value is set to zero if it is negative (and give a warning telling the user to inform the help desk). In the medium term, you should fix the faulty calculation that sets a quantity to negative in the first place.

Telling the end user the value they have entered is incorrect and guiding them as to what to actually enter is all well and good, but we can take this to the next level. What if the code was so clever that it could recognize a mistake in the input data and correct it automatically? Let us look at two examples.

Fuzzy Searches

The most obvious example of such a thing is in word processing software, where if you spell a word slightly incorrectly it changes to the right spelling, most likely without your even noticing. So-called fuzzy searches as used by Google and even the HANA database are another good example—you spell what you are looking for with missing letters, or letters in the wrong order, but what you are looking for is found anyway.

Spreadsheets

Even in the year 2020, custom SAP programs all across the globe still seem to spend an inordinate amount of time uploading spreadsheet data into SAP. Given that this phenomenon isn't going away anytime soon, the question becomes this: What is the most common input error that causes programs to behave unexpectedly?

The answer is easy—you give someone a template with the columns in a certain order and the data starting at a certain row, and the upload program is expecting this format. Then someone decides to add a few blank columns or rows at the start, and maybe rearranges the column order for some reason, and then naturally the upload program goes into meltdown (or worse, processes the data and produces nonsense as a result), and the SAP system gets the blame.

In this situation, it is possible to be really clever. The trick is to upload the spreadsheet via the open source ABAP software ABAP2XLSX. Using that mechanism, you not only have the data in the spreadsheet, but you also have the metadata, such as what values are in what exact cells.

Thus, you can go hunting to see if there are any blank rows at the top and ignore them. You can then hunt for the cells with the column headings. Unless the person changing the spreadsheet has gone totally bananas and changed the heading names, you can see if any column is missing and raise an error, and if the columns have been moved into the wrong order it does not matter—you can programmatically determine in which column what sort of data lives based on the name in the heading row. You can also programmatically tell where the data starts; i.e., dynamically find the first non-empty row after the heading row.

You can also run checks on the actual data to see if somehow a text value has been entered in a cell in a column full of quantities.

Problems That Are Likely to Happen

Here, we look at several areas where at runtime the ABAP system is desperately trying to tell you there is a problem, but your code is ignoring that warning.

SY-SUBRC

One year, I did an analysis on a large SAP system where the idea of quality had been somewhat sacrificed to make way for pumping out working software as fast as possible, which is not actually all that unusual.

As a—predictable—result there was a very large number of short dumps in production every day and also a lot of unneeded database access. I produced a great, detailed report on all the problems, but given that a picture is worth a thousand words, I found I could summarize the root cause of 95 percent of the errors in one picture.

My colleague told me there was a meme generator on the internet where you could generate a picture of Bart Simpson writing something on a blackboard again and again.

In this case, I filled the blackboard with the words "CHECK SY-SUBRC EQ 0." That seemed to sum up the underlying nature of the problem perfectly.

I would say that SY-SUBRC's being changed to a value other than zero after an ABAP statement is executed is something that is *likely* to happen.

The most common situation is having a large string of routines that read a few database tables, do some calculations with the result, read some more database tables based on that result, do some more calculations, read yet more database tables, and so on. Most of the time everything is fine, yet every so often a bizarre result is returned.

The problem is that programmers often make assumptions that all the database reads will always return a result and all the reads on internal tables will also always return a result. You could be reading a configuration table, for example, and you know for a fact that all the entries are there—so why bother checking for SY-SUBRC after a database read to get the values, or after an internal table read on the table that stores those retrieved values? It's always going to work, so adding a SY-SUBRC check is boring, is a bit like effort, wastes valuable time, and is totally pointless. Maybe so—right up until the point some new configuration is added, and it is incomplete; e.g., a new plant with some organizational assignments missing.

At that point, everything goes pear shaped. As there are no checks after every database read or internal table read that fails, the program *thinks* it has succeeded and has no idea it is in trouble. It carries on its merry way, trying to process the non-existent or incorrect data, and the more processing there is after the first failure the stranger the end result will be.

After the event, the programmer says, "Well—who could have predicted *that*?" I just did. I always go to the airport early so I don't miss my flight. There is not usually a heatwave in South Australia so strong it melts the tram tracks and thus public transport is out so all the taxis are booked, and there is not usually a madman who takes a whole bus hostage thus blocking the bridge leading to Melbourne Airport, but on the two occasions those things did actually occur I was really glad I had allowed myself a load of extra time.

Neither of the last two things actually falls into the "likely to happen" basket, but the point is that when you start thinking about it there are very few things you can say are 100 percent certain to work every time—and 99.9 percent doesn't cut the mustard, because after six months of testing where everything has worked fine, on go-live day of course the very first end user does the one thing in a thousand where the entry is missing.

This is why there is the extended program check that asks you to always check the SY-SUBRC. At the very minimum, it makes you think. A failure may not actually be a problem—you could be writing a report that checks for deliveries with no invoices yet, in which case you are looking for failures when trying to get the invoice for a particular delivery. In such a case, you can write code to the effect of IF SY-SUBRC NE 0 then CLEAR LD_INVOICE_NUMBER. The point is, you are reacting to the failure and you are thinking about it.

A heinous crime many are guilty of is just adding an empty IF SY-SUBRC <> 0 block just to make an extended program check error go away. In the same way, when you generate a function module call using the "pattern" function you get an automatic IF SY-SUBRC <> 0 block generated with the comment "Insert suitable error handling here," and then very few people actually do—they even leave the generated comment there as evidence they don't care.

That does not help at all. If it (SY-SUBRC <> 0) really does not matter, then explain why, using a comment at the very minimum.

The gotcha is that different ABAP statements set SY-SUBRC differently in the event of an error, and some don't set it at all. As an example, if you do a read on a standard internal table and it fails, then SY-SUBRC is set to 4. If a read on a sorted table fails, however, SY-SUBRC is set to 8. The way around that is to always check if the value is 0 or not 0; that way, it does not matter what the failure value is.

Statements that do not set SY-SUBRC when they fail are more difficult to deal with. Luckily, the extended program check will warn you in such cases.

BAPIs

If you are lucky enough to have a BAPI to create the business object—e.g., sales order— then you know for a fact whether it succeeded or not, but you have another problem. Often, you want to create another object straight away; e.g., a delivery based on the new sales order. In theory, when you do a COMMIT WORK AND WAIT the word *wait* is supposed to mean that the program pauses until the database has been updated. However, quite often that does not happen, processing continues instantly, and the database is updated five seconds later. By that time your program has already tried to create a delivery based on a sales order that does not yet exist in the database and naturally fails.

Worse, this behavior varies randomly depending on the exact standard BAPI you use. There are myriad reasons why this happens—people have written huge essays on the internet explaining it—but the long and short of it is that even if you know the BAPI has succeeded you cannot make use of the new object until you know for a fact it is in the database, so you have to run around in a loop checking the database every second until the object is actually there.

BDCs

In the same way, I do not trust that the return code will not call a transaction via a BDC. You may instantly say, "Oh, come on, you should have stopped using BDCs 20 years ago!" When I first encountered them back in 1999 I made a vow that as soon as SAP released a BAPI for each transaction where I used a BDC, I would replace the BDC with a BAPI call. This I did, and yet 20 odd years on there are still some really common transactions with no BAPI; e.g., receipt inbound delivery (VL32), although you can use a BAPI to receipt an outbound delivery!

So, BDCs are still in use. The problem is this (and again, this is a real-life example): If the program called a BDC to create a customer in "errors only" mode, and some small thing went wrong and a mandatory field was not filled, that screen popped up in front of the end user. They did not know what to do and so pressed the Exit or Cancel button. The transaction terminated, and—amazingly—the BDC considered that a success and so the return code was set to zero. Then the program read the parameter ID KUN to get the newly created customer number, but because no customer had actually been created, the value was either blank or whatever customer number happened to be in memory at the time. That customer number then got written to a custom table. Oh, dear. As can be imagined, that caused all sorts of problems, and it happened so rarely it took me—literally—years to figure out what was going on.

Ever since then, I pretty much totally ignore the return code from a BDC and read the database instead to determine whether or not it succeeded.

Field Symbols

In Listing 4-17 you see two statements that appear to be identical.

Listing 4-17. Seemingly Identical Statements

```
FIELD-SYMBOLS: <LD_ANY_VALUE>.
FIELD-SYMBOLS: <LD_VALUE> TYPE ANY.
```

In both cases, you have a field symbol that can be assigned a value of any type. However, there is a subtle difference. Before using a field symbol, often you do a check to see if it is actually assigned, as in IF <LD_ANY_VALUE> IS ASSIGNED.

If neither was assigned, the one symbol that was declared as TYPE ANY would tell you it was not assigned, but the one that was declared with no type would lie and say it was assigned—i.e., IS ASSIGNED would return TRUE—and then you would try to read the value of the field symbol and would get a short dump. There is no logical reason for this; it is just something you have to be aware of. Happily, the extended program check warns you about this problem.

Here comes another problem with IS ASSIGNED. Take a look at Listing 4-18.

Listing 4-18. Problem with IS ASSIGNED

```
ASSIGN COMPONENT 'EQUNR' OF STRUCTURE <entity> TO <field>.
IF sy-subrc = 0.
  <field> = ls_equi-equnr.
ENDIF.
ASSIGN COMPONENT 'EQTYP' OF STRUCTURE <entity> TO <field>.
IF <field> IS ASSIGNED.
  <field> = ls_equi-eqtyp.
ENDIF.
```

In this example, the first assignment succeeds because there is a component called EQUNR in the <ENTITY> structure. However, the second one fails because there is no EQTYP component in the <ENTITY> structure. Is <FIELD> still assigned? Yes, it is—it is pointing to the EQUNR field in the target structure. As a result, the EQUNR field in the target structure (which was previously correct) would get overwritten with the EQTYP value from the source structure.

This is one case where it really is better to always evaluate SY-SUBRC!

Problems That Really Shouldn't Happen

In the preceding two sections, we talked about problems that you could predict would happen often—you could cause these "expected errors." Problems that you don't really expect to happen, but that you can imagine happening, are described as "exceptions" and should be handled with the ABAP classes of the same name—exception classes.

A real-life example is that while living in the United Kingdom I can reasonably expect that it might rain, and so I carry an umbrella to deal with the potential "error" in the weather. On the other hand, I wouldn't expect to be in the office looking out of the window one day and see a lightning strike hit the village a mile away and not realize it was my house that got hit and that the lightning bolt went right through the phone wires and threw my wife (who was on the landline phone at the time) across the room and also burnt out our modem, though the phone itself was fine. The call did not even get disconnected. Anyway, the latter definitely counts as an exception, and the exception handling there is that you have insurance against that type of thing.

In IT terms, these types of exceptional situations can arise when an interface to an external system breaks down, for example. You could also classify February 29 as an exception because three years out of four entering that value should cause an error.

In OO ABAP you are supposed to declare there has been an exceptional situation by raising an exception, which is then "caught," as in Listing 4-19,

Listing 4-19. Catching an Exception

```
TRY.
  me->talk_on_the_house_phone( ).
CATCH CX_LIGHTNING_STRIKE.
  me->contact_insurance_agent( ).
ENDTRY.
```

In these examples, not having any error-handling code in the CATCH statement for the exception is a million times worse than not having any error-handling code after a SY-SUBRC check. In this case, you know for a fact that something highly unusual is happening and so you really should deal with it.

This unusual situation might be so drastic that you need to bring the part of the program being executed (it could be a user command) to a graceful end, or maybe even the whole application. If you are lucky, however, you might be able to recover from the problem.

In science fiction spaceships and robots can often "self-repair," and your program may be able to do this as well.

Self-Repair: Example 1

In Listing 4-20, the user is asked to enter one or more sales orders on a selection screen, and they get a list of all the changes to those orders. When reading from the database while trying to get all those changes, if the program gets into trouble it "recovers" and tries a different approach.

Listing 4-20. Recovering from an Unexpected Situation

```
TRY.
    SELECT objectclas objectid changenr FROM cdhdr
       INTO TABLE lt_hdr
      WHERE objectclas = 'VERKBELEG'
        AND objectid   IN lr_objectid
        AND change_ind = 'U'.
  CATCH cx_sy_open_sql_db.
    COMMIT WORK.
    "possibly too many entries in lr_objectid.
    "Try 'for all entries' instead.
    SELECT objectclas objectid changenr FROM cdhdr
       INTO TABLE lt_hdr
        FOR ALL ENTRIES IN lr_objectid
      WHERE objectclas = 'VERKBELEG'
        AND objectid   = lr_objectid-low
        AND change_ind = 'U'.
ENDTRY.
```

If there are too many entries in a selection range, when you pass that into a SQL query a fatal exception is raised. However, there is no upper limit on how many rows you can have in a FOR ALL ENTRIES table, so if the first database read fails due to an excessive number of entries then a second database read is done using FOR ALL ENTRIES.

This is an exception situation because you only expect the user to enter a handful of order numbers and it would take many thousands to cause the exception. You don't expect that, but it is in theory possible because the user could upload a gigantic spreadsheet of order numbers into the section option box.

Self-Repair: Example 2

Let us say that all delivery locations (ship-tos, in SAP speak) need geocoordinates, and 99 percent of them have those fields filled at creation time. During the processing of an application, let's say the program comes across one with those fields blank—the code could have a "resumable" exception that calls some sort of web service to get those missing coordinates, update the master data, and then return to the line after the exception was raised and continue processing—without the user even knowing anything had gone wrong.

In a more general sense, if there is some sort of vital master data or configuration data missing, then, if the user is authorized, the program could pop up a message with a hyperlink to the transaction where the missing data can be entered, and then resume processing, or send some sort of automated message to whoever looks after missing data, tell the user what is happening (what is missing and who to chase up), and then gracefully abort processing.

Problems That Should Never, Ever Happen

The earlier problems in this "robustness" section were out of the hands of the custom program—they were caused by users or external systems; i.e., the supplier of external data was to blame for the problem.

However, with custom programs, as with life, sometimes, no matter how hard you try to pretend otherwise, there is no one to blame but yourself. This is what we are talking about now—clear bugs in the program. When you encounter such a problem you don't need to handle it—you need to terminate the program by forcing a dump. This is what the standard SAP "Message Type X" was designed for. Programs with bugs like this should never get to production . . . yet somehow they do.

In programs, as in life, we rely on assumptions. If those assumptions turn out to be incorrect in both cases (real life and programs), we get into serious trouble. American author Samuel Clemens (better known as Mark Twain) put it thusly:

> *"What gets us into trouble is not what we don't know. It's what we know for sure that just ain't so."*

> —Mark Twain

In other words, the program makes a presumption that, if incorrect, causes a dump or utterly incorrect behavior. The most common example is trying to do a division and the divisor turns out to be zero (which is "impossible"), leading to a dump.

In real life, one cannot check basic assumptions all the time—every time I go up to the bar I cannot check the beer I just bought for poison, and when I get back to my chair I don't check underneath each time in case someone put a bomb there whilst I was gone, and so on. That's just paranoid. In the programming world, however, we can be paranoid, and that's a good thing because things go wrong in programs a lot more than they do in real life (and that's saying something).

Spotting the Impossible

Taking the "this value will never be zero" assumption as an example, there are several ways you can treat this assumption in your code.

- You could write a comment to the effect that this value will never be zero, so everything will always be fine. This won't stop the problem, but at the very minimum if every developer documents all their assumptions it gives a clue to the next person maintaining the code. The problem, of course, is that comments go out of date very quickly.

- You could do an IF statement such that if the value is zero then do not do the division. That would stop the dump, but what would you do instead? Output an error message saying, "The impossible has happened!" Some standard SAP messages say just precisely that, and it does not help the end user one bit.

- You could write an ASSERT statement as in ASSERT DIVISOR NE 0. If the value is zero, a short dump will occur. This is far better than a comment because it actually has an effect if the assumption is not true and naturally can never go out of date. Such dumps are good. If a program dumps like there is no tomorrow in DEV and QA then you are forced to fix it before it goes to production.

- In higher levels of ABAP (7.53 and above) you can throw an exception with the RAISE SHORTDUMP addition, and that way you can pass a lot more information about the values that caused the "impossible" situation than could normally be ascertained when looking at a short dump.

Dealing with the Impossible

In the real world, when there is a fatal problem of some sort a common approach to dealing with it is to hold endless meetings trying to point the finger and find someone to blame, thus tying up the very people who could fix the problem and making sure the problem is not fixed for as long as possible—but at least you have someone to blame.

As might be imagined, that does not work too well, but when it comes to programs we absolutely do need to assign blame, and as quickly as possible, because the guilty party has to have major surgery on the spot (which usually does not happen to an office employee who has made a mistake).

In a program, we are not dealing with people—we are dealing with routines. The routine where the error actually occurred is on trial and presumed to be guilty, but when all the routines are gathered in the drawing room and the detective delivers a long speech detailing who has committed the crime, there are actually two possible guilty parties:

- The routine that called the routine on trial. That could be guilty of the horrible crime of not passing in the correct data to allow the routine on trial to do its job properly.

- The routine on trial. It just did not do the job it was supposed to be doing despite being given everything it needed to do that job.

In IT terms, this concept is known as "design by contract." This idea was invented by Bertrand Meyer, and you can find a link to the original article at the end of this chapter. As always, this concept is analogous to real life—if I want something from someone else then we have a "contract" (even if never explicitly stated) in that I want something specific from that other party and in return they want something from me.

246

In programming terms, there are three major strands to "design by contract":

- A "precondition" — This is the absolute minimum information a routine needs to do its job properly. If all of this information is not supplied or it is incorrect in some way, then a fatal error should be raised right at the start of the routine.

- A "postcondition" — This is when a routine has failed to do what it is supposed to do when given all the tools to do its job. This should be checked right at the end of the routine, and a failure should raise a fatal error.

- A "class invariant" — This is specific to OO programming and states that even when a routine has done its job correctly, if, along the way, it has somehow changed something that has made the class instance inconsistent (say, changing the number of tentacles for an octopus instance to nine) then a fatal error should be raised.

In the academic article about design by contract mentioned at the end of this chapter, a special programming language called Eiffel was created that had these three concepts built into the method signatures. Naturally, no other language has these built-in features, but the concept has been applied by Microsoft and can be added to languages like Java and JavaScript and most of the "cool" new web programming languages.

In ABAP there is no direct equivalent, but there is nothing to stop you from writing "precondition" and "postcondition" checks at the beginning and end of any method where you are making assumptions, or from having a failure raise a fatal exception. It is important that such an exception identify whether it was the calling routine that was at fault and needs changing (failed precondition) or the routine being executed that needs changing (failed postcondition).

So, you would need two different custom exception classes—one for preconditions and one for postconditions. If the impossible situation that caused the error happened halfway through the routine, you would raise the "postcondition" exception right there and then (as opposed to an ASSERT statement) rather than at the end.

Then, you would need unit tests to trigger those "contract violations"—to simulate the situations where "impossibly incorrect" data was passed in, or the impossible situation where the routine could not deal with correct data being passed in. Remember: We are dealing with bugs—fatal errors—here. If such things are remotely possible then you need a test to make sure the code can deal with them, even if dealing with them means a dump. A unit test run can handle the situation where a short dump would occur without actually making the dump happen. That would count as a failed unit test, which would force you to fix the production code.

Raising exceptions handles the first two strands of design by contract—the preconditions and postconditions—but what about the class invariant concept? There is no equivalent in ABAP at all. Since I like the whole concept of design by contract so much, I could not let that one go.

When I was 14, instead of playing games on my 1K computer like most of my friends did, I used to read *Computer and Video Games* and see what new features had been added to games and check if I could incorporate them into the things I was writing. I have not changed in the intervening 30-year period, so when I saw a concept that was alien to ABAP—namely, the class invariant—I thought, "How can I do that?"

Once you think about it, the concept of a class invariant is fairly easy to apply to almost anything. Classes are supposed to be models of the real world, so after each method call you can say that certain general "house rules" must be true; e.g., a lift (*elevator* for Americans) object cannot be higher than the highest floor in the hotel object (you would hope).

In one of my existing procedural programs I had added assorted unit tests in a test class, and this had weeded out no end of errors. So then I thought to myself—is there anything that must always be true in this program after any operation, no matter what it is? The answer came straight back: the program dealt with grouping items together, so at any given point there must either be no groups yet, or the groups that did exist must follow certain rules, like all items belong to the same customer, all items sum either to zero or within tolerance, and one or two others. I did not do anything dramatic, just added a recurring method at the end of each unit test. Note: This was a procedural program, so there was not even a "class" to be invalidated, but the idea was just the same as the "invariant" concept.

The result can be seen in Listing 4-21.

Listing 4-21. Adding a Class Invariant to a Test Method

```
* The fifth line is an invoice from a different month so should
* not have been cleared
    READ TABLE gt_alv_output ASSIGNING <ls_output> INDEX 6.
```

```
cl_abap_unit_assert=>assert_equals( exp = gc_no_matching
                                    act = <ls_output>-clear
                                    msg = 'Multiple payments for a
                                    months invoices cleared an invoice
                                    from the wrong month'(056) ).

    class_invariant( ).

  ENDMETHOD.                        "clear_2_plus_pmnts_vs_1_month
```

The CLASS_INVARIANT method ran a bunch of tests on the program data as a whole and then called CL_ABAP_UNIT_ASSERT_FAIL in the event of problems. Naturally, the guts of the tests called routines from the core program, routines that did not exist until I decided what tests I needed and then placed them in the real program at appropriate points.

As sure as eggs are eggs, as soon as I ran the unit tests I got several failures, including one where, instead of summing to zero, the group summed to a million dollars. How embarrassing would that be if an end user spotted that result before I did?

So, I very much like the "design by contract" part of those computer science articles and all the associated assertions, as it protects me from my own stupid programming mistakes. The importance of not looking like a fool cannot be overstated!

Dealing with Instability: Using Humans

There is one thing I would urge every single programmer on your team to do, every single day. If there is not anything 100 percent vital you have to do first thing in the morning, then just after you have sat down at your desk in the morning whilst you are (a) eating toast and drinking coffee, or (b) eating a doughnut and drinking coke, or (c) not eating anything and swigging down a bottle of whiskey because you hate your job and can't handle it sober, log into production and have a look at the results from transaction ST22 (short dump analysis) for the preceding day.

This is not often seen as a programmer task—the idea is that the BASIS department should monitor this and forward any problems to whomever. Nonetheless—why not be proactive? If I see a division-by-zero dump in production I instantly send an email to the responsible business analyst to raise a ticket saying this needs to be fixed.

Another thing I would like you to try is what I have been doing at work lately—when I change some old code and I come across an obvious or not so obvious error, I take a screenshot of the code and email it to all my programming colleagues with the subject, "What's wrong with this?"

People like to show how clever they are and so vie to be the first one to respond with the correct answer, so this is a sort of fun game, and educational as well.

Let us look at two "What's Wrong?" examples to see if you can spot the problem (there may be more than one problem).

What's Wrong #1

Have a look at Listing 4-22 and see if you can spot the problem. The clue is that the "slump" value has leading zeroes in the database, but the equivalent variant configuration characteristic does *not* have leading zeroes; therefore, they need to be removed before doing a comparison.

Listing 4-22. What's Wrong with This Picture?

```
IF NOT mvke-mvgr5 IS INITIAL. "slump
  CALL FUNCTION 'CONVERSION_EXIT_ALPHA_OUTPUT'
    EXPORTING
      input  = mvke-mvgr5
    IMPORTING
      output = ld_slump.
* if we have no entries left then we need to check slump
* variations. Basically we see if the quote line can be
* varied to the value entered by the user
    IF lo_av IS NOT BOUND.
      CREATE OBJECT lo_av.
    ENDIF.

    LOOP AT t_cvbap INTO ls_cvbap.
* does the contract allow a slump variation?
      CHECK ls_cvbap-slump_variations IS NOT INITIAL.
      REFRESH lt_item_numbers.
      ld_value = mvke-mvgr5.
```

```
  lf_yes   = lo_av->is_value_allowed(
             id_quotation    = ls_cvbap-vbeln
             id_item         = ls_cvbap-posnr
             id_char_name    = 'VMC_12'   "slump
             id_value        = ld_value ).
  IF lf_yes = abap_false.
    DELETE lt_batch_codes
    WHERE batch_code = ls_cvbap-zzbatch_code.
  ENDIF.
 ENDLOOP.
ENDIF.
```

The answer cannot be that obvious, because it sat in a production system for four years after the original error was made (by me) and before it was discovered (by me). In this example, a huge effort is made to remove the leading zeroes and put the result in a new variable—and that variable is not actually used! The extended program check tells you when there are no reads on a variable, which is how I picked this up.

The corrected code can be seen in Listing 4-23.

Listing 4-23. Corrected Code

```
IF NOT mvke-mvgr5 IS INITIAL."slump
  "The characteristic Values of VMC_12 (Slump) have no
  "leading zeroes
  CALL FUNCTION 'CONVERSION_EXIT_ALPHA_OUTPUT'
    EXPORTING
      input  = mvke-mvgr5
    IMPORTING
      output = ld_slump_no_lz."<======
* if we have no entries left then we need to check slump
* variations. Basically we see if the quote line can be
* varied to the value entered by the user
  IF lo_av IS NOT BOUND.
    CREATE OBJECT lo_av.
  ENDIF.
```

```
  LOOP AT t_cvbap INTO ls_cvbap.
    "Does the contract allow a slump variation?
    CHECK ls_cvbap-slump_variations IS NOT INITIAL.
    ld_atwrt = ld_slump_no_lz."<=======
    lf_yes   = lo_av->is_value_allowed(
               id_quotation     = ls_cvbap-vbeln
               id_item          = ls_cvbap-posnr
               id_char_name     = 'VMC_12'   "slump
               id_value         = ld_atwrt )."<======
    IF lf_yes = abap_false.
      DELETE lt_batch_codes
      WHERE batch_code = ls_cvbap-zzbatch_code.
    ENDIF.
  ENDLOOP.
ENDIF.
```

In the revised version, I did not like the idea of calling a variable LD_VALUE, because if you think about it every variable has a value so that is not a very meaningful name. In any event, in Listing 4-22 the value without the leading zeroes is in fact used, leading to a much better result.

What's Wrong #2

I don't want to give too much away about this next example. It's a simple ALV report that attempts to read some data from the database, and if the query succeeds then the retrieved data is displayed in an ALV grid in a container on screen 0100. Very simple, and nothing could possibly go wrong . . . or could it?

Have a look at Listing 4-24 and think about what might go wrong.

Listing 4-24. Code with Hidden Problem: Part One

```
PERFORM select_data.

IF sy-subrc EQ 0.
  PERFORM other_data.
```

```
  CALL SCREEN 0100.
ELSE.
  MESSAGE i035."Nothing to display.
ENDIF.
```

At first glance, everything seems straightforward. You read the database to get some data, and if you do in fact get some data you display it; otherwise, tell the user there is no data. I am sure for years this worked just fine. Then one fine day someone improved the code in SELECT_DATA, as demonstrated in Listing 4-25.

The clue here is that at runtime parameter P_SAME is usually INITIAL.

Listing 4-25. Code with Hidden Problem: Part Two

```
        AND t7~kdatb LE sy-datlo
        AND t7~kdate GE sy-datlo.

SORT t_config BY werks matnr reswk.

IF p_same IS INITIAL.
  DELETE t_config WHERE autet IS INITIAL.
ENDIF.

ENDFORM.                         " SELECT_DATA
```

The problem the users were reporting was that sometimes the data appeared and sometimes it did not, regardless of the entries made on the selection screen. The result would even change from hour to hour.

The reason was that when the statement to DELETE entries in the table was executed and there were no matching entries to be deleted, then SY-SUBRC was set to 4. Back in the calling program the fact that SY-SURC was not zero made the code think that the database read had failed and so the results were not shown.

After a little bit of fixing the corrected code looked like Listing 4-26.

Listing 4-26. Corrected Code

```
PERFORM select_data.
PERFORM other_data.
IF t_config[] IS NOT INITIAL.
  CALL SCREEN 0100.
ELSE.
  MESSAGE i035."Nothing to display.
ENDIF.
```

In the OTHER_DATA routine, a check was made such that if the main table was empty no attempt was made to get related data. This example is a clear demonstration that you should not rely on the value of SY-SUBRC remaining stable. So many things can change it. If you need the value of SY-SUBRC later on then you should store it in a variable the instant it is set; e.g., directly after the database read.

Conclusion

In this chapter, you heard about the second pillar of code quality—namely, stability. No program can have a happy life if it does not behave in a reliable and consistent manner. Sadly, a lot of programs actually tend to behave somewhat erratically, to say the least, leading to lots of very confused and unhappy end users.

First, you heard about some famous theories about common ways programs can be made to behave in an unpredictable/unstable fashion.

> The Principle of Least Astonishment — This is when the way a program behaves is so far removed from what the user expects they are *astonished*; we looked at what causes that.

> Programming by Accident — This is when a program full of errors still works perfectly when it really should not, and we discussed how this can lull you into a false sense of security.

> Don't Repeat Yourself — This is when code is duplicated within and across programs with horrific results.

After moving on to look at other common causes of instability that did not fit neatly into any of those baskets, we started to look at how to deal with such problems.

As you saw, how to deal with such errors programmatically varies with how likely any given problem is to occur—the way you treat a problem that is virtually certain to occur is very different to how you deal with a problem that should absolutely never occur.

At the end was a sort of "call to action"; i.e., a recommendation to proactively check ST22 dumps every day and also to share any horrible code problems you find with your colleagues.

At this point in the book, we have dealt with two of the three categories raised by the static code encountered in the BLUE phase—clarity and stability. We now move on to the third pillar—performance.

Recommended Reading

Anti-Fragile: This book is nothing to do with software, but the underlying idea is 100 percent relevant. The idea is that you can make your programs get *better* over time as opposed to *worse*, which has always been the case up until now.

`https://www.goodreads.com/book/show/13530973-antifragile`

ABAP2XLSX — Creating and reading Excel spreadsheets from SAP. Even after ten years this is still virtually unknown so the more people who discover it the better.

`https://github.com/sapmentors/abap2xlsx`

"Design by Contract" — This is a life-changing article (at least in regard to programming) so please read it!

`http://se.ethz.ch/~meyer/publications/computer/contract.pdf`

CHAPTER 5

Performance: The Third Pillar of Code Quality

Knowing that your program works perfectly might make you think everything in the ABAP garden is rosy. However, no program is good if it takes forever to run—even if it gives the correct result. Therefore, a common IT mantra is, "First make it work—then make it good—then make it fast." In this chapter, you will learn about the third part of that statement—once the code is clear and correct, how to make it run as fast as possible—by highlighting dozens of common performance traps in code that programmers often fall into.

Let's say you spend ages crafting the most elegant program in the world. It meets the clarity and stability guidelines covered in the previous two chapters and does whatever it is supposed to do every time. It goes live, and you are expecting the end users to arrange a ticker-tape parade for you, at the end of which you will be given a medal and a sack of gold. In real life, that generally does not happen.

More puzzling, there are no bug reports or requests for enhancements. This is not because the program is so great, but because the application takes forever to run so the users never go near it. They instead find a workaround that does not involve them staring at the screen for hours on end waiting for a result.

The best possible way to learn about dealing with performance problems is to find an existing custom program that falls into this basket—i.e., it takes forever to run or always times out—and then fix it.

I find fixing such programs to be one of the most fun activities I get to do in my day-to-day job, and, moreover, it is "Hollywood programming," so you actually *do* get a medal at the end of it.

© Paul David Hardy 2021
P. D. Hardy, *Improving the Quality of ABAP Code*, https://doi.org/10.1007/978-1-4842-6711-0_5

Hollywood Programming

A lot of programming involves refactoring existing programs or writing batch jobs or external interfaces—things the users will never see. You could do the most brilliant job in the world and never be noticed. Then one day you change something so it does exactly the same thing as before but now has a pretty user interface, and now you are a hero. That's Hollywood programming.

The SAP head of UX (user experience) once talked about the concept of perceived performance. Some web pages distract the user with flashing lights and bells and whistles whilst the important data is loading so the user doesn't notice how slow the site is. I am sure that works, but that is not actually how you want to solve the problem.

What you really want to do is delight the user. One day last year, I had to add some extra fields to a report that traditionally had horrible performance problems. As well as adding the extra fields, I messed about with the performance (in a good way) as best I could.

My changes went into production on the weekend, and on the Tuesday afterward I emailed one of the key business users, whom I suspected was the main user of this report based on my analysis of the usage logs. In any event, I asked her if it was running faster or slower since the weekend, and she said the following:

> *"I noticed there were additional fields added today, definitely quicker, I said earlier wow what's going on!!!!!"*

That is the ideal outcome—the program does more than before, and much faster at that.

The following sub-sections aim to give you a guided path to achieving similar positive outcomes yourself. You'll start off with the general concept of continuous improvement of existing code—the so-called CPO (Custom Program Optimization) concept. Next, you'll hear about the three types of performance checks you will find yourself doing on Z code: static checks, runtime checks, and "postmortem" checks.

To round things off, you will read about a whole bunch of sneaky tricks I have discovered over the years in regard to making programs run faster—some might really surprise you!

CPO Concept

Twenty years ago, the organization for which I work had a new SAP implementation, and six months after go-live the system was in serious trouble. We were having a major production crisis near daily, and there is nothing worse than frantically staring at the problems occurring in production whilst assorted senior-management types are looking over your shoulder, all expecting you to magically fix everything on the spot.

Our implementation could not be described in any way, shape, or form as "vanilla"— there was Z code all over the place. Like most organizations, we had started off with the goal of a "vanilla" implementation and throughout the project a steady trickle of "minor" enhancement requests had eventually eroded the mountain of "vanilla-ness" into a sea of "Z-ness." I know for a fact most SAP implementations end up this way, much as people like to deny it.

In any event, SAP offers a service called Custom Program Optimization whereby you pay SAP and they send out an expert for a week to look at the performance problems in your Z code. More important, that expert does not just give you a fish (i.e., analyzes the problems and tells you how to fix them); they teach you how to fish (i.e., how to diagnose such problems yourself going forward).

When it comes to "bang for your buck," that was probably the best return on investment we ever got. I remember one of the IT managers at the time practically jumping up and down and saying, "Look how much we are getting out of this!"—and how right he was. The knowledge got deeply embedded throughout the IT department, right down to the help desk doing daily checks on production each morning. Ever since, there has not been one major performance problem in production that we have not been able to solve ourselves.

Apart from daily morning checks, two changes were made to the way we programmers worked: having someone always be on "dump watch," which involves looking at the daily short dumps, and an annual in-house CPO (Custom Program Optimization) exercise. These are changes I would call progressive, but which would probably horrify some IT managers.

Daily Dumps

One programmer is always on "dump watch," by which I mean they spend the first hour of every morning looking at the short dumps from the day before in transaction ST22. If the problem is deemed to be technical, then they encourage the business analyst in charge of that functional area to raise a change request to let us programmers fix the technical problem. If it is a time out on a report, then the business analyst still gets bothered, but this time has to do a bit more work; i.e., contact the end user and work out what they were trying to do. Most likely, the end user was trying to retrieve six years of line items at once, and there is usually a better way to get the information sought.

In both cases we are being proactive. Often the problem is solved before the end user even complains. I also cannot over-emphasize the public relations benefit you get if you email an end user and explain you noticed they got a dump (you have to tell them what a dump is; i.e., when their screen goes all white and they get a strange message in German) and you are trying to stop that happening to them again, so can they remember what they were doing at the time? People are not used to anyone caring about their problems, let alone a total stranger from IT, so when someone does, they are pleasantly shocked.

Sadly, you are never going to get down to no dumps ever, but it is possible to get to the stage where they do not happen every day. The very first time you have a "dump free" day in production it is a cause for breaking out the champagne.

Annual In-House CPO

With any sort of newly acquired knowledge, if you don't keep using it, then it will fade away until eventually you cannot remember anything about it.

So every year for a day and a half, every single programmer at my company downs tools and gets together in the same room, and the team as a whole goes through a checklist of the various things you check in a CPO, which by a staggering coincidence are the types of things mentioned in this chapter.

The reason I said some managers would be horrified by this is that at first glance it appears to be a huge waste of time and money, as there is no specific problem actually happening—rather like the way they regard TDD! However, since the cost of a serious production problem can be enormous, the calculation has been made that the one-off annual cost of this CPO exercise is much less than the cost of a string of fatal problems in production.

In fact, right at the start we did this three times a year, but as time has gone by the quality of the custom code has improved such that once a year is enough. It would be easy to become complacent though, so the once-a-year minimum will never change. We *always* find at least one new serious problem each time.

Static Checks

It seems like a million years ago now, but when the code inspector first came out the biggest difference between it and the extended program check was that the code inspector had a section on potential performance problems.

If you are developing using test-driven development (TDD), then all the database access will have been extracted into a helper class, so the only remaining errors you will see during the BLUE phase will be in regard to internal table processing. However, as you will see, these can be just as deadly.

As always, every single such error or warning should be investigated and dealt with. Then you should check the database access class as well, but for now let us concentrate on the two killer problems with processing internal tables: geometric loops and not using secondary indexes with internal tables.

Geometric Loops

Since computers can perform a vast number of calculations really quickly, usually the performance bottleneck is database access—but not always.

If you give the system a truly enormous number of records to process, it is going to take a long time even though there is no database access at all. Mix the two together—vast amount of records plus database access—and the world ends.

You can see this in Listing 5-1, where there is an outer loop on one internal table (IREPO), and for every row of that table that is processed an inner loop is done on another table (GT_VBFA).

Listing 5-1. Nested Loops

```
LOOP AT irepo.
  lv_tabix = sy-tabix.
  LOOP AT gt_vbfa WHERE vbelv = irepo-vbeln
                    AND posnv = irepo-posnr.
    irepo-rfmng = irepo-rfmng + gt_vbfa-rfmng.
    SELECT SINGLE abgru INTO @DATA(lv_abgru)
    FROM vbap WHERE vbeln = @gt_vbfa-vbeln
    AND posnr = @gt_vbfa-posnn.
```

In Listing 5-1, GT_VBFA is a standard table. For each row in IREPO, there could be 0 to many corresponding records in GT_VBFA.

When I debugged this in production, GT_VBFA had 276,813 records. IREPO had 35,557 records.

Because the inner table (GT_VBFA) is a standard table, and even though the rows in the inner table are only processed if there is a match on the WHERE condition, for every row in IREPO every single row in GT_VBFA has to be evaluated to see if it matches.

Given the table sizes in this example, that means that 9,842,639,841 rows have to be processed. Obviously that takes forever. Put another way, the runtime of the program is based on the size of the outer table multiplied by the size of the inner table—a geometric progression. Imagine if there were yet another standard table being looped over in the middle of the inner loop (and sadly I have seen this).

The most important fix that needs to be made is to change the runtime from a geometric progression to a linear progression; i.e., have the runtime increase based on the sum of the size of the two tables rather than on the product (multiplication) of the size of the two tables.

This can be done by defining the inner table as a SORTED table, as shown in Listing 5-2. Note I have also changed the name of the table to reflect its actual contents, as SAP table VBFA can contain information on many different document types.

Listing 5-2. Defining a Table as SORTED

```
DATA: lt_orders TYPE SORTED TABLE OF g_typ_vbfa WITH NON-UNIQUE KEY vbelv
posnv vbeln posnn.
```

Notice that the first two fields by which the table is sorted—VBELV and POSNV—are the same as the fields used in the inner loop to determine matches. This is what will prevent the inspection of every row in this table with each loop through it.

The secondary problem is the repeated database access on VBAP inside the inner loop. This can be fixed by adding the ABGRU (rejection reason) field to the definition of the former GT_VBFA, thereby getting all the values at once, as shown in Listing 5-3.

Listing 5-3. Getting All the Rejection Reasons in One Hit

```
*** Primary key of VBFA is VBELV
  SELECT vbfa~vbelv, vbfa~posnv, vbfa~vbeln, vbfa~posnn, vbfa~rfmng, vbfa~erdat,
         vbap~abgru
    FROM vbfa
    INNER JOIN vbap
    ON   vbap~vbeln EQ vbfa~vbeln
    AND vbap~posnr EQ vbfa~posnn
    INTO TABLE @lt_orders
    FOR ALL ENTRIES IN @lt_sales_key
    WHERE vbfa~vbelv    EQ @lt_sales_key-vbeln
    AND    vbfa~vbtyp_n EQ 'C' "Document category of subsequent
    "document i.e. sales order in this case
    AND    vbfa~rfmng    NE 0.
```

Lastly, it is always good to loop into a field symbol as it speeds things up just that little bit. Then the nested loop construct can be slightly rewritten, as shown in Listing 5-4, and there will be no performance problem at all.

Listing 5-4. Nested Loop Code with No Performance Problem

```
  LOOP AT irepo ASSIGNING <ls_repo>.
    "SORTED table so no problem with nested loops
    LOOP AT lt_orders ASSIGNING FIELD-SYMBOL(<ls_orders>)
      WHERE vbelv EQ <ls_repo>-vbeln
      AND    posnv EQ <ls_repo>-posnr
      AND    abgru IS INITIAL."i.e. not a rejected order item
      <ls_repo>-rfmng = <ls_repo>-rfmng + <ls_orders>-rfmng.
```

In conclusion, whenever I am doing a code inspector check on a program I treat the performance section as very important indeed and always make a habit of looking at the "Nested Sequential Access to Internal Tables" entries, as shown at the end of Figure 5-1.

D..	...	E...	Tests	Error	Warn...	Infor...
ℹ			List of Checks	756	301	455
ℹ			code pal for ABAP	4	218	0
ℹ			Performance Checks	62	9	84
ℹ		⇨	Analysis of WHERE Condition for SELECT	0	0	0
ℹ		⇨	Analysis of WHERE Condition in UPDATE and DELETE	0	0	0
ℹ			SELECT Statements That Bypass the Table Buffer	0	6	0
ℹ		⇨	Search problematic SELECT * statements	9	1	1
ℹ		⇨	Search SELECT .. FOR ALL ENTRIES-clauses to be transformed	1	0	1
ℹ			Search SELECT statement with DELETE statement	23	0	1
ℹ		⇨	Search DB Operations in loops across modularization units	29	0	1
ℹ			Changing Database Accesses in Loops	0	0	0
ℹ		⇨	EXIT or no statement in SELECT...ENDSELECT loop	0	0	5
ℹ			SELECT Statements with Subsequent CHECK	0	0	0
ℹ		⇨	Low Performance Operations on Internal Tables	0	2	0
ℹ		⇨	Nested Sequential Accesses to Internal Tables	0	0	42

Figure 5-1. *Code inspector performance checks*

Secondary Indexes for Internal Tables

The concept of having secondary indexes on internal tables has been around for a very long time—over 15 years—and yet even now they are hardly ever used. The point is that you may have one internal table in your program that is accessed in several different ways—for example, it could be an internal table of sales order items that is accessed most of the time by getting a single record based on VBELN and POSNR. Thus, the table is defined as a hashed table with a unique key.

However, at various points in the program the table needs to be looped over using the reference document item—VGBEL and VGPOS. This would cause a full table scan, so the way around this is to define a secondary sorted index on the table with VGBEL and VGPOS as a non-unique key (as many rows have the same VGBEL/VGPOS values).

You can have as many secondary indexes on an internal table as you want—each new such index adds a bit of processing time when records are inserted, but if the internal table is likely to grow to a large size then the benefits of having every single read on that table use some sort of index cannot be overstated.

Runtime Checks

Once the application you are writing gets to the stage where data is being retrieved from the database and then displayed or processed in some way, you can perform runtime checks upon it to see how well it is performing.

In this section, you will start with an introduction to the ST05 transaction, which is the tool you use for this exercise. You will also see the specific problems that ST05 will highlight and how to handle them.

You will hear about three variants of the same problem—transferring more data from the database to the application server than is needed. These take the form of identical selects, reading more data from a given table than you actually need, and reading the same table multiple times.

The second half of the section will deal with specific issues that cannot be grouped together—problems with the FOR ALL ENTRIES method of database access, the poor design of custom database indexes, nested SELECT statements, and lastly "bad" joins on database tales.

ST05 in General

Where I work, we have a sequence of approvals a change has to go through before it even gets to test. The notable thing is that the developer doesn't just sign off that they have finished the development and are done with basic testing. They have to sign off that they have done all that *plus* a SQL trace.

Transaction ST05 is the go-to transaction for doing a SQL trace on one of your custom programs. You open up the application you are testing on one screen and the ST05 transaction on another screen. In ST05 you press the Activate Trace button and then run the transaction, and once it has finished you press Deactivate Trace and then Display Trace in ST05.

You could be running this trace on a new piece of code you have written or tracing an existing program because the end users have been complaining. In either case, a surefire sign of a problem is if as soon as you press Display Trace you see the pop-up shown in Figure 5-2.

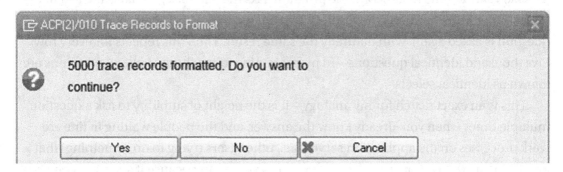

Figure 5-2. Very bad sign indeed

265

If you see that question presented to you, that is not good. Generally, no program should be doing so many database reads that the message is triggered. It is a sign of lots of little database reads in a loop or some such.

Sometimes if you say "yes" to the preceding question the whole transaction crashes because there is just so much data. What you should do is say "yes" just to see, and if everything blows up in your face then try again and say "no" the next time.

Once you are presented with a gigantic list of SQL statements, just do a bit of scrolling up and down at random, and the worst culprits will jump out at you and slap you in the face with a wet fish, screaming, "Here I am! Here I am! Doing as many database reads as I can!"

In the next few sections, you will see the sorts of problems that arise when doing an ST05 analysis and how to deal with them.

Identical SELECTS

The very first time I go into a new pub I usually ask the bar person their name and maybe some questions about what sort of special beers they have and maybe what they recommend from the menu. If I go up to the bar a further six times that evening, I certainly don't ask the exact same set of questions again. That would annoy the bar person to no end, and whilst they were answering me for the fifth time with the exact same answers as before they would be tied up and unable to serve the other ten people waiting in line.

We don't do that sort of strange behavior in real life, so why do we often write programs that do just that? Let us say we have some sort of report that lists sales orders. The end user asks for all the orders for customer XYZ for the month of May. It turns out there are five thousand such orders, so the program reads all of them out of VBAK/VBAP in one go and then runs round in a loop "decorating" the report with the values of fields not in VBAK/VBAP. For the first record, the program asks the database, "What is the text name of Customer XYZ?" and gets the result. When the second record is reached, the same question is asked again, with naturally the same result. Then this repeats for every row. Five thousand identical questions—in programming terms these identical questions are known as identical selects.

This is an exact match for my analogy—it is the height of stupidity to ask a question multiple times when you already know the answer, and the people waiting in line are work processes on the application server (i.e., other users trying to do something) that are getting held up because one report takes forever to run because it spends so much time asking the database pointless questions.

How to Spot the Problem

Thus, when presented with the SQL list from ST05, the very first thing you should do is take the menu option *Trace* ➤ *Value-Identical Selects*. When the list comes back, sort it in descending order based on the number in the "Total Number of Executions" column; the result looks like Figure 5-3.

Performance Analysis: Value-Identical Statements

Σ Executions	Σ Duration	ΣRec...	Dur./Exec.	Rec./Exec.	Dur./Rec.	Dur./Rec.	Lngth	Buffe...	Table Ty...	Object Name	Statement
7,239	55,99...	23...									
27	335,434	27	12,423	1.0	12,423	376	1,122		TRANSP	KLAH	SELECT WHERE "MANDT"=
27	15,180	0	562	0.0	562	0	0		TRANSP	AUFK, AFKO, A...	SELECT <JOIN> WHERE "
24	767,888	0	31,995	0.0	31,995	0	0		TRANSP	AUFK, AFKO, A...	SELECT <JOIN> WHERE "
21	12,134	0	578	0.0	578	0	0		TRANSP	AUFK, AFKO, A...	SELECT <JOIN> WHERE "
21	11,381	0	542	0.0	542	0	0		TRANSP	AUFK, AFKO, A...	SELECT <JOIN> WHERE "
18	11,125	0	618	0.0	618	0	0		TRANSP	AUFK, AFKO, A...	SELECT <JOIN> WHERE "
18	9,918	0	551	0.0	551	0	0		TRANSP	AUFK, AFKO, A...	SELECT <JOIN> WHERE "
18	7,443	0	414	0.0	414	0	0		TRANSP	LIKP, VBUK, LIPS	SELECT <JOIN> WHERE "
16	859,730	0	53,733	0.0	53,733	0	0		TRANSP	LIKP, VBUK, LIPS	SELECT <JOIN> WHERE "
16	13,308	0	832	0.0	832	0	0		TRANSP	AUFK, AFKO, A...	SELECT <JOIN> WHERE "
15	11,227	0	748	0.0	748	0	0		TRANSP	AUFK, AFKO, A...	SELECT <JOIN> WHERE "
15	9,882	0	659	0.0	659	0	0		TRANSP	AUFK, AFKO, A...	SELECT <JOIN> WHERE "
15	7,901	0	527	0.0	527	0	0		TRANSP	AUFK, AFKO, A...	SELECT <JOIN> WHERE "
14	5,637	0	403	0.0	403	0	0		TRANSP	LIKP, VBUK, LIPS	SELECT <JOIN> WHERE "
14	5,445	0	389	0.0	389	0	0		TRANSP	LIKP, VBUK, LIPS	SELECT <JOIN> WHERE "
12	7,747	0	646	0.0	646	0	0		TRANSP	AUFK, AFKO, A...	SELECT <JOIN> WHERE "
12	6,168	0	514	0.0	514	0	0		TRANSP	AUFK, AFKO, A...	SELECT <JOIN> WHERE "
12	5,391	0	449	0.0	449	0	0		TRANSP	LIKP, VBUK, LIPS	SELECT <JOIN> WHERE "
12	4,879	0	407	0.0	407	0	0		TRANSP	LIKP, VBUK, LIPS	SELECT <JOIN> WHERE "
10	9,013	0	901	0.0	901	0	0		TRANSP	LIKP, VBUK, LIPS	SELECT <JOIN> WHERE "
10	4,534	0	453	0.0	453	0	0		TRANSP	LIKP, VBUK, LIPS	SELECT <JOIN> WHERE "
10	4,206	0	421	0.0	421	0	0		TRANSP	LIKP, VBUK, LIPS	SELECT <JOIN> WHERE "
10	4,190	0	419	0.0	419	0	0		TRANSP	LIKP, VBUK, LIPS	SELECT <JOIN> WHERE "

Figure 5-3. *Lots of identical select statements*

Sometimes the number of identical selects can be in the hundreds, but really anything above two or three is bad. If there are none at all you can dance around the room with joy.

Strategies to Deal with the Problem

Taking the example of a customer name's being queried 5,000 times, there are several way to deal with this; we will take them from the least good approach to the best.

- You could add the customer name to the database query; i.e., join the customer master table KNA1 to the transactional tables VBAK/VBAP. That would work and avoid the identical selects, but that is not a good solution for technical reasons we will deal with at the end of this section.

- During the loop you could use internal buffering—either use a standard SAP function module like V_KNA1_SINGLE_READ or have your own code that stores the results of previous queries in an internal table and reads the table first to see if the answer is already there before going to the database. Note that some standard SAP functions have a really small buffer size. In this example, with 5,000 records for the same customer, this would work perfectly. With about 100 different customers there may be identical selects if the buffer size is less than 100.

- You could build up a list of customers based upon the results of the transactional database read, and then do a mass read to get all the names at once. Then, during the loop, the internal table is read rather than the database, and if you make that table a hashed table based on customer number all will be well.

Don't Make a Hash of Things

It's been over 20 years since sorted and hashed internal tables were introduced into ABAP, but sadly they are still not used very much. If an internal table exists for the sole purpose of getting individual records read one at a time, and that table has all the key fields of the underlying database table, then there is no logical reason at all *not* to define it as a hashed table.

Real-Life Example

Once upon a time whilst looking at an ST05 trace on a report, I noticed a vast number of identical selects on KNVP/KNA1. This turned out to be the program looking for details of a particular partner function—a so-called project—in a loop. The original programmer had had the foresight to create a buffer table to prevent a database read to get the name of the project multiple times after it had been found once. This is very common; you can see the code in Listing 5-5. If an entry exists in the buffer table, hooray, that is used, and otherwise off we go to the database.

Listing 5-5. Projects—Using Internal Buffering—V1

```
READ TABLE gt_proj INTO ls_proj
WITH KEY kunn2 = pa_kunnr.

IF sy-subrc = 0.
  pa_project = ls_proj-kunnr.
  pa_project_name = ls_proj-name1.
ELSE.
  SELECT kunn2 knvp~kunnr kna1~name1 UP TO 1 ROWS
    INTO (ls_proj-kunn2, ls_proj-kunnr, ls_proj-name1)
    FROM knvp
      INNER JOIN kna1
        ON knvp~kunnr = kna1~kunnr
      WHERE knvp~parvw = 'WE'
        AND knvp~kunn2 = pa_kunnr
        AND kna1~ktokd = 'ZPJT'.
  ENDSELECT.

  IF sy-subrc = 0.
    pa_project = ls_proj-kunnr.
    pa_project_name = ls_proj-name1.
    APPEND ls_proj TO gt_proj.
  ENDIF.
ENDIF.
```

Here is where the example gets really strange. The decision was made some years back by a business analyst that some delivery addresses (ship-tos, in SAP speak) would have "project" partner functions added for each one-off multi-year project.

So at that time, many years ago, the request came in to alter the report in question such that the project number and name were added to every line. All well and good, but no actual projects were created in the SAP system for the next three years. Every time the report was run in that period, which is a gigantic number of times a day by very many people, there were a large number of database reads looking for something that was just not there.

As a result, if there is no project, which was 100 percent of the time for three years, and even now that a few have been created is still the case the vast majority of the time, the buffering does not work. If you set a Z database table to have single-record buffering, then the system is clever enough to buffer negative results as well, avoiding identical selects, but in this example the programmer is coding the buffering themself.

I made two changes—I buffered the negative results to avoid identical selects, and also altered the internal table to be hashed to speed up the read on it, even if only by a microsecond. The end result can be seen in Listing 5-6.

Listing 5-6. Projects—Using Internal Buffering—V2

```
*-----------------------------------------------------------------------*
* NB 99.99999% of ship-tos do not have a project associated with them
* Thus it is quite important to buffer negative results
*-----------------------------------------------------------------------*

  CLEAR: pa_project, pa_project_name.

  READ TABLE gt_proj INTO DATA(ls_proj)
  WITH TABLE KEY kunn2 = pa_ship_to.

  IF sy-subrc = 0.
    pa_project      = ls_proj-kunnr.
    pa_project_name = ls_proj-name1.
    RETURN.
  ENDIF.

  SELECT kunn2 knvp~kunnr kna1~name1 UP TO 1 ROWS
    INTO (ls_proj-kunn2, ls_proj-kunnr, ls_proj-name1)
    FROM knvp
      INNER JOIN kna1
        ON knvp~kunnr = kna1~kunnr
      WHERE knvp~parvw = 'WE'
        AND knvp~kunn2 = pa_ship_to
        AND kna1~ktokd = 'ZPJT'.
  ENDSELECT.

  IF sy-subrc <> 0.
    "Buffer negative result
```

270

```
  ls_proj-kunn2 = pa_ship_to.
  INSERT ls_proj INTO TABLE gt_proj.
ELSE.
  pa_project        = ls_proj-kunnr.
  pa_project_name = ls_proj-name1.
  "Buffer positive result
  INSERT ls_proj INTO TABLE gt_proj.
ENDIF.
```

Stuttering

In the same way that you can waste both the program's time and the database's time by asking the exact same thing again in a loop, it is also possible to ask the same question dozens, perhaps hundreds, of times all at once in one single SQL statement. As might be imagined, the database does not like this either.

This problem is highlighted in the ST05 trace, but most people do not notice it, because they are not looking for it.

Let us say someone has read the database to get an internal table full of all the deliveries for the month to a particular location. Then a bit later in the program they need the header details of all the sales orders that were the "parents" of those deliveries.

In programming terms that is easy enough—the preceding document for a delivery lives in field LIPS-VGBEL, so you write something like Listing 5-7.

Listing 5-7. Getting All Related Entries

```
SELECT *
FROM VBAK
INTO parent_orders_header_data
FOR ALL ENTRIES IN delivery_list
WHERE VBELN EQ DELIVERY_LIST-VGBEL.
```

That works perfectly. If you debug and look at the result, you see you have a unique list of sales order headers; everything appears to have gone swimmingly. However, "under the hood" something is rotten in the State of Denmark.

If you look at the ST05 trace for such a query, at first glance everything looks normal. Such a query is broken into about five (depending on how your database is configured) reads at a time from the selection list, and each such group of five shows up as a separate line on the ST05 trace. Put another way, if the selection list contains two hundred values there will only be one database read called from the program, but that will show up as 40 lines on the ST05 trace, each line showing a query with five values.

Solving performance problems is detective work, and as any great detective will tell you the key to success is to look at something and to see not what you expect to see but rather what is *actually there*. Since human brains are basically hard-wired to do the former, great detectives are very rare and cunning criminals (in this case a bad SQL query) can hide things in plain sight and generally get away with the crime.

In this example, if you manage to look at the trace with "fresh eyes," you will see something like:

```
FROM VBAK WHERE (A1 = '1234' OR A1 = '1234' OR A1 = '1234' OR A1 = '1234')
```

This what I call "stuttering," as in, "I want to know what the value of X-X-X-X-X-X-X is!" In other words, the same value can appear in the query multiple times. You will only get one result back, but you are giving the database far more work than it needs to do.

What is happening here is that one sales order for (say) 1,000 tons of bananas can have 50 deliveries of 20 tons each. If your internal table of deliveries has every row referring to the same parent sales order, then the query will be in effect asking for the same header details 50 times.

What you need to do here is not to pass the results of the original query (in this example table DELIVERY_LIST) directly into the next query, but instead to build up a selection list of unique values. This can be seen in Listing 5-8; when the "for all entries" query is done there will be no multiple database requests for the same value.

Listing 5-8. Ensuring a Unique Selection List

```
DATA: lt_selection_table TYPE STANDARD TABLE OF sales_key.

CHECK delivery_list[] IS NOT INITIAL.

LOOP AT delivery_list
  ASSIGNING FIELD-SYMBOL(<delivery_data>).
  INSERT VALUE #(
  vbeln = <delivery_data>-vgbel )
  INTO TABLE lt_selection_table.
ENDLOOP.
```

```
SORT lt_selection_table BY vbeln.
DELETE ADJACENT DUPLICATES FROM lt_selection_table
COMPARING vbeln.

SELECT *
FROM vbak
  INTO parent_orders_header_data
  FOR ALL ENTRIES IN lt_selection_table
  WHERE vbeln EQ lt_selection_table-vbeln.
```

Asking Stupid Questions

If you were to ask a panel of scientists how many flying purple crocodiles there are in the Amazon basin, the vast majority of those scientists would tell you that (a) no crocodiles are purple and (b) none of them can fly, and thus the most common answer is "none." If you ask someone who doesn't know anything about crocodiles the same question the chances of getting an answer are even lower.

In the same way, if you asked a sports expert, "Who won the 100m women's sprint in the Olympics?" they would ask you "Which Olympics—what year?" and if you answered, "I don't know," then they would not be able to answer your question.

In both cases, those are stupid questions—not only will you not get an answer, but you are wasting the time of whomever it is you are asking. Hopefully we do not ask such questions in real life, but the programs we write might be doing just that.

The analogy to the flying crocodile question is (to follow on from our previous example) when we have a big list of deliveries and some of the predecessor documents were sales orders and some were schedule agreements, and the program queries all of those numbers against table VBAK. All the schedule agreement numbers will return no result, because schedule agreement header details do not live in table VBAK but rather table EKKO.

So at the same time you are making sure there are no duplicate VGBEL (predecessor document) entries you actually have to split them into two selection lists—sales orders for table VBAK and schedule agreements for table EKKO. That way, you can ask the right "person" the right question.

The analogy to the Olympics question is that some of the deliveries may have no predecessor document at all (that is possible in SAP). If you forgot to remove blank values from the selection list then you will be asking the database to give you the values for sales order number zero, which obviously does not exist. Ninety-nine times out of a hundred the database will be clever enough to treat that question with the contempt it deserves and return a null result in a fraction of a second. Sadly, I have seen cases—in production—where asking the database for a blank value causes it to have a nervous breakdown and do a full table scan looking for that blank value, which takes forever and usually causes a short dump.

It is rather like the famous case where someone kept getting letters from their credit card company saying they had an overdue balance of zero dollars and zero cents. After some months that letter threatened legal action if the balance was not paid. So the person in question wrote out and sent off a check for zero dollars and zero cents. That did in fact satisfy the credit card company computer, but caused the IT system of a major US bank to crash when it tried to process the check.

The moral of the story is to not pass in zero/null values to a query in fields where a value is always expected. Doing that sort of thing always ends in tears.

Reading More Data Than Needed

One of the "Golden Rules" of writing SQL queries is to minimize the amount of data transferred between the database and the application server. This applies even to the HANA database. Once again, I have some analogies.

The reason it takes so long for everyone to board a plane is that everyone has to go through the narrow entrance at the front one at a time. If all passengers could magically drop into their seats from above all at once, things would be a lot faster, but amazingly no one has found a way to make that happen yet.

Now imagine that all 400 passengers have finally gotten on the plane, and just before takeoff 399 of them decide they want to get off. You have the same problem as before, only in reverse, and the plane gets so delayed as a result it misses its flight window. The one remaining passenger has to wait another two hours on the tarmac for the next flight window.

This sort of thing hopefully does not happen on most flights, but most certainly happens virtually all the time in computer programs—I would say in almost all of them. Happily, it does not have to be this way.

There are three aspects to this: selecting more columns then you need, selecting more rows than you need, and existence checks.

Selecting More Columns Than You Need

Keeping with the airline analogy, if you wanted to fly from London to Paris you would not buy tickets for every single seat on the plane (at enormous cost to yourself) and then give all but one away to total strangers because you only in fact need one ticket. However, many programs do something very similar in that they do a SELECT *, which reads every single column from a database row.

Chances are, especially for very wide tables like VBAK and VBAP, there is no way in the world you are going to need all of those values. The code inspector is clever enough to actually look at your code and see how many values you actually do use. If you are doing a SELECT * and only use ten fields, you will get an error message like "Only 1% of fields used." You can drill into that message to find what fields are getting used, and then you can change the SELECT * into a SELECT with a list of just the fields that are actually needed.

Going back to the aircraft analogy, this has the effect of drastically reducing the number of passengers (fields) all trying to get on the aircraft (from the database to the application server) all at once, and thus the plane can take off a lot faster.

On a HANA database a SELECT * on a wide table is poison. This is because it is a column-based database as opposed to a row-based database, which is brilliant when you are just interested in a few columns, but the database goes into meltdown when you ask for three hundred columns at once.

Professor Hasso Plattner, one of the founders of SAP and inventor of HANA, once wore a T-shirt at the conference SAPPHIRE NOW that read "SELECT * is for Losers."

Selecting More Rows Than You Need

This is the analogy where 400 passengers get on the plane and then 399 get off just before takeoff. In a programming sense, this is where you do a database SELECT on a table and get back 400 rows from the database (i.e., 400 passengers have to go through the narrow entrance) and then do some checks on that retrieved data and decide you do not actually need 399 of those rows and so delete them from your internal table (they get off the plane).

The code inspector will warn you about this as well with the message "SELECT with subsequent DELETE," and when you drill into the message you will be shown the SELECT statement and where the rows are deleted later on.

There are three possible situations here: that behavior never made sense, that behavior used to make sense but does not anymore, and that behavior is sensible.

The Behavior Never Made Sense

This is where, for example, you select all the rows from VBAK created today and then 20 lines later decide to delete all the rows that are not sales orders (VBTYP <> 'C').

That makes no sense at all. In such a case, you should add the condition VBTYP <> 'C' to the WHERE clause in the SELECT statement, thus reducing the number of passengers getting on the plane at once. I have seen this sort of thing far too often.

The Behavior No Longer Makes Sense

Program logic is usually not as simple as checking for specific values in fields when doing a SELECT. Traditionally, the main reason we moved a load of data onto the application server and then did all sorts of tests and calculations within ABAP was because the options in a SQL query in ABAP were very limited.

This is no longer the case, starting with ABAP 7.40 and increasing at a rapid pace ever since a bucket load of new options were added to the ABAP SQL syntax (not to mention CDS Views and ABAP Managed Database Procedures); e.g., CASE statements within SQL queries. A lot of tasks you had to do in ABAP before can now be done on the database side.

This is partly due to SAP's no longer being database agnostic—if the only database the SAP system supports is HANA, then it no longer has to cater to the lowest common denominator of all supported databases—but mainly due to the new "Code Pushdown" paradigm where you are encouraged to let the database take as much of the programming strain as it can.

In this case, we want as much filtering logic as possible to take place on the database side to reduce the number of records coming back. There is no room here to list the million new features available in ABAP SQL, but suffice it to say you need to check if reading a record from the database and then deleting it later is being done, because while once that was the only technique possible, now it is not, so the database query needs to be changed.

Not New

The Code Pushdown idea is not as new as you might think. Even on a non-HANA database you can do this test. Write a test program that gets a million records back from the database and then adds up some value (quantity, say) in ABAP to get the total. Then write another one that uses the aggregate SUM function in the SQL query. Then compare performance. The second one will only return one record rather than a million and will be a great deal faster. That's Code Pushdown, and ABAP programmers have been doing that for ages.

The Behavior Makes Sense

No matter how many extra goodies SAP adds to the ABAP language, there are always going to be cases where you cannot perform all the filtering logic on the database prior to returning the records to the application server. There are always going to be exceptions to every rule, and sometimes the most logical thing to do is in fact to get more records than you need and then discard some later.

However, as the years go by and the ABAP language gets better and better, this category is going to get rarer and rarer.

Existence Checks

Imagine that you wanted to know if Fred Bloggs was on the plane. You would want to look at the passenger list to get a simple yes/no answer. You would not expect Fred Bloggs to actually get off the plane to prove to you he exists. You most certainly would not expect every single one of the passengers on the plane to disembark just to prove that one of them was Fred Bloggs.

In the same way, often you just want to know if a database record exists and could not care less about any of its contents. One example might be when you want to see whether a sales document is incomplete, and if it is highlight it in red on a report or something. If a sales document is incomplete in SAP then it will have at least one entry in table VBUV. So if you do not care why the document is incomplete, just that it is, armed with the document number you can go looking for a VBUV record.

The worst thing you could possibly do is a SELECT *, as in Listing 5-9

Listing 5-9. Getting All Records and Columns as an Existence Check

```
SELECT *
FROM VBUV
INTO INCOMPLETION_DETAILS
WHERE VBELN = CONTRACT_NUMBER.
```

That would be the equivalent of making everybody get off the plane, along with all their luggage. You have gotten all the column values in that row and are not going to do anything with them.

Traditionally, the best way to do an existence check would be the one shown in Listing 5-10.

Listing 5-10. Using COUNT as an Existence Check

```
SELECT COUNT( * )
FROM VBUV
WHERE VBELN = CONTRACT_NUMBER.
```

That way, SY-SUBRC is set to zero if any records exist and SY-DBCNT is set to the number of records in VBUV that match. However, you don't care about the latter, and so that is the equivalent of making Fred Bloggs get off the plane. However, that used to be the best way to do an existence check.

From ABAP 7.50 and up, however, there is a much better way (using @ABAP_TRUE), as can be seen in Listing 5-11.

Listing 5-11. Best Way to Do an Existence Check

```
SELECT @ABAP_TRUE
FROM VBUV UP TO 1 ROWS
INTO @DATA(RECORD_EXISTS)
WHERE VBELN = CONTRACT_NUMBER.
ENDSELECT.
```

In this case, no data at all is transferred between the database and the application server, just the yes/no result. That's a lot faster and is the equivalent of looking at the passenger list to see if Fred Bloggs is on it.

Multiple Reads on the Same Table

Yesterday, my wife sent me out to buy ten lemons from the supermarket. The shop is not very far away, maybe a five-minute walk to get there and a five-minute walk back (providing I don't stop at the pub on the way back). However, even if I did stop at the pub, that is a 40-minute round trip altogether.

But what if I decided to make ten trips to the supermarket and buy one lemon each time? The end result would be the same, but it would take over six hours, and I would be really drunk at the end having stopped off in the pub ten times.

You would hope that since more than 99 percent of programmers in such a situation would get all ten lemons in one go that they would apply the same logic to their programs. Sadly, that is often not the case. Just today I had to look at a program written only last month, and after a short while I burst into tears and screamed, "He is reading the database in a LOOP!"

To understand why I got so upset, let us look at three examples of "loopy" behavior.

Contract Example

In this example, I was doing an ST05 trace on an ALV report that produced a big list of sales orders based on whatever the user requested on the selection screen.

After noting the initial SQL query on VBAK/VBAP—which I was expecting and did not take very long at all—the next thing I noticed in the ST05 trace was a massive amount of reads on VBAK. I found the code that was doing this, and it was looping round a fairly large internal table doing a SELECT SINGLE each time, as shown in Listing 5-12.

Listing 5-12. Getting Contract Data in a Loop

```
SORT t_contract.
DELETE ADJACENT DUPLICATES FROM t_contract.

LOOP AT t_contract WHERE vbeln IS NOT INITIAL.
  SELECT SINGLE ktext INTO t_contract-ktext FROM  vbak
         WHERE  vbeln  = t_contract-vbeln.

  MODIFY t_contract INDEX sy-tabix.

ENDLOOP.
```

The good news was that the T_CONTRACT had been sorted and condensed such that there was only one entry per VBELN. Presumably the logic of not including the KTEXT in the main join was that not every sales order was created with reference to a contract.

The internal table T_CONTRACT only had two fields—VBELN and KTEXT—inside it. What I did here was replace the looping with a FOR ALL ENTRIES, so there would be only one request to the database. There will still be lots of lines in the ST05 trace, but a small fraction of what was there before. The revised code can be seen in Listing 5-13.

Listing 5-13. Getting the Contract Data All at Once

```
SORT t_contract.
DELETE ADJACENT DUPLICATES FROM t_contract.

* Now is the time for a self-referential SELECT as opposed to a SELECT in a
loop
SELECT vbeln ktext
  FROM vbak
  INTO CORRESPONDING FIELDS OF TABLE t_contract
  FOR ALL ENTRIES IN t_contract
  WHERE vbeln EQ t_contract-vbeln
  ORDER BY PRIMARY KEY.
```

That's a quick fix. Going forward, I could do a test to see if a LEFT OUTER JOIN in the main SELECT statement would (probably) be faster than just looking for contracts you know exist. When you encounter this sort of thing, it's well worth experimenting to work out which is faster.

Partner Function Example

In one system I was analyzing at some point in the past, it was decided by a business analyst that some sales documents could have different "bill-tos" (KUNRG) and "payers" (KUNRE) than the actual customer (KUNNR). Again, all well and good, no doubt a valid business requirement. One customer was set up this way, and thus it remained for many years.

The development department was told to add the bill-to and payer numbers and names to an ALV report. The programmer assigned thought the easiest way to do this was to pick somewhere the program was looping over the main output internal table and add in two database reads from VBPA: one for the RE function and one for the RG function (i.e., doing repeated database reads inside a loop).

As mentioned earlier, doing lots of database selects in a loop is bad, so the obvious next step was to move the selection on VBPA outside the loop such that all the RE and RG data was retrieved at once; however, before I did that I was struck by another idea.

What I wanted to know was if the partner function table—VBPA—was being read elsewhere in that same program. It turned out that there were two separate reads on VBPA—all at once for PERNR using a FOR ALL ENTRIES based on a list of sales orders, and then one by one in a loop for RG and RE. Going back to the aircraft analogy, going to query the same database table twice in different areas of the same program is like all the passengers getting on the plane, then all getting off again, and then all getting back on.

The obvious solution was to move the RG/RE reads into the initial read on VBPA, thus getting all three partners at once.

Whilst I was doing that, I also encountered some very strange code that, in effect, added a few extra random values to the list of partner functions getting read from the database query on VBPA. That code had been there forever, and no one had ever questioned it. Since the random values were not valid partner functions, nothing had ever been returned. So I got rid of that code. There was probably a purpose for it originally, a purpose that obviously failed, and someone signed off on it as working anyway, but since the change was so very long ago, and not documented anywhere, getting rid of it could have no downside.

The moral of the story is to check the number of records returned in ST05—if it is always zero, no matter what, then the code needs some serious analysis.

Shipment Cost Example

Many times in the past I have had the BASIS people tell me that a batch job was still running after 16 hours, and ask if that was normal. Obviously not—nothing should ever take that long. The IT department decided to have the expected runtime be part of the batch job name; e.g., a suffix like _H01 for one hour or _M05 for five minutes.

Due to this, the nature of how BASIS reported the problem to me changed. One day, I was told a batch job that started at three o'clock every morning was taking five hours to run and was thus having negative effects when the vast bulk of users logged on (which was at seven o'clock every morning). The batch job name ended with _M10, so something must be wrong; i.e., it should only take ten minutes, not five hours. If the batch job name had ended with _H05 they would have let it be.

As it transpired, I had written the original program and many years ago had based the ten-minute estimate on how long it usually ran in production. Tying up one work process for ten minutes at 3 a.m. had seemed a safe thing to do. So the question became—what had caused the runtime to balloon out from ten minutes to five hours?

The nature of the program was to loop over a huge number of shipment costs and make assorted FI/CO postings if need be, based on incredibly complicated logic. Naturally, there is no business logic so complicated that it cannot be made even more complicated from time to time, and that is what had happened in this case.

The new rule needed data from three tables—LFA1 (Vendor Master), LIPS (Delivery Item), and VBAP (Sales Order Item). The programmer who implemented the change had a crystal-clear understanding of the new business requirement and implemented it perfectly. From a functional point of view, this was 100 percent successful. From a performance point of view, clearly not so.

Listing 5-14 is the code after the change. It is aiming to get data from four tables: LFA1, VBKD, LIPS, and VBAP. As you look at the code, you may think to yourself, "One of these things is not like the others," and how right you would be. Extra information routine GET_VENDOR reads LFA1 (using the standard SAP buffer module), and routine GET_TRUCK_TYPE reads LIPS (using a standard buffer module) to get the order item that spawned the delivery, and then reads VBAP (using a standard buffer module) to get the sales order item detail. The ALL_COSTS table has 300,000 records. So, can you spot the problem?

Listing 5-14. Code That Worked but Ruined the Program's Performance

```
LOOP AT all_costs.
* Get SAPG's
   PERFORM get_vendor USING    all_costs-tdlnr
                      CHANGING all_costs-dlgrp.
* Set pricelist type
   READ TABLE lt_vbkd INTO ls_vbkd
   WITH TABLE KEY vbeln COMPONENTS vbeln = all_costs-vbeln.
   IF sy-subrc = 0.
     all_costs-pltyp = ls_vbkd-pltyp.
   ENDIF.
```

```
    "Get Truck Type
    PERFORM get_truck_type USING     all_costs-vbeln
                           CHANGING all_costs-zzvtype.

    MODIFY all_costs.
  ENDLOOP.
```

Having so many records using the buffering module did not help at all—very rarely were the values being queried the same. Moreover, a lot of the "sales order" numbers queried are actually schedule agreements (the "stupid question" problem discussed earlier) and so never returned a result but caused database overhead nonetheless.

Silly Comment

The German acronym DLGRP translates to "Service Agent Procedure Group." The comment in Listing 5-14 does not in fact explain this—or what such a concept means—but instead translates the meaningless German acronym into a meaningless English acronym (SAPG).

I managed to get this back down from five hours to ten minutes. It wasn't even all that difficult—if you look at Listing 5-14 you will see the clue is the read on an internal table full of VBKD values, an internal table with a TABLE KEY thus optimized for fast access. Reading such an internal table during a loop is a zillion billion times faster than doing a database read for each row.

Since access to VBKD was already optimized, the next step was to extend such optimization to the other three tables. First came the access to LFA1. In Listing 5-15, I built up a unique list of vendors from the huge table and then only retrieved the two fields of interest—the key and the "DLGRP."

Listing 5-15. Getting All the Vendor Data in One Hit

```
FORM fill_vendor_buffer.
* Local Variables
  DATA: lr_lifnr TYPE RANGE OF lfa1-lifnr.

* Preconditions
  CHECK all_costs[] IS NOT INITIAL.
```

```abap
REFRESH ilfa1.

LOOP AT all_costs
ASSIGNING FIELD-SYMBOL(<ls_all_costs>) WHERE tdlnr IS NOT INITIAL.
  INSERT VALUE #(
  option = 'EQ'
  sign   = 'I'
  low    = <ls_all_costs>-tdlnr ) INTO TABLE lr_lifnr.
ENDLOOP.

IF lr_lifnr[] IS INITIAL.
  RETURN.
ELSE.
  SORT lr_lifnr BY low.
  DELETE ADJACENT DUPLICATES FROM lr_lifnr COMPARING ALL FIELDS.
ENDIF.

PERFORM message USING 'Get Haulier Vendor Data'(028).

* LFA1–Primary Key = LIFNR
SELECT lifnr dlgrp
  FROM lfa1
  INTO CORRESPONDING FIELDS OF TABLE ilfa1
  WHERE lifnr IN lr_lifnr.

IF sy-subrc NE 0.
  RETURN.
ENDIF.

ENDFORM.
```

The internal table storing the vendor data is hashed, so reading entries back from it will be lightning fast. Next came optimizing the reads on LIPS/VBAP. I know a little bit about the SAP data model, so I know that if a row in table VFKP (shipment costs) has the field VKORG (sales organization) blank, then there is no sales order involved. The moral of this story is that every ABAP programmer should become familiar with what the data in the underlying database tables looks like for different business scenarios.

Thus armed, I built up a unique list of shipment costs that relate to sales orders (i.e., have a VKORG). Then, instead of getting every field of LIPS in a loop, and then using that to get every field in VBAP in that same loop, and then only making use of one solitary field from VBAP, I did a join on LIPS and VBAP and returned the bare minimum of information; i.e., the delivery number and the associated VBAP field I was interested in. The result can be seen in Listing 5-16.

Listing 5-16. Joining LIPS and VBAP as Opposed to Reading in a Loop

```
FORM fill_truck_type_buffer.
* Local Variables
  DATA: lr_vbeln TYPE RANGE OF likp-vbeln,
        ld_first TYPE lips-posnr VALUE '000010'.

  "VKORG indicates a sales order based delivery
  LOOP AT all_costs
  ASSIGNING FIELD-SYMBOL(<ls_all_costs>) WHERE vkorg IS NOT INITIAL.
    INSERT VALUE #(
    option = 'EQ'
    sign   = 'I'
    low    = <ls_all_costs>-vbeln ) INTO TABLE lr_vbeln.
  ENDLOOP.

  IF lr_vbeln[] IS INITIAL.
    RETURN.
  ENDIF.

  SORT lr_vbeln BY low.
  DELETE ADJACENT DUPLICATES FROM lr_vbeln COMPARING ALL FIELDS.

  PERFORM message USING 'Get Truck Type Data'(032).

* LIPS–Primary Key = VBELN / POSNR
* VBAP–Primary Key = VBELN / POSNR
  SELECT lips~vbeln
         vbap~zzvtype
    INTO CORRESPONDING FIELDS OF TABLE gt_truck_types
    FROM lips
    INNER JOIN vbap
```

```
  ON  lips~vgbel = vbap~vbeln
  AND lips~vgpos = vbap~posnr
  WHERE lips~vbeln IN lr_vbeln
  AND   lips~posnr EQ ld_first.

IF sy-subrc NE 0.
  RETURN.
ENDIF.

ENDFORM.
```

All that remained was to change the main loop such that the buffer tables are read using hashed internal tables instead of lots of single selects on each loop pass. To add some icing on the cake and make this just a little bit faster, I changed the main loop so that a field symbol is used as opposed to a work area. The result is shown in Listing 5-17.

Listing 5-17. Reading from Internal Tables, Not the Database

```
LOOP AT all_costs ASSIGNING FIELD-SYMBOL(<ls_all_costs>).
  "Get SAPG's
  PERFORM get_vendor USING     <ls_all_costs>-tdlnr
                     CHANGING <ls_all_costs>-dlgrp.

  "Get pricelist type
  READ TABLE lt_vbkd INTO DATA(ls_vbkd)
  WITH TABLE KEY vbeln COMPONENTS vbeln = <ls_all_costs>-vbeln.
  IF sy-subrc = 0.
    <ls_all_costs>-pltyp = ls_vbkd-pltyp.
  ENDIF.

  "Get Truck Type
  READ TABLE gt_truck_types INTO DATA(ls_truck_types)
  WITH TABLE KEY vbeln = <ls_all_costs>-vbeln.
  IF sy-subrc EQ 0.
    <ls_all_costs>-zzvtype = ls_truck_types-zzvtype.
  ENDIF.

ENDLOOP.
```

After that change went into production, the runtime decreased from five hours to ten minutes. You can't always achieve these sorts of performance improvements, but when you do you feel great and people will think you are a miracle worker. The downside, of course, is that from that point on you will be expected to fix every single performance problem anywhere in the system as soon as someone reports it.

Using FOR ALL ENTRIES

In the previous example, you saw the common trick of using the contents of one internal table to build up a selection list—i.e., a list of the database keys of whatever it is you are interested in—and then using that selection list in a FOR ALL ENTRIES (hereafter FAE) query on one or more different database tables. In effect, you are saying to the database, "Give me certain information about every sales order (or whatever) on this list."

In the real world, if you walked into a library and said to the librarian, "Can you please lend me all the books on this list," and then handed the librarian an empty list, they would get puzzled and tell you not to be so stupid and not give you any books.

However, if the ABAP runtime were the librarian, you would be given every single book in the library. That is because a blank FAE is interpreted as "give me everything." This is an obvious bug and makes no semantic sense at all.

Some people say, "Oh, this is just like an empty SELECT-OPTION—if that is left blank you get everything as well." I say that comparison is nonsense—a SELECT-OPTION is an *exclusion*—if you leave it blank you are saying exclude nothing, whereas with a blank FAE it is an *inclusion*—i.e., include nothing. Thus, instead of being the same thing they are in fact polar opposites.

I stand by my assertion that the FAE behavior for a blank list is a bug. Moreover, SAP refuses to fix it, and they (in the form of Horst Keller, who writes the ABAP documentation) have even told me why SAP will not fix it. Prior to S/4HANA and ABAP in the Cloud, every new ABAP release had to be downward compatible with lower releases. Thus, there was the remote possibility that some programs were actually relying on the buggy behavior of FAE, and if it were suddenly fixed the program would start behaving differently.

I would say that not only does nobody in the entire universe rely on the bug in FAE, but on the contrary there are tens of thousands of programs hat don't work properly because of this bug, and they could all be fixed overnight. However, that is never going to happen, so you must always manually check that the selection table is not empty. The code inspector will tell you if no such check exists.

Having just said that nobody relies on the bug in FAE, I will now give an example of some code that worked *because* of the bug—but was in fact an accident waiting to happen.

Look at the code in Listing 5-18 and see if you can spot the error.

Listing 5-18. Code with an Error

```
DATA: lt_tesys_down   TYPE STANDARD TABLE OF zsd_tesys_down.
DATA: lt_bzirk        TYPE STANDARD TABLE OF ltyp_bzirk.

* get all dispatch groups
SELECT * FROM  zsd_tesys_down INTO TABLE lt_tesys_down.

CHECK sy-subrc EQ 0.

* now get all the plants
* get the concrete plants that supply the dispatch group.
SELECT werks bzirk geo_x geo_y plant_type tolling_type
       vkorg prim_pion_plant
  FROM  zt001w INTO TABLE gt_werks
  FOR ALL ENTRIES IN lt_tesys_down
       WHERE   plant_type      IN ('A','B')   "agg/concrete
       AND     plant_category  IN ('1','2')   "agg/concrete
       AND     pioneer_plant   = 'X'
       AND     bzirk           = lt_tesys_down-bzirk.

* add tolling plants-concrete
SELECT werks bzirk explant vkorg
       FROM zt001w_tolling ##too_many_itab_fields
       INTO CORRESPONDING FIELDS OF TABLE gt_tolling
       FOR ALL ENTRIES IN lt_bzirk
       WHERE bzirk = lt_bzirk-bzirk.
```

The bug is not that difficult to spot—the table LT_BZIRK is declared but at no point is it filled. Thus, when that table is used, the selection list is empty and every record from the target table is retrieved.

However, this code worked fine—but it was "programming by accident." It turns out it was important that the GT_TOLLING table had a record for every BZIRK in the LT_TESYS_DOWN table. Since GT_TOLLING had every single record in the database table, naturally it had all the required records (and a lot more besides, which it did not need).

The "accident waiting to happen" bit is because at some point in the future someone might decide to actually put some entries in LT_BZIRK, and they would have no clue that this would make everything fall down in a heap because the correct functioning of the program is 100 percent dependent on a hidden bug.

The change I made, which you can see in Listing 5-19, is not so much a fix (because the program already worked) as a refactoring—the behavior of the program is unchanged, but now it is much more obvious what is going on, and the code is more resilient to future changes.

Listing 5-19. Code with the Error Fixed

```
DATA: lt_tesys_down   TYPE STANDARD TABLE OF zsd_tesys_down.

* get all dispatch groups
SELECT * FROM  zsd_tesys_down INTO TABLE lt_tesys_down.

CHECK sy-subrc EQ 0.

* now get all the plants
* get the concrete plants that supply the dispatch group.
SELECT werks bzirk geo_x geo_y plant_type tolling_type
       vkorg prim_pion_plant
  FROM  zt001w INTO TABLE gt_werks
  FOR ALL ENTRIES IN lt_tesys_down
      WHERE  plant_type     IN ('A','B')    "agg/concrete
      AND    plant_category IN ('1','2')    "agg/concrete
      AND    pioneer_plant  = 'X'
      AND    bzirk          = lt_tesys_down-bzirk.

* add tolling plants—concrete
SELECT werks bzirk explant vkorg
       FROM zt001w_tolling ##too_many_itab_fields
       INTO CORRESPONDING FIELDS OF TABLE gt_tolling
       FOR ALL ENTRIES IN lt_tesys_down
       WHERE bzirk = lt_tesys_down-bzirk.
```

In Listing 5-19, I get rid of LT_BZIRK altogether and use the same selection table for both database reads; that way, they will always be in synch.

The recommendation is that if something is working by accident, change things such that it works explicitly. If it had turned out that every single record in the target table was needed, then rather than rely on a blank selection table I would have just removed all the selection conditions and given a direct explicit instruction to read in the whole table.

FAE in HANA

In a HANA database the FAE problem goes away because it works as follows: You have a selection table with a hundred sales orders in it. You do a FAE on VBAK/VBAP. The HANA database actually creates a new temporary database table with one hundred rows, fills it with the selection table, and calls it XXXX or something. It then does an INNER JOIN on VBAK/VBAP/XXXX. That way, you only have one line on the SQL trace, and it is a zillion times faster. The book *ABAP Programming for HANA* describes tons of little tricks like that which HANA does.

Indexes

In a HANA database, generally you don't need indexes of any sort—but sometimes you do! There is no hard and fast rule, sadly. In all other databases that SAP supports, the use of indexes is always vital.

In this section, you will read about three topics all in regard to using the correct index when reading database tables. First, you'll see a tip about how to make it obvious whether every SQL statement is using an index or not, and then you'll review two related topics—why it is really important to always supply the first field in an index when doing a database select, and then an exception to that rule!

Indexes: Always Using One

In the checklist I drew up for myself in the days before the code inspector even existed, I put the following entry:

> *"Make sure every database SELECT uses an index—and state which index is going to be used as a comment in the line before the SELECT statement."*

Doing this forces you to think about performance with every single SELECT statement you write, and also makes your intention clear to someone coming along afterward to optimize the query (if performance problems in production have been identified, for example).

I also wanted to include the nature of the table being queried (e.g., is it a fully buffered table?) as well as the primary-key fields. It gets a bit tedious having to manually look that up and copy it into a comment before the SELECT statement, so being a good (i.e., lazy) programmer, I decided to automate the process.

Surprisingly, many ABAP programmers don't know you can define your own "patterns" that can be inserted into programs. Patterns were originally intended for something like adding a copyright notice at the start of every program; i.e., you could automatically insert the same bunch of comments into a program every time with the press of a button. To define your own pattern, call up transaction SE38, and when you are inside a program take the menu option *Utilities ➤ More Utilities ➤ Edit Pattern ➤ Create Pattern*.

I wanted to create a pattern to automatically describe the key fields and buffering attributes of any given database table, so I called the pattern ZTABLEKEY and defined it with one (seemingly very strange) line of code, as shown in the very short Listing 5-20.

Listing 5-20. What Is This Strange Command? It's a MUSTERY!

```
*$&$MUSTER
```

MUSTER? What in the world does that mean? Are we talking about Herman Munster? What this actually means is that a function module with a similar name to the pattern name is going to be called whenever you try to insert the pattern.

The function module has the words _EDITOR_EXIT after the pattern name, so in this case it is going to be called ZTABLEKEY_EDITOR_EXIT. That function module needs to have a very specific interface, otherwise you will get a short dump when the ABAP editor tries to call it dynamically. The interface must be that shown in Listing 5-21.

Listing 5-21. Interface Definition for a Pattern Function Module

```
*"----------------------------------------------------------------
*"*"Local interface:
*"  TABLES
*"      BUFFER TYPE  RSWSOURCET
```

```
*"  EXCEPTIONS
*"       CANCELLED
*"----------------------------------------------------------------------
```

The BUFFER parameter is an internal table of strings. Inside the function module you fill that internal table with whatever you want, and the result is returned to the ABAP editor and inserted as a comment.

In the code in Listing 5-22, I am doing the following:

- Asking the user (programmer) to type in a table name

- Querying the database to see if that table is buffered at all and, if so, what sort of buffering is defined

- Querying the database to see what the key fields of the table are

Listing 5-22. Function to Insert Comment Describing Key Fields of a Database Table

```
FUNCTION ZTABLEKEY_EDITOR_EXIT.
*"----------------------------------------------------------------------
*"*"Local interface:
*"  TABLES
*"       BUFFER TYPE   RSWSOURCET
*"  EXCEPTIONS
*"       CANCELLED
*"----------------------------------------------------------------------
* Local Variables
  DATA: lt_sval    TYPE STANDARD TABLE OF sval  WITH HEADER LINE,
        lt_ddo3l   TYPE STANDARD TABLE OF ddo3l WITH HEADER LINE,
        ls_ddo9l   TYPE ddo9l,
        ld_string TYPE string.

  lt_sval-tabname    = 'DDO2L'.
  lt_sval-fieldname = 'TABNAME'.
  APPEND lt_sval.
```

```abap
CALL FUNCTION 'POPUP_GET_VALUES'
  EXPORTING
    popup_title     = 'Enter Table Name'
  TABLES
    fields          = lt_sval
  EXCEPTIONS
    error_in_fields = 1
    OTHERS          = 2.

IF sy-subrc <> 0.
  RETURN.
ENDIF.

READ TABLE lt_sval INDEX 1.

CHECK lt_sval-value IS NOT INITIAL.

SELECT SINGLE * FROM dd09l
  INTO ls_dd09l
  WHERE tabname EQ lt_sval-value.

CHECK sy-subrc = 0.

CONCATENATE '*' lt_sval-value INTO buffer SEPARATED BY space.

IF ls_dd09l-bufallow = 'X'."Buffering Switched On
  CASE ls_dd09l-pufferung.
    WHEN 'X'.
      ld_string = 'Fully Buffered'.
    WHEN 'P'.
      ld_string = 'Single Record Buffering'.
    WHEN 'G'.
      ld_string = 'Generic Buffering'.
    WHEN OTHERS.
* Should never happen
  ENDCASE.
ENDIF.
```

```
IF ld_string IS NOT INITIAL.
  CONCATENATE buffer ld_string INTO buffer SEPARATED BY '-'.
ENDIF.

SELECT * FROM dd03l
  INTO CORRESPONDING FIELDS OF TABLE lt_dd03l
  WHERE tabname    EQ lt_sval-value
  AND   keyflag    EQ 'X'
  AND   fieldname NE 'MANDT'.

SORT lt_dd03l BY position.

IF lt_dd03l[] IS NOT INITIAL.
  CONCATENATE buffer 'Primary Key =' INTO buffer
  SEPARATED BY '-'.
ENDIF.

LOOP AT lt_dd03l.
  IF sy-tabix = 1.
    CONCATENATE buffer
  lt_dd03l-fieldname INTO buffer SEPARATED BY space.
  ELSE.
    CONCATENATE buffer
    lt_dd03l-fieldname INTO buffer SEPARATED BY ' / '.
  ENDIF.
ENDLOOP.

  APPEND buffer.

ENDFUNCTION.
```

The end result is a comment that says the table name, followed by buffering information, followed by a list of the key fields.

Say I was doing a SELECT on the plant master data table T001W. I would put my cursor on the blank line before the SELECT statement, press the Pattern button at the top of the screen, and then in the "Other Pattern" box at the bottom of the pop-up that appears enter ZTABLEKEY and press Enter. In the next pop-up box, I would enter T001W and presto!—a comment is inserted into my code as follows:

* T001W–Generic Buffering–Primary Key = WERKS

Indexes: Missing the First Field

The code in Listing 5-23 does not say what index is being used and what fields are in that index, which is most likely what caused the problem I want you to try to spot.

The index on the Z table being read starts with DOCUMENT_TYPE/VBELN/POSNR. Have a look at Listing 5-23 and see what is wrong.

Listing 5-23. Something Is Missing

```
FORM check_ptmover_ride .
  LOOP AT SCREEN.
    IF screen-name = 'T_VBAP-ZZBATCH_CODE' AND
       t_vbap-zzbatch_code IS NOT INITIAL.
     DATA: lf_no_over_rides  TYPE abap_bool.
     DATA(lo_ptm) = NEW zcl_vc_ptm_over_rides( ).
     SELECT SINGLE * INTO @DATA(ls_ptm_over_rides)
        FROM ztvc_ptm_overide
        WHERE vbeln = @t_vbap-vbeln
        AND   posnr = @t_vbap-posnr.
     IF sy-subrc = 0.
       lf_no_over_rides =
       lo_ptm->has_no_over_rides( ls_ptm_over_rides ).
     ELSE.
       CHECK t_vbap-vgbel IS NOT INITIAL AND
             t_vbap-vgpos IS NOT INITIAL.
       SELECT SINGLE * INTO ls_ptm_over_rides
         FROM ztvc_ptm_overide
         WHERE vbeln = t_vbap-vgbel
         AND   posnr = t_vbap-vgpos.
     ENDIF.
    ENDIF.
  ENDLOOP.
```

You have probably worked it out already—the first field (document type) of the index is not being used in the selection condition in either read on the Z table. That means the index will be ignored, and most likely a full table scan will be done.

What is criminal about this example (as always, a real-life example) is that the program knew what the VGTYP (SAP speak for document type) was—because the T_VBAP table only contains sales order items—thus, in the first read the document is always a sales order (VGTYP = C). For the second read, table VBAP has a special field saying what the reference type of the predecessor document is, VGTYP. Adding the first field of the index to the selection conditions made a huge performance improvement—the changed code can be seen in Listing 5-24.

Listing 5-24. Adding the First Field of the Index

```
FORM check_ptmover_ride.
  LOOP AT SCREEN.
    IF screen-name = 'T_VBAP-ZZBATCH_CODE' AND
       t_vbap-zzbatch_code IS NOT INITIAL.
      DATA: lf_no_over_rides TYPE abap_bool.
      DATA(lo_ptm) = NEW zcl_vc_ptm_over_rides( ).
* Check for overrides at the ORDER level
* ZTVC_PTM_OVERIDE-Single Record Buffering-
Primary Key = DOCUMENT_TYPE / VBELN / POSNR
        SELECT SINGLE *
           INTO @DATA(ls_ptm_over_rides)
           FROM  ztvc_ptm_overide
           WHERE document_type EQ 'C'
           AND    vbeln = @t_vbap-vbeln
           AND    posnr = @t_vbap-posnr.
        IF sy-subrc = 0.
          lf_no_over_rides =
          lo_ptm->has_no_over_rides( ls_ptm_over_rides ).
        ELSE.
    "Check for overrides at REFERENCE DOCUMENT level
    CHECK t_vbap-vgbel IS NOT INITIAL AND t_vbap-vgpos IS NOT INITIAL.
        SELECT SINGLE *
           INTO  ls_ptm_over_rides
           FROM  ztvc_ptm_overide
           WHERE document_type = t_vbap-vgtyp
```

```
    AND    vbeln       = t_vbap-vgbel
    AND    posnr       = t_vbap-vgpos.
  IF sy-subrc = 0.
```

Indexes: SKIP SCAN

You are probably going to think I am the world's maddest madman, madder even than Jock McMadman, the Mad Scotsman, winner of the All Scotland Madness competition ten years running, because in the previous section I was going on about how important it is to always use the first field in an index and I am now going to say it doesn't matter all that much—at least in some circumstances.

One fine day, I found an index had been created on the standard SAP "Change Header" table—CDHDR; you can see the index definition in Figure 5-4. Note that "Username" is the first (proper) field.

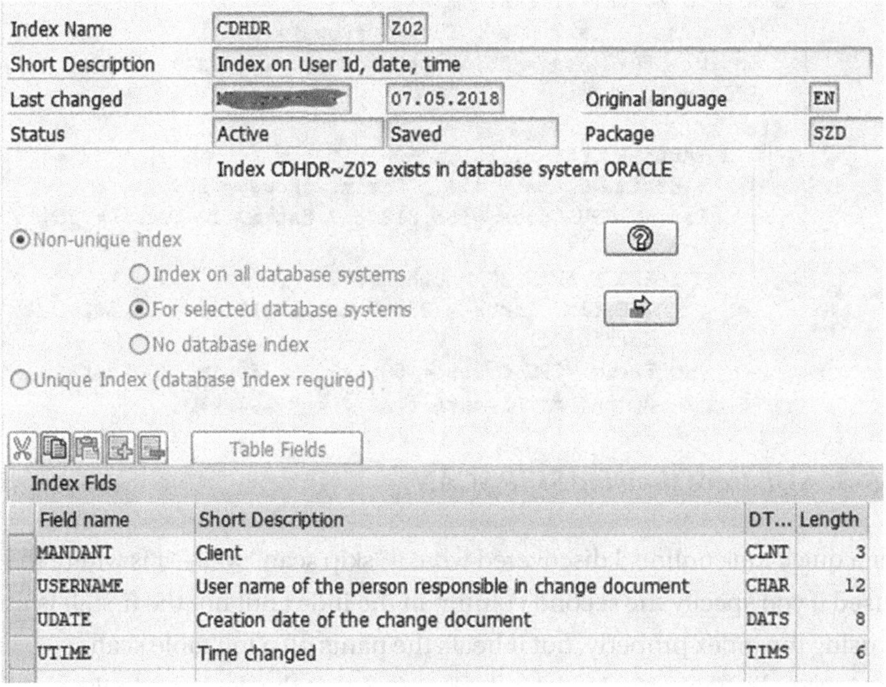

Index Name	CDHDR	Z02		
Short Description	Index on User Id, date, time			
Last changed	▓▓▓▓▓▓	07.05.2018	Original language	EN
Status	Active	Saved	Package	SZD

Index CDHDR~Z02 exists in database system ORACLE

⦿ Non-unique index
    ○ Index on all database systems
    ⦿ For selected database systems
    ○ No database index
○ Unique Index (database Index required)

Table Fields

Index Flds

Field name	Short Description	DT...	Length
MANDANT	Client	CLNT	3
USERNAME	User name of the person responsible in change document	CHAR	12
UDATE	Creation date of the change document	DATS	8
UTIME	Time changed	TIMS	6

Figure 5-4. Index on CDHDR

As might be imagined, in a productive system the number of records in table CDHDR would be truly gigantic. As a result, a full table scan would always result in a "time out" dump. Imagine my surprise when I ran transaction SE16 on the CDHDR table with the only selection criteria being database field UDATE with a value of today. Since that field is not the primary key or the first field of any index, I expected a "time out" dump. Instead, the results came back almost at once.

That puzzled me greatly, so I did a SQL trace on the SE16 query; the result can be seen in Figure 5-5.

```
Existing Plan Hash Values with Parse Timestamps:
───────────────────────────────────────────────────────────
424869326 09.JAN.2021 07:50:39 v$sql_plan
───────────────────────────────────────────────────────────
SELECT STATEMENT ( Estimated Costs = 372 , Estimated #Rows = 200 )
    │
    └─▣ 4 VIEW
    │     ( Estim. Costs = 372 , Estim. #Rows = 200 )
    │     Estim. CPU-Costs = 58,812,657 Estim. IO-Costs = 354
    │     Filter Predicates
    │
    └───▣ 3 WINDOW NOSORT STOPKEY
    │        ( Estim. Costs = 371 , Estim. #Rows = 200 )
    │        Estim. CPU-Costs = 58,812,657 Estim. IO-Costs = 354
    │        Filter Predicates
    │
    └────▣ 2 TABLE ACCESS BY INDEX ROWID CDHDR
    │          ( Estim. Costs = 371 , Estim. #Rows = 200 )
    │          Estim. CPU-Costs = 58,812,657 Estim. IO-Costs = 354
    │
    └──────1 INDEX SKIP SCAN CDHDR~Z02
              ( Estim. Costs = 351 , Estim. #Rows = 21,682 )
              Search Columns: 2
              Estim. CPU-Costs = 58,649,358 Estim. IO-Costs = 334
              Access Predicates Filter Predicates
```

Figure 5-5. *SQL trace showing SKIP SCAN*

After a quick look online, I discovered what a "skip scan" was—it is where the index can be used if you specify the second column in the index but not the first. It is not as good as using the index properly, but it beats the pants off a full table scan.

What is actually happening "under the hood" is that the database looks to see how many values exist for the first field in the index—"username," in this case. Let us say it finds five hundred different values for "username" in the table. The database then proceeds (internally) to do 500 different scans—one with User A and the specified date, one with User B and the specified date, and so on. Since the combination of those two fields is incredibly selective, the five hundred queries take a very short time. You only see the one query in the ST05 trace; the five hundred different queries are done deep inside the database.

So the advice to always specify the first field still stands. In the preceding example, specifying the username and date would be five hundred times faster than just specifying the date alone, but if you really do not know the value of the first field in the index and there is a relatively limited number of possible values for that first field, then the database will try to help you out by doing a skip scan. As might be imagined, if the first field is something like VBELN with ten million different possible values, a skip scan is not going to help at all.

Nested SELECTs

Earlier in the chapter, you heard about geometric loops on internal tables and how to avoid potential performance problems with nested loops; i.e., a LOOP within a LOOP within a LOOP.

There is only one thing worse than the geometric runtime progression caused by the incorrect usage of nested loops on internal tables—and that is any sort of nested loop on database tables.

As you know, you can either do a SELECT all in one go or you can do a SELECT/ENDSELECT construct where one database row at a time is returned. You can write all sorts of code using the data in that row, and then when the ENDSELECT is reached the process starts again with the next row until all required values have been returned. It's like looping over an internal table with a work area, but in this case the work area is a read-only database row.

I never, ever use the latter unless I am also using the UP TO 1 ROWS addition. This is quite a common scenario—I don't know all the values for the primary key of the table, but any row with the values that I do know will meet my program's need.

Going back to the aircraft analogy, a SELECT all in one go opens the aircraft door, then lets all required passengers (records) through, then closes the door. A SELECT/ENDSELECT loop opens the door, lets one passenger through, then slams the door in the face of the next passenger, shouts "Ha ha! You can't come through yet!", counts to ten, and then opens the door again. As might be imagined, the second method takes rather longer than the first.

Doing this for a read on one table is bad enough, but it could be a million times worse. Have a look at what is going on in Listing 5-25.

Listing 5-25. Nested SELECTs within a LOOP

```
    LOOP AT int_ebeln.
* ZMM_EKET-Primary Key = EBELN / EBELP / ETENR
    CLEAR zmm_eket.
    SELECT * FROM  zmm_eket
            WHERE   ebeln        = int_ebeln-ebeln
              AND   ebelp        = int_ebeln-ebelp
              AND   eindt        GE  date
              AND   deleted      EQ space.

* ZMM_DELIVERY-Primary Key = VBELN
* Index on EBELN / EBELP / ETENR
      CLEAR zmm_delivery.
      SELECT * FROM zmm_delivery
        WHERE   ebeln   = zmm_eket-ebeln
          AND   ebelp   = zmm_eket-ebelp
          AND   etenr   = zmm_eket-etenr.
      IF sy-subrc EQ 0 AND zmm_delivery-wemng = 0.
        IF zmm_delivery-wamng IS INITIAL.
* load has not yet been issued/weighed
          CLEAR l_lfimg.
          SELECT lfimg INTO l_lfimg FROM  lips
                WHERE   vbeln  = zmm_delivery-vbeln.
            pcd_current_stock = pcd_current_stock + l_lfimg.
            quarry_stk        = quarry_stk + l_lfimg.
          ENDSELECT.
        ELSE.
* load has been issued/weighed
          pcd_current_stock =
          pcd_current_stock + zmm_delivery-wamng.
          quarry_stk        = quarry_stk + zmm_delivery-wamng.
        ENDIF.
      ENDIF.
    ENDSELECT.
```

```
    IF sy-subrc NE 0 AND
       gl_mrp14 EQ 'X'.
      "keep a record of what has been ordered
      gs_zmm_eket = zmm_eket.
      APPEND gs_zmm_eket TO gt_zmm_eket.
    ENDIF.
  ENDSELECT.
ENDLOOP.
```

In Listing 5-25, the program is doing a loop over an internal table. For every row in that table, a connection is opened to database table ZMM_EKET, and one row at a time is retrieved. For each such row, a database connection is opened to table ZMM_DELIVERY, and one row at a time from that table is retrieved. Then potentially we can go down another level, opening a connection to table LIPS.

That's like going up to an aircraft, waiting for the door to open, running through the plane, getting off the other end, then running up to a second aircraft and waiting for the door to open, running through that second plane and off again the other end, then running up to a third plane and waiting for its door to open, going inside, getting what you want, and then running all the way back again through the three aircraft, pausing every time you encounter a door—then repeating the process for each row in the internal table.

Back in the computer world, if you use the "running from plane to plane" technique using nested SELECTs but use primary keys or indexes for every table, then the response time can in fact be fairly reasonable, but it is still a somewhat silly way to go about things.

A better way to proceed would be as follows:

- Loop through the internal table, building a section table for ZMM_EKET.

- Then get all the ZMM_EKET records at once into an internal table.

- Then either do a FAE to get all the ZMM_DELIVERY records at once or do an INNER JOIN if you can into another internal table.

- Then use that table to get all required records from table LIPS at once into another internal table. Once again, it may be possible with all the fancy new ABAP constructs to do one mega-query on all three tables.

If you cannot do any joins, then you end up with three internal tables, one for each database table. Replace the SELECT/ENDSELECT loops with loops on sorted or hashed internal tables. The result comes out looking like Listing 5-26.

Listing 5-26. Replacing SELECT/ENDSELECT with LOOPS

```
LOOP AT int_ebeln.
  "SORTED Table by EBELN / EBELP
  LOOP AT gt_zmm_eket_prefill
          ASSIGNING FIELD-SYMBOL(<ls_zmm_eket>)
          WHERE   ebeln         EQ int_ebeln-ebeln
              AND ebelp         EQ int_ebeln-ebelp
              AND eindt         GE date
              AND deleted       EQ space.

    "SORTED Table by EBELN / EBELP / ETENR
    LOOP AT gt_zmm_delivery_prefill
      ASSIGNING FIELD-SYMBOL(<ls_zmm_delivery>)
      WHERE ebeln   = <ls_zmm_eket>-ebeln
      AND   ebelp   = <ls_zmm_eket>-ebelp
      AND   etenr   = <ls_zmm_eket>-etenr.
      IF <ls_zmm_delivery>-wemng = 0.
```

As an aside, SAP always recommends looping into a field symbol even if you don't intend to change the values in the row of the internal table, as this is faster and uses less memory. The code inspector will highlight loops where you do not use field symbols.

In any event, if you do a SQL trace before and after such a transformation (i.e., changing nested SELECT statements to loops on sorted or hashed internal tables), then you will see a dramatic performance improvement.

"Bad" Joins on Database Tables

I was once asked by a colleague if doing an inner join on a large number of tables at once was considered a bad thing. The rumor was that SAP was advising against such behavior. I don't think that rumor is true—if anything the reverse is true. The code inspector looks for situations where a database table is read, and then the results of that query are later used for a FAE, and then if that situation is found a warning is issued that the two queries can possibly be combined into one join.

I am not convinced doing a join on many tables at once is the end of the world in and of itself. I had a colleague who used to stuff the JOIN full of as many tables as he could, and it never caused too much grief. His position was that he was telling the database exactly what he wanted, and it should be clever enough to obey in a fast and efficient way. This is of course exactly what SAP is now advocating in two ways:

- "Pushing down" selection logic to the database, often using CDS views

- Where CDS views are used, the idea is to assemble them into a sort of pyramid (views on views is what SAP calls this), where at the base are views on individual tables, and each layer of the pyramid above this combines the views below until at the top of the pyramid only one mega-view remains, which is in effect joining all the tables below it.

I don't think it is the *number* of tables being joined that can potentially cause problems so much as the *nature* of the tables being joined. For example, buffered tables like T001W should never be in a join. The data is already in memory, so it is silly to go and get it again from the database. This is true even for a HANA database—everything is in memory, but buffered tables are in a different bit of memory (the cache on the application server), which is easier and faster to access.

Text tables should never be in a join, as there might be entries missing in some languages. Thus, the result of the same SQL query would give a different result depending on what language you were logged into.

Transactional tables like VBAK/VBAP should never be joined to master data tables like MARA or KNA1. There is a really complicated technical explanation of why that is a really bad thing to do, and I could prattle on for ten pages explaining it, but maybe it is better to summarize just the concept, which is all to do with how many database "blocks" need to be processed. The example is a join on VBAP/MARA where every single VBAP entry has the same material number—in such a case, it is faster to go to MARA just once.

If you were to follow the SAP Community website, you would see that a lot of ABAP programmers try to avoid FOR ALL ENTRIES like the plague and instead try to do a join if it is at all possible. It is easy to see why—if you do a SQL trace on a program that does a join and then a FAE you will see one line in the SQL trace for the join and then five hundred for the FAE, each line fetching five results (or more or less depending on the length of the SQL query—put another way, a FAE with a where condition that contains criteria other than the fields in the selection list is non-optimal).

Each line of the FAE on the trace has the retrieval time against it, and often those add up to a large number. If everything were in one join, then probably (but not always) the total retrieval time would be less.

In other words, when the code inspector says, "Query can be transformed" and wants you to do a join as opposed to a FAE it is worth a look to see if the recommendation does in fact make sense.

As always, I like to give an example of a problematic query, and in Listing 5-27 you will see a SQL query that took forever to run.

Listing 5-27. Badly Performing SQL Query

```
select vbap~vbeln vbap~posnr vbap~werks vbap~matnr vbap~kwmeng
         vbap~arktx vbap~zzfirstload_dt vbap~spart
         vbak~kunnr as kunag
         kna1ag~name1 as agname
         vbpa~kunnr as kunwe
         kna1we~name1 as wename
         mara~bismt
         zsd_altplant~travel_time
         zsd_altplant~road_dist
         t001w~land1
         vbap~zzmaxload
         vbap~cuobj
         vbak~vbtyp
         vbap~zzvtype
         zmm_plant_master~dispatch_group
         vbak~erdat
         vbak~erzet
         zmm_plant_master~plant_gradient
         zsd_altplant~zzshipto_gradient
      into corresponding fields of table et_sales_data
      from vbap
      inner join vbak
        on vbak~vbeln = vbap~vbeln
      inner join kna1 as kna1ag
        on vbak~kunnr = kna1ag~kunnr
```

```
inner join vbpa
  on vbpa~vbeln = vbap~vbeln
inner join kna1 as kna1we
  on vbpa~kunnr = kna1we~kunnr
inner join t001w as t001w
  on t001w~werks = vbap~werks
inner join zmm_plant_master as zmm_plant_master
  on zmm_plant_master~werks = vbap~werks
left outer join mara
  on mara~matnr = vbap~matnr
left outer join zsd_altplant
  on zsd_altplant~spart = vbak~spart
 and zsd_altplant~ship_to = vbpa~kunnr
 and zsd_altplant~plant = vbap~werks
where vbap~vbeln in go_selections->mt_vbeln
  and vbap~matnr in go_selections->mt_matnr
  and vbap~werks in go_selections->mt_werks
  and vbpa~parvw = 'WE'
  and vbpa~posnr = '000000'
  and vbak~kunnr in go_selections->mt_soldto
  and vbak~auart in go_selections->mt_doctype
  and vbpa~kunnr in go_selections->mt_shipto
  and vbap~zzfirstload_dt in go_selections->mt_1stload.
```

In Listing 5-27, the problem was the large number of master data tables being joined—T001W/KNA1 and MARA plus two Z master data tables. When the query was rewritten to just join the transactional tables, all the performance problems melted away.

Postmortem Checks

Thus far, we have looked at static checks, which can be done whilst you are writing new code, and runtime checks, which you can do either just after writing the new code or after a problem is reported.

Now we move on to "postmortem" checks, which are done when you know (or suspect) there is a performance problem.

First, you will hear about standard SAP transactions that can help you in this quest. Next, you will move on to the technical attributes of database tables. Last, two postmortem "tricks" are described that can help you analyze and fix performance problems that you may find in this stage.

Standard SAP Transactions for Troubleshooting Performance Problems

We will start with the "go-to" solution for analyzing performance problems in a particular program, namely transaction SAT (the transaction formerly known as SE30). Then, we will expand this to look at how to find performance problems in the system as whole via transaction ST04. Then, we will have quick look at transaction SRTCM, which is designed to find really specific problems in production.

SAT

As you have seen, performance problems are not always related to database access. Poorly written ABAP code can cause them as well; e.g., nested loops on standard internal tables. Sometimes you just cannot tell where a performance problem is coming from, and so it is time to call out the "big guns," by which I mean doing a runtime analysis using transaction SAT.

As an example, this year one of the analysts told me he'd had to change the frequency of a batch job that used to run every five minutes to only run every ten minutes, because it had started taking longer than five minutes to run. I was really puzzled—I had written most of the code that was called, and I had taken great pains to consider the performance aspects of the code. Just to be sure, I did a code inspector analysis on the core program and an ST05 trace, and everything looked fine. I was really perplexed.

It was time to call up transaction SAT (Runtime Analysis). There are loads of options on the initial screen—enough to make you take one look and run away screaming—but the simplest is just to enter the transaction code for whatever it is you are analyzing into the "In Dialog" box, as shown in Figure 5-6, and then press the Execute button at the bottom.

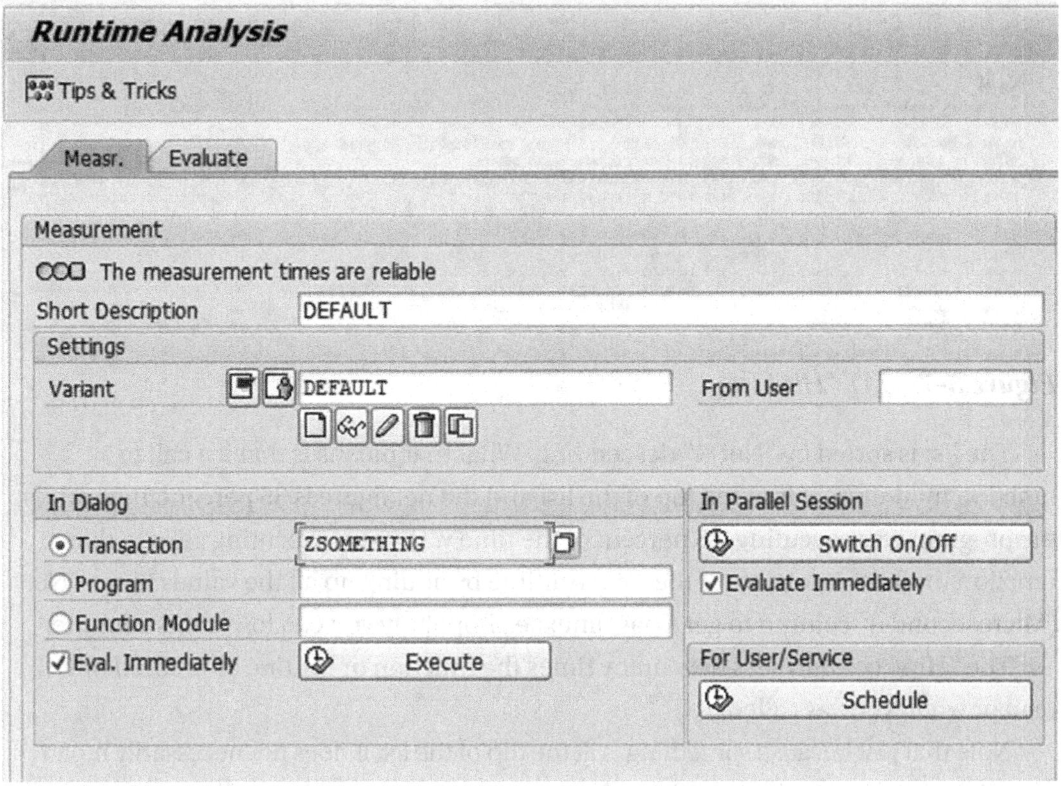

Figure 5-6. *Transaction SAT*

You are then taken to the initial screen of the transaction you specified (ZSOMETHING), and you execute that program just as you would normally. However, when you are finished (e.g., an ALV list appears), press the green "back" arrow and instead of going back to the main menu, after a few ominous messages at the bottom of the screen you are taken to a result screen, which at first glance contains so many tabs and options and tables of information that you are totally lost and wonder how this can ever help you.

There is plenty of documentation on the internet on how to use this; here, I will just concentrate on the simplest approach to take so as not to melt your brain. My recommendation is to navigate to the "Hit List" tab, as shown in Figure 5-7.

	Hits	Gross [microsec]	Net [microsec]	Gross [%]	Net [%]	Statement/Event	Program Called
	3,349,783	10,181,958	10,181,958	7.01	7.01	Call M. {0:63*ZCL_BC_PARAMETER}->CONSTRUCTOR	ZCL_BC_PARAMETER=============CP
	399,202	9,581,523	9,581,523	6.59	6.59	Call M. {0:1*ZCL_MATERIAL_MASTER_SHMO_ROOT}->GET_MATERIAL	ZCL_MATERIAL_MASTER=========CP
	399,202	8,287,860	8,287,860	5.70	5.70	Call M. {0:25*CL_SHM_AREA}->_DETACH	CL_SHM_AREA================CP
	51,342	7,978,264	7,978,264	5.49	5.49	Call Function Z_MRP_CALC_MULTI_SSW_AND_SSQ	ZMM_MRP_MULTIDAY_SCHEDULES_DIS
	50,901	15,693,019	6,519,353	10.80	4.49	Perform PROCESS_REQUIREMENTS_TODAY	ZMM_MRP_MULTIDAY_SCHEDULES_DIS
	134	5,231,480	5,231,480	3.60	3.60	DB Buffer: Fetch TABL FETCH(Q)	ZCL_VC_CONSTRAINTS_PL========CP
	380,972	4,005,116	3,982,441	2.76	2.74	Perform READ_OLDMAT	SAPLLMGT
	399,202	3,200,223	3,200,180	2.20	2.20	Call M. {0:25*CL_SHM_AREA}->_ATTACH_READ71	ZCL_MATERIAL_MASTER_SHMO=====CP
	399,202	6,038,606	2,320,640	4.16	1.60	Call M. ZCL_MATERIAL_MASTER_SHMO=>ATTACH_FOR_READ	ZCL_MATERIAL_MASTER=========CP
	99,698	10,551,791	2,228,960	7.26	1.53	Call M. {0:99*ZCL_VC_BOM_PERS_LAYER}->GET_COMPONENT_BLEND_MATERIALS	ZCL_VC_BOM_SIMULATOR========CP
	194,548	13,780,784	1,985,045	9.49	1.37	Call M. ZCL_MATERIAL_MASTER=>READ	ZCL_VC_BOM_PERS_LAYER========CP
	154,072	3,985,186	1,858,774	2.74	1.28	Open SQL ZTVC_CAGG_SETS	ZCL_VC_BOM_PERS_LAYER========CP

Figure 5-7. *SAT "Hit List"*

The list is sorted by "Net %" descending. What that means is that if a call to function module XYZ is at the top of the list and the net figure is 35 percent, then whilst the program was executing, 35 percent of the time was spent executing calls to that function module. Take note of the total runtime by adding up all the values in the "Net (Microseconds)" column to get a baseline; i.e., hopefully you can lower this runtime.

The "Hits" column says how many times the function or routine or method or DB read or whatever was called.

Note that just because something is at the top of the list it does not necessarily mean that it is inefficient. You have to divide the net runtime by the number of hits to find the worst culprits. If something is only called once and takes 50% percent of the runtime, that is bad, but if it is called half a million times and takes 50 percent of the runtime, maybe it is OK.

So, you start at the top of the list and work down. For each entry you ask yourself two questions:

- Does it really need to be called as often as it is actually being called?

- Is it performing in an optimal manner?

With luck you can often address both problems in parallel—for example, you could improve a call to a SQL statement by using a better index and then buffer the result so as to reduce the number of times that SQL statement is called.

In my batch job example, I found that right at the top of my list was a routine with a net runtime of 32 percent and 15,000 calls. Upon investigation, it turned out a complex evaluation was being done constantly, which returned a negative result 100 percent of the time. It was looking for a situation that could not possibly happen, so the whole thing was pointless. You do not often find such obvious candidates, but when you do you feel really happy fixing them, in this case by not calling the evaluation in the first place.

The good thing is—provided you have enough data in development—you can make a change and then re-run the SAT analysis and see what is at the top of the list now (and also prove your change worked, because the previous top entry has vanished to a thousand places lower in the hit list). Thus, this is an iterative process, knocking over problems until all the entries at the top of the list are deemed to be optimal in both number of executions and performance.

The next thing that popped to the top of my list was a function module that was called 48,000 times. I checked to see if that was by accident or design, and in fact it was by design; it was called from deep within some nested loops. However, I noticed it did a read on a large internal table that was a standard table without even so much as a BINARY SEARCH. I turned that table into a sorted table and—boing—the call to the function module dropped off the top of the list.

What came up next was a read on database table CABN executed a vast number of times, which was odd as the code was trying to buffer the result. It turned out the buffering code did not work, so that got fixed, and then what remained at the top of the list was a bunch of database reads, none of which appeared to be called an excessive number of times and all of which used good indexes.

At that point, it seemed a good idea to compare the new total runtime with the baseline, and I was happy to see it was running about three times faster than before—due to some trivial changes I never would have picked up on without the SAT analysis.

ST04

Thus far, you have been hearing about how to determine performance problems in specific programs—you were checking either because you had just written or changed the program yourself, or because someone was complaining.

At the start of this chapter, you heard about the CPO concept, which is all about being proactive and going looking for performance problems in custom programs even if no one has complained. It is a common perception that end users complain about everything that is wrong in the system, but that's not true—and I of course have a story by way of example.

Once I was on a site visit with some IT colleagues, and the plant manager told us to wait in reception—he said he was with a driver and would be with us once he had finished. Half an hour later, he called us in and said he was sorry about the wait, but it had taken 15 minutes for the report to run in SAP to detail the driver's earnings for last month. I instantly said, "Never mind about why I am here. Can I have the selection criteria for that report? There is no way it should take 15 minutes for one driver for one month." Fifteen seconds is what I would expect. That night in my hotel room, I replicated the problem and did some magic to fix it. The point was, though, that we only found out by accident. The manager had presumed that the report in question took forever to run because that was just the way it was.

The question now becomes how to find the worst-performing SQL queries in the entire live SAP system. Some will be custom programs that you can do something about, some will be standard SAP programs, which of course you cannot change (but you might be able to come up with a custom solution to whatever problem the end user is trying to solve). Either way, the way to find such evil queries is via transaction ST04—the "Performance Overview."

This transaction does ten billion different things and is usually used by the BASIS department. Here, we are going to concentrate on the "Shared Cursor Cache"—the option shown in Figure 5-8. (Note: In the screenshot it says "Oracle"—for you that will change to whatever database you actually use).

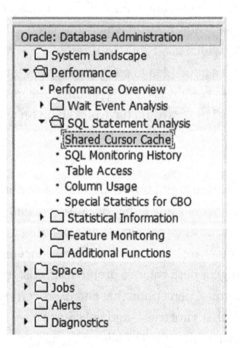

Figure 5-8. *ST04 options with "Shared Cursor Cache" selected*

As soon as the database starts up, every single SQL statement executed is recorded, together with its execution plan and how efficient the query was in real life. That is what the "Shared Cursor Cache" refers to.

If you double-click on the "Shared Cursor Cache" option, you will get a pop-up box with half a billion options. As we are talking about production, you probably want to exclude queries that are not executed very often—say less than 100,000 times since database startup. The result list can be sorted lots of ways as well. It doesn't hurt to start by sorting that list by "Elapsed Time" so long-running queries are at the top. In fact, whatever options you choose, the "bad players" will end up at the top, but if you just restrict the total number of executions then the pop-up box will look like Figure 5-9.

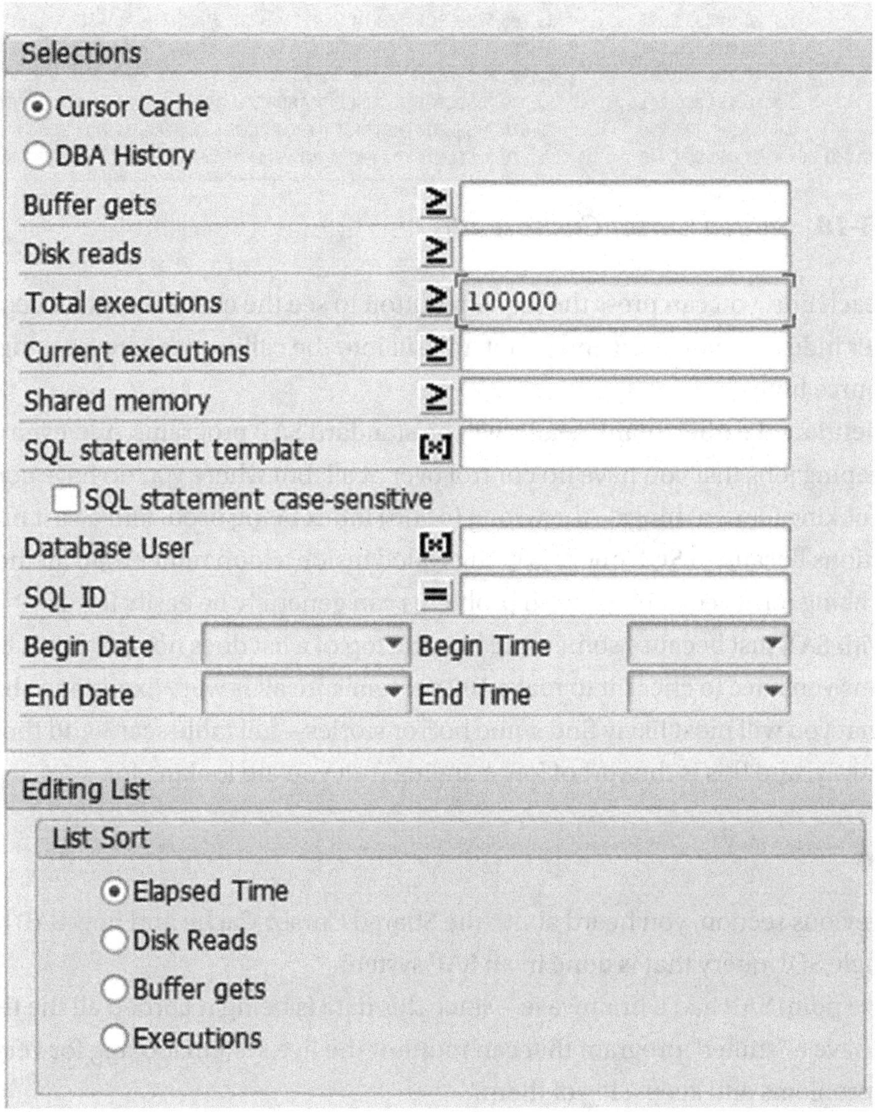

Figure 5-9. *Shared Cursor Cache selections*

The result screen will be overwhelming, with numbers all over the place, as shown in Figure 5-10. As a general rule, the higher the value for any number at all (apart from number of executions) on that screen, the worse things are.

| | EXPLAIN | ABAP Source | Analysis Report | Table Filter | Reset point | Since reset | Since DB-start |

Rproc/Exec	Bgets/row	Elapsed Time	Elapsed Time/Exec	SQL statement
5.0	8.1	83,368,560,797	30,541.9	SELECT "ZLAB_VBAP"."VBELN","ZLAB_VBAP"."POSNR","ZLAB_VBAP"."
8.8	0.9	28,948,205,215	43,934.6	SELECT DISTINCT * FROM "RESB" WHERE "MANDT"=:A0 AND "RSNUM"
10.5	0.8	28,174,581,511	42,866.7	SELECT DISTINCT "MANDT","LEDNR","OBJNR","GJAHR","WRTTP","VER
9.8	1.0	28,145,238,595	31,766.5	SELECT * FROM "JEST" WHERE "MANDT"=:A0 AND "OBJNR"=:A1 ORDER
209.4	0.3	24,469,226,281	51,786.7	SELECT * FROM "BSAD" WHERE "MANDT"=:A0 AND "BUKRS"=:A1 AND "
21.1	0.9	20,270,762,662	32,955.1	SELECT * FROM "VBFA" WHERE "MANDT"=:A0 AND "VBELV"=:A1 AND "
12.9	1.1	16,457,866,241	12,489.2	SELECT DISTINCT "MANDT","LEDNR","OBJNR","GJAHR","WRTTP","VER
9.7	0.6	15,517,727,838	23,676.7	SELECT DISTINCT * FROM "COKA" WHERE "MANDT"=:A0 AND "OBJNR"
0.0	41,403,684.4	13,950,969,948	79.3	SELECT /*+ FIRST_ROWS(1) */ * FROM "TBTCO" WHERE "JOBNAME"=:

Figure 5-10. *Shared Cursor Cache result*

For each line, you can press the Explain button to see the execution plan; i.e., to see if a proper index is being used and, if not, to drill into the calling code by pressing the ABAP Source button.

As mentioned earlier, many results will be standard SAP programs, and even system housekeeping jobs that you have no control over at all, but where you do have control you are looking for two things—the wrong (or no) index being used, and a vast number of executions because a SQL query is being called inside a loop rather than all the records' being retrieved at once. Both problems can generally be easily fixed.

As with SAT, just because something is at the top of a list does not mean it is bad—it just means you have to check it to make 100 percent sure all is well. Experience has shown that you will most likely find some horror stories—full table scans and the like—straight away, and this is the sort of low-hanging fruit you are looking for.

SRTCM

In the previous section, you heard about the Shared Cursor Cache and how SAP logs every single SQL query that is done in an SAP system.

At one point SAP had a brainwave—since this data is being recorded all the time, why not have a "sniffer" program that can monitor the live system looking for very specific problems and keep a log of them?

The result is transaction SRTCM, which is the runtime check monitor. The idea is that you switch it on looking for individual problems, it logs them in real time, and after a few weeks it automatically switches itself off until you manually activate it again. In actual fact, I have found that after less than a week you have a list of the problems that need to be addressed.

At time of writing, there are only two problems that this transaction checks for, but I imagine more will be added over time.

Those problems are as follows:

- Empty table in FOR ALL ENTRIES clause — As mentioned earlier, this causes a full table scan. The static code checks tell you if this *might* happen in production, and the SRTCM log tells you if they *actually do* happen in production.

- Missing ORDER BY or SORT after SELECT — This is all to do with the fact that in a HANA database the records in a SQL query come back in a random order, as opposed to in the order of the primary key like they do in a row-based database. This means any code that does not sort the data itself but rather implicitly relies on the data's being in primary-key order will break after an upgrade to a HANA database.

In Figure 5-11, you can see an example of transaction SRTCM where the FAE check is currently not activated but the SORT check is.

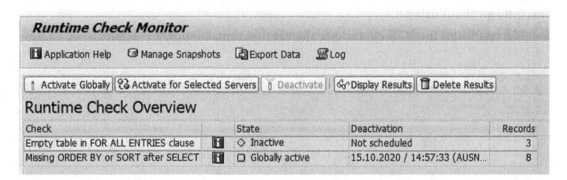

Figure 5-11. *Transaction SRTCM*

If you put your cursor on the inactive check and press the "Activate Globally" icon, then you will get a little pop-up box asking you when the check should switch itself off; it defaults to four weeks' time from today. When you press the green tick, the "State" column changes to "Globally Active." Then the Deactivate button is enabled, and you can switch off the check earlier if you so desire.

Naturally, even after deactivation the results are still available—strangely enough, you see those results by pressing the "Display Results" icon. For the FAE check they look like Figure 5-12.

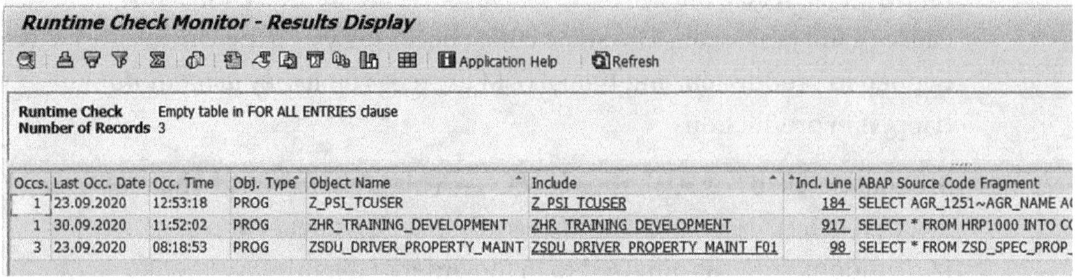

Figure 5-12. *FAE check results*

Here, you can see programs that have executed a full table scan in production due to the result table's being empty in the FAE query. More important, you are told the program with the problem right down to the line in the routine where the SQL query was called, and you can even drill into that code. As soon as you spot such a result, you should instantly go about fixing it.

The results for the SORT check look slightly different, as shown in Figure 5-13.

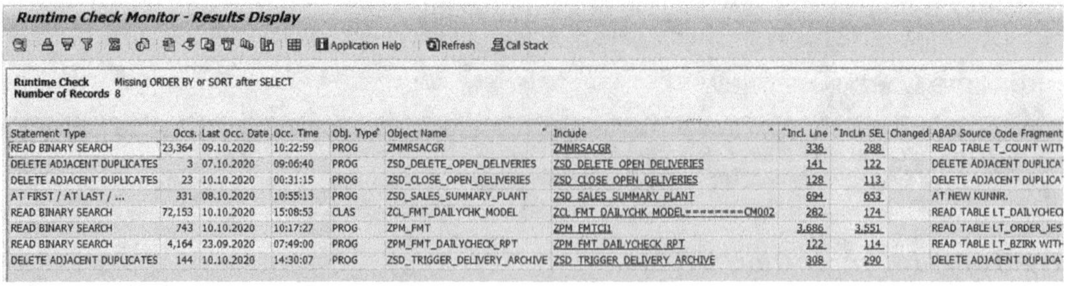

Figure 5-13. *SORT check results*

This time, in the very first column the nature of the problem is stated—for example, BINARY SEARCH will not work if an internal table is not sorted, nor will DELETE ADJACENT DUPLICATES (because they will not be adjacent) and so on. You will note there are two line numbers this time: the line of the code where the SQL SELECT takes place and the line of the code where the evaluation (e.g., BINARY SEARCH) takes place.

Unless you are upgrading to a HANA database tomorrow, these are not fatal problems in the same way the FAE problem is, but nonetheless they all need to be solved because you will be upgrading to a HANA database sooner or later.

Technical Attributes of Database Tables

In this section, first you will read about the subject of custom indexes on database tables and how to ensure these are designed optimally, and then the concept of table buffering will be introduced, along with a mechanism to ensure your Z tables are always optimally buffered.

Indexes

If you find a SQL statement that is performing badly, then one possible way to solve the problem is to create a secondary index on the database table in question. You would design the index using the selection fields in the query that is causing problems. However, to use a mixed metaphor, indexes can be double-edged swords, and so you could end up shooting yourself in the foot by creating a new one, and in the worst case could blow the whole system up.

In the following sections you will see examples of a pointless index, a terrible index, and a really good index, and as an added bonus a description of how you can tell if an index is going to be good or not before you create it.

Pointless Index

At some point long, long ago, in an SAP system far, far away, an index was placed on profit center line item table GLPCA in order to speed up "Report Painter" reports. The index looked like Figure 5-14.

NONUNIQUE Index GLPCA~Z1	
Column Name	#Distinct
RPRCTR	821
RACCT	858
POPER	14
RYEAR	21

Figure 5-14. *Good index on GLPCA*

That index worked really well. There were lots of profit centers and lots of GL accounts, and accountants usually ran a report looking for several years' worth of items for one GL account in one profit center, so the report went like lightning. Even better, since this index contained both month (POPER) and year (RYEAR), the index was "stable."

I cannot stress enough the importance of having a stable index; i.e., one that contains "Date" fields. If there were no such fields in the index—in this example, if the index were just on profit center and account, for example—then over time the performance of the SQL query would just get worse and worse as more and more records had to be checked to see if they fit the date selection (and accounting transaction queries always have a date selection).

As a tip, if you have an actual "date" field (e.g., ERDAT for creation date or LFDAT for delivery date), then put it at the start of the index. Over time, as the days go by, this will make it the most-selective field, plus the records added for each day will sit close together in the database as opposed to being scattered all over the place.

For an example, imagine you are in a library researching old newspapers (in the days before they were all digitized). The newspapers are filed in date order, so if you are just interested in one week you just have to go to one place. If you are looking for all stories about elephants, for example, even if you have an index that says in which paper each elephant story lives, you have to run up and down the aisles as the newspapers in question are nowhere near each other.

This is just for traditional row-based databases, by the way. With a HANA database—which is column based—all the elephants are clustered together, which is why you don't usually need secondary indexes with HANA.

Getting back to the point, at one stage someone decided that they could "turbo boost" the performance of another report by creating the index shown in Figure 5-15. Have a look at that index and compare it to the first one, and something should spring out at you.

NONUNIQUE Index GLPCA~Z3	
Column Name	#Distinct
RVERS	1
RLDNR	1
KOKRS	4
RYEAR	21
POPER	14
RPRCTR	821
RACCT	858

Figure 5-15. *Pointless index on GLPCA*

That's right—the second index contains every single one of the fields from the first index, plus three totally non-selective ones. This is bad for several reasons, as follows:

- It does not help at all. Whichever index the optimizer chooses, the performance would be the same. This can be proved by doing tests in development using database hints.

- It confuses the optimizer. The more indexes there are on a table, the more confused it gets. That might seem a bit abstract, but my experience has been that when an optimizer gets confused it has a nervous breakdown and picks something totally inappropriate to use in a SQL query.

- With every new index a slight performance hit is caused when an entry is written into the underlying table (to update the index). Since almost every single transaction in an SAP system updates GLPCA, a new index on this table would slow the whole system down.

- GLPCA is one of the largest tables in an SAP system. When a new index is created, this will absorb a vast amount of memory. The DB administrator will be wondering why they have to spend a million dollars on extra memory hardware but presumes it is for a useful purpose, but in this case it is not. It's just an extra million dollars— every so often—to benefit nobody and slow the whole system down.

Terrible Index

Just to belabor the point, I want to give a similar example of an index that is not only completely useless but also causes the mental breakdown of the database optimizer I alluded to earlier. This example is all about reporting on sales orders where the data lives in header table VBAK and item table VBAP.

Often, end users wanted to see what orders were due out of a given plant on a given date (or usually a range of dates), and thus an index was created on the item table VBAP on the supplying plant (WERKS) and the requested delivery date. Since the date was the first field, this index was stable and worked like lightning.

Then one day, after I was away for some years and went back to the same system and ran the same query, it took forever and sometimes timed out. The original good index was still there—what could be going on?

In the intervening period no less than eleven different Z indexes had been added to VBAK, and five more on VBAP. Some of the indexes had totally different fields than the others, and that is fine—that means they are for totally different purposes and cannot get in each other's way. The problems tend to start when there are several indexes with overlapping fields and so the optimizer struggles to pick one.

As it transpired, if you put in one plant and one date the proper index was used. However, if you wanted the orders for a range of plants—all on one day—then the report ran very slowly indeed. The way to work out what was going on was to do an ST05 trace on the report twice—once with the criteria that gave the fast result, once with the criteria that gave the slow result.

With the query for one day and one plant, the optimizer correctly chose the index on date and plant. However, for a vast range of plants, even though only one date had been asked for—which would have made a query using the good index really fast—the optimizer thought something like, "That is a lot of plants, maybe I can find something better," and so it went off looking at all the other indexes and picked the one in Figure 5-16.

Index Flds			
Field name	Short Description	DT...	Length
MANDT	Client	CLNT	3
VKORG	Sales Organization	CHAR	4
VTWEG	Distribution Channel	CHAR	2
VBTYP	SD document category	CHAR	1
AUART	Sales Document Type	CHAR	4
VKBUR	Sales Office	CHAR	4

Figure 5-16. *Terrible index*

In the query, the VKORG and VTWEG were specified, and so the optimizer decided for no logical reason to go with the index shown in Figure 5-16. As you can see, there are no date fields in that index, and so it is "unstable," and VBAK is a very big table and there are not that many distinct values for VKORG. As a result, the performance was terrible.

In the next section we will look at the opposite case and talk about how to avoid creating such horrific indexes.

Really Good Index

SAP table KEKO contains details of "Product Costing," which is used in the "Cost of Goods Sold" calculation for profit margins. Once upon a time, there was a custom report that queried that table and was taking a really long time, and so the programmer decided to see if an index was needed.

The programmer knew the fields used with the SQL query in the Z ABAP program. The question was—would creating an index on those fields help or make things a million times worse?

The trick is to go into the live system and call up transaction DB05. This allows you to analyze how good a potential index would be using the actual data from the live system, before you have to create an index. You can "try before you buy," as it were.

In Figure 5-17, the programmer has nominated the table—KEKO—and then in the bottom of the screen listed the fields they are proposing to include in the index.

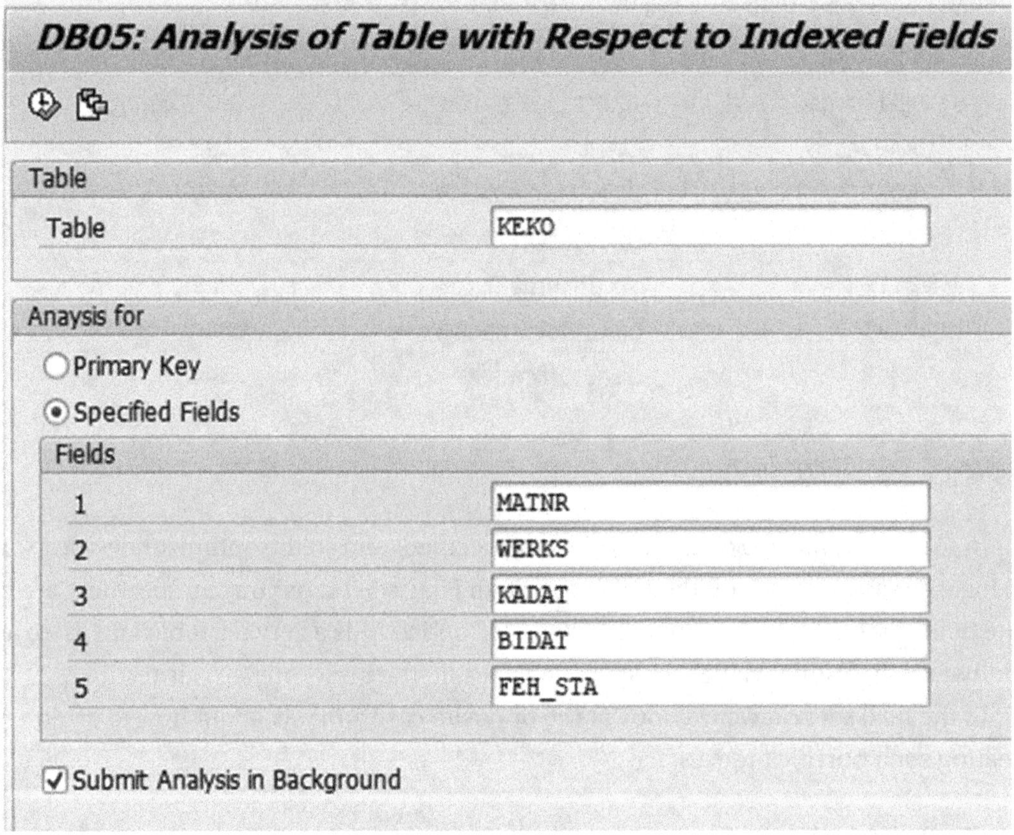

Figure 5-17. *Analyzing a proposed index*

The job runs in the background in case the table is gigantic. Generally, though, the results come back reasonably quickly. You go to transaction SM37 and see that a job is running under your name called (in this case) TABLE_ANALYSIS_KEKO.

When that job finishes, you have a look at the spool request it generates. The result will look something like Figure 5-18.

Rows per generic key	Distinct values	1 - 10	11 - 100	101 - 1,000	1,001 - 10,000	10,001 - 100,000	100,001 -1,000,000	more than 1,000,000
Key fields		Number of areas that are specified by the generic key and contain the given number of rows						
1 MATNR	64,383	4,284	18,266	35,194	6,131	433	67	8
2 WERKS	353,182	41,490	180,351	127,091	3,012	1,209	29	
3 KADAT	21,844,167	20,764,765	1,048,965	29,153	1,271	13		
4 BIDAT	23,616,548	22,541,618	1,045,336	28,311	1,270	13		
5 FEH_STA	23,691,462	22,618,299	1,043,695	28,185	1,270	13		

Figure 5-18. *DB05 results for table KEKO*

As usual with SAP transactions, there are numbers all over the place, so I will try to explain what they mean.

In this case, there are roughly 64,000 possible values of the material number MATNR. For four thousand of those combinations, the SQL query would have to only scan less than ten database "blocks," so the result would come back really quickly, but if any of eight "unlucky" materials were specified the query would have to scan more than a million blocks, which would not be anywhere near as good. This is like the library analogy again—if everything you want is in one newspaper then great, if it is scattered across a million newspapers it is going to take you a while to get everything you need.

Moving along to the second line, if the query had specified both the MATNR and the plant (WERKS) then there would be 353,000 possible combinations. Of those combinations, 41,000 of those values would need less than ten blocks scanned, the next 180,000 would need less than 100 blocks, and so on.

If the query had specified MATNR + WERKS + KADAT (costing date from), then everything dramatically changes. This time there are 22 million possible combinations, and 21 million of those need less than ten blocks. So you are 95 percent likely to get a really good result, and most of the remaining million options require less than 100 blocks, so therefore this is a really good index.

In fact, the query in the program being written provided all five of the fields shown in Listing 5-18. The ones after KADAT didn't make that big a difference so they are more trouble than they are worth and should not be included.

Now, let's do the same exercise for the index on VBAK that was causing problems. In Figure 5-19, you can see the DB05 settings to analyze the index (which in this case already exists).

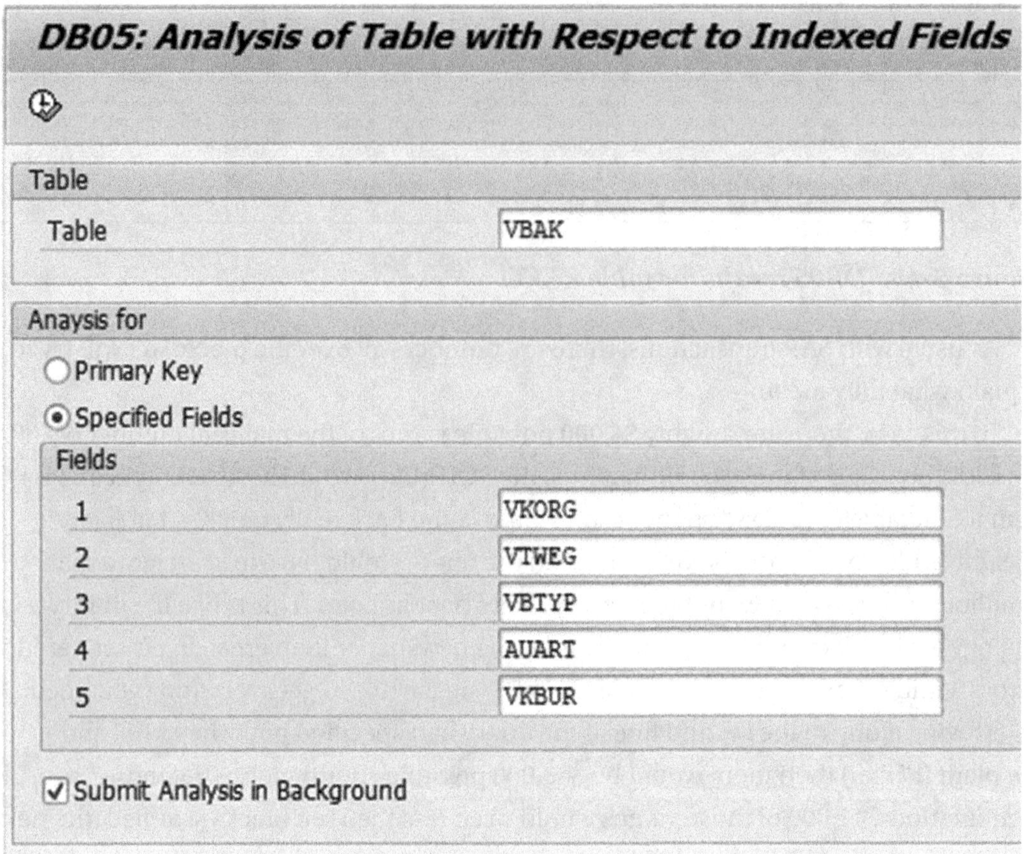

DB05: Analysis of Table with Respect to Indexed Fields

Table

Table	VBAK

Anaysis for

○ Primary Key
◉ Specified Fields

Fields

1	VKORG
2	VTWEG
3	VBTYP
4	AUART
5	VKBUR

☑ Submit Analysis in Background

Figure 5-19. Analyzing a problematic index

The result can be seen in Figure 5-20, and you can tell at first glance the number distribution is very different than in the last example.

	Rows per generic key	Distinct values	1 - 10	11 - 100	101 - 1.000	1.001 - 10.000	10.001 - 100.000	100.001 -1.000.000	more than 1.000.000
	Key fields		Number of areas that are specified by the generic key and contain the given number of rows						
1	VKORG	132	6	7	11	22	30	47	9
2	VTWEG	170	10	11	13	40	35	52	9
3	VBTYP	647	114	133	129	127	76	60	8
4	AUART	1.245	272	243	276	242	135	68	9
5	VKBUR	5.729	2.368	1.418	1.021	607	233	77	5

Figure 5-20. DB05 result for a non-optimal index

In this case, none of the values are very distinctive and so even adding extra combinations does not help very much. Even on the last row, a figure of 6,000 unique values on a gigantic table like VBAK is not unique in the slightest.

Even if the query specified all five fields, there is a less than 50 percent chance that only ten blocks would need to be scanned, and still a chance that more than a million blocks would need to be queried. This index is therefore useless, as it speeds up no queries, slows many queries down, gets worse every day because it is unstable, takes up a huge amount of space on the database (i.e., costs money), and delays sales order entry by a fraction of a second each time. It needs to be deleted.

Buffering

The term *buffering* refers to the ability of the SAP system to store the data of some database tables locally on the application server. That way, when an ABAP program does a SQL query, the data is read from a cache rather than the database, which is one billion times faster. Even better, if a record is *not* found that fact is remembered (and buffered) as well. You have to do the latter manually if programmatically buffering internal tables.

In this section, first you will read about the various possible buffering settings you can make on your custom Z database tables, and then you will see an example of how this can help performance. Next, we will move on to a really common misconception about buffering that may come as a surprise, and lastly you will hear about how to decide which of your Z tables to buffer.

Possible Buffering Settings

There are three types of buffering, as follows:

- Full Buffering — The very first time such a table is queried after database startup the entire contents are loaded into the cache.

- Generic Buffering — In this case, only some fields of the primary key are specified as relevant for buffering. The most common example of this would be text tables—the primary key is the language and the value, and the first time a query is done every entry for that language is buffered.

- Single Records Buffering — In this case, individual records are buffered as and when a query is done using every field of the primary key.

In the first case, after the initial load, every single query is read out of the cache; in the latter two cases, similar queries are read out of the cache and new queries are read out the database the first time. Let us get a little more specific to see how this can help.

Example of How Buffering Can Help

When a table is buffered you would expect to see in an ST05 trace that table name no longer pops up because the data is not being read from the database. If the table name does appear then the buffer has been "bypassed" in some way (e.g., join) or the query does not use the primary key (single record buffering) or the specified fields (generic buffering). You therefore need to fiddle with the code until the tables no longer appear in the ST05 trace. Here comes an example of this.

In Listing 5-28, you can see that the nature of the tables has been commented (automatically using the trick described earlier in the chapter) above the SQL queries. In this case, the requirement is to get every single possible "patternset" (it does not matter what a patternset is) into an internal table, and then fill another table with all the values for that patternset. It would be inadvisable to do a join on the two tables, as they are both buffered.

Listing 5-28. Initial SQL Query on Patternset Tables

```
* ZTVC_PSETS–Fully Buffered–Primary Key = PATTERNSET
  SELECT *
    FROM ztvc_psets
    INTO CORRESPONDING FIELDS OF TABLE et_patternsets.

  CHECK sy-subrc = 0.

* ZTVC_PSET_VALUES–Generic Buffering–Primary Key = PATTERNSET /
COUNTER–Buffering on PATTERNSET
  SELECT *
    FROM ztvc_pset_values
    INTO CORRESPONDING FIELDS OF TABLE et_patternset_values.
```

This code was called an enormous number of times in the live system, and it was code I had written. I was expecting there to be no database access at all. However, after this had been in production a while I was horrified to see that the read on the second table was causing a bucket load of database access all the time—the buffer was not being used at all.

Where was I going wrong? Well, a generic buffered table will not add anything to the buffer unless it gets a query with the field(s) that have been specified. In this case, one field had been specified—the field PATTERNSET. The query in Listing 5-28 has no selection fields at all, thus the condition to add records to the buffer was never met.

Before ABAP 7.50 the solution would have been to run round in a loop, doing a query for every row in the first table and thus implicitly adding the entries to the buffer. As from 7.50 and above, FAE no longer bypasses the buffer, so instead of a loop a FAE query can be used, as shown in Listing 5-29.

Listing 5-29. Improved SQL Query on Patternset Tables

```
* ZTVC_PSETS–Fully Buffered–Primary Key = PATTERNSET
* Fully buffered so should be no database access at all
  SELECT *
    FROM ztvc_psets
    INTO CORRESPONDING FIELDS OF TABLE et_patternsets
    ORDER BY PRIMARY KEY.

  IF sy-subrc NE 0.
    RETURN.
  ENDIF.

* ZTVC_PSET_VALUES–Generic Buffering on PATTERNSET–Primary Key = PATTERNSET
/ COUNTER
* Generic buffering and FOR ALL ENTRIES should use buffering, so in theory
no database access at all
  SELECT *
    FROM ztvc_pset_values
    INTO CORRESPONDING FIELDS OF TABLE et_patternset_values
    FOR ALL ENTRIES IN et_patternsets
    WHERE patternset EQ et_patternsets-patternset.
```

You will note in the comments in Listing 5-29 I said "in theory" there would be no database access; happily that turned out to be the case in reality as well.

In general, the main task you have is to take buffered tables out of joins. It is much faster to get all the data you need from normal tables in a join and then add the data from the buffered tables afterward, as that reduces overall database access.

Common Misconception About Generic Buffering

As mentioned earlier, generic buffering is when you set the number of fields needed to trigger buffering to fewer fields than the primary key. It would be silly to choose generic buffering and then specify all the primary fields, because in that case the table would in fact be single record buffered. Thus, the system does not let you choose all the fields. Instead, if you have five fields in the primary key, when you choose generic buffering you must choose a number between one and four in regard to how many fields of the primary key trigger buffering. That is, if you choose four and only the first three fields are supplied in the query the buffer will not be used/triggered.

So far so good—but here comes a common mistake virtually everybody makes, including the developers at SAP. As you know, the vast majority of database tables in SAP are client dependent—that is, they have different data in each client. Thus, the first field of such tables is the client field MANDT. In Figure 5-21, you see a standard SAP table TVKOT that contains the text descriptions of sales organizations.

Transparent Table	TVKOT		Active			
Short Description	Organizational Unit: Sales Organizations: Texts					

Attributes	Delivery and Maintenance	Fields	Input Help/Check	Currency/Quantity Fields

Srch Help   Built-In Type

Field	Key	Ini...	Data element	Data Type	Length	Deci...	Short Description
MANDT	✓	✓	MANDT	CLNT	3	0	Client
SPRAS	✓	✓	SPRAS	LANG	1	0	Language Key
VKORG	✓	✓	VKORG	CHAR	4	0	Sales Organization
VTEXT	☐	☐	VTXTK	CHAR	20	0	Name

Figure 5-21. *Definition of text table TVKOT*

Text tables are wonderful candidates for generic buffering. The names of the sales organizations are defined in customizing and very rarely change, plus there are not very many of them, and the text table is accessed all the time, so reading the values from the buffer instead of the database makes a lot of sense. However, let us say at one point you had six countries active and now you only have four, yet the text names are set up in all six languages. It would be a waste of space to store the texts for the two languages that are never used in the buffer.

As you can see from Figure 5-21, the primary key of the table is language (SPRAS) and sales organization (VKORG), and the result is the text description of the sales organization (VTEXT). The programmer rightly decided to use generic buffering, and the intention was that the first time any query was done on TVKOT that specified the language of the user logged on then every single record in that table that had a corresponding SPRAS would be loaded into the buffer, but *only* records for that particular language.

When the programmer set up the technical settings for TVKOT they were asked by the system how many key fields to use. The programmer thought to themselves, "The language is the only important field so the answer to that question is one field; i.e., the language field." The result can be seen in Figure 5-22.

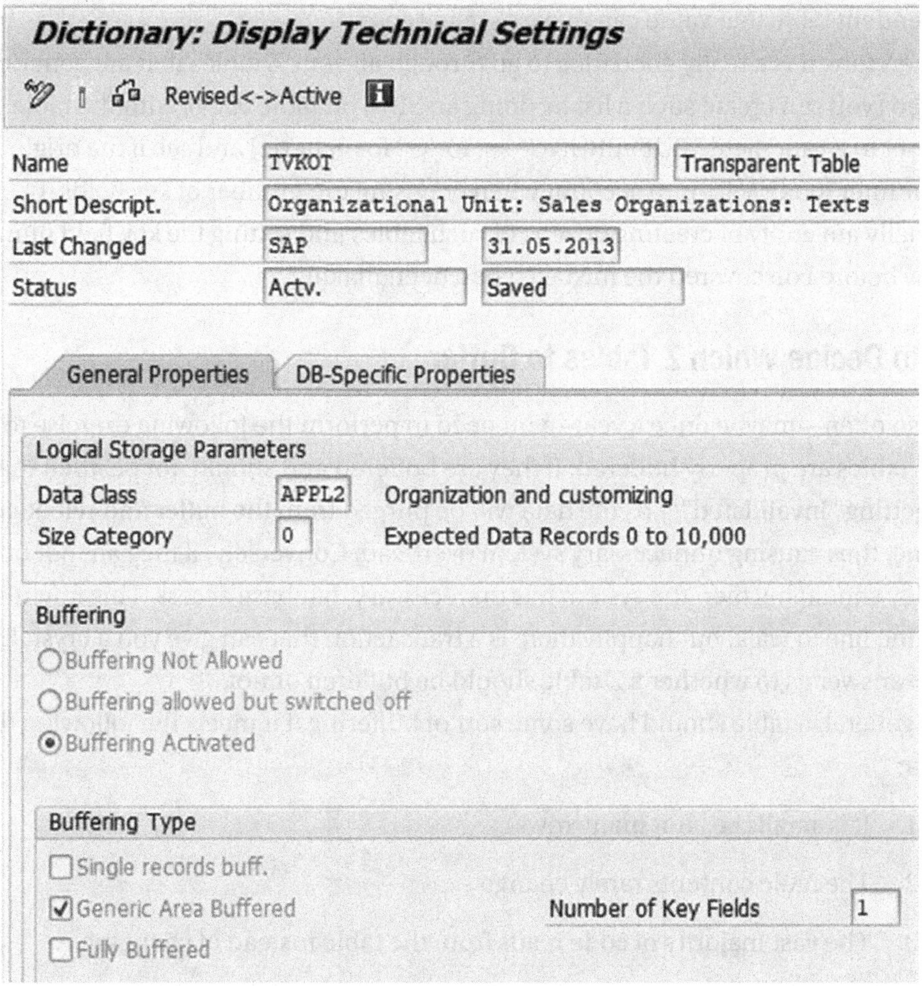

Figure 5-22. *Technical settings for table TVKOT*

However, unfortunately the answer "one" is the wrong answer because the client field MANDT counts. Setting the value to one means the table is buffered on MANDT. Setting the value to two means the table is buffered on MANDT + SPRAS. As discussed, you cannot set the value to 3.

Since every ABAP SQL query implicitly adds the MANDT field when accessing client-dependent tables, the very first time any query on TVKOT occurs everything in the table with the same client field as the client the user is logged on to is loaded into memory. Since there is usually only one client in production, that means that in the live system this table is effectively fully buffered; i.e., stores more records in the buffer than are actually needed. I am 100 percent positive that was not the original intention.

So you may ask, why allow the value of 1 at all? The answer is that for a client-independent table that value can make perfect sense.

Therefore, it is a really good idea to go through all your Z tables that are generically buffered (you can create such a list by doing an SE16 on table DD09L with the table name set to Z* and field "PUFFERUNG" set to "G" for generic) and see if the original programmer took MANDT into account when choosing the number of key fields. I personally am guilty of creating dozens of such tables and setting the key field number too low before I discovered the mistake I had been making.

How to Decide Which Z Tables to Buffer

Every so often—maybe once a year—you need to perform the following exercise to see if your Z tables are properly buffered. If they are buffered and should not be, then they will keep getting "invalidated"; i.e., the data will be purged from the buffer and reloaded all the time, thus causing unnecessary system overhead. Conversely, if they are not buffered and they should be, then the system has unnecessary database access. This might seem like a fine line to walk, but happily there is a transaction that can give you a crystal clear yes/no answer as to whether a Z table should be buffered or not.

In general, a table should have some sort of buffering if it meets the following three criteria:

1. It is small (i.e., not many rows).

2. The table contents rarely change.

3. The vast majority of code reads from the table instead of changing or adding to it.

All customizing tables meet those criteria, and all transactional tables fail all three.

That answers the buffering question on the spot for those two types of table, but for many tables things are not quite so clear cut. Luckily, there is a transaction to help you— transaction ST10. You can do the analysis directly in production. This procedure will not cause the universe to explode, and the results come back very quickly.

Call up the transaction and change the default setting until they look like the ones in Figure 5-23. If your SAP system is truly enormous you may want to limit the time period to "previous month."

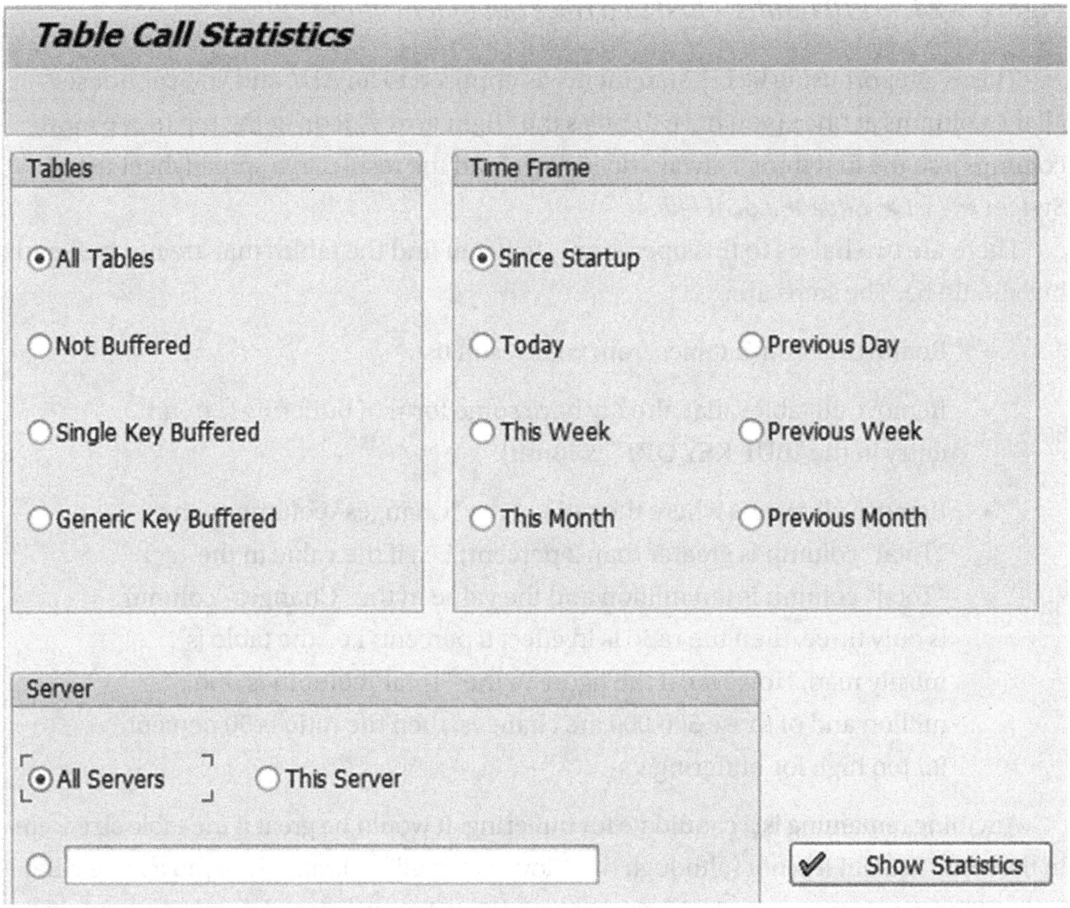

Table Call Statistics

Tables	Time Frame	
⦿ All Tables	⦿ Since Startup	
○ Not Buffered	○ Today	○ Previous Day
○ Single Key Buffered	○ This Week	○ Previous Week
○ Generic Key Buffered	○ This Month	○ Previous Month

Server	
⦿ All Servers	○ This Server
○ [ ]	✓ Show Statistics

***Figure 5-23.** Transaction ST10*

When you press the Show Statistics button, a gigantic list of every single table in the system that has had a SQL query since database startup appears, as shown in Figure 5-24.

Performance analysis: Table call statistics

Choose   Generic buffer   Single record buffer   Not buffered   Sort   Analyze table   Servers <-> tables   🖫   Reset   Refresh

System: All servers   All tables
Date & time of snapshot: 11.10.2020   14:01:00   System Startup: 13.09.2020 13:51:15

| Table | Buf key opt | Invali- dations | ABAP Processor requests | | | | DB activity | |
			Total	Direct reads	Seq. reads	Changes	Calls	Rows affected
Total		*023999	266410950053	87532205085	177847656866	1031088,102	25024983938	134056623361
/ALG/GENTK001		0	1,157	1,049	98	10	2,496	1,108
/ALG/GENTK001T		0	314	302	2	10	630	312

Figure 5-24. *ST10 results—first two rows out of ten billion zillion*

This is a report using WRITE statements as opposed to an ALV, and you cannot see all the columns at once (you have to press the "right arrow" icon at the top to see more columns), so the first thing I always do is download the results to a spreadsheet using *System ➤ List ➤ Save ➤ Local File.*

There are two halves to this operation—first you find the tables that are not buffered but should be. The steps are:

- Remove all non-Z tables from your result list.

- Remove all tables that already have some form of buffering (i.e., an entry in the "BUF KEY OPT" column).

- Remove all results where the ratio of the "Changes" column to the "Total" column is greater than 2 percent; i.e., if the value in the "Total" column is ten million and the value in the "Changes" column is only three, then the ratio is in effect 0 percent; i.e., the table is mostly read. However, if the figure in the "Total" column is one million and of those 500,000 are changes, then the ratio is 50 percent, far too high for buffering.

Anything remaining is a candidate for buffering. It would be great if the table size were in the result list, but it is not (although the "Rows Affected" column gives you a huge clue). To be 100 percent sure, do an SE16 on each candidate to see the total number of rows in production. There is no "magic number," but generally if there are more than 50,000 rows it is probably not a good candidate for full buffering. Generic or single row buffering might be appropriate; you will just have to use common sense once you get a good understanding of how the table is used. This is a fine example of why developers need a good understanding of the business process in order to optimize the system technically.

The second half of the exercise is to find tables that are buffered but should not be. This is basically the reverse of the first process.

- Remove all non-Z tables from your result list.

- Remove all tables that have no buffering.

- Remove all results that have a zero or trivial number in the "Invalidations" column.

An "invalidation" is where the table has been changed such that the buffer needs to be refreshed. If this is happening a large number of times, then maybe the table should not be buffered. There is no magic threshold number or ratio that can be used here; investigation on a case-by-case basis is needed. Usually you find that a transactional Z table has been buffered by accident.

SELECT * on Buffered Tables

Some programmers advocate always using `SELECT *` on buffered tables. The argument is that there is no need for field lists, as all fields in the table are already in the buffer. That is undoubtably true, but the counter-argument is that listing just the fields you need makes it clearer what the code is using the database selection for.

Postmortem Tricks

In this section you will find two little tricks to help when dealing with performance problems reported in the live system. The first is all about changing programs than run in batch, while the second is to do with a common task developers often forget to do.

Batch Jobs

Often, you will get reports that a batch job running a Z program is taking a long time to run. A good approach to take as an initial step is to make some non-invasive changes in the program before changing anything major. So change that program such that before each major database read a message is output saying what data is being retrieved. I created a class that took such a message, and if the program was online it output that information to the user at the bottom of the screen via the SAPGUI_PROGRESS_INDICATOR, but if the program was running in batch the message was output as an "S" message so it would appear in the SM37 log of the batch job.

That way, if a user runs the program online you might—if you are really lucky—have them tell the help desk "the program pauses for ages after the XYZ message." Regardless, if such messages are output, and the program is run in batch, and you look at the SM37 log, then you will see something like the log in Figure 5-25.

Date	Time	Message text
21.07.2020	02:03:18	Step 002 started (program ZFIR_CARTAGE, variant PIONEER2, user ID SSCBATCH)
21.07.2020	02:03:18	Get Shipment Cost Data
21.07.2020	06:49:37	Get Shipment Data

Figure 5-25. *SM37 batch job log*

In Figure 5-25, you can see there is a four-hour gap between one database read and the next. No database read should take four hours, so you are given a clue that you need to concentrate your analysis efforts on the code between the two message statements. In the preceding example, it turned out there were nested loops over non-sorted internal tables causing a geometric increase in the runtime.

Deadlocks

Once upon a time, I had two seemingly unrelated problems on my list—the BASIS department had reported that the database log showed there were "deadlocks" on a Z table, and an analyst had reported that a certain batch job usually ran really quickly but occasionally paused for half an hour for no apparent reason. These two problems turned out to be one and the same.

A deadlock is where two programs try to update the same database rows at the same time, and each SQL update request pauses until the other one is finished, and so neither ever finishes. The result is usually a short dump that mentions a deadlock specifically (if the process is in the background) or a "time out" short dump (if the process in is in dialog). That makes it obvious what is going on.

In this case, however, it seems the database every so often was clever enough such that after a (long) while it managed to break the deadlock and let one of the two competing processes complete. I am not sure that is supposed to happen, but it did explain the half-hour pause followed by the batch job completing normally.

In any event, the solution was trivial—this sort of thing never happens with standard SAP tables, because of the locking mechanism. All standard SAP transactional tables have a "lock object," and before attempting any database change the program tries to lock the object. If it cannot (because the database row[s] are locked by another program) then the program does not even try to do the database update but instead gives an error message or whatever.

In this case, the Z table was indeed a transactional table and got updated every ten minutes but had no lock object at all. This is a very easy problem to fix. Generating a lock object out of a database table takes only a few minutes—you can do it straight from transaction SE11. This will generate two function modules to lock and unlock the object, and then you insert those in your Z code at the appropriate places, and the deadlock problem goes away.

Sneaky Tricks

This section is going to be a "mixed bag" in which you will hear about some tricks to improve performance in your programs that you most likely are not aware of. The various tricks have no relationship to each other and are in no particular order.

Database Reads in a Loop

I once had a help-desk call where the problem was that an accountant was trying to run a line-item report for profit center line items for a combination of profit center + account for a three-year period. It always timed out.

In theory, this should not have happened, as the index on GLPCA was on profit center + account + posting period + year.

It was possible to replicate the problem in the development system, as it had a large enough amount of data to cause the performance problem. I could tell by the ST05 trace that the correct index was being used, but it still took a really long time for the data to come back.

As an experiment, I changed the code such that if only one profit center was chosen and only one GL account and the user chose (say) a three-year period, then 36 different database reads were done in a loop—one for each month in that three-year period.

Normally, doing a database read in a loop as opposed to all at once is the opposite of what you should be doing. However, in this case I was amazed to find the performance improvement was nothing short of miraculous.

I can only imagine this was because each of those 36 queries had unique values for the four fields of the index and a query on one unique combination out of a possible 800 x 800 x 12 x 20 is a very unique selection indeed and so took no time at all. This is similar to how the INDEX SKIP SCAN described earlier in the chapter works.

I would still recommend starting with trying to get all the values from the database in one hit, and only if that does not seem to work at all (as in this case) do an experiment to see if reading in a loop helps.

Using Standard SAP "Buffering" Modules

There is a whole bucket load of standard SAP function modules that read standard tables and automatically buffer the results; e.g., SD_VBAK_SINGLE_READ, MARA_SINGLE_READ, ME_EKKO_SINGLE_READ. It would be nice if the naming convention were a bit more standardized as that would make it easier to find such modules.

In this section, first you will hear about when it is a good idea to use these modules, then about a sneaky trick for a specific function that reads customer data, and lastly about a tip on how to optimize database access when you do decide to use such function modules.

When to Use Them

The downside of using such modules is that every single field from the table in question is read instead of just the ones you need, and the upside is that if your program calls standard SAP functions (e.g., a BAPI) or is inside a user exit in a standard SAP program, chances are that the standard SAP program uses such buffering modules and so the buffer is shared between your Z code and the standard SAP code. That can make a big difference to performance.

Sadly, there is often more than one standard SAP function module for buffering for a given table, so if you call one or more standard SAP functions or classes they might use more than one buffering module for the table, and this reduces the benefit. Thus, you need to look at the standard SAP code you are calling to see what exact function modules it uses.

Anyway, in the first case (100 percent standalone code) it is better to write your own buffering code, and in the second it is better to use the standard SAP buffering modules.

KNA1_SINGLE_READER

One standard module to read customer header details is KNA1_SINGLE_READER. You might decide to use this in one of your programs to read data from KNA1 and then be surprised when you do an ST05 trace and still see a very large number of database reads on KNA1. That is because for that particular module there is a maximum buffer size—and the default value is hard coded to one hundred records only.

There are lots of standard function modules that read customer header data in a buffered manner, and all have different buffer sizes. KNA1_READ_SINGLE only buffers five records, and V_KNA1_SINGLE_READ also buffers one hundred, but it is best to use KNA1_SINGLE_READER because in that case you can set the buffer size yourself.

When using KNA1_SINGLE_READER, the default value of 100 might not be anywhere near the amount you need to have in memory at once, so you can set the maximum buffer size with your program prior to the first call of the function. This works by setting a parameter ID (PID), which is then picked up by the function module and used to change the maximum buffer size. How to set the PID is shown in Listing 5-30.

Listing 5-30. Setting the Maximum Buffer Size for KNA1_SINGLE_READER

```
"Set buffer size for customer reads-picked up by Function Module KNA1_
SINGLE_READER
 DATA ld_value TYPE xuvalue VALUE '5000'.
 SET PARAMETER ID 'VS_GEN_READ_BUFFER' FIELD ld_value.
```

Prefilling Buffers

If you are going to use such standard SAP modules, you could do worse than copying a trick that you often see in standard SAP programs. Your program may start off with a big internal table that has a purchase order in each row. You know that you need all the header PO data for the values in that table, and then later on in the program possibly more purchase order values might get added that are not in the list. At the end you call a standard SAP program (e.g., RSNAST00 to send an IDoc) that at some point uses the standard SAP function module ME_EKKO_SINGLE_READ to get purchase order header details.

Instead of reading all the unique entries' values from table EKKO one at a time, in a loop over an internal table, it is far more efficient to read them all at once, as shown in Listing 5-31.

Listing 5-31. Prefilling the EKKO Buffer

```
FORM prefill_ekko_buffer.

  DATA: lt_selection_table TYPE STANDARD TABLE OF ekko_key.

  CHECK gt_all_sources[] IS NOT INITIAL.

  LOOP AT gt_all_sources ASSIGNING FIELD-SYMBOL(<ls_sources>).
    INSERT VALUE #(
    ebeln = <ls_sources>-ebeln )
    INTO TABLE lt_selection_table.
  ENDLOOP.

  SORT lt_selection_table BY ebeln.
  DELETE ADJACENT DUPLICATES FROM lt_selection_table
  COMPARING ebeln.

  CALL FUNCTION 'ME_EKKO_ARRAY_READ'
    TABLES
      pti_ekko_keytab           = lt_selection_table[]
    EXCEPTIONS
      err_no_records_requested = 1
      err_no_records_found      = 2
      OTHERS                    = 3.

  IF sy-subrc <> 0.
    RETURN.
  ENDIF.

ENDFORM.
```

Once the "array read" has been done from the database, all the initial values are stored, and any time ME_EKKO_READ_SINGLE is called by either your Z code or the standard SAP program the buffer will be used, and if the entry is not already there the buffer will be appended.

Constants

A top tip that Horst Keller from SAP once gave in a comment to a blog on the SAP Community website is that when you have a proper immutable constant, don't declare it as a local constant but rather as a global one. That way, if you have 54 instances of the program running in different user sessions, the ABAP runtime system will use black magic to only have the value of the constant existing in one place in shared memory and all the user sessions will read the value from there. The amount of memory this saves is miniscule, but the more microscopic savings you make the better—they all add up.

You could even have a global interface just full of (related) constants—I see a lot of standard SAP classes like that. This is for when such a constant needs to be read by more than one program. The "clean code" guidelines are against this approach—those guidelines say to use "enumerations" instead of a constants interface. All well and good, but at time of writing (2020) virtually nobody outside of SAP has a cutting-edge ABAP version where enumerations are available.

INTO CORRESPONDING

When you do a SELECT statement on a database table, you can specify the target using INTO and then you have to make 100 percent sure the structure of the target is an exact match for the order of the fields in the SELECT statement.

The alternative is to list the fields in the SELECT statement in any order you feel like and then use the INTO CORRESPONDING FIELDS OF variant, and that way you can be sure that every database field in the selection list will find its way to the correct identically named field in the target internal table or structure.

The urban myth is that using the INTO CORRESPONDING variant causes a performance problem as the system has to spend extra time working out where to put each database field in the target structure.

I had always suspected this was nonsense, because as far as I could tell from the experiments I did, whichever variant I used seemed to have the same performance. I always preferred INTO CORRESPONDING for stability reasons—you never knew when someone was going to add another field to the end (or in the middle) of the list of fields to be retrieved, and in that case if INTO CORRESPONDING was *not* being used the whole program would break.

It turns out the database is a lot cleverer than you might think—provided you define a target structure or table with only the fields you actually need from the database. In Listing 5-32, you will see the two possible selection methods—a straight SELECT INTO and then the same thing but with SELECT * and INTO CORRESPONDING FIELDS OF.

Listing 5-32. Two Ways of Reading Fields from Table MARA

```
TYPES: BEGIN OF l_typ_material,
         matnr TYPE mara-matnr,
         matkl TYPE mara-matkl,
         meins TYPE mara-meins,
       END   OF l_typ_material.

DATA: ls_material TYPE l_typ_material.

* Use Field List
SELECT SINGLE matnr matkl meins
  FROM mara
  INTO ls_material
  WHERE matnr = '000000000000001086'.

* Use INTO CORRESPONDING
SELECT SINGLE *
  FROM mara
  INTO CORRESPONDING FIELDS OF ls_material
  WHERE matnr = '000000000000001086'.
```

You would expect the second query to try to read every single field in MARA and then pass the lot back to the application server and spend a load of effort trying to put the three relevant fields in the correct places in the target structure.

In fact, when you do an ST05 trace on the preceding code you will get the SQL query seen in Figure 5-26—for *both* SELECT statements.

```
SQL Statement

SELECT
/*+
   FIRST_ROWS(1)
*/
   "MATNR","MATKL","MEINS"
FROM
   "MARA"
WHERE
   "MANDT"=:A0 AND "MATNR"='00000000000001086' FETCH FIRST 1 ROW ONLY
```

Figure 5-26. *SQL statement generated from both types of reads on MARA*

If the SQL statement is the same, then the performance is going to be the same. Moreover, with the INTO CORRESPONDING variant you can add an extra field into the target structure, and it will automatically be populated by the existing query.

In conclusion, there is no actual performance problem with using INTO CORRESPONDING, and you can even use SELECT * provided you specify the target structure/table correctly.

DDIC Information

Every so often you may find yourself doing some sort of dynamic programming whereby the exact name of the table you are dealing with is not known until runtime. The preferred way to deal with such a situation is to employ RTTI (runtime type identification) using the subclasses of CL_ABAP_TYPEDESCR. However, you may feel the burning urge to do a direct read on database table DD03L, which contains a list of all the fields in a given DDIC table.

If you look at the technical settings of any of the DDIC metadata tables you may wonder why they are not buffered—after all, they very rarely change, or are not that large in IT terms and are always read and never written to in production outside of an incoming transport request.

This is because SAP uses another mechanism entirely whenever a standard SAP program wants such information. For example, if a standard SAP program wanted the contents of DD03L it would call function DDIF_NAMETAB_GET. Deep in the bowels of that function you will see the code shown in Listing 5-33.

Listing 5-33. How Standard SAP Programs Get Table Information

```
system-call import nametab x030l_wa x031l_tab id tabname.
```

As you can see, standard SAP programs use some sort of black magic call to the kernel to get the table information, and that causes no database access. As might be imagined, the RTTI classes use the same mechanism. Thus, trying to reinvent the wheel and access the DDIC metadata tables directly is somewhat counterproductive from a performance point of view.

Using Standard SAP Functions Incorrectly

This section has talked about reusing standard SAP function modules. This can be helpful in some scenarios, but you need to be 100 percent sure of what the function does and especially that it causes no side effects. As usual, I will tell you a horror story about when the misuse of such functions can make everything go terribly wrong.

Once upon a time, a business analyst thought it would be good to add the document-clearing status of the invoice to a particular report because it would help one person, once a month, with reconciliation. This new field to be added would tell the end user whether an invoice had been cleared, partially cleared, or was still outstanding.

This did not seem an unreasonable requirement—after all, you can see that status quite clearly on the document flow. You could say the underlying problem is adding more and more fields to the same report every single year, giving that report more responsibilities. We don't like that in program design—the so-called Single Responsibility Principle—so do we like it in applications? The Fiori paradigm seems to go the other way, replacing monolithic applications that do hundreds of things with lots of applications that do one thing each.

In any event, when this was assigned to a programmer they had a problem—the invoice-clearing status was not in document flow table VBFA. If it had been, all would have been well. The obvious question was then—if the value is not in the document flow database table, how in the world does that value show up in the document flow? So the programmer debugged the document flow to find out.

It turned out the standard SAP function module RV_DOCUMENT_FLOW_INFORMATION is used in the standard SAP document flow code and returns an enhanced VBFA table that does indeed contain the invoice-clearing status, amongst a *lot* of other data. So a big chunk of standard SAP code was copied into the custom program, ending with a call to that standard function, and then evaluated the invoice-clearing status bit of it to fill the new field. That worked fine: the correct result was returned for the new field, the change went to production, everyone was happy.

However, looking at the "bigger picture" there were three problems with this new change:

- This report was run many times a day by a great many people—hundreds, in fact. Of those only one person cared about the new field, and then only once a month, yet the field was derived every time the report was run and stored as a hidden field.

- The standard SAP module to get the invoice-clearing status was called in a loop, once per record in the main internal table, and there were usually a great many records in that internal table.

- The standard SAP module read about 30 or 40 different SAP tables, ending with BKPF and BSEG, which it used to see if the invoice was cleared.

When a SQL trace was done on the report, it transpired that the assorted database reads inside the repeated calls to the RV_DOCUMENT_FLOW_INFORMATION function module were taking up the vast majority of the runtime. There were so many of them that this caused the "5000 records already, do you want to continue?" message to pop up when doing an ST05 trace, even on a small selection of data.

To make matters worse, the vast bulk (99.99 percent) of the data being brought back from the database in that standard function call was not even getting used, just one field from one of the very large number of tables being read. In a loop.

I had the radical idea that if we are only interested in the results from the BSEG table, then maybe what we should do is just read the BSEG table, and maybe only once, not in a loop? Now, BSEG is a horrible table to read, as it is a cluster table, at least until you get onto HANA, but the upside was whatever change was made, the result could not be worse than before.

Next, I did a search on this huge report program to see if BSEG was already getting read, and yes it was, all in one go. However, this only happened if the end user ticked "Do you want invoice information?" on the selection screen. I asked the business analyst if the one user who needed the clearing status ticked that box, and yes that user did.

The end result was, for eight years, there was a performance problem with the report in production. That eight-year period was the time between the extra field (and the repeated calls to the standard module) being added and a performance ticket being raised, which caused me to come along and look at the program.

During that period, if an end user ran the report and did not tick the "invoice information" box, then the program made ten billion un-needed database reads plus one sort of useful one on BSEG. If they did tick that box, they got the same ten billion reads, and this time two identical reads on BSEG, to get the same invoice-clearing information; at one point in the program the data was retrieved all at once, at another point the data was retrieved a bit at a time in a loop.

So, I moved the logic to populate the invoice-clearing field to just after the read on BSEG that was already happening if the user pressed the "invoice" tick box and got rid of the call to the standard SAP function module altogether.

The end result was that the report ran much faster for the one person looking for the clearing information, and much faster yet again for the 99.99 percent of people who did not care and thus did not tick the "invoice" box.

The moral of the story is that using a standard SAP function that appears to do exactly what you want can actually cause more harm than good if you don't have a clear idea of everything it actually does.

The second moral of the story is that once any given program gets over a certain level of complexity, then horrible things can easily get added and no one is ever the wiser, possibly for many years.

Going back to TDD (as I always do), some people have said that an ALV report like the one in this example has no need to be written in an OO manner. When this program started out, no doubt that was true. However, as it got more and more complicated it started to break down and decay. Now, you could say that would have happened in an OO program as well.

There is nothing magical about OO programs that makes them read the database in a better way. All the horrors about reading data far too many times could well have happened if methods were used rather than FORM routines.

However, a well-written OO program would have had automated unit tests. You might think tests are crazy in a read-only report. However, it would have been much more obvious that there were two almost identical routines getting virtually the same invoice information.

Conclusion

This chapter has been about the third pillar of code quality—performance. First, you were introduced to the over-arching concept of custom program optimization and how it is the duty of every developer to proactively monitor the performance of every custom program in the live system.

Then, you moved on to the three types of performance checks that you carry out—static and runtime checks, which are generally done whilst creating or changing code, and "postmortem" checks, which are generally done after a problem has been reported for a program already in production.

The chapter ended with a bunch of sneaky tricks that can help with performance problems.

At this point in the development cycle, you might be forgiven for thinking you are done with the BLUE phase of the TDD process. The code is easy to understand (clarity) and does what it is supposed to do every time (stability) very quickly indeed (performance).

However, there is one more aspect to be addressed before the code can truly become great—an aspect that is overlooked the vast majority of the time. This aspect of user friendliness is the subject of the next chapter.

CHAPTER 6

User Friendliness: Ensuring UI Quality

Making an application user friendly is sadly often the last thing on a programmer's mind.

SAP applications in the past traditionally had the UI done with DYNPRO (Dynamic Program) or the ALV (ABAP List Viewer), and people made a lot of mistakes with that approach, thinking that if a tool does everything for you then you cannot possibly go wrong; i.e., you don't need to even think about the UI. You can't normally go horribly wrong using the ALV, but some programmers managed it, and the DYNPRO screens are what got SAP its bad UI reputation in the first place.

These days, technology has dramatically advanced. As a result of using UI5 and an XML/JavaScript approach, the scope for doing the wrong thing with the UI is in fact much greater, so the need to think about the UI—which has always been there—has gotten more important.

In this chapter, you will learn how to increase the quality of the UI regardless of the technology used. As with the previous chapters, a large number of concrete examples will be shown.

This chapter comes at this point in the book because the nature of the UI is addressed after the backend code works properly and is fast enough to make an application responsive. Going back to TDD (as I always do), for traditional ABAP programs the UI is an often overlooked part of the BLUE phase. With UI5, the UI can be developed in a 100 percent TDD manner using the built-in test tools in JavaScript.

Thus far, we have dealt almost exclusively with the backend code. In a good program the user interface is totally decoupled from the business logic. This is difficult but not impossible in traditional ABAP (DYNPRO/ALV) and is actually enforced in modern ABAP (Web Dynpro/UI5).

345

© Paul David Hardy 2021
P. D. Hardy, *Improving the Quality of ABAP Code*, https://doi.org/10.1007/978-1-4842-6711-0_6

This chapter starts with a discussion of various philosophical aspects of user friendliness that are completely independent of the technology in use. Each subsequent section starts off at the abstract level, but all the examples are SAP specific.

Next comes the subject of consistency—the idea that every application should behave the same way as far as possible. This leads into the next topic, which is ease of use—the idea that the consistent way of behaving should be the way that is easiest for the end user.

We then move on to the subject of errors—first, how to prevent them from happening in the first place, and then if they do happen how to make the experience as painless as possible for the end user.

Last, you'll hear about the boring (to developers) subject of documentation and why it is so vital to making life easier for not only the users but also—surprisingly—the developers themselves!

General Philosophy

There are about 20 million billion computer applications that people have to use, but one thing binds them all together—there is always a human on the other end trying to use the application, and nine times out of ten they curse each and every application they have to use.

To get an understanding of why this might be on a general level, first we look at the difference between UI and UX and see which of the two is actually the important one, then move on to the most famous concept in the computer usability world, namely, "Don't Make Me Think."

Lastly, the nature of traditional IT projects is explored to try to understand why they have never ended up delivering products humans can use.

Difference Between UI and UX

Before I even start, I want to clear up the misconception about the terms *UI* and *UX*. Many people think they are one and the same.

- *UI* stands for "user interface" — This is the technology the end user uses to access the application you have written. It could be UI5 or Web Dynpro or the ALV or traditional DYNPRO or even WRITE statements.

- *UX* stands for "user e**X**perience" — That is, how easy it is for the end user to use the application; e.g., how fast they can complete the transaction, how intuitive the screen is, how easy is it to recover when errors occur, etc.

- The two things are totally unrelated. The first relates to the technology used, while the second relates to how well that technology was implemented (programmed). Thus, you could have an application written with `WRITE` statements (old-fashioned UI) that is user friendly (good UX) and an application written using UI5 (modern UI) that is user hostile (bad UX).

Don't Make Me Think

No doubt there have been about half a billion books written on the subject of user interfaces, but in my opinion the most important one was *Don't Make Me Think!* by Steve Krug, which was all about the user friendliness (or not) of websites (`https://www.amazon.com.au/Dont-Make-Think-Steve-Krug/dp/0321344758`).

The book was written in the year 2000, but like so many books that state the "obvious" (i.e., it is obvious only after you have heard the concept) it is still as relevant today as it was then, and barring some sort of radical change in the way human brains work I can't see it ever being *not* relevant.

You may have seen the Steve Martin movie where in order to test if he is drunk or not the police officer first makes him walk on his hands whilst reciting the value of pi to 15 decimal places, and then when he manages that the officer has him juggle three balls whilst doing a tap dance and singing a specific opera song all at the same time.

The basic premise of *Don't Make Me Think!* is the opposite—any sort of user interface must be so obvious that you can instantly spot what you need to do to achieve any given task—even if you *are* drunk.

A bad example is one furniture website in Australia whose sole purpose is to sell furniture, yet even if you had the highest IQ in the universe you would not be able to work out how to buy the items shown on the screen. To make matters worse, there is a "go to shopping cart" button in the top right-hand corner, but seemingly no way to fill that cart. There probably is a way, but if you have to spend an hour working out how, you likely will not bother and will go to a competitor website that also sells furniture.

Back in the SAP world, imagine an application that asks you to approve/reject a purchase order. You would want to see all the (very few) pieces of important information at once (and then be able to go looking for more information only if you need to), right in your face, and there should be two big, obvious Approve/Reject buttons.

Approving a purchase order in the SAP GUI is not quite like that. The word *approve* is not there (it is called "releasing"), but instead every single piece of purchase order information (95 percent of which you don't care about) is shown to you all at once. Most important, how to actually approve the purchase order is not obvious at all. The more modern Fiori applications for achieving the same task are much more streamlined.

Waterfall Projects

The traditional method of dealing with an enormously complicated SAP project is to take the original user requirements, go and lock yourself and your team in a room for two years to build something, and then give the finished product to the user who wrote the original requirements and be really shocked when they say, "This is not what I wanted at all," and then you have to tell them, "Sorry, this is what you asked for, therefore what you're getting; the project has run out of money, we're doing a new one next week."

This is the "waterfall" method, and it is how most of the major SAP implementations I have observed over the years have worked. A few years either side of the year 2000 a lot of consulting companies made all the money in the world using this method. The secret to their success was they could hand over the finished product and then run out the door.

The inherent problem is that the customer—be they external or internal to your organization—is a human. Therefore, they (usually) don't really know what they really want, and even if they did they would not be able to articulate it properly. As a result, the requirement you as a developer get is pretty much never going to reflect the actual requirement in the real world.

This disconnect was identified a long time ago. The proposed solution was to move from a waterfall approach to a so-called agile approach.

What does the term *agile* here mean? Sadly, it means something totally different to every single person you ask. The simplest way of describing the concept is that you demonstrate what you have developed thus far at regular intervals to the customer (i.e., whoever it is that will be using the application in real life) so when (not if) they change their mind as to what it is they want you know far earlier in the development process.

If you looked on the internet you would think that the waterfall methodology is a thing of the past—nowadays surely everyone uses variants of the agile methodology, such as "extreme programming/scrum," in the same way all ABAP programmers use OO programming. Now, is that true? No.

One compromise is that if you absolutely have to use a waterfall methodology, then go live with the development but only let one or two users have access to it. Then those key users would come back with a non-stop stream of bug fixes and enhancements until the development was fit for a human to use. Then everyone else could have it. You might think one or two users is not a broad enough base to be representative, but it is a hell of a lot better than zero users looking at it before it goes live for the whole company, as appears to be the normal state of affairs, according to anecdotal evidence from all over the world.

Consistency

As you have seen, the idea is to stop people having to think when they are using applications. The less the end user has to think, the more user friendly the application is.

If you were to look at the UI in the ERP system J.D. Edwards, you would immediately notice that the screens in the different modules all look exactly the same—rather like a spreadsheet with lots of extra buttons. Conversely, if you were to look at the screens in different SAP modules—e.g., VA01 (Create Sales Order) in SD, ME21N (Create Purchase Order) in MM, and F01 (Enter GL Document) in FI—they look so different that you would be hard pressed to identify that they all belong to the same, integrated ERP system. There are historical reasons for this—the SAP modules were created over a large time period by different teams, and the J.D. Edwards modules were created all at once, as it were, but nonetheless it is not a good look for SAP. This is one reason SAP is trying to move users away from the SAP GUI and toward Fiori apps instead, which should (in theory) all look the same.

However, even if your job involves creating programs that run in the SAP GUI, there is no reason at all you cannot strive to apply consistency in those programs.

In this section, we first focus on the positive, looking at how usage of standards can ensure your applications are user friendly. Then, we focus on the negative, looking at some examples of how inconsistent behavior in various aspects of an application can lead to non-user-friendly applications.

Standards

One good way of achieving consistency in your programs is to follow standards such that the various elements of the application are where people expect them to be and the icon or text description clearly indicates what the function does.

As an example, in SAP the Save button is always at the top of the screen, and its icon looks like a floppy disk. Younger users may never have seen a floppy disk in real life, but they get used to the icon and what it represents. If the Save button were in a different position in different transactions and had a different icon each time, then users would have to spend time hunting for the button all over the screen.

In this section, we look first at using industry standards to make life easier for the end users, and then at some examples of how not using standards can make their life much more difficult.

Applying Industry Standards

You really cannot go wrong by looking at which companies have more or less a monopoly in their chosen field and then, rather than fighting it, using the same UI standards they do.

One good example of this is that up until version 4.6 of SAP all the "easy access" standard menu trees for accessing transaction codes (Logistics/Accounting/Human Resources, etc.) were located across the top of the screen. However, that was not the way Microsoft did it—the File Explorer menu was always at the left-hand side of the screen.

So eventually SAP caved in, and their main menu jumped to the left-hand side of the screen as well. That way, users who were in SAP half the day and Office half the day did not keep jumping from one user experience to the other.

In the same way, a lot of websites have standardized putting elements like search fields and the shopping cart in the same place Amazon does, purely because so many people use the Amazon site.

Therefore, the recommendation for your application is to not invent your own standards but rather follow a set of guidelines.

SAP has always had a set of online guidelines for DYNPRO applications, with code inspector warnings when they are breached. Usage of the ALV ensures all list reports look the same with the same row of icons at the top of the screen in the same position, and the "Floor Plan Manager" gives Web Dynpro a consistent look and feel.

In SAP UI5, the Fiori guidelines for good UI design are even stricter than the GUI ones (a good thing), and you have the equivalent of the Floor Plan Manager (Fiori Elements), which lets you automatically generate templates to ensure applications that perform the same function (e.g., list reports) look the same.

Non-Standard Icon Appearance

One of the strangest (and most short-lived) experiments that SAP did was to introduce a new GUI theme called Blue Crystal. A GUI theme sets the fonts and colors on the standard SAP screens, how the icons at the top of those screens appear, and so on. As a baseline, the SAP Signature Theme looks like Figure 6-1.

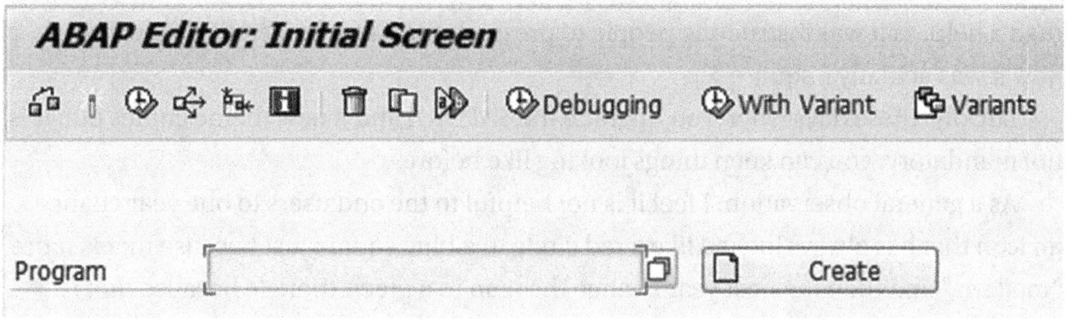

Figure 6-1. *SAP Signature Theme*

There were about five different themes created over the years, but none of them looked that radically different from the others. However, if you changed your theme (as recommended by SAP) to Blue Crystal, then the screen shown in Figure 6-1 suddenly looked like that in Figure 6-2.

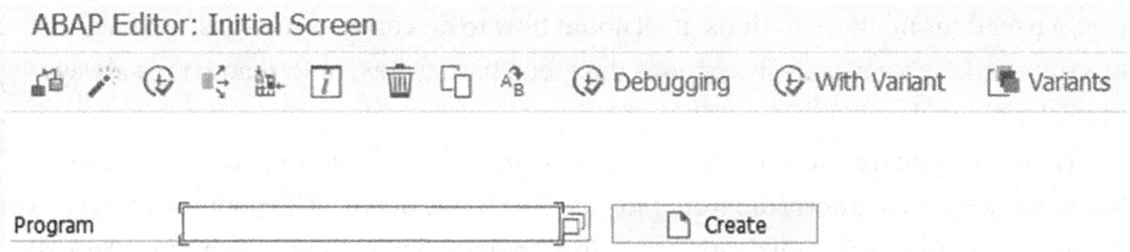

Figure 6-2. *Blue Crystal Theme*

Most of the icons looked vaguely similar, but some of them were utterly different, so much so that you had to spend a lot of time looking at the menu bar at the top of the screen wondering what icon was the one you wanted—something that used to be so easy it did not bear thinking about.

After about an hour, I could not take it anymore and wanted to revert back to the normal theme—and the irony was that the icon that let you switch themes had changed in appearance so much I could not find it for a while.

As a very similar example, in an SAP implementation I was on in the year 2000, all the training documentation was ready and had been mailed out to all the locations and was sitting on people's desks. An online version of all that documentation was available as well. Then a week before go-live the SAP GUI was upgraded. That changed the look of all the icons so much that the training documentation suddenly was more of a hindrance than a help, as it was instructing people to press a button that looked like a circle and now it was actually a square.

Luckily, these days when you upgrade the SAP GUI and a new theme comes out, it is not mandatory; you can keep things looking like before.

As a general observation, I feel it is not helpful to the end users to one year change an icon that has always looked like a red circle to a blue square just because that is more "modern," and then the next year change the icon to a green triangle because *that* is more "modern," and then the next year change it back to a red circle to give it a "fresh, new look."

Non-Standard Icon Usage

In the vast majority of cases, SAP has gone out of its way to ensure that in every application the same icon means the same thing; e.g., the icon that is supposed to look like a floppy disk always means "save," as indeed it does in Microsoft applications. That way, a user does not have to think at all about how to do certain functions—to back out of a transaction the user always presses the green back arrow, or to search they always press the binoculars icon.

Therefore, you would be crazy to develop your own application and use the normal "save" icon for some utterly different purpose like "page down." The poor old end users would not know if they were coming or going. To demonstrate a bad example, take SAP transaction MIRO, which is for entering supplier invoices. You can see a screenshot from that transaction in Figure 6-3.

Figure 6-3. *Screenshot from transaction MIRO*

In Figure 6-3, the third icon from the left, which looks a bit like two arrows chasing each other in a circle, usually means "refresh"; i.e. "update the current transaction with the latest data." However, in this transaction (and only in this transaction) that icon actually means "delete." That is a great surprise for the users.

The moral is clear—SAP was big enough to follow standards set by Microsoft and use the same icons for the same functions. In the same way, in your applications you should always use the icons in the same way SAP software does.

Inconsistency

SAP GUI transactions have traditionally been "all things to all people," containing a vast amount of functionality and hence a vast amount of screens and fields and assorted application-specific behavior. Nonetheless, certain aspects of the application are always supposed to behave the same way between applications (and indeed within the same application).

Let us take a look at three examples where that does not happen—F4 helps, pop-up screens (dialog boxes), and master data transactions.

Inconsistency in F4 Helps

If you press the same button in a transaction, then regardless of what field your cursor might be resting in, you expect the same behavior. You would be astonished otherwise. As an example, in the SAP GUI, pressing F1 should always bring up the documentation for whatever field your cursor is on, and F4 should always bring up a list of possible entries for whatever field your cursor is on. Sadly, it is possible in custom programs to deliberately assign the wrong function key to standard functions (you do get warned about this in the extended program check).

However, even if the correct function key is assigned, you sometimes get varying behavior by field based on the data element or some other factor. Take standard SAP transaction VD51 as an example. You can see what that transaction looks like in Figure 6-4.

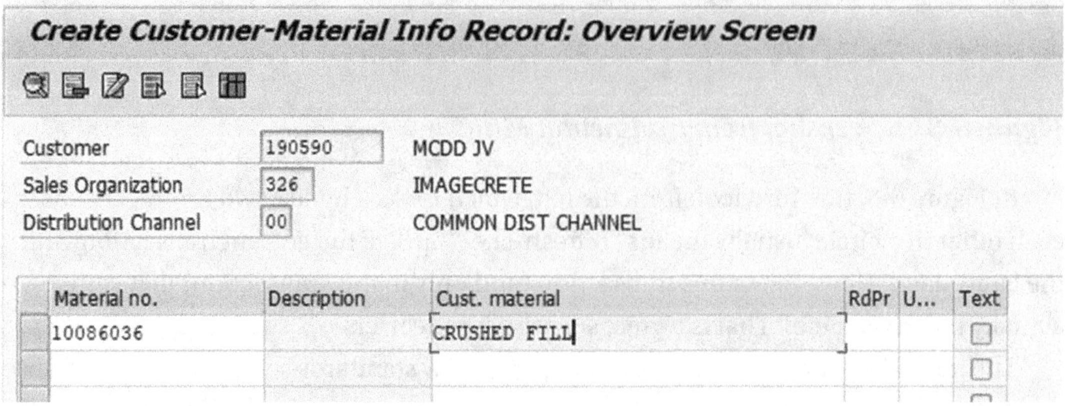

Create Customer-Material Info Record: Overview Screen

Customer	190590	MCDD JV
Sales Organization	326	IMAGECRETE
Distribution Channel	00	COMMON DIST CHANNEL

	Material no.	Description	Cust. material		RdPr	U...	Text
	10086036		CRUSHED FILL				☐
							☐
							☐

Figure 6-4. *Transaction VD51*

In Figure 6-4, you can see two small columns on the right side of the table control, the ones where you cannot tell what the headings mean (e.g., "U..." is not very meaningful). Both fields have drop-down arrows for possible values. If the two configuration tables that the two fields point to are both empty, then when you press F4 on the first field it says, "No possible entries," and if you press F4 on the second field it says, "No entries exist—would you like to create some?"

If a user sees a drop-down arrow, then they will probably press it and get puzzled that there are no entries to choose from. Worse, if they are asked if they want to create a possible entry value they might say yes and then get told they are not authorized—a puzzling and confusing experience whichever way you look at it.

When you have a custom program, the ideal situation would be to programmatically determine if there were any possible entries for a field and, if not, suppress the F4 help for that field; e.g., in a DYNPRO like this one set SCREEN-VALUE_HELP to 0.

Inconsistency in Pop-Ups

In one program I had to maintain there were about 50 different places where pop-ups were shown to the user, sometimes three or four in a row; i.e., in one pop-up the user chooses an option, thus triggering another pop-up, and so on.

These pop-ups were mostly called with CALL SCREEN STARTING AT X Y mixed in with a few POPUP_TO_CONFIRMS. As an academic exercise, I looked to see how many of the CALL SCREENS started at the same coordinates. It was none of them. So if a user went through four pop-ups, the boxes would be all over the screen like a mad wombat's breakfast, and the end user would have to chase the box with their cursor each time a new one appeared.

One of my colleagues suggested this was intentional, to force the user to move their eyes around the screen so they would pay attention to the contents of the box. I suspected the truth was that every pop-up box had been coded by a different person over a ten-year period and they each just picked a start position at random.

The recommendation is that since the standard POPUP_TO_CONFIRM defaults to appear at column 25 and row 6, then, unless there is a really good reason otherwise, that is a good place to have your pop-ups appear so as not to shock the user; i.e., avoid the situation whereby you have one pop-up in the top right of the screen, then the next in the bottom left, and so on.

In the same way, the code inspector warns you when a function key other than F12 is used for "cancel." In the program I was looking at, about 15 different function keys on different screens pointed at "cancel," but F12 was nowhere to be seen.

Happy ENDING

Often when programming a pop-up screen, the code will say CALL SCREEN STARTING AT A B ENDING AT X Y. The programmer often makes a guess as to how big that pop-up needs to be, and if that area turns out to be smaller than the screen definition then the end user will have to scroll up and down and/ or left and right in order to see all the fields. However, if you remove the ENDING AT part of the declaration then the pop-up box will automatically expand to the exact size needed to display all the fields at once. Thus, you should only use ENDING AT when it is important for whatever reason that only part of the screen be visible at once.

Inconsistency in Master Data Transactions

In virtually every master data key field in SAP the data is case insensitive—for example, if your system allows free text for customer numbers you can enter "Octopus" for the customer number, and it will be interpreted as OCTOPUS. It's the same for vendors—in fact, it is the same for every single master data field in the SAP system.

There did used to be an exception though, in the Plant Maintenance module, and that serves as a wonderful example of what not to do. In prior releases of SAP, the key field EQUNR for "equipment number" was case sensitive. That meant you could have two pieces of equipment called abc1234 and ABC1234 for the exact same piece of equipment. Someone would try to update the equipment master, have their caps lock off, and so type abc1234, find it did not exist (because only ABC1234 did), and then create abc1234 to solve the "problem."

SAP fixed this for their own application—EQUNR is now case insensitive—but it serves as a warning: Never make key fields of master data objects case sensitive.

Ease of Use

What makes an application "easy to use" is in many ways a value judgement that is impossible to measure, but you can apply some "hard" measures; e.g., it is fair to say that if a task in one application takes six button clicks but the same task in another application only takes one, then the second application is easier to use. This is why ATM PIN numbers are generally four digits long as opposed to twenty-four. The latter would make using your bank card a nightmare.

Humans have a natural tendency to anthropomorphize computers; i.e., treat them as if they were human or there was a little man inside reacting to the input they give. In recent years, devices like Alexa and Cortana just reinforce that perception. The end user does not blame the programmer for any bad behavior on the part of the program—they blame "the computer," hence the UK phrase "Computer says NO."

Given that fact, the examples in the next section ("Laying Traps for the User") would be perceived as the computer actively being evil, doing its best to stop the user from doing their job.

The examples in the subsequent section ("Confusing the User") would be perceived as the computer not really caring either way, giving vague hints to the user as to what to do but clearly having something more important on its mind.

In the last section ("Explaining Things to the User"), we will explore how to make it seem like the computer is actively trying to help the user achieve whatever it is they are trying to do.

Laying Traps for the User

In recent years, SAP (amongst others) has made much of "design thinking," where you try to imagine what the user of your software might want/like/need by creating a "persona" that represents the end user so you can "empathize" with them. Obviously, if you can actually go to where the end user actually is and ask them directly that is better, not that they often know themselves.

In this section, you will see some examples of how to not consider at all what an end user might want/need to do.

Hiding Icons for No Reason

Let us start with transaction ST05—the SQL trace analysis tool. The steps taken by an end user would be as follows:

- Start the trace.

- Run the transaction that is to be analyzed.

- Stop the trace.

- Call up the trace results.

- Look for identical SELECTS ("Value-Identical Statements").

- Sort the result list in some way, usually by number of executions.

To be honest, after choosing the "Value-Identical Statements" option I would have expected the result list to be sorted by number of executions in descending order by default (because an identical SELECT executed a million times is worse than one executed twice), but it is not. Therefore, you would want to manually sort the list. Unfortunately, when you choose the "Value-Identical Statements" option at the top of the screen a row of icons appears, as shown in Figure 6-5.

Figure 6-5. Icon list for "Value-Identical Statements" in ST05

The icon on the far left side in Figure 6-5 (the one that sort of looks like an arrow pointing right) is supposed to indicate that if you press that icon then a load of other icons that are currently hidden will appear. Those hidden icons would be the ones that are actually useful, like "sort," and indeed in lower versions of SAP those icons appeared by default. There is no logical reason at all to hide 90 percent of the icons. There is more than enough room on the screen—even after the extra icons appear there is still an ocean of emptiness to the right of the last icon, as shown in Figure 6-6.

Figure 6-6. *Icon list for "Value-Identical Statements" after expansion*

It could be argued that seven icons are less confusing than (say) twenty, but if that is the logic then hide the icons people don't use rather than the ones they always do. In this case, the "people" are developers!

Moreover, if we are talking about consistency, then the fact that no other SAP applications hide icons by default makes this the odd one out.

The moral of the story is to not hide icons—provided you have room to show them all—and even if you do not have room ask the end users which ones they use most often and do not hide those.

Hiding Fields for No Reason

I once stayed in a hotel in the United Kingdom, and in the breakfast area was a row of fruit-juice dispensers, but seemingly no glasses to put the juice in. After wandering around the room twice I found the cupboard the glasses were hidden in. I initially presumed someone had just forgotten to put them out, but every day that week I saw each and every hotel guest (the ones not yet in on the secret) wandering around looking for the glasses. We wondered if the hotel staff was watching from behind a one-way mirror, laughing.

In the same way, if there is a field that the user absolutely has to fill with a value or the transaction will not work at all, then it is probably a good idea to have that field in a prominent place, somewhere the user cannot possibly miss it.

Conversely, deliberately hiding that field from the end user and then laughing at them as they go frantically looking for it is not the way forward. Let us consider two examples of this behavior.

Slightly Hidden Field

Transaction VI05 is used to "settle" shipment costs; in other words, to do a good's receipt against the driver's purchase order so they get paid whatever the system has calculated for each load they have delivered.

There was a time—round about the year 2000—when I had to go into this transaction many times a day. As far as I am concerned, one of the most important options on the selection screen can be seen in Figure 6-7.

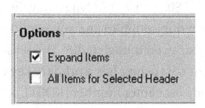

Figure 6-7. *Most important VI05 options*

As it turns out, due to there being so many possible selections on the VI05 selection screen, the options in Figure 6-7 are not at the top of the selection screen. The selection screen is so big you have to page down to see it. Back in 2000, before monitors got bigger, you had to page down twice to get to it.

Naturally, the "most important" fields are a value judgement—you have to actually talk to the prospective users of the application (or the actual users once that application is live) and see what fields they fill out on the selection screen, and if the selection screen spans more than one page, put the most common ones near the top.

If you don't want to talk to the end users (most programmers don't), then after the application is live have a look at what selection-screen variants people are saving in production, and that will tell you what fields are important to them.

Totally Hidden Field

If you are an accountant and work with SAP it is likely that every so often you want to look at the definition of a cost center. The transaction to do this is KS03. For many years, the screen looked like Figure 6-8.

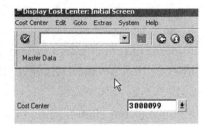

Figure 6-8. *How transaction KS03 used to look*

Sometimes in transaction KS03 you would type in a value of a cost center you knew for a fact existed ("3000099," in our example) and you would get the message "Cost Center 30000099 does not exist," even though it did. The reason for that fake message was that the database table for cost center has a primary key consisting of two fields—controlling area (KOKRS) and cost center number (KOSTL). Without the controlling area being specified, the system could not find the cost center, even if you gave the correct number—and there was no way to specify the controlling area on the main screen; the field was just not there.

What you used to have to do was take the menu option *Extras* ➤ *Set Controlling Area* and then a pop-up box would appear, and you could enter the controlling area. In other words, a vital field had been totally hidden, and the end user had to go hunting to find it.

It eventually occurred to SAP that the big blank area above the cost center number field would be just the place to add the controlling area field, and now the screen looks like Figure 6-9.

Display Cost Center: Initial Screen

Master Data

Controlling Area	CZ01
Cost Center	3000099

Figure 6-9. *Slightly improved KS03 screen*

That is a little bit better in that the controlling area is now visible, so you can see if the value is wrong, but as the controlling area field is grayed out, you still cannot change the value without going to the menu, and you still get the false error message "Cost Center does not exist." It does exist, just not in the controlling area currently specified. The long text in the error message does mention the controlling area, but I would say that there is room in the short text to improve the error message; i.e., to something like "Cost Center X does not exist in Controlling Area Y." Making the controlling area field editable would not hurt either—you have to enter two values, and you have to enter each value on a different screen. That adds three extra clicks to get a task done, for no logical reason whatsoever.

The recommendations are obvious here:

- All vital selection fields should be in the main screen. Making the user go to the menu to select the value in the pop-up is not sensible, especially when the main screen has loads of room for other fields.

- You really need to make sure that the error message is not "lying," as in this example. The user knows the cost center exists, as they can see it in reports, and yet the system says it does not exist.

Incorrect Use of Check Boxes

Sometimes programmers can get confused about the difference between radio buttons and check boxes on selection screens. To recap:

- Radio buttons are for when one option must be chosen, but only one; e.g., "Do you want to see open orders, closed orders, or both?"

- Check boxes are for when zero to many options can be chosen, and they are unrelated; e.g., "email results," "run in background," "suppress zero values," and so on.

The problem comes when a programmer decides to have check boxes that are contradictory; e.g., one box says, "Show open orders" and another box says "Hide open orders." With check boxes it is quite possible to select both.

In that example, if the user ticks both the "show" and "hide" boxes, then it is not obvious at all what the program will do. Maybe it will show everything. Maybe it will hide everything. Maybe it will dump. What it will probably do is issue an error message telling the user off for being stupid and ticking both boxes.

What you, as a programmer, should be aiming for is to make it literally impossible for a user to enter contradictory values and thus get an error message. The worst-case scenario is when it is not obvious at all if the options are contradictory. Look at Figure 6-10, which shows a standard SAP selection screen.

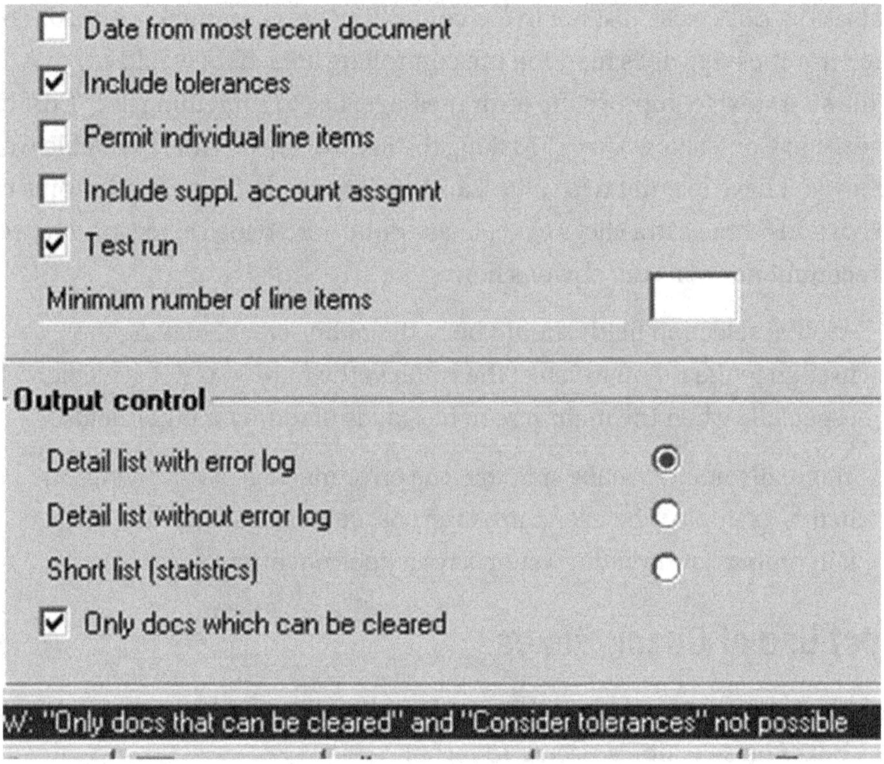

Figure 6-10. *Selection screen designed to confuse users*

In Figure 6-10, the user has ticked both the "Include tolerances" and "Only docs which can be cleared" boxes, which they are not supposed to do. Therefore, a little blue message appears at the bottom to tell them that what they have chosen is not possible. So why let them do it in the first place? If the two options are contradictory then they should be radio buttons.

As an aside—did you notice that in Figure 6-10 the field on the screen is called "Include tolerances" and yet in the message at the bottom of the screen that field is referred to by the different name "Consider tolerances" just to make it slightly less obvious to the user what they have done wrong.

Confusing the User

In this section, we look at three examples where the end user is presented with some information on a screen and is supposed to do something with that information but ends up having no idea at all how to proceed, apart from making a wild guess.

Giving Incorrect Options

This next one is going to seem obvious, but it can't be as obvious as all that, because one tends to see the problem every single day on one website or another.

Often an application will ask the user to choose between two or more options. If the application is being helpful, it will explain exactly what choosing each option entails. If the application is *not* being helpful, it will list options that do not exist.

See if you can spot what is wrong with Figure 6-11.

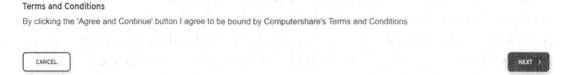

Terms and Conditions
By clicking the 'Agree and Continue' button I agree to be bound by Computershare's Terms and Conditions

CANCEL   NEXT >

Figure 6-11. *Hunting for the Agree and Continue button*

That's right—the text refers to an Agree and Continue button, but the actual button reads "Next." You see this sort of thing all the time.

What probably happened is that at one point the long description and the button text were the same, but then one was changed and the other was not.

In SAP there is an easy way to avoid this—use the same text symbol in both the definition of the message or pop-up box that lists the available buttons and the definitions of the button(s) in question. It is always possible in GUI screens to have dynamic text on push-buttons and icons (and indeed menu options) rather than static text.

If (when) you need to change the desired description, all you need to do is change the text symbol, and the screen output will be updated in both places at once.

Giving No Options at All

I recall that once whilst I was working at a very bureaucratic organization in Europe I broke some sort of illogical rule that I did not even know existed. When my boss at the time criticized me for breaking that secret rule, I said I would obey the new (to me) rule from that point forward and summed it up thus:

> *"You don't have to tell me twice. But you do have to tell me at least once."*

Life in general is the only area where you have to learn the rules as you go along, and even then there are (hopefully) people to guide you—parents/teachers, etc.

In any other area—playing a game for the first time or, more important, starting a new job—you would be pretty upset if you were told, "There are a lot of rules you have to follow—but you are not going to be told what they are. You will know when you break one because then you will be *punished*." Most people would think that was quite unfair.

As with many other examples in this book, you would not want that to happen to you in real life, so you had better take care not to inflict this horrible situation on anyone else whilst coding an application. Let us look at an example of having to learn the rules by breaking them.

Traditionally, in SAP systems you would have to log on every morning using your username and password. As time went by, many companies moved to single sign-on (known as SNC in the SAP world), whereby the fact that you had logged on to the system using your Windows (or whatever system you use) password was good enough to allow you to log on to SAP as well.

That is wonderful; but there are times when you—as a programmer as opposed to an end user—want to attempt to log on to SAP using a password to test some obscure technical thing out. The SAP logon pad defaults to single sign-on, but you can choose password log-on if you so desire.

That's great, but of course passwords expire after a certain amount of time, which is fair enough. When your password expires, and you try to log on to the SAP system again the next day, you get the screen shown in Figure 6-12.

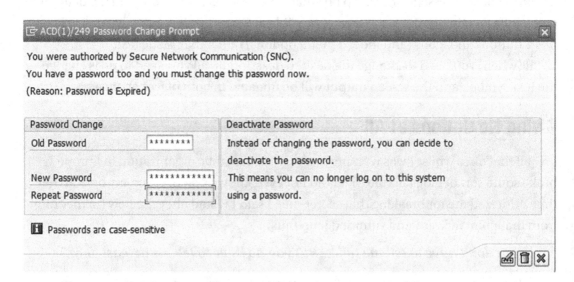

Figure 6-12. *SAP screen asking you to change your password*

The positive news is that you are told that passwords are case-sensitive. For many years in SAP they were not. For the sake of this example, let us say you try to enter "octopus" as your new password. You enter it in both the second (new) and third (repeat) boxes. You would get an error saying the password must be at least eight characters long.

You then change the password (in both boxes) to be "octopus23" to meet the length criteria you now know about. First, you get a false message that the passwords in both lower boxes must be identical (they are). Then, you get another message saying that the passwords must contain an uppercase letter.

Now that you know this extra rule, you change the value in both boxes to "Octupus23." You get a false message that the passwords in both lower boxes must be identical (they are). Then, you get another message saying that the passwords must contain a special character.

Now that you know this extra rule you change the value in both boxes to "Octupus23!" You get a false message that the passwords in both lower boxes must be identical (they are). As it turns out, there are no more hidden rules, but nonetheless you get another message saying, "Please enter password."

What that means is that you have to reenter your old password once again in the top box, as the value you originally entered has somehow been blanked out, though that is not obvious in the slightest. After that, you are fine, apart from having a sore throat from screaming at the screen for the last ten minutes.

In this day and age, you probably have about 50 passwords on various systems and websites, each of which has subtly different rules; e.g., some want special characters, some don't. So there is no "obvious" set of standard password rules that you can guess.

My guess is that whoever programmed the SAP example never had to go through the process themselves, but even if they did they would have known the rules and so would not have gotten the error messages, and so would not have realized the problem.

Therefore, for custom programs the recommendation is as follows:

- If there are rules the end user has to follow, tell them what those rules are.

- Test your own program by putting in wrong values (this is known as "gorilla testing") and see what happens, before releasing it to QA.

Accessibility

Using computer applications has become such a vital part of life that it is essential that the UI for an application is accessible. For example, there are checks in the SAP screen painter that all fields have some sort of text description so that someone who is visually impaired can get an audio representation of what a given field means.

Something often overlooked is the need to accommodate people with color blindness by avoiding the use of colored text (particularly red) in reports, transaction screens, and/or graphics. An alternative method would be to highlight text using background colors instead and keep the text black.

Where I work, we have someone in the accounts department who is color blind, and we run all BI reports by him to see if he can make out the figures in colored cells. If not, then the UI design is not good, even for people who are not color blind.

Explaining Things to the User

Thus far, we have only talked about examples of applications that are hard to use. Now is the time to turn that on its head and look at how to program a UI such that the user never has to wonder what they are looking at or what to do—the computer equivalent of writing "Pull" on a door.

Avoiding Abbreviations

Going back to the "Don't Make Me Think" principle once again, if there are text names on the screen just to the left of a value in a certain field, then it should be obvious to the user what that text description means. Therefore, if there is enough space on the screen to fit an entire word or phrase—e.g., "Required Delivery Date"—then do not write something cryptic instead, like "RDD."

In fact, if there is room then there is no need at all to shorten words, like the example in Figure 6-13 from SAP transaction VA01.

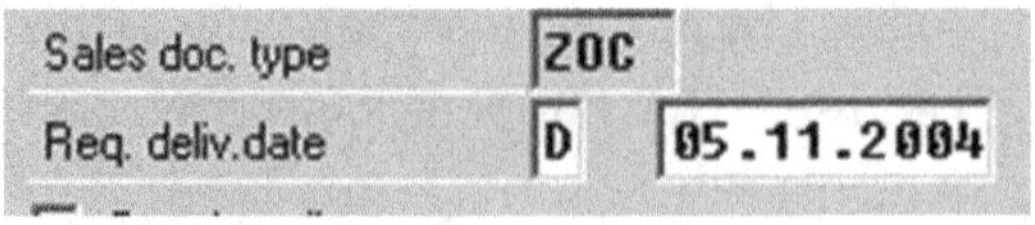

Figure 6-13. *SAP transaction VA01*

There is room on the screen, so why not say "Sales Document Type" and "Required Delivery Date"? In this case, the reason could be that the transaction was written a very long time ago and SAP screens used to be a lot smaller, by which I mean both the maximum size you were allowed to specify when designing an SAP screen was smaller and also the physical size of the monitors on people's desks was smaller.

In recent SAP releases, you can define screens to be much bigger than you could (say) 20 years ago, and in addition end users tend to have two (or three) monitors now, each 36 inches wide.

A lot of standard SAP transactions have not caught up with that technology change, however. For example, when you define a parameter transaction to do table maintenance of a Z table via SM30, all the important information is squished up in a box at the bottom left of the screen, and you have to keep scrolling left and right whilst entering data into a two-column-wide table, all whilst looking at acres of empty space on the right of the screen, as shown in Figure 6-14.

Figure 6-14. *Important fields squished together despite loads of empty space*

Table Maintenance Generator

When you use the table maintenance generator to create a DYNPRO program that can be called from SM30 to update the data in a DDIC table, due to that tool's not being updated for over a decade (because no one is supposed to use the GUI anymore), the resulting generated screen will be far too thin. You will need to manually go into the generated function group and expand the definition of the screen so it is wide enough that the end user does not have to keep scrolling to the left and right all the time.

I am sorry to report that even in the very latest SAP web applications this problem is still occurring. For example, when you log in to ABAP in the Cloud (which only came out in 2019) you get a tiny box in the middle of a huge, empty gray screen in which to put your email address and password, and that box is far too short to display the whole email address at once without scrolling. On a mobile device, that maybe would make sense, but who programs on their phone?

If you 100 percent have to shorten the names on the screen, you can still take steps to help the end user. In an ALV grid you have the "tooltip" field that you can set to provide a description that will appear when the user hovers their cursor over the column (this description usually defaults to the long description of the underlying data element).

So that the user gets the description when they hover over the button or icon, it is vital in DYNPRO programs that you define a tooltip in icon fields and tooltip fields, as shown in Figure 6-15.

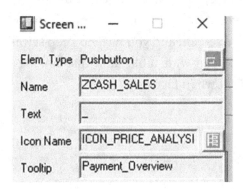

Figure 6-15. *Defining a tooltip for a push-button*

This is vital for two reasons:

- No icon is self-explanatory—the symbol it shows means different things to different people. You may think a red "x" clearly means cancel, but just to force the issue make it say "cancel" when the user hovers over it. That way, if one day SAP decides to change the icon to look like a banana the user will still know what it means when they hover over it.

- An easy mistake to make is to choose an icon for your custom screen and then forget to manually enter the tooltip. If you don't do this, the tooltip field will be automatically populated with the default SAP description of the icon, which often is nothing at all to do with what the icon actually does in the application at hand. In Figure 6-15, the programmer has changed the tooltip to "Payment Overview" to reflect what the button does in the application. If they had left the default value, it would have said "Material Price Analysis," which would have confused the user to no end.

Custom Data Elements

On standard SAP screens in the GUI—be it a DYNPRO or an ALV—often there is a field with an obscure name, and the user has no idea what that name means. In theory, in that situation the end user should be able to press the F1 button and get a clear explanation of what that term means. Sadly, in most standard transactions—and virtually all custom ones—if you see a field called "Self-Sealing Stem Bolt" and press F1, either nothing happens at all or you get a pop-up saying, "Self-Sealing Stem Bolt" and nothing else. Or, worse, you get a pop-up saying "Character Field—Length 10" or (even worse) a pop-up with a false definition; e.g., "Purchase Order Number" plus a description of what a purchase order is.

The description the user sees when pressing F1 depends on the data element that underlies the field in question. Thus, it is vitally important that you take a little time to think when defining internal tables and database tables.

If everything in the internal table or database table is only ever going to be used "internally"—i.e., by one or more programs—then defining fields using the built-in SAP types such as CHAR5 or SY-UZEIT or even VBELN is fine. The question is—are these values ever going to be user facing? Is a user going to have to look at or enter them on a screen, maybe with an F4 help, or are those fields ever going to pop up on some sort of report that the user looks at, or maybe in a table maintenance dialog?

If the answer is "yes" or even "maybe," then you need to start creating custom data elements. I can hear the screaming already: what a waste of time, so much extra effort, just use standard SAP elements of the same type and length or built-in types. To make things worse, I am going to insist that whilst creating the data element you take the path less followed—GOTO ➤ DOCUMENTATION ➤ CHANGE—and then describe what this field means semantically; i.e., what the values in this field are used for in the business process.

A lot of developers would rather crawl over a thousand miles of broken glass than write one word of documentation in the SAP system. Many would be puzzled by why I (as a developer) would even *care* what the field means in semantic terms; I have the algorithm in the functional specification, don't I? I know if it's an integer or a string, so if it's a four-character string just pick EKPO-BSTAE—that's a four-character string, surely that's good enough, and so much easier.

That's not good enough! If you have a field that is going to appear on a user-facing screen and you define it as type STRING, then no F1 help is going to appear at all. If you define the field based on data element CHAR10 then the F1 help is going to say, "Character Field—Length 10." If you define every ten-digit numeric field as EBELN then the F1 help is always going to say, "Purchase Order."

Thus, if your user-facing field actually does have a 100 percent semantic match with a standard SAP field, then naturally you should type it according to that relevant SAP standard data element, but if that field is something specific to your organization then you should define a custom data element—and *document it*.

By this point, you will have gathered that the idea is that for every single field on the screen, if the user gets puzzled as to what that field means, they should be able to put their cursor on that field and press F1 and have a box pop up with a detailed explanation of what the purpose of the field is.

As a test, after your application is ready move your cursor all around the screen and press F1 on each field in turn. If you get a detailed explanation, fine.

If you don't get a detailed explanation:

- If the field points to a Z data element then go to the definition of the Z data element and add the documentation.

- If the field points to a standard data element like CHAR05 create a Z data element specific to the data use and document it.

- If the field points to a standard SAP data element that just parrots the name of the field with no further details, or does not point to a DDIC element at all (and it has to stay that way), then you can program a custom F1 help.

Custom F1 Help

In a DYNPRO program, in the same way that you can program custom F4 helps on specific fields for drop-down lists that override any standard F4 help that is attached to the underlying data element, you can also specify custom F1 helps for any fields you so desire via the PROCESS ON HELP-REQUEST command, as shown in Listing 6-1.

Listing 6-1. Defining Custom F1 Help on a DYNPRO Screen

```
*---- P O H ----*
PROCESS ON HELP-REQUEST.
  FIELD t_vbap-stext MODULE f1_sales_text.
  FIELD t_vbap-zz_test  MODULE f1_testing_flag.
  FIELD vbak-zz_tel_num MODULE f1_site_contact.
  FIELD vbak-zz_contact_name MODULE f1_site_contact_nm.
  FIELD box_plusload MODULE f1_plus_load.
  FIELD box_balance  MODULE f1_balance_load.
```

Normally, pressing F1 on a screen field would call up the F1 help of the underlying data element. If you override that by specifying the field in the PROCESS ON HELP-REQUEST section, then obviously, in the routines or methods your PAI F1 modules call, you can program anything you want to get the explanation to the user. Listing 6-2 shows three possible mechanisms for displaying a custom F1 help to a user.

Listing 6-2. Three Ways of Calling a Custom F1 Help

```
MESSAGE 'Does this order line item require testing?'(030) TYPE 'I'.
 CALL FUNCTION 'SWF_HELP_LONGTEXT_SHOW'
    EXPORTING
      in_workarea = 'ZSD'
      in_message  = '314'.
 CALL FUNCTION 'HELP_OBJECT_SHOW_FOR_FIELD'
    EXPORTING
      doklangu         = sy-langu
      called_for_tab   = 'VBAK'
      called_for_field = 'VKORG'
    EXCEPTIONS
      object_not_found = 1
      sapscript_error  = 2
      OTHERS           = 3.
```

First, you could just output an information message (so that it appears in a pop-up box like a real F1 help). However, that limits the amount of detail you can show the user.

You could define a custom message with a big, long text and then call function module SWF_HELP_LONGTEXT_SHOW, which would directly pop up the long text for that message.

Lastly, you could "redirect" the F1 help to a standard or custom data element by using the function HELP_OBJECT_SHOW_FOR_FIELD and specifying a database table/field combination that uses the data element you want to show the help for.

In an ALV grid, the easiest way to ensure the user has a proper F1 available for every field is to have the field catalog definition point to the required reference table/field combination, but just like a DYNPRO you can override this if need be. The CL_GUI_ALV_ GRD has an event called ONF1 for which you can declare a handler method, and in the CL_SALV_TABLE you can define a handler method for the BEFORE_SALV_FUNCTION event of the CL_SALV_EVENTS object to achieve the same. In both cases, in the handler method you would then use the same techniques as with the DYNPRO in order to pop up your custom F1 documentation.

Custom Domains

The next question becomes—if you have a custom (Z) data element, does it need a Z domain as well? I have seen a lot of custom Z domains that are carbon copies of standard SAP ones, which seems to add no benefit whatsoever. For example, if you have a custom TEXT20 domain how is that different than the standard SAP TEXT20 domain?

Whilst there is no purpose in creating a new Z object that adds no value, creating a custom domain can in fact help the user-friendliness aspect to no end, and here comes an example.

One day, I created a custom domain for a Z data element, pointing to a Z table full of possible values, and then all throughout the system F4 helps and "foreign key checks" magically sprang up for that field, even in standard transactions like VK11 and TK11. For the preceding *13 years* people (users) had no F4 drop-down on that field and could put in any value they wanted without getting an error, and I was able to fix both of these things in about five minutes in dozens of programs without touching them, just by changing the Z data element definition so it used my new Z domain. That is the "open/ closed" principle all over.

Error Prevention

You are bound to have heard the phrase, "Prevention is better than cure," in that it is a million times better not to have the disease in the first place than to have the disease and then be cured of it. That's why we have the concept of vaccination—a pre-emptive strike to stop a disease before it starts.

In the same way, you can be proactive in your coding when it comes to user friendliness. This idea might seem strange at first glance, so let us look at a few examples.

Once again, we will move from the negative to the positive. To start off, we will look at the way some programs appear to go out of their way to get the user to make a mistake and can even have "self-destruct" buttons. Then, we will move on to the positive—how to stop short dumps before they happen and the idea of building in a "self-service" facility to let the user solve a potential problem on their own without having to bother the IT department. Last, we will see a sneaky trick regarding how to ensure the filter function on an ALV report always works.

Inviting Errors

One good way to prevent errors before they happen is to not design your screen such that the slightest mistake from an end user will cause the universe to explode. This concept is going to need some examples to explain, but the idea is that when designing your screen you should position function keys that can cause the most serious consequences far away from low-consequence and high-use keys. For instance, an exit function key (which takes you totally out of the transaction and thus is rarely used) should be positioned far from a page down function key (which just shows you more records and is used all the time).

Here are some other examples of what not to do:

- In an early version of the SAP Master Data Management application where you had a list of vendor numbers, the "delete" icon was next to the "display" icon, and if you pressed the "delete" one by accident then the record was deleted without even an "Are you sure?" prompt.

- For a long time in the standard SAP transaction STMS (which moves transport requests between systems), there were two almost identical icons right next to each other, both looking like trucks. If you pressed the first icon only the transports you wanted went to production. If you pressed the other icon every single transport in the queue went to production, ready or not; you could only look on with horror as all sorts of untested changes marched unstoppably into the live system, with disastrous consequences. As a result, companies started modifying that standard STMS transaction to suppress the "evil" button until eventually SAP suppressed that icon in the standard system.

- For a non-SAP example: Every evening I switch my PC off. I have a Windows operating system, so I press the Start button to switch my computer off. Then I press the Power button, and there are three options all on top of each other, two of which are "Switch Off" and "Restart"—since "Restart" is at the bottom and thus presumably the one that is most commonly used, I press that by accident instead of "Switch Off" a lot of the time, and then have to wait ages for the PC to restart, and then I try to switch the PC off again—this time taking care to pick the correct option.

Therefore, the recommendation is to position harmless and frequently used buttons such as Search far away from buttons with serious consequences like Exit or Delete or Self-destruct to avoid the "fat finger" problem whereby someone presses the button to the right of the one they actually want. Speaking of "self-destruct" buttons . . .

Self-Destruct Button

In a previous chapter (about performance), you saw the concept of proactively stopping short dumps by looking at ST22 every morning to see what went wrong the day before. Whilst doing this over a protracted period I was really puzzled by a series of short dumps that did not happen very often and were spread over a wide range of custom programs. They were all TIME OUT short dumps, and the clue was that it always seemed to be happening during F4 processing; i.e., when the user presses the F4 key to get a list of possible values.

It took a lot of investigation, but in the end the root cause was identified—what was happening was that the end user had put their cursor on a read-only field (either in a DYNPRO or a read-only ALV report) that contained a value like sales order, material document, accounting document, or the like, and then *by accident* had pressed the F4 button. The so-called fat fingers problem whereby you press a key close to (or sometimes nowhere near) the key you actually wanted to press, or maybe even put a coffee cup down on the keyboard, thus pressing a button unintentionally.

If a field contains a document number, then the underlying table—VBAK for sales orders, MKPF for material documents, GLPCA for profit center documents—will be gigantic. Pressing F4 without any filter caused a full table scan on these huge tables, usually leading to a TIME OUT dump.

From the user's point of view, seemingly at random the application would freeze for ten minutes (literally) followed by a short dump. As you might imagine, this is both annoying and confusing. In effect, there are one or more "self-destruct" buttons in the application—if they are pressed, the application explodes.

Happily, this is easy to fix. In a DYNPRO program if you have a field that is based on sales order number (VBAK-VBELN) then the definition automatically generated by the "screen painter" will have the same search help as the underlying data element.

In such situations—where users are getting dumps—it is best to blank that value out, as shown in Figure 6-16, and then even if the user presses F4 nothing will happen.

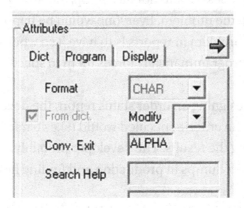

Figure 6-16. Blanking out the Search Help field

In the same way, in an ALV report if a field refers to the underlying table and field—e.g., VBAK-VBELN—then the search help will be inherited as well. In the various ALV technologies available to you there is always a way to switch the F4 help off.

For CL_GUI_ALV_GRID, for example, you need to pass a space (i.e., the value FALSE) to field F4AVAILABLE in the field catalog. If using CL_SALV_TABLE, you can use method SET_F4 of the "column" object to TRUE (X) or FALSE (space) to influence the F4 behavior. In the SALV, however, the default behavior is that the F4 is not active (because the grid cannot be editable), so you are usually OK.

Stopping Dumps Before They Begin

One thing an end user finds frustrating is when they run a report online and then stare at the screen for ten minutes waiting for it to finish, only to find they get a short dump—in other words, they have wasted their time. They have also unwittingly tied up a work process for ten minutes, potentially blocking one of their colleagues from running another report or creating a sales order or something.

In this situation, when the complaint comes into IT, one approach is to find out what selection criteria the user entered, find out it was a ridiculous amount of data—e.g., line items for seven years—and then advise them that if they *really* want such a vast amount of data (often they don't and there is a better way to get the information they need, but sometimes they do) then the only way is to run the report in the background.

How much better would it be if we could stop this problem before it began? That way, the end user would not have to waste ten minutes of their life and then get really unhappy, and the work process would not be tied up, and the IT person would not have to spend time diagnosing the problem. Everyone would be happier.

The way around this problem in reports is to have it so when the user tries to run the report online the report programmatically forces them to specify enough search criteria to ensure finite runtimes.

Let's say that when designing an order status report, the developer knows that running it with no selection criteria specified would take 40 minutes and would actually time out before generating the results. The developer probably knows that from having looked at half a ton of short dumps in production and finding how long the same query takes in batch.

Therefore, the program should be changed to issue an error message instructing the user to specify selections if the report will be run in the foreground, while allowing the report to be run in the background with no selections.

You might think that just making some selection fields (e.g., the ones on indexed fields in the main table being read) obligatory would do the trick, but no—when confronted with an obligatory date range some people are going to put in 01/01/2000 to 12/31/9999, which doesn't really help.

That's not to say you shouldn't make such fields obligatory—you certainly should— but you also need to evaluate what has actually been entered. The best way to do this in an ALV report is by using the AT-SELECTION-SCREEN event. This event fires not only when the user presses the Execute button to run the report online but also when they submit the report in the background. The latter is important because if the amount of requested data is truly ridiculous then the batch job might run for three days or more, and you don't want that happening either, because the background work process thus occupied might block other potentially more vital batch jobs from running.

"How much is too much" is not an exact science—you will have to make some sort of guess as to how much requested data will cause a time out based on your experience. In Listing 6-3, you will notice that in FORM routine CHECK_FOR_BIG_RANGE I made up some arbitrary formula to see if the selections were too big. In this case, the table index is on plant (WERKS) and delivery date (LFDAT). Both selections are compulsory, and if only one value for each is selected the result comes back lightning fast. If six years' worth of data is requested for ten plants, however, things do not work so well.

Listing 6-3. Checking for Excessive User Selections

```
AT SELECTION-SCREEN.
  PERFORM authority_check USING p_werks[].
  PERFORM check_variant   USING p_vari.
  PERFORM check_for_big_range.
FORM check_for_big_range.
  "Local variables
  DATA: l_size  TYPE i,
        l_limit TYPE I,
ls_lfdat LIKE LINE OF S_LFDAT.

  "Check makes no sense when we are running in background
  CHECK sy-batch EQ space.
  "Only make check if the user has pressed "execute" or "execute in
  background"
```

```
IF sy-ucomm = 'ONLI'.      "On-Line    - 5 Months
  l_limit = 150.
ELSEIF sy-ucomm = 'SJOB'. "Background - 24 months
  l_limit = 730.
ELSE.
  RETURN.                  "User has not pressed a processing option
ENDIF.

SELECT COUNT( * )          "count the plants selected
  FROM t001w
  INTO l_size
 WHERE werks IN p_werks.

l_size = l_size / 5.

READ TABLE s_lfdat INTO ls_lfdat INDEX 1.

l_size = l_size + ls_lfdat-high - ls_lfdat-low.

IF l_size > l_limit.
  IF sy-ucomm = 'SJOB'.
    MESSAGE
'Selection too big even for background processing'(036) TYPE 'I'.
  ENDIF.
  MESSAGE e020(zz)."For large selections run report in Background
ENDIF.

ENDFORM.                        "CHECK_FOR_BIG_RANGE
```

Self-Service

As mentioned earlier, it is always great when end users are "empowered" to solve problems themselves and do not have to go cap in hand to the IT department. It saves everyone time, and afterward the users feel content rather than frustrated. Let us look at two examples of how this might be achieved.

Logging

There are some situations in an SAP system where an incredibly complicated calculation is done in the background with hundreds of steps. One example could be variant configuration, whereby the bill of materials (ingredients) for a product are dynamically calculated based on customer requirements, or MRP (Material Replenishment Planning), whereby what raw materials you need and when are dynamically calculated.

In both cases, what annoys the users is that if the result is incorrect in some way then they do not know *why*—the whole process is a "black box" to them.

Often when there is an error the cause of the problem can arise from several places— it could be an error in the ABAP code, it could be an error in configuration, it could be an error in master data, the list goes on. If the user does not know, they will inevitably assume the problem is in the code, and so a ticket will be raised for IT to solve the problem. Then, after a while, you discover that a material has not been extended to a certain plant (or whatever); i.e., the problem is not a coding problem at all.

How much better would it be if the end user could somehow know the nature of the problem themselves (hence "self-service"), and thus would not have to waste their time and yours? Everyone would be happier.

This is where the standard SAP application log comes in. I once had to write a variant configuration application where the code had at least a thousand steps, probably a lot more. I made the decision that after every piece of ABAP logic—IF/ELSE statement, CASE statement, or database read—I would log the result. This was an online transaction, so I did not need to persist the log, but after the calculation the end user could view the result; i.e., every step in the "thought process" the computer had used to come up with the final result.

The downside was that (rather like unit tests) this doubled the amount of code and hence the time taken to write that code. The upside was that by looking at the detailed log the end user could do the following:

- Tell if some master data was wrong (because they could see the result of a database read on a master data table) and then fix the problem themselves without having to bother IT and wait a long while

- Tell if some configuration data was wrong (because they could see the result of a database read on a configuration table) and then get the analyst to fix it directly without having to get the programmer to work out it was a configuration problem and then after a while inform the analyst

- Tell if the problem was actually in the algorithm itself and if so tell the programmer which area needs to be fixed

This approach, whilst taking longer initially during the build, more than paid for itself in terms of both time and number of tickets raised. Moreover, having the logic 100 percent visible led to problems in that logic (which had been there forever but were now suddenly visible) getting fixed.

Linking Errors to Training Material

One wonderful recommendation I found on the internet—not specific to SAP—was that after you've finished the application, have the people writing the training documentation write the long texts for the error messages, and then have the long text have a hyperlink to the relevant training material at the end.

This is the sort of really good idea that is never applied in practice as it involves different departments (i.e., training and development) actually talking to each other, instead of trying to stab each other with knives.

Sneaky Trick: ALV Filter Not Working

Speaking of things that can really annoy the end user, there is a wonderful example regarding the "filter" function.

What happens here is that the user is presented with a list of results and then decides they are only interested in certain customers (say) and thus presses the Filter button to filter out all customers except the one they are interested in, as shown in Figure 6-17.

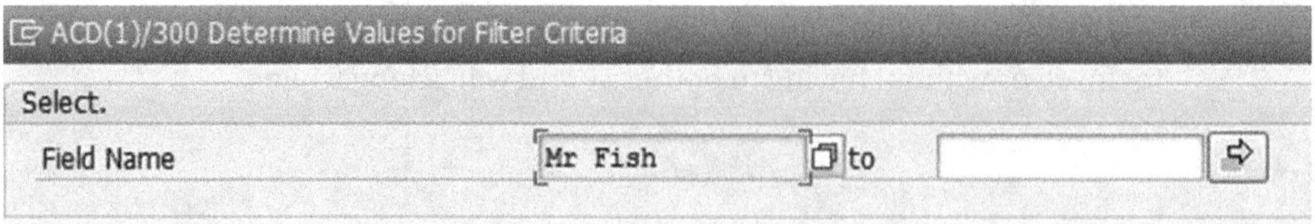

Figure 6-17. *Setting a filter criteria*

You even get a drop-down list of all the possible values in the field you are trying to filter, so you do not even have to type the name manually—you can just pick it from a list. Wonderful!

Then, after you have picked the value you want and pressed the green tick or Enter, every single row in the report vanishes, including the ones you wanted to remain. How can that be? You picked the name from an F4 list, so you cannot possibly have spelled it wrong!

This problem is more common than you might think and seemingly happens at random; i.e., the filter works on some fields in a report and not on others, and, even worse, the filter works on a field in report A but not the same field in report B! This drives the end users up the wall.

What is causing this is the program definition of the internal table. You usually define an internal table field with reference to a data dictionary table field, which in turn points to a data element, which in turn points to a domain. The question is—does that domain support case-sensitive fields?

As an example, I had a request to build a totally custom version of the standard SAP report that displays changes to customer master records. The change log is always going to come from the tables CDHDR and CDPOS, but there needed to be a half a ton of business logic added on top dictating what fields to show or suppress. The important thing was that the ALV table had the field name referenced to standard SAP data element FIELDNAME, which points to standard domain FDNAME, which is *not* case sensitive.

However, that field was getting populated with the value from database table DD04T-SCTREXT_M (medium text description of a data element), which points to domain SCRTEXT_M, which *is* case sensitive. The end result was that the column in the ALV contained values with a mixture of upper- and lowercase letters, but the filter did not work because it was expecting everything to be in uppercase.

There are two ways to fix this—the most obvious is to change the definition of the internal table field such that it points to a data element that points to a case-sensitive domain. However, there are times that—for whatever reason—you don't want to change the definition of your internal table. You can still fix the problem.

Presuming you are using CL_SALV_TABLE to display the ALV list, you need to add code similar to that shown in Listing 6-4.

Listing 6-4. Forcing an ALV Column to Accept Lowercase Values

```
data MO_COLUMN type ref to CL_SALV_COLUMN_TABLE .
data MO_COLUMNS type ref to CL_SALV_COLUMNS_TABLE .
 methods SET_LOWERCASE
   importing
     !ID_FIELD_NAME type LVC_FNAME .

METHOD set_lowercase.

  TRY.
      mo_column ?= mo_columns->get_column( id_field_name ).

      mo_column->set_lowercase( abap_true ).

    CATCH cx_salv_not_found.
      MESSAGE 'Report in Trouble' TYPE 'E'
  ENDTRY.

ENDMETHOD.
```

In Listing 6-4, the MO_COLUMNS variable is an instance of class CL_SALV_COLUMNS_ TABLE, which is one of the attributes of CL_SALV_TABLE, and MO_COLUMN is of type CL_ SALV_COLUMN_TABLE.

The result is that even though the internal table definition still refers to a domain that is case insensitive, the ALV column definition gets explicitly changed and thus the filter now works properly.

Error Handling

You have probably heard the saying, "To err is human, to forgive divine." Users are humans and are therefore going to input incorrect values every so often; in fact, probably more often than not. Your job as a programmer is to make life as painless as possible whenever that inevitable situation occurs.

In this section, we will start with a recommendation to treat the end user with respect and not shout at them via rude error messages. Then, we will move on to look at some "anti-patterns" - in this case various ways that programs can actively prevent the end user from fixing the problem once your rude error message has told them there is a problem. Lastly, you will see some good ways of actually helping the user instead.

Shouting at the User

Usually, young children think that a good way of getting people to do what they want is to shout and scream as loud as possible. Then, as they get older most people come to realize that is in fact not the best way to get what you want; a bit more subtlety is needed when communicating with your fellow human beings.

As mentioned earlier, the end users are going to input incorrect data into your program from time to time. When this happens, the program should not attempt to tell the user off or blame them or punish them. It should instead try to help them achieve whatever it is they were trying to do when they got into trouble.

You might think this is obvious, but if so, then why do so many error messages in computer software shout and scream at the end user?

As an example, let us say we have two fields, ABC and XYZ. The user must enter a value in one of them, but not both, and by accident they fill in both fields.

What should happen in such a case is that they get an error message that, if they read the long text,

- explains the *technical* reason they are getting the error message in the first place; i.e., because both fields have been filled in;

- explains the *business* reason why filling in both fields makes no sense and hence why there is an error message when both are filled;

- explains what the user should do to solve the problem—in this simple example, pick which value they actually want and delete the other; and

- says "Please" as in "Please fill in the missing field and try again." As many mothers have said throughout the ages, "Being polite never hurt anyone."

What the program should not do, in increasing order of "badness," is any of the following:

- Use ambiguous words such as *THAT* or *IT* as in "Do it again." This just confuses the users. It is better to say, "Try to save the order again." In the ABC/XYZ field example, if the message says, "Fill in one of those fields," the user will think, "What fields?"

- Issue a terse error message (with no long text) blaming the user, such as, "You filled both the ABC and XYZ fields."

- Issue an error message that uses violent/hostile language attacking the user, such as, "Why did you fill both the ABC and XYZ fields?" That message might as well have "you idiot" on the end, as it would mean the same thing.

- Issue an error message with an exclamation mark at the end. That is in effect shouting at the user. The message, "You filled both the ABC and XYZ fields!" has an exclamation mark at the end and so is equivalent to shouting, "You filled both the ABC and XYZ fields. You are so stupid!"

- Issue an error message in uppercase. That is the equivalent of screaming at the user, as in, "YOU FILLED BOTH THE ABC AND XYZ FIELDS! YOU ARE SO STUPID!"

- Do a short dump to punish the user for being so stupid and make them start the transaction all over again

When reading the preceding recommendations as to what not to do, you might think, "None of my custom error messages are anything like that," but I would urge you to check them nonetheless. You may find more uppercase messages and exclamation marks than you might like.

Preventing the User from Fixing the Problem

Here, we will look at two examples where a program can force the user to start from scratch if they run into a problem; i.e., have to back out of the transaction, then go back in and reenter all the data again.

Making the User Reenter Data

On some web pages, if you make one mistake, all the fields that you have entered thus far are deleted. This could be described as a sort of "nuclear option" and as might be imagined is the most annoying thing possible from an end user's point of view, especially if they have just spent 15 minutes filling in data.

SAP transactions in the GUI have traditionally had a huge number of fields that needed to be filled in, and the last thing anyone needs is to fill out 99 of those fields and then be prevented from saving the data because of a problem with the one-hundredth field, and then have to enter all one hundred values again once that problem has been solved.

A concrete example of this would be transaction MIRO (Logistics Invoice Verification). A supplier has sent you an invoice with one hundred line items. Each line item has a unique reference, which your users would have entered during the goods-receipt process. The AP clerk manually types the details of all one hundred line items into MIRO—that takes ages. Then, the invoice cannot be saved because one of the line items has not yet been goods receipted. The AP clerk tries to phone up the person who should have done the goods receipt but cannot get through.

Invoices can be "parked" but only at header level. Thus, the AP person has to wait until the final goods receipt has been done and then type in the one hundred lines again. That is very demoralizing.

In the latest releases of ABAP, SAP has come up with the "draft concept" in technologies such as the Business Object Processing Framework (BOPF) and the ABAP RESTful Application Programming Model (RAP). The idea here is that all data entered is constantly updating a "draft" table, and thus nothing is ever lost. This is like the auto-save option on Excel spreadsheets and Word documents. It really helps if you are on a train doing a transaction and halfway through the train goes into a tunnel and you lose internet connectivity.

Only when all mandatory fields have been entered and there are no data errors is the data moved out of the draft table(s) into the real table(s). The wonderful thing is that you do not have to write half a ton of code yourself each time to enable this—you just have to switch on this draft facility in new applications by uncommenting a so-called annotation at the start of the business object definition and specifying a database table name in which to store the draft (this table is automatically created).

There is no such facility available in traditional DYNPRO programs—you would have to program it yourself (which is what I did with a custom MIRO wrapper program to ensure no one ever had to enter one hundred line items twice).

Making It Impossible to Fix the Problem

Another incredibly annoying behavior sometimes seen in software applications is where the user makes a mistake and then the program goes out of its way to explain what the problem is, and how to fix it, and then will not let the user actually fix the problem.

The user might be told they need to change a value in field XYZ only to find that field XYZ has been grayed out. They have no option but to back out of the transaction and start again.

Sometimes things are even worse, and the user cannot even back out of the transaction. An example of this would be if you are entering a sales order that has a configurable material. What you should do is use the Configuration button to choose various options to configure the material. However, you might forget to do this and just save the order. At that point, you would get the "Incompletion Log" pop-up that would ask if you want to complete the missing data. Saying "yes" to that would be a big mistake. A pop-up box would appear where it looks like you can add the missing configuration data, but you cannot—and furthermore you cannot back out of that box or cancel it. You would have to use Task Manager to terminate all your SAP sessions. That is the only way you would be able to escape.

Let us go back to looking at why a field the user might need to change gets grayed out in the first place, preventing them from solving the problem. In this case, we are talking about a traditional DYNPRO program in the SAP GUI, be it standard or custom.

As an example, the program might look up the nature of the customer that was entered and decide that because the customer is of a certain type (field KNA1-KTOKD), the XYZ field becomes mandatory, and so the program sends an error message to the user asking them to fill in the XYZ field. At that stage, every field except the XYZ field goes gray; i.e., you cannot enter or change the values in those gray fields.

At that point, the user realizes that they have entered the wrong customer number—but they cannot change the customer number because the customer number field has gone gray. One way around this would be to put some random value in the XYZ field, but that might trigger another error. Usually, the only possible option is to back out of the transaction and start again.

What SAP expects you to do is to issue such error messages as part of a CHAIN, as shown in Listing 6-5.

Listing 6-5. Issuing an Error Message as Part of a CHAIN

```
CHAIN.
    FIELD: t_vbap-pstyv, t_vbap-uepos
      MODULE check_pstyv_uepos ON CHAIN-REQUEST.
  ENDCHAIN.
```

What happens with a CHAIN is that when the error message is issued, any fields mentioned in the CHAIN list remain open for input (and are highlighted). In the example in Listing 6-5, there is deemed to be a relationship between PSTYV (item category) and UEPOS (higher-level item), such that a problem in one of those fields could be fixed by changing the value in the other; thus, you would want them both to be open at once.

So, in our example, the programmer would code a CHAIN that included the customer field and the XYZ field so that if the user had actually put in the wrong customer the customer field would not be gray and thus could be changed.

Enabling the User to Fix the Problem

Here, we will look at how to help the user via two tips. The first is how to handle mandatory fields, and the second is how to exploit the oft-overlooked features of SAP error messages.

Mandatory Fields

Usually, there are a number of mandatory fields that have to be filled out before the transaction can be saved. It would be logical to think that an error message should be issued whenever such a field has been left blank. In actual fact, that drives the end user up the wall—if there are five missing fields they want to be able to fill them all in at once (plus any other optional fields they want to fill in), as opposed to everything on the screen except one missing mandatory field going gray, and then that process repeating many times.

Standard SAP programs don't behave like this, so neither should your custom programs. Instead, when checking for mandatory fields, some sort of flag should be set to ensure the transaction cannot be saved yet, and then a message issued telling the user what field to fill in next and placing the cursor there—but not an error message. Amazingly, you send a success message!

That sounds bonkers, but when you send a message of type "S" for success that message appears at the bottom of the screen so the user can see it, but it does not lock any fields for input. Nonetheless, you want the user to know it is an error; i.e., they cannot save the data until it is fixed.

How you square this circle is via a sneaky trick—you define an error message as shown in Figure 6-18.

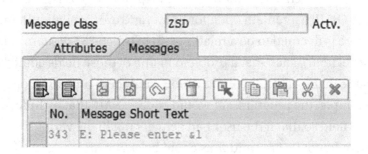

Figure 6-18. *Sneaky error message trick*

If you issue a success message that starts with "E:" then the letter E and the semi-colon are not output—rather the error symbol is output instead, as demonstrated in Figure 6-19. Thus, the message *looks* like an error message to the end user even if does not behave like one.

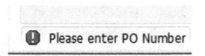

Figure 6-19. *A success message pretending to be an error message*

Taking the User to the Source of the Problem

Once I was in a shop and for whatever reason the customer before me had taken out his house keys and put them on the counter whilst paying, and then after he had bought whatever it was he walked out of the shop, forgetting his keys.

When I realized what had happened I could have just done nothing. Then he would have found out the problem when he tried to get into his house and would have had no idea at all at what point he lost his keys.

Or I could have left the keys on the counter and run after him and when I caught up said, "Your keys are back in that shop you just went into," forcing him to walk back to the shop.

What I actually did was pick up his keys and run after him up the street (which quite disturbed him), and when I caught up with him handed him his keys.

Translating that into the SAP world, when an end user encounters a problem, be it incorrect data they have entered or some sort of missing master data or any sort of problem, really, you as a programmer have the same three choices:

- Don't send any sort of message at all; e.g., IF SY_SUBRC <> 0 then "do nothing" or CATCH an exception and then do nothing. Don't let the user know anything is wrong; let them carry on merrily down the path to disaster.

- Send the end user a message saying what is wrong and telling them, "Go into transaction XYZ, enter ABC on the first screen, and then fix the underlying problem."

- Send the end user the message saying what is wrong plus a hyperlink to the transaction they need to call and in that transaction default the ABC value.

Most SAP error messages—be they standard or Z messages—are flagged as self-explanatory (which 90 percent or more are not) and thus have no long text. That is a huge pity, as the options you have in the long text of a message are amazing—there are a dozen or more links you can insert into the long text; e.g., you can highlight confusing terms by providing a link to the data element description. Most important, you can put a hyperlink in the long text that calls the transaction the user needs so they can fix the problem themselves (if they are authorized) or a hyperlink to a display transaction where the user can find out what the problem is and then ask whoever is authorized to fix the problem to do just that.

Moreover, you can insert a "call transaction and skip first screen" link to the transaction the user needs to fix (maintain a customer master maybe). In the calling program where the error occurred, the program can set the parameter ID (PID) to the customer number just prior to raising the error message so when the user follows the hyperlink they will jump straight into the correct customer.

A wonderful example of this technique follows.

Example: IDoc Application Log

The good thing about this example is that it is both a good and a bad example—once upon a time it was a bad example, then SAP fixed it, and now it is a good example.

The scenario is thus: an IDoc has come into your SAP system from an external system trying to update some data. In this case, the data to be updated is the material master.

You go into transaction WE05 to see if the IDoc was processed successfully, and it turns out it was not—the IDoc is in an error status. When you call up the long text of the error message you see the screen in Figure 6-20.

Messages have been issued: number 0000000221250199

Message no. MK101

Diagnosis

During inbound processing for the IDoc, messages have arisen while checking material data.

System Response

The system has filed these messages in the form of an application log with the number 0000000221250199.

Procedure

View the application log.
Proceed

Figure 6-20. *Error message from an IDoc that failed*

If you look at the error message shown in Figure 6-20, you can spot two positive things—the word *IDoc* has been highlighted in blue, which means if the user does not know what an IDoc is then they can click on the word and a definition will appear.

Secondly, the word *Proceed* is also in blue—if the user clicks on this they will be taken to the transaction to display the application log. Looking at IDoc errors has to be done in two stages because there could be half a dozen or more error messages issued during IDoc processing. Hence, the top-level error message just indicates that one or more such errors occurred, and you have to go somewhere else to look for them.

So far so good—the error message has a hyperlink that takes you to the application log transaction. However, for years when you clicked on "Proceed" to be taken to the application log, you landed on the transaction to display application logs, but the log number was blank. Then you had to type in the huge number manually, and you had to add all the leading zeroes, or the application log transaction could not find the entry.

Happily, SAP identified the problem, and these days the parameter ID of the IDoc is programmatically set, and when you jump into the transaction to display the application log the number is therefore pre-populated; you do not have to manually type it out again complete with leading zeros. To make this perfect, the next thing SAP has to do is to skip the first screen, and then you will not even see the first screen of the application log transaction; you will be taken straight to the list of error messages.

Hopefully, the moral is clear—don't make the person reading the error message run back to the shop to get their keys—give them the keys.

Documentation

If the end user is really lucky, then when on the selection screen of a report transaction they will see a little blue icon that looks like the lowercase letter "i." If they put their cursor over it, then the text says, "Program Documentation (Shift + F1)." If they press that button, then they will see a (hopefully) helpful document explaining how to use the transaction at hand properly, as shown in Figure 6-21.

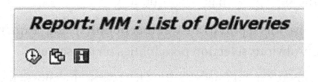

Figure 6-21. Report with Documentation button

Most programs have no such documentation. In order for that end-user documentation to exist in the first place, the programmer has to actually go into transaction SE38 for their program and choose the "Documentation" radio button and press the Change button.

Historically, many programmers do not do that ever, because (a) it is not compulsory and, more important, (b) they have no idea what to write, and (c) it is documentation and you know how programmers feel about writing documentation.

Just as with data elements, when the screen comes up to write your documentation SAP provides some ready-made section titles such as "Integration." Sadly, this usually seems to confuse developers more than help them.

This section will first provide some suggestions regarding (a) what sort of thing the programmer should write in such online documentation and (b) the sort of terminology they should use. Then, after a sneaky trick dealing with how to provide such documentation for dialog transactions (where there is no selection screen), we will end by considering a neglected group of people who really need documentation but rarely get any.

Documentation Guidelines

To address this problem of documentation, the following guidelines can be used when creating online documentation for a program—or you might ignore them and come up with better ones of your own. Either way is fine, as long as the documentation is actually created.

- What is the business need? E.g., to find out how much money we are making

- What question am I asking? E.g., how much did we sell?

- What is the key figure? E.g., sales quantity

- How do I use this report to answer that question? E.g., explain some of the non-obvious selection possibilities on the screen

- How can I make the report run quickly? I.e., performance hints; e.g., which fields are indexed (don't use that term to an end user, just say filling that field in helps) or use a list of profit centers rather than a range.

- Why not use standard SAP? The users don't actually care what is standard SAP and what is custom, but answering this question is a useful exercise in and of itself. The answer to the question might be "standard SAP doesn't cater for this at all" or "standard SAP only gives half the data we need." If the developer or analyst cannot answer this question, then we must ask why we are writing this program in the first place.

Documentation Terminology

If you add some standard SAP terms in your documentation, that might really confuse people. A fine example of this is that the terms *vendor* and *ship-to* do not come naturally to an employee of an English-speaking company until they are forced to use SAP. One way around this is to write in documentation something like "Vendor (supplier)" or "Ship-To (delivery address)" so it is obvious to people new to SAP what the strange terms mean.

Documentation should explain things using concepts and terminology familiar to users. The greatest (good) example of this I have ever seen was a help sheet that told a driver what buttons to press on a truck radio device at what stage of their journey to tell the central SAP system where they were located in their journey (this was well before the days of reliable GPS).

That help sheet showed cartoon pictures of the truck arriving at the customer's site and the customer waving "hello" (the instruction was "press the ARRIVE CUSTOMER SITE button") and then a picture of the driver waving "goodbye" when they left the customer site (the instruction was "press the DEPART CUSTOMER SITE button"). You might think that is childish and condescending, but it did make everything 100 percent obvious—especially for people who had no computer experience at all. This was in the year 2000, well before smartphones and the like. Nonetheless, even now the importance of making things obvious to all cannot be overstated. Put another way: It is better if the documentation is far too obvious than not obvious at all.

Documentation for Dialog Transactions

When programming a dialog transaction (i.e., where the user starts on a nominated DYNPRO screen as opposed to the selection screen of a report transaction) it is still possible to program online documentation so the user gets an information button on the initial screen just like they would with a report transaction.

It is a little more work, but not much. To do this, add an icon to the application toolbar of the "status" that appears on the initial screen (and the corresponding new menu option) and call the function code something like ZINFO. The result will look like Figure 6-22.

393

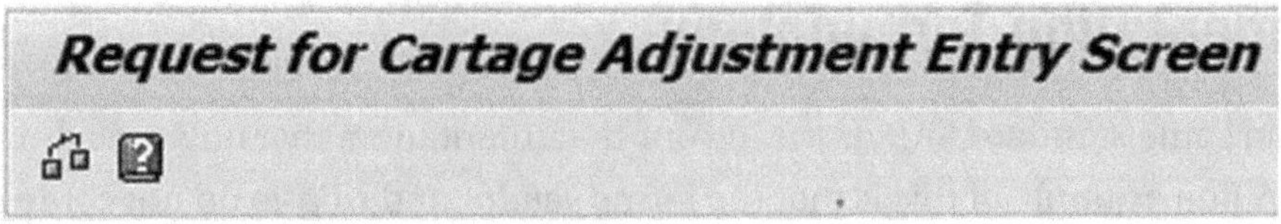

Request for Cartage Adjustment Entry Screen

Figure 6-22. *Self-defined help button on a DYNPRO screen*

This is a real example I created many years ago. Looking back, I should have chosen the same icon that you get on a selection screen—the blue one (`ICON_INFORMATION`)—rather than the red one I actually chose. The other important setting (to ensure consistency) is to have the user be able to trigger the function by pressing SHIFT + F1, which is the keyboard shortcut that triggers the information icon in a report program.

The next step is to add some code in the PAI module that handles user commands to process the ZINFO button when the user presses it. Listing 6-6 shows how to do this.

Listing 6-6. How to Invoke Documentation for Dialog Transactions

```
WHEN 'ZINFO'. "Help Button
      CALL FUNCTION 'DOCU_CALL'
        EXPORTING
          displ      = 'X'
          displ_mode = '2'
          id         = 'RE'
          langu      = sy-langu
          object     = 'SAPMZMM_CART_ADJ'
          typ        = 'E'.
```

This code will display the program documentation that is defined in transaction SE38 for the top-level program in the module pool, which in the example above is SAPMZMM_CART_ADJ.

Documentation for Developers

Developers need documentation too! Example: SAP function modules. It drives developers mad when they try to use a standard SAP function module and find there is no documentation. The problem is 1000 times worse for BAPIS. So developers moan and groan and curse, but when *they* create a custom function module they don't document it either.

You can (hopefully) work out what a function module or class does from looking at the code, but it is so much better if any ABAP construct (function module, class, and so on) is documented so the next programmer that comes along knows why it was created in the first place and what the desired outcome is. Otherwise, if all someone has to go on is the code, then they have to presume that the code was written the way it currently is deliberately, whereas in reality it could be full of faulty logic. Most developers are too scared to change anything if they think there may be a reason for the current behavior— even if they don't know what that reason is (and neither does anyone else).

So, the next time you are creating a function module, class, or some sort of non-user-facing database table, be sure to document it so when you come back to it in five years' time you can work out what it is for, and if it is doing what it is supposed to.

Conclusion

This chapter started with a discussion of the various philosophical aspects of user friendliness that are completely independent of the technology in use. In essence, in a user interface everything should be so obvious the user can navigate it without thinking, in the same way I can use the keyboard without looking at the keys.

Next up was the subject of consistency—the idea that every application should behave the same way as every other application—even between different software systems. That also involves the usage of icons being consistent.

This led into the topic of "ease of use"—an application should be going out of its way to help the end user perform their task rather than actively fighting them and making that task as hard as possible.

Next up was the subject of errors. We looked at how to prevent such errors from happening in the first place, but since some are going to happen anyway, we looked at how to make the experience as painless as possible for the end user.

Last came the subject of documentation and why it is so vital to make life easier for any human being trying to use the system—and not just the end users.

This chapter takes us to end of the BLUE phase of the TDD cycle. At this point, the application does what it should do, the code is easy to understand, performance is excellent, and the user experience is exceptional.

In the next few chapters, we will look at niche subjects—still to do with improving code quality but in very specific areas—starting off with the subject of user exits.

Recommended Reading

Steve Krug, *Don't Make Me Think!* (in regard to user-friendly web pages):

```
https://www.amazon.com.au/Dont-Make-Think-Steve-Krug/dp/0321344758
```

CHAPTER 7

User Exits: Defusing a Potential Time Bomb

Your SAP implementation probably started with the aim of being "vanilla"—i.e., having no Z code and making no changes to the way standard SAP works. In real life, things never turn out that way, and you end up with tons of Z programs and user exits all over the place that also use Z code.

How can you avoid this? To be honest, you cannot, so if you need lots of Z code it might as well be good Z code; hence, this book. The preceding chapters have all been about Z programs, which sit apart from standard SAP code. Now, we turn to user exits. A user exit sits inside standard SAP code; it is a means by which you can influence the way standard SAP transactions work in a code-based way, going beyond what can be achieved by configuration in the IMG (SAP Customizing Implementation Guide) alone.

Configuration is all well and good, but the ability to "go beyond" is one of the strengths of SAP. The idea 30 years ago when SAP first came out was that instead of a software provider building one ERP system for banking in Poland and then building another ERP system from scratch for turkey farming in Kentucky and so on, it could have one integrated ERP system for all industries in all countries by using the following mechanism:

- Configuration — By means of the IMG, it would be able to alter the behavior of the system with no code changes at all to move from the "neutral" vanilla behavior to a system that behaves 90 percent of the way your particular country/industry requires.

- User Exits — By providing "hooks" in the standard SAP code on which customers can "hang" their own code, should be able to change standard system behavior to 99 percent of what is required (don't laugh).

397

© Paul David Hardy 2021
P. D. Hardy, *Improving the Quality of ABAP Code*, https://doi.org/10.1007/978-1-4842-6711-0_7

- Custom Programs — Z programs were then supposed to plug the remaining one percent gap (stop laughing).

As we know, reality is somewhat closer to almost every transaction's being a Z transaction, but nonetheless a lot of these Z transactions are wrappers around standard SAP transactions, and thus configuration and user exits are as important today as they have ever been.

This chapter is all about user exits. Sadly, for historical reasons, there are about ten billion different types of user exits, and people tend to use them at random and get into all sorts of trouble. In this chapter, you will learn the safest way to implement user exits and how to ensure the robustness of the custom code in the user exit, as well as how to prevent its breaking the behavior of the surrounding standard SAP code.

First, we will go on a musical trip through time, examining the various mechanisms that have evolved over the years to enable customers (us) to insert our own ABAP code inside the standard code in traditional SAP systems, and considering the pros and cons of each.

Next, we will look at the seeming contradiction that is "user exits in a cloud system." In a cloud system, the ERP code base is shared between different customers and is thus unchangeable, so you can't possibly have user exits—or can you?

At this point, you might be thinking, "What about the bomb mentioned in the title? What is that bomb and how do I defuse it?" You will see this at the end of this chapter when I describe my grand plan to unify all user exit code using a "one ring to rule them all"–type framework where you apply the same technique no matter what type of user exit you choose—and do the coding in a Test Driven Development manner as per Chapter 2.

User Exits in On-Premises SAP Systems

SAP first came out in 1972—the same year in which digital watches were introduced—and in that year the company Atari had enormous success with the state-of-the-art arcade game *PONG*, as shown in Figure 7-1, which simulated table tennis on a video screen. At the time, *PONG* blew people's minds. They just could not believe a video game could be that good.

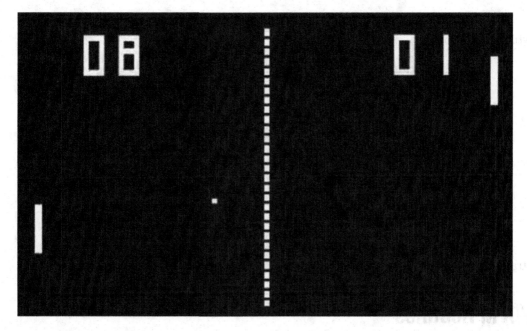

Figure 7-1. PONG Arcade Game from 1972

Given the state of computer technology in 1972, it could be said that the founders of SAP were well ahead of their time in actually bringing to market their vision of an integrated ERP system that could serve all industries and countries.

As we know, over the following 50 years computer technology advanced far faster than anyone could have ever expected, pretty much following Moore's Law (doubling in capacity every 18 months).

SAP had the idea of user exits right from the start, and as technology improved SAP introduced improved versions of its user exit technology. However, since the requirement was always that SAP code be downward compatible (i.e., after an upgrade everything that worked before would keep on working), the previous user exit technologies were never removed, and so we have ended up with six (major) different ways of coding a user exit. There are also a billion different minor ways, but it would take far too long to go into each of those, and in any event the miracle solution at the end of this chapter applies to the minor ones as well.

In this section, we will look at each of the main six user exit technologies in turn, which are as follows:

- VOFM Routines

- Repairs

- FORM-based User Exits

- CMOD User Exits

- BADI User Exits

- Enhancement Framework

We will finish with an excursus as to why you might want to take the seemingly strange step of introducing user exits to your own custom programs.

VOFM Routines

The term *VOFM* refers to an SAP transaction code. Within that transaction you can define (hopefully) small ABAP routines that can influence standard SAP processing in the areas of pricing, billing (invoicing), copy control (such as when a delivery is created based upon a sales order), and output determination (printing/emailing).

The ABAP routine in question is defined by the developer by using transaction VOFM. SAP provides a large number of examples in each area that are in fact used by standard SAP programs and can thus be copied, providing a template for customers to enhance the business logic. An example of such a routine can be seen in Listing 7-1.

Listing 7-1. Example VOFM Routine

```
FORM KOBED_669.
*{   INSERT            ACBC984559
 sy-subrc = 4.
  if komp-kposn ne 0.
    check: komp-prsfd = 'X'.
    check: komp-kznep = space.
    if not komt1-bergl is initial.
      check: komt1-bergl = komp-bergl.
    endif.
```

```
  endif.
  sy-subrc = 0.

  DATA:   ld_return type sysubrc.
* Requirement - bypass this requirement/condition, If customer group is
cash & payment terms is CCSH  . This requirement should trigger for Account
customers
    perform check_cash_customer changing ld_return .
    if ld_return <> 0.
       sy-subrc =   ld_return.
       return.
    else.
       sy-subrc = 0.
    endif.

*
*}   INSERT
ENDFORM.
```

In Listing 7-1 (which is an example of a VOFM routine known as a requirement), the routine determines whether a certain shipping pricing condition should be executed or not. The first half of the code is copied from standard SAP routine 051, which contains logic common to all shipping pricing conditions. Then, this is enhanced in the second half of the code such that the condition will only get calculated if the customer is an account customer (pays when they get an invoice) as opposed to a cash sales customer (has to pay straight away).

Next, the business analyst makes use of these VOFM routines—be they standard or custom—when configuring the pricing procedure. In Figure 7-2, you can see the configuration for a shipment cost pricing procedure for charging the customer for freight costs. The "Requirement" column contains the number of an ABAP routine that decides whether the pricing condition is calculated or not, and the "Basic Type" column (if filled) contains the number of an ABAP routine that alters the value that a standard SAP would normally calculate for the pricing condition.

Procedure			ZCONAU Concrete Charges AU										

Control data

Reference Step Overview

Step	Co...	CTyp	Description	Fro	To	Ma...	R...	St...	P	SuTot	Reqt	CalTy...	BasType
20	0	ZMNI	Mini Truck Surcharge	0	0	☐	☐	☐	S	51	0	0	
30	0	ZMVN	Mini Tk Surcharge S	0	0	☐	☐	☐	S	51	0	0	
40	0	ZCBA	Con. Base AU	0	0	☐	☑	☐	S	51	0	0	
55	0	ZREA	Returned Loads AU	0	0	☐	☐	☐	S	610	0	606	
60	0	ZHRA	Hourly Hire AU	0	0	☐	☐	☐	S	51	0	0	
70	0	ZHRM	Hire Metres/Km AU	0	0	☐	☐	☐	S	51	0	0	
75	0	ZCBB	Con. Base Extras AU	0	0	☐	☐	☐	S	51	0	604	
80	0	ZLOA	Load Charge AU	0	0	☑	☐	☐	S	51	0	0	
100	0	ZFR2	Freight Cost CO	0	0	☐	☐	☑	S	51	0	0	
400	0		Total Freight Charges	10	99	☐	☐	☐		0	0	0	

Figure 7-2. *Configuring a pricing procedure using VOFM routines*

The code in Listing 7-2 (routine 604) is an example of a "Basic Type" routine. In this case, the base volume for pricing is determined from the delivery document, but the ABAP routine 604 will possibly change that value based on various logic. What you should take note of is how the code goes about changing the volume to the value of 1 if it is currently less than three. We will come back to this shortly.

Listing 7-2. VOFM Routine to Change the Basis for Pricing

```
FORM FRM_KOND_BASIS_604.
*{   INSERT          ABCK917512
*** Condition ZCBB will cater for odd rules in various states
*** In NSW it will be used for extra cartage over 25KM
*** Between 1 and 3 the volume will be changed to 1M3
*** Between 3 and 4 the volume will be changed to 4 - X
*** Over 4 it will be set to 0
*** This will be multiplied by the load size to get the extra
*** cartage amount to be added on to the real extra cartage
*** New South Wales - Pioneer - Charge Customer
IF ( KOMK-REGIOA = 'NSW'
OR KOMK-REGIOZ = 'NSW' OR    "New South Wales
   KOMK-REGIOA = 'ACT'
OR KOMK-REGIOZ = 'ACT'  )    "ACT counts also
```

```
AND KOMK-VKORG = '026'.
   IF KOMP-VOLUM EQ 0.
* Let it be if it is zero, most likely a service material
   ELSEIF KOMP-VOLUM LE '3000'.
      KOMP-VOLUM = '1000'.
   ELSEIF KOMP-VOLUM GE '4000'.
      KOMP-VOLUM = '0'.
   ELSE.
      KOMP-VOLUM = '4000' - KOMP-VOLUM.
   ENDIF.                               "Check on volume size
ENDIF.                                  "Check for NSW Relevance

*}    INSERT
ENDFORM.
```

As a result of the somewhat antiquated nature of VOFM routines, there are several things worth noting, all of them bad to an extent:

- Most companies have a separation of concerns between who does the configuration (business analysts) and who does the programming (developers). Thus, the two people actually have to talk to each other, a prospect both often find horrifying.

- More important, I have seen cases where the ABAP routine is deleted but is still referred to in the configuration. I would have expected this to cause a dump, but it does not; instead, the pricing routine is not calculated and you see the cryptic message "Condition was determined, but not set" in the pricing analysis.

- You will notice from Listing 7-1 that the "requirement" routine works by setting the value of system variable SY-SUBRC. If that value is set to 0, the pricing condition is calculated; if SY-SUBRC is set to 4, then the condition is not calculated. In modern ABAP you are strongly advised to never change the values of system variables, and in ABAP in the cloud it becomes impossible.

- When you create a new program you will notice there is a checkbox called "Fixed Point Arithmetic," which defaults to "on." With that flag active, the program can handle numbers with decimal points. Originally, SAP programs could not handle decimals, and VOFM routines are still that way today, 50 years on. Thus, in Listing 7-2, in order to change the volume to "1" you have to set it "1000." The numbers you play with in a VOFM routine have to be a thousand times higher than their actual value. This can be really confusing, especially for new programmers.

- It is almost impossible to spot syntax errors in such routines. Amazingly, you can activate a VOFM routine with no errors and then get a short dump with a syntax error when the code runs for real.

- In Listings 7-1 and 7-2 you can see the generated comment "INSERT" at the start and end of the code. This is because the names of the VOFM routines are automatically generated and fall into the standard SAP name space; i.e., they do not start with a Z. Therefore, to add your code you need to make, in effect, a modification to the standard SAP, a so-called repair (more on this concept shortly), and thus you need to register the generated program name (RV62AXXX or whatever) in the SAP Service Marketplace. Many developers do not have authority for that and have to get their boss to do it for them. Either way, being forced (by SAP) to pretend you are modifying a standard SAP program when you are not is a very painful process.

- How these VOFM routines work is that SAP generates code in INCLUDEs in standard SAP programs that call the VOFM routines. This is "supposed" to happen automatically upon creation of the VOFM routine and when such routines are transported into a new system, but this does not always happen, leading to (in the best case) the VOFM routine's not getting called or (in the worst case) short dumps in dozens of standard SAP business-critical SAP transactions, like VA01 and VA41. To fix either problem, run SAP report RV80HGEN in the system where the problem is occurring to regenerate the code. A good idea is to create a Z transaction to call this report so authorized developers can run it in production in the event of a crisis (because you are most likely not allowed to run transaction SE38 directly in production). In addition, you can add an XPRA entry to transports containing VOFM routines such that RV80HGEN is automatically run when the transport arrives in the new system. As you will have gathered by now, the fact you have to build in such safeguards is because the whole concept is not as stable as one would ideally like.

Repairs

In the past, there was no way you could describe anything SAP-related as open source—all its code and concepts were 100 percent proprietary, and very few "community" contributions ever made it into the SAP standard code base. Nonetheless, SAP was somewhat unusual amongst its peers in that since the vast bulk of the standard code (apart from the kernel) was written in ABAP, every SAP customer could examine all that code.

Moreover, it is also possible for SAP customers to change anything in the standard SAP code base they feel like. This is known as a repair, though that term is very misleading—*mutilation* would be more accurate. When you make such a change you are "repairing" the tree that is the SAP system by cutting off a branch and replacing it with an umbrella. You may get the result you want, but the tree as a whole is worse off. More specifically, the effort at upgrade time (or support stack time) is increased geometrically by the number of "repairs" you have made to your system.

As such, SAP has always recommended—and I wholeheartedly agree—that you only make repairs as a very last resort. There are just so many other user exit options available that you should really never have to do this. And yet in every single on-premises SAP installation in the world, you will see such repairs, even in organizations that swear blind they would never do such a thing. Due to this fact, I am going to class repairs as a form of user exit, and at the end of the chapter when I talk about treating all forms of user exits the same, repairs will fall into the same bucket.

FORM-Based User Exits

Anyone who has been programming in SAP for a while will have come across standard program SAPMV45A, which is one huge monster of a program. Several dozen transactions all call this program—sales order, contract, and quotation maintenance, for example.

I think it is fair to say that every single organization that runs SAP and uses the system to process sales orders is unhappy with some aspect of the standard system and so wants to change something. The first technique SAP came up with for enabling this was the so-called FORM-based user exit. Using SAPMV45A as an example, there are a bunch of INCLUDES in that standard program with one or more "Z" characters in the name (e.g., MV45AFZZ) that are a series of blank FORM routines with the word *USEREXIT* at the start of the routine names into which you can insert your own code.

These FORM routines are then called by the standard SAP program; e.g., USEREXIT_ SAVE_DOCUMENT_PREPARE is called before the document is saved (so you can abort the save process if you want), and USEREXIT_SAVE_DOCUMENT is called after the document is saved—specifically at the point when you know the newly created order number (so you can update Z tables with that order number, for example).

This is all well and good and works very well indeed. There are, however, some points that are worth noting:

- Once again, this counts as a modification (repair) to the standard SAP as INCLUDES such as MV45AFZZ lie in the standard SAP namespace; i.e., they do not start with a Z. Thus, any changes you make have to be registered in the SAP Service Marketplace.

- At upgrade time, the system will want to reset INCLUDES like MV45AFZZ back to their blank state; i.e., remove all the Z code you added. The so-called SPAU exercise is supposed to catch this but does not always. Sometimes you have to manually add everything back again.

- You have access to every single global variable in the SAPMV45A program. That's great in regard to flexibility but can be incredibly dangerous if you don't know what you are doing—the amount of damage you could potentially do is astronomical.

- All the different user exits are in the one INCLUDE. If you have anything other than a really small organization then you are going to find that every day of the year there are going to be three or four different change requests all needing to change one of the user exits in that same INCLUDE.

The last point is the most important. There are 12 different user exits in MV45AFZZ. As a very first step, the recommendation is to put no code at all directly into the routines; instead, for each such routine, you should have one line of code only, and that line will declare an `INCLUDE`; e.g., `INCLUDE ZSD_MV45AFZZ_DELETE_DOCUMENT`.

That way, you can have 12 different developers working on 12 different user exits in 12 different transport requests all at once, without getting in each other's way. Moreover, as all the Z code is safely in the Z namespace it will not get over-written at upgrade time. If for whatever reason the SPAU mechanism does not work and the MV45AFZZ is reset to its initial state, instead of having to manually paste back in all the Z code you just have to re-insert the one line per routine with the `INCLUDE` statement.

Naturally, you still have the problem that 12 different developers all want to work on the *same* user exit at the same time, perhaps for different countries. There are many ways to solve this, and if you get it wrong you can do more harm than good. Happily, the "miracle" solution at the end of the chapter deals with this issue.

CMOD User Exits

The next step in SAP's user exit evolution was to move from FORM-based user exits to function module–based user exits. There are two transactions that handle this type of exit—SMOD for exploring the options open to you, and CMOD for creating such user exits via so-called projects.

With the CMOD concept, every so often in standard SAP programs a call is made to a function module with the word *exit* in its name; for example, `EXIT_SAPLKMA1_001`. Into this function module you can place your own Z code. The standard SAP code does not call the exit function by name; rather, it will say `CALL CUSTOMER-FUNCTION '001'`, which will magically invoke function `EXIT_SAPLKMA1_001`.

In the screen shown in Figure 7-3, a so-called CMOD project has been defined to add an extra field into the standard cost center master data maintenance transaction. There are several elements to this, as follows:

- Function Exits — One or more function modules called from standard programs where you can add Z code

- Menu Exits — Where you can add extra user commands into standard SAP menus

- Screen Exits — Where SAP provides screens or sub-screens that you
  can fill with your own fields, and these screens can then be shown in
  standard SAP transactions

- Include Tables — This is where you add some Z fields onto the end
  of a standard SAP database table (CI_CSKS extending standard table
  CSKS in this example). This is the best way to extend standard SAP
  tables, because that way SAP knows what you are doing and can
  automatically convert the data when you move to S/4HANA—even if
  the table being converted no longer exists in the new system. In such
  a case, the append will be directed to the table where the data now
  lives.

Project		☐		ZCOMKS01 Cost Center Menu Exit for Classification		
Enhancement	Impl	☐	Exp	COOMKS01 Customer Fields for Cost Center Master Data		
Function exit	✓	☐	🖹	EXIT_SAPLKMA1_001		
	✓	☐	🖹	EXIT_SAPLKMA1_002		
Menu exit	✓	☐		SAPLKMA1	+CU1	
Screen exit	✓	☐		SAPLKMA1	0399 CUSTFLDS SAPLXKM1	0999
	✓	☐		SAPLKMA1	3399 CUSTFLDS SAPLXKM1	0999
Include tables	✓	☐		CI_CSKS		

Figure 7-3. *Definition of a CMOD project*

Until the project has been activated in the transaction CMOD, the Z code in the
function modules will be totally ignored. In the debugger you will see the function
module being called, but the Z code inside effectively does not exist.

The first point to note is that there is one line of code already there in each "exit"
function module. That line declares a "Z" INCLUDE, which has a name (defined by SAP)
such as ZXKM1U01, and that INCLUDE is where you add your custom code. As that name
of the INCLUDE lies inside the customer namespace (even though it was created by SAP),
your Z code cannot get over-written at upgrade time.

Secondly, the code lives inside a function module with a defined signature; i.e., you
only have access to the parameters in that signature as opposed to being able to read
and modify any global variable in the entire standard SAP program, as is the case with
FORM-based user exits.

This means the whole concept is far less risky—you can only see what SAP wants you to see and change what SAP allows you to change. In theory, this limits the amount of damage that function module–based user exits can do.

Of course, since you can do a "Where-Used List" on the function module and thus see where it is called inside the standard SAP program, you can determine the name of the standard SAP program and, using the "dirty trick" with field symbols (which I am *not* going to go into here), read and modify any global variable in that program just like you could with a FORM-based user exit. That should, however, be a last resort.

BAdi User Exits

In the year 2000, SAP started a push to have everyone develop in an object-oriented manner. As you have seen, that did not work too well in terms of adoption, but the next logical step in user exit technology was to move on from function module–based user exits to class-based user exits—hence the Badi, or Business Add-in, user exit concept was born.

I am happy to say the concept was implemented in a proper OO fashion. This time, the standard SAP programs do not know if any user exits exist. They do know about the interface (in the SE24 sense of the word) that such user exits would implement should they exist. So at certain points in standard SAP programs, the code goes looking for any classes that implement the BAdi interface. Sometimes only one implementation can exist at a time, but more often you can create dozens of implementations (classes) of the same user exit if you so desire, and then the calling program will execute them one at a time.

That way, there is no way the user exit can ever be locked. If two people want to work on the user exit at the same time they just create two different classes that implement the interface (you do this via transaction SE19, by the way).

Moreover, there is the concept of a "filter Badi," where you can specify in the definition that a particular class that implements the BAdi interface is only ever called for Poland (for example). That way you can have 12 developers all looking after different countries working on the same user exit all at the same time, and if the developer working on the Polish exit makes a change it cannot possibly affect what the developer working on the Moroccan user exit is doing and vice versa.

The Enhancement Framework

All the prior user exit technologies worked well, but it is the nature of humanity to never be satisfied. Thus, no matter how many places in standard SAP programs calls to user exits were made, it was never going to be enough. Someone would always want to influence the behavior of a standard SAP program in a place where there was no user exit available.

As you saw earlier, traditionally, when no user exit was available, such changes were made by so-called repairs. SAP concluded that if people were going to make such changes anyway then why not give them a better way of doing so—and thus the enhancement framework was born.

You could best describe this concept as "user exits everywhere." Enhancements are categorized as either implicit or explicit. As with the prior concepts, there are a large number of places where SAP expects you might want to make a change—these are called explicit enhancement points. More important, when you are in SE80 looking at a standard SAP program, press the Enhancement button and then choose the menu options *Edit* ➤ *Enhancement Operations* ➤ *Show Implicit Enhancement Options*. Then, at several points in the standard program, you will see a string of quotation marks with black arrows pointing at them, as shown in Figure 7-4.

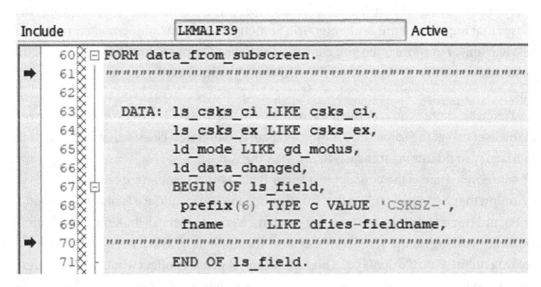

Figure 7-4. Implicit enhancement options

The line of quotation marks shows where an implicit enhancement option exists. In such places, you can insert some of your own code, just like a repair. You get such options at the start and end of every single FORM routine and—as you can see in Figure 7-4—at the end of every structure definition inside a FORM routine; i.e., you can add your own fields to standard SAP structure and internal table definitions.

However, if you want to change something right in the middle of a FORM routine, you are stuck. If standard SAP routines were all really short that would not be a problem, but sadly most standard routines are really long. If confronted with such a situation, you have to use the traditional "repair" mechanism.

The enhancement framework is of course just as dangerous as the "old-fashioned" way of modifying standard SAP code, but this time your added code lives in a Z namespace and so is far easier to handle at upgrade time. Moreover, you do not need to register each change in the SAP Service Marketplace.

User Exits in Your Own Z Programs

This next concept is going to seem very strange at first glance, but hopefully the light bulb will go on sooner or later.

Thus far, we have talked about changing standard SAP programs by inserting your own Z code through one method or another. This is because standard SAP code is locked against customers' making changes in order to prevent chaos.

Now, when it comes to your own Z programs, those are in your own namespace, so you can make whatever changes you want wherever you want. Therefore, there is no need at all for user exits in a Z program. That would seem to be madness.

However, a point that has been raised several times in this book is that programs start off small and simple—such as a read-only report—but gradually have more and more functionality added until it ends up with fifty thousand lines of code and is used to run half your business.

Imagine you have such a program (I don't have to imagine this; I have to live with two such programs) and that you work for a multi-national corporation operating in 50 different countries all out of the same SAP system. In such a situation, a business-critical program such as this will have outstanding change requests from all 50 countries at once—continually, forever. It doesn't even have to be a multi-national company; you could have ten different business lines all using the same program and all wanting changes at once.

You have two options here:

- Process the changes one at a time, not starting on the next until the previous change has progressed all the way to production and been signed off on as working perfectly. In such a situation, you will have 49 countries waiting in a queue all the time, so 98 percent of your internal customers are really unhappy all the time. That is not really a sensible option—any given country could end up waiting for two years for their change to go through, by which time the requirement would have totally changed.

- Bundle the requirements and do a bunch of changes at once, then release them at regular intervals—quarterly or monthly. That keeps everybody happy, but the downside is when something does go wrong it is much more difficult to isolate which of the myriad changes is to blame.

In both cases, you also have the problem that a change made for Iceland can break something that was working fine in the Dominican Republic. Moreover, in SAP you cannot have two people working on the same ABAP code at the same time (due to objects' being locked in transport requests), so you cannot speed up the number of changes being made at once by hiring one hundred developers and spreading all the requests evenly amongst them.

As you have seen in the list of various possible user exit techniques available in SAP, there is one that stands out as an obvious solution to the "50 countries" problem. That is the filter BAdi.

In such a situation, you would add hooks (BAdi calls) at various points throughout your custom program in the exact same way SAP adds hooks to their standard programs. When that point in the program is reached, it goes looking to see how many (if any) classes have implemented the BAdi interface in question and how many of these are relevant based on filter conditions (the country of the user running the program, for example). Then, if any such classes exist, they are looped through and a call is made to the same method of each class.

The idea is that just adding dozens of BAdi calls to classes that may or may not exist all throughout your program should have very little risk. The simplest way is to add such "exits" where it is obvious they will be needed and then add extra "exits" as and when they are needed rather than undergo a desperate effort to try to cater to every possible situation in advance.

Having your custom program full of user exits gives you the following benefits:

- If each class used by the BAdi call has a clear single responsibility (e.g., mango growing in Australia), then a change to that class cannot possibly break a totally unrelated class (e.g., a class dedicated to a donkey sanctuary in the United Kingdom).

- Leading on from that, it is obvious where the problem is; if something suddenly stops working for Tunisia, you can be fairly certain the problem lies with the Tunisia-specific class.

- You can in fact have 50 different developers working on 50 country-specific classes at the same time; the objects are totally separate, so the developers do not block each other.

- The life cycle of each country-specific class can be 100 percent separate from that of the core program that calls these exits. You can have small changes going up each week (or more often) as opposed to a "shotgun blast" of changes every three months.

You do not have to use filter BAdis to achieve this—you could build your own framework (more on this at the end of this chapter), but BAdis are well worth investigating if you are currently suffering from some variety of the "50 countries" problem.

User Exits in Cloud SAP Systems

Unless you have been hiding under a rock for the last few years, you will no doubt be aware of this horrible thing called the cloud that has come along. The days of on-premises systems (i.e., the way we have always done things) are supposedly numbered.

Instead, the idea is to use Software as a Service solutions such as Office 365 or Ariba or Success Factors or S/4HANA Cloud. If you use such a service, then the code base is shared between you and a million other customers, and you get an upgrade every three months automatically, whether you want it or not.

In fact, at the time of writing 99.9 percent of SAP customers that have done system conversions from SAP ECC 6.0 to S/4HANA have chosen the on-premises version; but let us leave that aside for now. Even though only a small percentage did not choose the on-premises option, that still means that plenty of organizations are now running S/4HANA in the cloud, and as time goes by the percentage of companies taking the cloud option when converting to S/4HANA gradually increases.

From a user exit point of view, the most obvious difference between an on-premises ERP system and a cloud one is that in an on-premises SAP system you can hack away at the source code via "repairs" as much as you want. That option vanishes if you are in the cloud and thus sharing the standard SAP code with a sausage factory in Tibet and NASA (who do run SAP, by the way) and half a billion other organizations.

This is also known as a "multi-tenant" or "shared tenant" situation. The analogy is that if you own your own house and it is just you who are living in it you can dig a huge hole in the floor of your front room if you want and turn it into a swimming pool. If, however, you live in an apartment block with dozens of other tenants, then your floor is someone else's ceiling, and so digging a big hole in your floor is not really a good idea, as the person below you would probably not appreciate it.

And naturally, when you move to the shared tenant environment you lose all your Z programs as well. Twenty or thirty years of non-stop custom development, gone in a puff of smoke. You are probably gathering why this option has not been as popular as SAP initially imagined it would be.

When SAP started up the cloud beanstalk, the claim was that all that "customization" (by which they meant Z code) was no longer needed, as the standard system would provide everything you could possibly need, and the way forward was for everyone to use "vanilla" SAP systems, such as the shared tenant version of S/4HANA, in the cloud, as that lowered the total cost of ownership, made upgrades incredibly easy, and so on.

That was also the message in the year 2000—i.e., everyone should use "vanilla" SAP systems. To be fair to SAP customers, I think every single SAP implementation has tried to do just that, at least at the start. Then they all added a minor "Z" tweak here, a minor "Z" tweak there, and before you knew it every single customer had more lines of custom code in Z programs and user exits than there were stars in the sky. Even if 75 percent of that Z code is not actually used, that leaves a vast amount that *is* actually used and is in fact business critical.

Realistically, everyone is going to want to add their own bits and pieces to their ERP system and to hang on to what they have built up over 20 to 30 years. So if you are such an SAP customer walking around with a big sack of Z code you can't afford to get rid of, does that mean you can never go to S/4HANA in the cloud? The answer is not as clear cut as you might think.

At first glance it seems obvious that if the code base is shared between all customers and is therefore unchangeable then everyone gets the exact same set of functionality. Enter the "Open/Closed" principle, where some piece of software is "Closed for Modification/Open for Extensions." S/4HANA Cloud naturally fits the first part—the code base is closed. The question then becomes, "How open is it for extension?" The answer is, "Very open indeed."

To start off with the obvious, even if the code base is shared, your master and transactional data is naturally private, and so you therefore have a vast amount of control over the way your ERP system behaves by means of your configuration (in the IMG sense of the word) settings. That's all well and good, as that is the way things have been since day one and it was never enough—so how do you fill in the remaining gaps?

What you have is the S/4HANA Extensibility Framework. This is in fact a huge topic, and I cannot possibly cover all of it here, but instead will give you a brief summary so you get the general idea. I'll include some links to relevant blogs at the end of the chapter for more information.

In essence, SAP appears to be aiming to have just as many user exits—if not more—in the S/4HANA Cloud version as you have been used to having in the on-premises SAP versions. You can also have custom Z ABAP programs via ABAP in the Cloud.

The difference is where the Z code lives. It is almost as if there are two databases (there are not, but it *seems* like there are), one where all the standard SAP code and standard SAP tables live, and one where all your Z programs and user exit Z code and custom Z tables live.

Due to the unchangeable nature of the S/4HANA Cloud code base and the automatic updates, there has to be an impenetrable barrier between the standard SAP code and all your Z code. Imagine two islands separated by a 20-mile bridge filled with armed guards and medical inspectors. The only way between those two islands is via the bridge, and due to all the guards and inspections nothing dangerous can possibly get through in either direction.

In SAP terms, the two "islands" (Standard Island and Z Island) can only communicate via strictly defined APIs. These APIs have to remain stable (as per the open/closed principle they can grow but anything existing cannot change), which lets the Z code be changed at any time without affecting the standard system, and the standard system can be updated automatically without affecting the Z code.

The areas where you can extend S/4HANA can be grouped into five basic types. We will look at each one in turn, listed in order of increasing flexibility. The first four are known as in-app extensibilities, and the last is known as a side-by-side extension.

UI Extensibility

Back in 1999, I first encountered the product GUIxt (not created by SAP), which was free and allowed you to change standard SAP fields in a code-free manner; i.e., you could rename them to something your users could understand (e.g., rename "Vendor" to "Supplier"), move fields around the screen, hide fields you did not need, add pictures, and so on. This worked by changing things at the SAP GUI level rather than the code level, and the changes lived in a file outside of SAP, thus not interfering with the core system. As an experiment, that year my colleague and I used GUIxt to make a standard SAP screen look exactly like the equivalent screen in the legacy system SAP was replacing—right down to the color scheme. As might be imagined, the users loved that.

Many years later, SAP came up with its own version of the same technology, called Screen Personas. This works via a web interface rather than the GUI, but the aim was exactly the same; i.e., rename standard fields and the like without touching the core.

S/4HANA also lets you do this to standard screens—here, the framework is called UI Extensibility.

Field Extensibility

Field extensibility is where you add custom fields onto the end of standard SAP tables—what we called append structures in the past. Now it is called a DDIC Extension Include, but it is the same thing in effect; since only you can see these fields, and not all the other customers using the shared code base, my guess is that behind the scenes SAP creates a new table just for you with the same primary key as the table being appended, and it only looks like there are new fields on the end of the standard table.

Custom Tables/Business Objects

Sometimes you want to have totally custom Z tables that have nothing to do with any standard SAP tables. You might well have a business object that is totally unique to your industry and/or country that needs to be represented by one or more Z tables. The extensibility framework in S/4HANA lets you create such tables and business objects.

416

Business Logic Extensibility

If you have custom tables and fields, then you need to fill them and make them interact with standard SAP transactions. That job has always been done by user exits in the past, and it still is in the new cloud world.

You can still have BAdis—they live in enhancement spots. For example, the good old FORM-based user exit MV45AFZZ is replaced by assorted BAdis (Business Add-In) that live in enhancement spot ES_SD_SLS_EXTEND. There are two caveats though, as follows:

- The version of ABAP you use to program the BAdis in the cloud pops up in a web-based editor and can be described as ABAP Light (Its official name is ABAP for Key Users); it has a very restricted set of editor commands available.

- At time of writing, there are not really that many places that in-app extensibility and enhancement spots are available in S/4HANA cloud. The number increases rapidly with each release of S/4HANA; thus far, approximately 100 new BAdis a year. That sounds like a lot (and it is), but given the amount of standard code in the entire ERP system it might be a while until you can extend every single area you want extended.

Custom Programs

Now we come to the side-by-side extension, where the code lives outside the S/4HANA Cloud system and communicates via a series of stable APIs; e.g., to read and update standard SAP objects like sales orders. External systems have been communicating with on-premises SAP systems via BAPIs for decades using this technique, so the concept is not radically new.

Until relatively recently, if you wanted to build a custom program that worked with S/4HANA in the cloud, then you could use any programming language at all you wanted— as long as it was not ABAP. There was—and is—a wonderful framework called the CAPM (Cloud Application Programming Model; you pronounce this "CAP," as the M is silent), which you could use to build such applications and software development kits (SDKs) for both Java and JavaScript to enable easy access to S/4HANA (and indeed to Ariba and SuccessFactors) business objects. However, the fact that you could not use ABAP to build such extensions led some to conclude that ABAP was dead and had no future.

Mark Twain once said, *"The rumors of my death have been greatly exaggerated,"* and so it was with ABAP. In September 2018, ABAP staggered back from the grave with the announcement of ABAP in the Cloud—sometimes called Steampunk. This, combined with the RESTful ABAP Application Programming Model (RAP), allows you to write custom programs for S/4HANA Cloud in the ABAP language—albeit a version of the ABAP language that is quite different from what you are used to.

The good news is that in theory you can reuse all your 20 or 30 years of custom development whilst still having a cloud ERP system. The bad news is that reality is not much like theory and whilst there is a defined process for migrating your code to ABAP in the Cloud you will have to rewrite most of it—which is why in the TDD Chapter 2 in this book we looked at running a static check on all new code to see if it would work in ABAP in the Cloud.

Tying This All Together—in a TDD Manner

In this section, we start by looking at two common problems: firstly, that to get the standard system working the way you want you need to employ user exits from a variety of the different technologies on offer; and secondly, that you want to develop using TDD and that is "impossible" when it comes to user exits.

Then, as might be expected, we move on to looking at an approach that can solve both problems at once.

Problem One: You Are Using a Mixture of Different User Exit Frameworks

If you have an SAP system that has been running for a long while—20 years or longer, for example—then it is quite likely that you have user exits in several or all of the categories mentioned earlier: FORM-based user exits, CMOD user exits, BAdis, and so on. Moreover, it is likely you will be using the current cloud-based user exits at some stage, and of course whatever new user exit frameworks SAP may invent in the future. Having user exits all over the place that use a mixture of technologies may seem messy, but there are two primary reasons that this turns out to be the normal situation for the vast majority of SAP customers.

Firstly, each new technology gets called from a set of predefined points inside standard SAP programs, and the list of areas you can enhance is not the same at all for each new technology. So, if you want to replace a FORM-based user exit with (say) a Badi, there may not be a suitable BAdi. Likewise, you cannot do all your exits via the enhancement framework as you might want to change some code in the middle of a standard SAP routine rather than at the start or the end, so you have to use (in the best case) a CMOD exit that lives in the middle of that routine or (in the worst case) do a repair.

Secondly, and maybe more importantly, whenever a new framework is released by SAP it is a bit of a thankless task converting all your existing code to use the new framework just for the sake of being "modern." It is difficult to justify changing something that already works and taking the risk of breaking it when there are so many other new change requests that actually bring a business benefit competing for attention.

For example, one company I knew had a load of custom HR applications running in the SAP GUI. The company SAP came along and said, that is so old-fashioned; you need to rewrite them so they run in the web using Web Dynpro JAVA. So that is what happened—all the applications were rewritten to use that new UI technology. No extra functionality was added,; just the enabling technology was changed. Then a few years later, SAP came along and said that Web Dynpro JAVA was obsolete, support for that will be removed, you need to rewrite all your HR applications in Web Dynpro ABAP. So they did another costly and time-consuming exercise with no apparent benefit. Then a few years later, SAP came along and said Web Dynpro ABAP is so old-fashioned, you need to rewrite all your HR applications using UI5. This time enough was enough, and the customer company flatly refused. You just end up going round in circles forever.

You can't attack SAP for constantly creating new frameworks that solve the same problem—each one is in fact better than the last, and the reason so many frameworks are created is that technology in general keeps improving, and at an ever-faster rate.

You just have to accept that new frameworks for pretty much anything will keep coming out, and if someone tells you something like "BOPF is the be-all and end-all of how to handle business logic, it will never be replaced," then take that claim with a pinch of salt.

The way around this—in any area—is to program in a framework-agnostic way. For example, I have model classes (that contain business logic such as derivations and validations) that can be used in SAP GUI DYNPRO programs, in Web Dynpro programs, in the BOPF, and in the new RESTful ABAP Application Programming model, and indeed can be reused in whatever framework SAP may invent in the future. This is because in each case there is very little code in the framework other than calls to the model class.

In other words, the application does not depend on the framework, the framework depends on the application; that's known as dependency inversion.

SAP itself recommends that you put no code in specific frameworks like PBO or PAI modules in DYNPRO programs, or in methods of gateway data provider classes; instead, in both frameworks the task at hand should be outsourced to reusable business classes. The latter advice was very sensible, as those data provider classes are already obsolete, so you would be sunk if you had put all your Z coding inside them.

Getting back to user exits—at long last—the principle is exactly the same. You have a whole bunch of frameworks that are all used to achieve the exact same task; i.e., to modify the behavior of standard SAP programs. Furthermore, it would not be the greatest shock in the world if in the future some new user exit frameworks were created by SAP.

So the first problem is that you really should not have any Z code in any user exit framework that is not a call to a reusable business class. Before we move on to the solution, let us look at the second problem.

Problem Two: You Can't Develop User Exits Using TDD

As you will have realized by now, I am a big advocate of using TDD for all ABAP development. Since a percentage of change requests relate to adding or changing code in user exits, then naturally I am saying you should use TDD here as well; i.e., write the test first in a test class and then write the actual code in the user exit.

You may be forgiven for thinking that this approach is crazy plus impossible. You can certainly easily add test classes to a class that implements a BAdi interface, and it might be just about possible for a CMOD function module–based user exit, but what about user exits that are right in the middle of a standard SAP procedural program like a FORM-based user exit or an implicit enhancement? Even worse—what about a VOFM routine or a repair?

At first glance, the idea of using TDD for these developments seems ludicrous, and therefore even the small number of ABAP programmers who currently use TDD agree that user exit code is an exception and that code can only be tested manually. That's a great shame, as making 100 percent sure that user exit code works is even more important than making sure your normal Z code works, because the scope for disaster is so much greater (disaster in the sense of stopping standard SAP programs from working properly).

Solution to Both Problems

Now is the time to defuse the user exit time bomb! Let us say you are adding a new country to your existing SAP implementation—the Ukraine, to pick a country at random. The analysts have various meetings with local business managers and come back with a list of country-specific requirements that have to be developed inside SAP, a list as long as an elephant's trunk.

In this example, you are in charge of ABAP developments for sales order enhancements and do a technical analysis. To your horror, you discover you need to create some user exits using loads of techniques—VOFM routines, FORM-based user exits, and so on—the whole kit and caboodle. Moreover, some existing custom programs used by many existing countries need Ukraine-specific logic added to them, which would best be done by adding some form of user exit to those Z programs.

In addition, you wish to do the right thing and develop all that new code in a TDD manner, which is of course "impossible" for user exits.

In this example, there is a long list of requirements, but one thing binds them all together—they all have to do with sales order processing in the Ukraine. This is a single area of responsibility, and thus a standalone class can be created to deal with this single responsibility. This class will implement the existing interface, which all sales order processing classes for the existing countries implement.

Thus, since it is possible to outsource processing in DYNPRO (or Web DYNPRO or SEGW or BOPF or RAP or any new SAP framework) by using a call to a common reusable Z class, why not do the exact same thing in the various user exit technologies?

In both cases, the idea is that in the same way a PAI module in a DYNPRO program or a method call in a SEGW class should have no actual code at all, just a straight call to a reusable business class, that should be the exact same procedure in any of the myriad user exit frameworks. No matter what user exit technology you are using, code no actual ABAP statements in the exit; just make a call to a method of the class that looks after the business logic.

A filter BAdi would know what specific class to call, while none of the other techniques would, so to ensure uniformity each exit would only know about the interface (in this example, the interface to the sales order business logic class) and dynamically determine what actual class to call based on the country or whatever using a factory method.

This gives the following advantages:

- Most important, the country-specific Z class can have a local test class and thus can be developed in a TDD manner.

- You have type safety—you just pass into the method call whatever information the user exit call point has that is relevant (as opposed to the entire global variable list in FORM-based user exits) and return what needs to be changed at the call point.

- It is much easier to run the extended program check and code inspector on code inside a standalone Z class as opposed to on user exit code that is inside a standard SAP program, like VOFM exits or FORM-based user exits (you generally cannot run a static code check on a standard SAP program).

- You can move the call from one technology to another. If a new BAdi comes out to replace a FORM-based user exit, then you can just move the call rather than having to cut and paste the code and potentially make a load of adjustments to make that code live in its new "home." Thus, the "bomb" that would go off when you move to a new platform like S/4HANA Cloud or ABAP in the Cloud will never explode.

- All the user exit code is in one place, irrespective of the exact technology that calls it. I used to maintain a spreadsheet (which went out of date quickly) with one worksheet for each type of user exit technology, and then I listed all the relevant exits on that sheet. Then, when making a change, the idea was to look at the spreadsheet to see what tool to use to change the user exit code. How much easier would that be if you always had to go to just the one place?

Lowest Common Denominator

In my opinion, the idea that SAP came up with for filter BAdis was wonderful. One or more classes are called based on some sort of filter value, be it country or business line or something else entirely. That is great, but sadly there is not always such a BAdi available for whatever sort of user exit you want.

If you really want a unified approach, i.e., to achieve the same sort of thing a filter BAdi does but for all past and future user exit technologies, you will have to build your own custom framework. There are two strands to this.

Firstly, the user exit code does not need to know about concrete classes that implement Ukraine-specific logic. It only needs to know about the interface. Then, some sort of factory method will return the correct class based on country (or whatever), and if there is no such class the user exit will do nothing. That way, when you add classes for new countries you do not need to change the call in the user exit.

Secondly, we come to the concept of "feature toggling," which is really common outside the SAP universe. As you know, in SAP when a transport goes into production and something horrible happens as a result you cannot just press a button and instantly change things back to the way they were before.

In this case, we are talking about some new user exit code that has just arrived in production and changes the behavior of a standard SAP program or maybe one of your Z programs. If you have designed the code properly this new thing will live in one specific method instead of in a method that handles ten different behaviors all at once.

You could create a custom Z configuration table—directly maintainable in production—that controls the class/method combinations flagged as dormant for user exits. Every user exit method would check this table, and if there were an entry it would return from the user exit code without doing anything.

If every method in the user exit class works perfectly (which you would hope would be the normal situation), then there are no entries in the "dormant" table. If something goes into production that causes a horrible problem, however, you could switch it off in a heartbeat.

You could even have some sort of PID that IT people could set that would activate dormant user exits—only for their user ID—so they could test the new code when it arrives in production before unleashing it on the unsuspecting user base.

Conclusion

This chapter has been all about user exits—a form of custom code usually treated 100 percent differently than the rest of the custom code that developers create.

First of all, you looked at the main user exit technologies available to modify the behavior of standard SAP programs (and indeed your own Z programs) in a traditional on-premises SAP system. Then, you looked at the equivalent options available in a cloud-based SAP system.

Lastly, you saw a proposal to unify the "mixed bag" of different user exit technologies—both past and future—by adopting a common approach to all of them.

The previous chapters have generally focused on custom code in SAP systems prior to S/4HANA. This chapter has discussed custom code in both environments. The next two chapters will deal with making sure custom code works in S/4HANA and beyond.

Recommended Reading

The following are links to is a very painful process, blogs on the SAP Community website on the subject of S/4HANA extensibility:

https://blogs.sap.com/2020/03/05/s-4hana-in-app-extensibility-end-of-classical-extensions/
https://blogs.sap.com/2015/09/30/the-key-user-extensibility-tools-of-s4-hana/

CHAPTER 8

Ensuring Code Runs in S/4HANA

Past upgrades have no doubt gotten you used to the idea that ABAP code is always 100 percent downward compatible, so that after an upgrade to a newer version of SAP your custom code keeps working without having to be changed. This is not the case when moving to S/4HANA, as it is in effect a totally new product, so you are not doing an upgrade but rather a re-implementation. In this chapter, you will learn how to ensure your custom code is of high enough quality to keep working after a move to S/4HANA.

Initially, the deadline for all customers (who wanted to stay with SAP) to convert to S/4HANA was 2025. This deadline was later extended to 2030.

Oracle thought this was the opportunity of a lifetime. Since every single SAP customer had to do an ERP re-implementation anyway, the logic was that some customers might jump ship and move to an Oracle ERP system. As it turns out, that never happened—Oracle claimed in an earnings call that during the next year they would announce some major "steals," but after that year was up they went very quiet. At that point, SAP announced they had not lost a single customer.

The year 2030 seems a long way away, but you have to bear in mind that SAP claims they stopped making new innovations in SAP ECC 6.0 in 2017. I am not so sure about that, as the list of what is included in each new ECC 6.0 EHP8 support stack certainly seems to contain things that look like new functionality, but the official position is "nothing new since 2017." According to that theory, if you wait till 2030 to move to S/4HANA, you will be, in some senses, 13 years behind the "early adopters" who made the jump the first year S/4HANA was out (which was 2015).

Therefore, if you are an ABAP developer, then the day will dawn when you go through a system conversion to S/4HANA.

© Paul David Hardy 2021
P. D. Hardy, *Improving the Quality of ABAP Code*, https://doi.org/10.1007/978-1-4842-6711-0_8

Two Flavors of S/4HANA   When you are converting to S/4HANA you have two choices. You can go for the on-premises version, where you can in theory keep most of your Z code; this option is the focus of this chapter. The other option is to convert to S/4HANA in the Cloud, where in theory you can keep none of your Z code; this option is the focus of the next chapter.

In this chapter, so far you have read about why it is a fantastic idea to start getting your custom code ready for the S/4HANA conversion right now, even if your organization isn't planning to start that conversion project until 2030 (or later). These incremental changes should be done as part of your normal TDD (Test Driven Development) process.

Next, you will hear about the types of automated checks you can do to verify your code for S/4HANA readiness—those available to you right now, the ones available during the conversion project, and those you can only do once your development system has been converted.

The last section will bring it all together. Various common issues you might find when converting custom code to S/4HANA are listed, along with, where applicable, which automated tests and fixes can help with each problem.

HANA and Her Sisters   Many people get confused by SAP's putting the name HANA in as many products as possible. Just to be clear, HANA is the underlying database—you could run your ECC 6.0 system on a HANA database if you wanted. S/4HANA is an ERP system that only runs on a HANA database, in the same way BW4HANA is a BW system that only runs on a HANA database.

TDD Recap

Having gotten eight chapters into this book, you will not drop dead of shock each time the subject of TDD rears its ugly head. In this chapter, the relevance is that after you have gotten each piece of new or changed code working, you go through the BLUE phase, where you make the code as good as it can possibly be.

Whilst going through that exercise, you run a bunch of automated static code checks and also do some manual code checks based on your knowledge of what is good and bad. At this point, it would be a good time to fix anything you can that you know for a fact will not work in S/4HANA.

As an example, in 2006 I added to my "finalization checklist" an instruction to switch on the Unicode checks in every Z program I changed; i.e., I ticked the "Unicode Check" box in the program attributes, which usually caused a load of syntax errors I then had to fix.

There was no need at all to do this at the time, but I knew sooner or later we would be moving to an SAP release where Unicode checks were mandatory, and I might as well deal with any problems that switch would cause on a program-by-program basis, years in advance (four years, as it turned out), rather than having to deal with ten billion problems all throughout the custom code base, all at once, during upgrade time whilst faced with a looming deadline.

In the same way, all the recommendations in this chapter are not intended to be used in one massive exercise just prior to go-live, but rather over a protracted period as part of the TDD cycle.

Types of S/4HANA Checks

Happily, you are going to be helped every step of the way on your journey to S/4HANA. In this section, you will look at what is available to you right now in your current system, what will become available to you once your conversion project starts, and lastly how ABAP in Eclipse can help with automated code conversion once your development system has migrated to S/4HANA.

Prior to the Conversion: ATC Checks in ECC 6.0

S/4HANA for ERP came out in 2015. At that point, it was clear that sooner or later every SAP customer would have to migrate, and so SAP added a bunch of new ABAP Test Cockpit (ATC) checks to the ECC 6.0 system to help people identify problems they might experience when moving to S/4HANA.

You can spot the checks that were added by invoking the code inspector (via transaction SCI) and looking at the check variants FUNCTIONAL_DB and FUNCTIONAL_DB_ ADDITION. You would generally not want to use those variants on their own as they only have a small number of checks.

An important point to note is that having a clean ATC check slate—i.e., you run the code inspector, and nothing pops up—can reduce the work needed in the conversion project by about a third. To be more exact, in most conversion projects when you get a big list of "things that need to be changed because we are moving to S/4HANA" about a third of the items on that list have been showing up in the ATC checks for years. Therefore, reducing the number of ATC errors and warnings now will save your management a heart attack later.

During the Conversion Project: Remote Checks

When your organization goes from thinking about moving to S/4HANA to actually getting the green light to go ahead, your BASIS department needs to set up a standalone ABAP system on release 7.52 (which is the highest release you are ever going to be able to have a standalone ABAP system on).

That new 7.52 system then needs an RFC connection to your current development system set up, and then your development system gets half a hundred OSS (SAP Support) notes installed.

Normally, an ATC check analyzes the code in the system where it is run. In this case, the ATC configuration is changed in the remote 7.52 system such that it analyzes a different system—i.e., your current development system.

The process for setting this up is quite complex; there is a link to a blog on the subject at the end of this chapter, if you are interested, even though this is a BASIS task.

SAP has created some standard ABAP Test Cockpit check variants like S4HANA_READINESS_REMOTE (general purpose) or S4HANA_READINESS_1909 (if you want to check for the specific release to which you are going to be converting).

In addition, you can check your customized open SQL queries for SAP S/4HANA readiness after implementing SAP Note 2942419—"Include ATC check 'S/4HANA: Readiness Check for SAP Queries'"—into your standalone 7.52 system.

What this check is looking for is custom (Z) SQL queries that use SAP standard objects that were "simplified" in SAP S/4HANA; i.e., they may no longer exist.

The important point about a remote ATC check is that the result list looks subtly different than that for the standard ATC checks you are used to. A new column is introduced that points to an SAP note for each finding. That note is supposed to guide you as to what to do about the problem and—credit where it is due—most of the notes are quite helpful.

The even more important point is that the remote ATC check will come back with a gigantic number of findings. This can lead people to believe that the effort involved in converting the custom code is astronomical. In fact, if you sort the result list by OSS note, you will find that there is in fact only a small number of recurring problems—and that each problem occurs a very large number of times.

I would advocate trying to get a 7.52 system set up before the conversion project kicks off—years before, if you can—and as part of the normal development process doing remote checks on the areas of Z code you have just changed. That way, you can chip away at the problem over time rather than having to boil the ocean all at once during a short project timeline.

After the Conversion: ADT Quick Fixes

At the end of the Open SAP Course on migration to S/4HANA there is a multiple-choice quiz. One of the possible answers to the question "How do you convert your code such that it works in S/4HANA?" is "Run program SAPFIXCODE."

Sadly, that is not the correct answer, wonderful though it would be. I wonder how many people have gone looking in their systems for that program. We also need the program SAPFIXBUGS, but that does not exist either.

Nonetheless, after your development system has been converted to S/4HANA you will find you do have access to a sort of "poor man's" version of the imaginary SAPFIXCODE program.

The "quick fixes" in ABAP in Eclipse (ADT) are intended to automate boring manual tasks such as creating an empty implementation for a local method definition. Since you are likely to have several hundred occurrences in your Z code of each S/4HANA-related problem that can be detected with an ATC check, the process of fixing seven hundred sections of code by doing the exact same thing for each easily falls into the "boring" category.

Eclipse in S/4HANA   If you have S/4HANA on-premises, then you can still use SE80 as per before. However, the automated quick fixes described in this section are only available when using ADT.

Thus, SAP has come up with a list of new "quick fixes" that are specifically designed to deal with such S/4HANA problems; e.g., automatically adding ORDER BY to existing database queries where appropriate. Moreover, you can run an ATC check on your whole Z code base at once and if you find seven thousand instances of the same problem you can fix every single one of them at the press of a button.

The important point to note is that such quick fixes are not available until *after* you have converted to S/4HANA. Thus, it could be argued that since many problems can be automatically fixed later on, it would be pointless to expend the effort to manually fix them in your current system.

There is no hard and fast answer to this—I would say that if you run a remote ATC check on your entire existing code base and find ten thousand problems that can be fixed at the press of a button after conversion, then there is no need to do anything, but when changing one small routine in the current system I would tend to make the manual "future-proofing" fix anyway on point of principle, as such changes make the code just that little bit better.

In the subsequent sections, you will see a list of specific problems that converting to S/4HANA brings to your code, and for each one you will be told whether some sort of automated fix is available and into which category it falls—checks available right now, checks available in the remote ATC check, or automated fixes after the conversion event.

Specific Issues to Be Dealt With

There are two broad areas that change when converting to S/4HANA, as follows:

- The underlying data — The nature of the fields in the database tables, the nature of those database tables, and the nature of the database itself

- The nature of the applications that work with this data

Field Changes

If you were to look online to see what the biggest change is when moving to S/4HANA, the answer always is, "The material number! It increases in length from 18 characters to 40 characters!" Whilst this is true, it is not the biggest change by any means—yet this is always the first example given.

In theory, this should not be a problem at all, provided you

- always type variables that store materials with reference to data element MATNR as opposed to CHAR18;

- always type parameters that pass materials using data element MATNR;

- always type custom fields in database tables that store material numbers using data element MATNR; and,

- when creating custom data elements that refer to material numbers, use the domain MATNR.

So, as long as you never directly specify an 18-character "holder" for a material number but rather always use the standard SAP data element/domain, you will be OK. If you come across a CHAR18 specification when changing existing code in your current system, there is no logical reason why you can't change the assignment to the standard MATNR right now.

In the same way, in ECC 6.0 and below there are about half a billion different domains and data elements for storing currency amounts. They all have different lengths and a different number of decimal places. SAP did an inventory of all these fields and found the longest one had a length of 23 and the maximum number of decimal places was two.

Therefore, in S/4HANA every single currency field has been increased to accommodate a length of 23 numerals with two decimal places. Once again, as long as all your custom code has currency fields that always refer to a standard SAP currency data element or domain, you should be OK. That way there is no possibility of data loss in your custom tables.

The remote ATC check will explode with findings in this area. If anything, it goes a little bit too far—even if you are doing the right thing and typing a material number variable using MATNR it will still show up as a "warning" when in fact there is no problem at all.

Table Changes

For historical reasons, the data model in standard SAP is incredibly complex. When you post an accounting document, for example, not only are FI tables BKPF (header) and BSEG (line items) updated, but about half a billion secondary tables as well; e.g., BSIK (Open Vendor Items), BSID (Open Customer Items) in FI, assorted tables in cost-center accounting, assorted tables in profit-center accounting, tables in profitability analysis, the list goes on forever.

This was mainly done for performance reasons. There was just so much data that the easiest way to satisfy assorted queries in an optimal manner was to store the exact same data in multiple places. The same is true of the data models in the areas of SD (Sales and Distribution) and MM (Materials Management) and in fact pretty much the whole SAP system.

Simplification of the Data Model

In the S/4HANA system there has been a dramatic reduction in the number of database tables. The fifty billion tables in the FI/CO area go down to just two, for example—BKPF for the header and ACCDOC for the line items. Similar "culls" of tables have been made in the SD and MM areas.

At first glance, you might find this information quite worrying—after all, 99.9 percent of your custom code is likely to be doing database reads on dozens of database tables that simply no longer exist in the S/4HANA system. Thus, you might expect a torrent of syntax errors along the lines of "Table BSID does not exist."

In actual fact, that is not going to be a problem. SAP has been very clever about this. The table definitions still exist for all the "dead" tables. There will be no data within them, and yet if you do an SE16 on such a table or even a SQL read from a custom program you still see the data—what is going on?

Something extra has been added to the table definitions for all the "dead" tables— namely a nominated "replacement object." To understand what a replacement object is, if you are inside an S/4HANA system and have a look at the "dead" table MSEG (for example) via transaction SE11, then take the menu option EXTRAS ➤ REPLACEMENT OBJECT, you will see the name of the CDS view that is actually called when a SELECT is done on that "dead" table. That CDS view will query the new table where the data lives and retrieve all the fields that were in the original table.

That way, not only will you not get any syntax errors in your existing custom programs that query the empty tables, but also the exact same data as before will be retrieved. The only way you can tell that something totally different than before is going on is by looking at an ST05 trace, where you will see the actual table the data is coming from.

Appends to Standard SAP Tables

The next area of worry is that you may well have added a customized (Z) append structure onto some of those tables that "no longer exist" in S/4HANA. Since those tables have all their data deleted upon conversion to S/4HANA, and the new tables have no idea about your Z fields, does that mean all the historical Z data in those tables will be destroyed?

The good news is that SAP provides "cookbooks" for each area (FI/SD/MM) with advice as to what to do if you have a custom append on a "dying" table. The exact mechanism varies from table to table. Sometimes the system is even clever enough to recognize you have added a Z append to a standard SAP "include" structure that starts with the letters CI_ (which stands for customer include) such as CI_COBL. Since SAP knows the entire purpose of those structures is to extend standard tables, equivalent extensions have to be added to the new tables, and often automatic data conversion is possible during the migration.

The remote ATC check will highlight areas where your SQL queries relate to "dead" tables and point you to SAP notes, which in turn point you to the "cookbooks," giving you precise instructions as to what to do.

Database Changes

Throughout this book, the advice has been to have all custom database access done by specialized database access classes. The primary reason for this was to allow unit testing, because such specialized classes can be replaced by test doubles during unit tests.

However, this approach also yields benefits when you need to change the database queries in your custom code. Instead of having to trawl through all your programs looking for SELECT statements, you just have to go through the database access classes.

At this point, you may be thinking, "Hang on—if all my SQL queries on dead tables are going to keep on working as before, why do I need to change anything?"

In theory you do not. However, there are two reasons why after the conversion you might like to change your custom queries so that they point to the actual data source table(s):

- From a purely semantic "clean code" perspective, it could be said it is clearer to the reader of the code if the code states the actual table the data is read from, as opposed to where it used to be read from in the prior system. You may get to the point ten years from now when a new programmer looks at a query on BSIK and asks "What is BSIK? That's not where open vendor items are stored!"

- On a more practical level, there will always be a performance overhead—however small—in retrieving data indirectly as opposed to directly. It's like putting an extra layer of wrapping paper on a birthday present. It doesn't make it much harder to unwrap, but it would be easier if it were not there.

The Golden Rules

For some time now SAP has had the concept of the "Golden Rules" of SQL queries. These rules were designed before the advent of the HANA database and were relevant to all databases then supported by SAP. Before HANA, the bottleneck occurred when transferring data between the disk-based storage on the database and data in memory on the application server. As HANA is an in-memory database, that bottleneck has gone away, so you might be forgiven for thinking that the previous "Golden Rules" (which were created to deal with a bottleneck that no longer exists) can now be safely ignored.

In fact, the rules are equally applicable to a HANA database; however, some of those rules are much less important now, and some are a million times more important. Let us look at each of the rules and how they change with the advent of HANA.

Minimize Amount of Transferred Data

What this is all about is only selecting the minimum number of *columns* from the database that you actually need.

When I first started programming in ABAP many years ago it was common to see developers declaring their internal table or work area based on a standard SAP table such as VBAP and then doing a SELECT * to get every single column in that table and then transferring those values to the internal table or work area. Then only a small number of the retrieved columns would actually be used in the custom program.

This is clearly a waste—it is like buying what you need for your weekly shopping from the supermarket plus a load of stuff you don't actually need. You have to endure the extra weight of carrying all the things you don't need home, and then throw them away as soon as you get home.

Hasso Plattner—one of the founders of SAP—once famously said "SELECT * is for losers." The correct way to behave is to have a work area not based on an SAP table but comprising only the fields you actually need, and then select only those fields from the table.

Importance in HANA World

This is much, much more important in a HANA database than in a traditional database like Oracle because HANA is a column-based database; the more columns you ask for, the more work the database has to do. Thus, if you throw a SELECT * for a table like

VBAP with over 400 columns at a HANA database you are in effect throwing a lit stick of dynamite at it.

Just to be clear: a SELECT * on a wide table in a column-based database like HANA will perform much, much worse than the equivalent query in a traditional row-based database.

ATC Check Support

The ATC check "Search Problematic SELECT * Statements" will tell you the percentage of fields being retrieved that are actually being used. Thus, if you do a SELECT * on VBAP and thereafter only use the primary key and one or two other fields, you will get a message like "Only 0.1% of fields used." The good thing is that the fields being used are actually listed, which will help you in changing your SELECT statement.

You also have to use a bit of common sense, as sometimes the result list table or structure has its components read dynamically or exports the result to somewhere the static code check cannot detect.

Minimize Number of Data Transfers

What this rule says is that if you have the numbers of 50 customers and need to get all their names, then get them all at once in one big database hit rather than looping through a table of 50 records and doing a SELECT SINGLE each time.

In the same way, if you want all the sales orders for Octopus Ltd for the month of June then you should not first go to the order header table (VBAK) to get all the headers, and then based upon that result get the order items (from table VBAP) in a separate SELECT statement. Instead, you should do an INNER JOIN on VBAK and VBAP and thus only go to the database once.

I like beer analogies—in this case, if I am out with four other people in a pub in England we have "rounds." Instead of everyone getting up individually to get their beers, one person at a time goes up and gets all five. It's much faster for the drinkers (calling program) and puts a lot less load on the barman (database).

Importance in HANA World

This rule is more important in a HANA database than it would be in a traditional database. To drastically over-simplify matters, I will say that the HANA database is optimized such that it handles a small number of really complex database queries rather better than it does a huge amount of simple database queries. There are lots of complex tricks built into the HANA database to deal with difficult queries like parallel processing and so on, and it cannot use any of this bag of tricks if presented with a simple query.

Put another way, HANA is rather like a circus clown who has been trained to juggle ten flaming brands at once whilst riding a unicycle across a rope over the Grand Canyon. If instead you ask him to pick up a piece of paper off the floor he feels his talents are being wasted.

ATC Check Support

There are several built-in ATC checks in the standard ECC 6.0 system to look for problems in this area.

The check "Search DB Operations in loops across modularization units" looks for SELECT statements that happen repeatedly in a loop—such as looping through an internal table and doing a SELECT using the data from each row. Moreover, even if the SELECT is "hidden" by the database read's being done within a repeated call to a FORM routine or method, that fact will be picked up as well. The solution here is to do one big read just before the loop instead of lots of little ones inside it.

The "Changing Database Accesses in Loops" check looks for situations where database records are deleted or updated one at a time in a loop. That is bad practice; instead, all database changes should be done in one hit based on an internal table containing all the required changes.

The check "Search SELECT .. FOR ALL ENTRIES-clauses to be transformed" searches for the situation mentioned earlier where there is a database read on one table and the results of that first read are used to do a FOR ALL ENTRIES on a second database table. In such cases, it is almost always faster to do a JOIN on the two tables instead. The check by default excludes buffered tables, as doing a JOIN on them bypasses the buffer.

Keep Results Sets Small

What this is all about is only selecting the minimum number of *rows* from the database that you actually need.

VBFA Example

As an example of getting more rows than you really require, take the requirement of getting all the outbound deliveries that were created with reference to one or more sales orders. That information lives in table VBFA, so the developer might decide to read in all VBFA entries that have the sales order as the preceding document or use the standard SAP function module to read such data.

However, only VBFA records that have the VBTYP_N field (type of subsequent document) set to "J" are valid for the requirement at hand. So, if records that do not fit that criteria are read in as well, the result set will be far larger than it needs to be. Data rows that are never going to be used are transferred into the program's memory, causing unnecessary processing overhead.

Aggregation Example

Sometimes you need what is called an aggregation, such as finding out the total invoiced quantity of a particular product for the month of March. One way to do this would be to read the thousand invoice item records that match the date and material you are looking for into an internal table, and then loop through that table adding up all the quantities.

Another approach would be to use the SQL aggregate function SUM as in SELECT SUM(FKIMG), and then only one row would be returned from the database. Thus, the result set would be a thousand times smaller. There have been case studies, using an Oracle database, that have shown that this approach changed a BW query from taking all night to taking 30 seconds.

Existence Check Example

Often, you only need to know if a row exists in the database; you are not actually interested in any of the contents. An example might be that you want to know if any invoices have been created for a sales order yet. You do not care at all about the details of the invoice(s); you just want to know whether any exist or not.

Traditionally, you could have done SELECT COUNT(*), where you were not actually interested in the number of invoices, just whether that number was zero or not. Some people like to do something like SELECT MANDT FROM VBRK UP TO 1 ROWS. Obviously, getting the client number is pointless, but if you did not get a result you would know the record did not exist. In both of these examples, if the record did exist then the result set would be one record (row) transferred back from the database.

From ABAP 7.50 and above you can achieve the same result by using SELECT @ ABAP_TRUE FROM VBRK UP TO 1 ROWS. In this case, you get a TRUE/FALSE result, but the important point is that even if the record does exist no rows at all are transferred back from the database, so the result set is zero rows—the ultimate example of keeping the result set small whilst still doing an accurate query for a database record.

Importance in HANA World

When moving to a HANA database, this rule is unchanged in importance—a small result set is a good thing no matter what database you are using.

ATC Check Support

The ATC check "Search SELECT statement with DELETE statement" looks for situations where an internal table is filled via a database read and then later on assorted records are deleted from that table based on certain conditions. In such a case, the idea would be to see if the records that get deleted could be excluded from the initial SELECT statement, thus lowering the size of the result set. Performing complex filters in an ABAP SQL statement becomes ever easier with every release of ABAP as the options in ABAP SQL constantly increase.

The ATC check "Search Problematic SELECT * Statements" will tell you if no fields at all from the selected row(s) are used by issuing the message "Existence Check – No Fields Used." In such a case, you can use the SELECT @ABAP_TRUE technique described earlier to avoid any result set at all.

Minimize Search Overhead

What we are talking about here is how much "work" the database has to do in order to search for the data the calling program has asked for.

Traditionally, this has been based on the correct usage of indexes in the calling program.

For small tables that very rarely change, the table can be buffered. This minimizes the search overhead, because if a query is done correctly on a buffered table then there is no overhead at all, as the result is read out of memory as opposed to having to go to the database.

For other tables, whether looking for one record or many, the calling program should ideally be using the primary key of whatever table(s) the query is being performed on, and if that is impossible then a (correctly designed) secondary index should be used.

If no index at all is used then the dreaded full table scan is done whereby the database has to check every single record in the table to see if it meets the query selection criteria, and for any table with more than a trivial amount of data this causes a "time out" short dump.

Importance in HANA World

When HANA first came out, many people said this rule was no longer of any importance whatsoever. Because HANA is a column-based database, in some sense you automatically have a secondary index on every single column in the table.

This is why when you have a custom "Z" index on a table and then go through any form of upgrade the system automatically flags your Z index as only being relevant for selected database systems; i.e., every database except HANA. This can be seen in Figure 8-1.

Dictionary: Display Index

Index Name	VBAP	Z1		
Short Description	Index on Creation Date / Plant			
Last changed	DDIC	25.04.2020	Original language	DE
Status	Active	Saved	Package	VA

Index VBAP~Z1 exists in database system ORACLE

⊙ Non-unique index

    ○ Index on all database systems

    ⊙ For selected database systems

    ○ No database index

○ Unique Index (database Index required)

Table Fields

Index Flds

Field name	Short Description	DT...	Length
MANDT	Client	CLNT	3
ERDAT	Date on Which Record Was Created	DATS	8
WERKS	Plant (Own or External)	CHAR	4

ACD(2)/249 Database-specific Index ☒

Create Index for Selected Database Systems

○ Selection List

⊙ Exclusion List

Database Systems

DBName	Short Description
HDB	SAP HANA Database

Figure 8-1. *Indexes being excluded from HANA databases*

To reiterate: that setting was made automatically by the system. The clear implication is that such indexes are only needed on traditional row-based databases and not on a column-based database such as HANA.

However, as time goes by it is looking increasingly clear that this is not a hard and fast rule. The revised rule is, "In HANA you don't need secondary indexes—until you do."

That is, you are recommended to start off with no secondary indexes and only reinstate them if you have performance problems. It is also worth noting that a HANA database is not a miracle cure for stupid queries. If your program does a query on all sales orders for a non-selective field like sales organization with a date range of "all time" then the performance is going to be terrible whatever database you use.

ATC Check Support

The main ATC check in this area has always been "Analysis of WHERE Condition for SELECT," whereby all SELECT statements are evaluated to see whether the selection criteria used in the SELECT statement would allow the optimizer to use any sort of index, be it the primary key or a secondary database index. If no index can be used then a full table scan will ensue.

There is also a similar check "Analysis of WHERE Condition in UPDATE and DELETE," which does the same thing but for database changes as opposed to queries.

Taking note of these checks is vital before your move to S/4HANA; afterward, you will have to evaluate each such query on a case-by-case basis.

In regard to table buffering, you have the ATC check "SELECT Statements That Bypass the Table Buffer," which tells you when a query goes to the database as opposed to reading the data from the buffer; e.g., a JOIN on two buffered tables.

You might be forgiven for thinking that since all of the HANA database data is in memory you would not even need a buffer. As it turns out, yes you do; even with HANA it is still faster to read from the buffer than from the database, in the same way it is still faster to read from an internal table than from the database.

Keep Load Away from Database

We are now venturing into what could be called philosophical territory. Since the very early days of SAP, developers were encouraged to follow what is now known as the "Data to Code" approach, which could be described as follows:

"Go into the database to get what you need, spend as little time in the database as possible, process all the results in the ABAP code."

With that approach the database had the single responsibility of storing data, and ABAP programs did not usually want the database to worry its pretty little head about having to "think" about anything. Maybe as a special treat every so often it would be allowed to add up some numbers using a SUM function in a SQL query.

Importance in HANA World

In recent years, everything has been turned upside down—now we have the "Code to Data" approach.

SAP has abandoned its "Database Agnostic" policy and as such database queries no longer have to cater for the "lowest common denominator"; the code knows that the database is HANA and what that database is capable of. Therefore, the number of options (i.e., logic that can be passed down to the database) in ABAP SQL queries and CDS views has increased dramatically from simple SUM operations to complex CASE conditions and more. Moreover, with ABAP Managed Database Procedures (ADMP) you can write complex code with loops and IF statements that can be executed inside the HANA database. You can write such code using the ABAP editor (even though the code you write is in the database-specific SQLSCRIPT language rather than ABAP).

ATC Check Support

There can be no automated support here—what logic makes sense at the ABAP level and what logic makes sense at the database level is pretty much 100 percent a value judgement.

Order in the House

In traditional row-based databases like Oracle or Microsoft SQL, you can virtually guarantee that if you do a SELECT statement on a database table then the results will come back in the order of the primary key. As a result, programmers often did not bother to sort the table afterward. After all, the most time-consuming sort is a sort on a table that is already sorted. They would then do a BINARY SEARCH or DELETE ADJACENT DUPLICATES or maybe read the first row, safe in the knowledge all of this would always work because the internal table filled from the database was correctly sorted.

With a column-based database like HANA, all bets are off. The data is stored in a totally different way and so although the correct records come back from the query they are effectively sorted totally randomly as opposed to in primary key order. So any assumptions made by the program as to the order of the records are no longer correct.

Therefore, you must always ensure you are 100 percent sure what order the records in any STANDARD table are in (for a SORTED table it is obvious what order the rows are in, and for a HASHED table it does not matter); otherwise, the BINARY search (or whatever) will fail.

ATC Check Support

Since this is a common problem—and moreover something everybody should have been doing since day one on any database—there are more automated checks for this than you can shake a stick at. For example:

- In the standard ECC 6.0 system you have the ATC check "Search problematic statements for result of SELECT/OPEN CURSOR without ORDER BY," which tells you when the sort of problems described in this section occur. Moreover, for a "cluster" table like BSEG or a "pool" table (such as some pricing tables) the warning is raised even if no BINARY search or whatever is detected afterward, the reason being that during conversion to S/4HANA, cluster tables and pool tables are converted into standard transparent tables and the order of the records is scrambled like an egg.

- In the standard ECC 6.0 system you have the Runtime Check Monitor (transaction SRTCM), which runs the same sort of "unsorted" check but actually logs every occurrence in production of an unsorted database query that is then followed by a BINARY SEARCH or some other problematic statement.

- After the conversion there is an automated "quick fix" that will add the ORDER BY clause to relevant custom SQL queries automatically.

Application Changes: "Missing" Modules

When it is said that something is "missing" or "no longer exists" in S/4HANA, the automatic assumption is that whatever it is has been totally removed from the S/4HANA system; that would be logical. Alas, life is never as simple as that.

So, I could say that table BSIK is no longer there in S/4HANA—but it actually is, it is just that it is empty.

I could say that the transactions to create customers or vendors no longer exist in S/4HANA (everything is a business partner now), but the KNA1 and LFA1 tables are still there (and full) and the old transactions (XK01 and so on) still work in batch input, even if you can no longer call them directly.

In the same way, in the next section you will see a list of modules that "do not exist" in S/4HANA; in fact, all the code is still there, but the problem is one of licensing. After

443

2025 you could keep using the "dead" modules, but if you did you would be breaching your licensing agreement with SAP. That date was not extended when the deadline to move to S/4HANA was changed to 2030.

You may ask, "Why are there dead modules—everything was always downward compatible in the past?" No longer. Where in the past there were three different ways to handle a business process in SAP, the decision has been made to "simplify" things and kill off two of those solutions, leaving only one solution for any given problem. This is great news if you are using the remaining solution, not so much if you are using one of the dead solutions. Furthermore, since the remaining solution is usually the *last* to be created (on the grounds that each new one is supposed to be better than the last) the longer you have been on SAP the more likely you are to be out of luck because you picked the only solution that existed at the time you implemented your business requirement—before one or more of the shiny new solutions were created.

The point here is that your custom code is very likely to be wrapped around some of the standard SAP code used by the modules that you are not licensed to use any more. You could split hairs and say, "It's only the transactions I am not allowed to use, not the underlying code," but I don't think SAP's lawyers would see it that way. Therefore, custom code in these areas will need to be changed sooner or later.

Standard Solutions

In this section, first of all we look at a (non-exhaustive) list of some modules that are "missing" in S/4HANA and then consider a possible way to "future-proof" your code.

Sample "Missing" Modules

It would be futile to list every single thing that is no longer supposed to be used in S/4HANA, so instead we will just look at four examples of the type of functionality that is being retired just to give you the general idea.

Sales Activities

A "sales activity" is a generic document in SAP used to capture all sorts of follow-up activities you pursue with your customers; e.g., follow-up sales calls. Some companies use them to track customer disputes. In any event, you are not supposed to use sales activities any more in S/4HANA—there are specialized documents for each possible activity; e.g., there is a specific type of document for disputes now.

Shipment Costs

A huge advance in SAP ERP 4.5 was the introduction of the "logistics execution" module whereby you had "shipments" to track inbound and outbound truck journeys and the "shipment cost document" to calculate what drivers should be paid for each trip and actually pay them via integration with the MM logistics invoice verification module. Back in the year 2000 this used to be my specialized subject, and I wrote half a billion lines of Z code wrapping all the standard shipment/shipment cost transactions. Oh dear! In S/4HANA everything changes! The replacement is the "transportation management" module (which used to be a separate add-on), which delivers the same functionality. The principle is pretty much identical, but everything is subtly different; e.g., different document types and so on.

SD Credit Control

This is for when you want to give customers a credit limit and put automatic blocks on their orders and deliveries when they go over it. Previously, this was part of the SD module, but in S/4HANA instead you use the "credit management" part of the "Financial Supply Chain Management" module, which I would note is available as part of ECC 6.0, so some SAP customers are already using it and so will be OK here upon conversion. As an example of a change: instead of one field in VBUK/VBUP storing the current credit status there is a whole separate document type (VBUK and VBUP don't exist in S/4HANA by the way).

HR/Payroll

It will come as no great shock to you that ever since SAP bought the company SuccessFactors in February 2012, their software was going to be the future of HR/payroll for SAP customers, in the same way that SAP pushes its customers to use another of its acquisitions (Ariba) for purchasing.

As such, HR/payroll is not officially a part of S/4HANA. The code is still there, but at some point—and the exact end year keeps changing—SAP customers who use the current Human Capital Management (HCM) part of SAP will have to move to SuccessFactors or one of its many competitors (e.g., Workday). For some companies that have HCM inside the ERP system this is a gigantic change, but on the other hand, best practice was always to have the HR/payroll system in a separate system than the ERP system; so for companies who followed this model things will not be that bad.

The remote ATC checks will highlight areas where your custom code has been deemed to be accessing SAP modules that "no longer exist."

Future Proofing "Missing Module" Code

Now that you have a general idea of the sort of seismic shift that moving to S/4HANA involves, you can see it is going to be more of a challenge for the business analysts than for the programmers. All these new modules that your organization was not using before and now has to use need to be configured, end users need to be retrained, and so on.

Nonetheless, if you had to write reams of custom code to enhance the former solution (which no longer exists), then naturally your organization will want that custom functionality to be available in the new solution. SAP would of course say that the new, improved solution will remove the need for all of the Z code you have written over the years. Sometimes that is true; sadly, more often it is not. SAP does a very good job of trying to cater for all industries and all countries at once, but it is a thankless task and there is always going to be the 5 to 10 percent gap that needs to be addressed by custom code.

So, do you need to totally rewrite 20 years' worth of Z development in (say) the area of SD credit control? Not really.

With both the Z code and the standard SAP code the "what is needed" has not changed; it is just the "how that need is delivered" that needs to change. With standard SAP code the "how" is a totally new module; with your Z code there are two situations:

- If you have user exits pointing at the modules that have "gone" then naturally those exits will not be much use anymore. New user exits will have to be implemented that point at the replacement standard SAP code. If by some miracle the interface (signature) is exactly the same in the new user exits then you could just cut and paste the code, but that is not very likely.

- If you have custom programs (interactive reports, batch jobs, or whatever) that wrap the standard SAP code in the module that is on "death row," then you are in a somewhat better position because you can most likely salvage your Z code using the procedure about to be described.

Going back to one of the recurring themes of this book, all database access (read or write) should be in a specialized class. The business logic (the "what" that we want) should be totally decoupled from the "how" code.

As an analogy, for a very long while there was never any proper standard SAP BAPI to create deliveries. As such, most companies used a BDC based on transaction VL01 to create deliveries. When SAP changed the transaction to VL01N, the BDC needed to be rewritten. Even back then, *hopefully*, the custom programs that created deliveries were all calling some sort of reusable Z function module to do so. So when transaction VL01N came along only one function module had to be rewritten, not the 20 Z programs that called it. Then, later on, when a proper BAPI finally came along saying "sorry I'm late," once again only the function, not the 20 Z programs, had to be rewritten. Of course, in real life 90 percent of companies had the BDC code duplicated all over the place.

One of the central tenets of object-oriented programming is to "separate the things that change from the things that stay the same." Let us say you have an interactive report that does all sorts of HR-related things—but it was designed to shield the user from having to go through the various current HR transactions. As such, the users only know the Z report. Many companies are like this, much to SAP's horror. Anyway, if the underlying HR system changes to SuccessFactors, then the Z report can stay exactly the same as far as the users are concerned—they do not care what it does "under the covers" as long the data is successfully retrieved/updated.

You as a programmer care what happens under the covers. Ideally, you would want to not have to change any of the Z programs that "wrap" standard SAP functions. You know for a fact what is going to change when you move to S/4HANA, so the idea is to make sure that each call to such an area is done via a method call, and, moreover, that the class to which that method call is made is typed via an interface rather than by a concrete class type. You achieve this by having a factory method that considers the SAP version as one factor when deciding what concrete class to pass back.

That way your code has become future proof—it works at the moment, and as soon as you have an S/4HANA development system you write new classes that implement the existing interface, but this time they interface with the new SAP modules rather than the old ones, by RFC or whatever (in the case of external systems such as SuccessFactors) if need be. Then, the assorted Z programs will automatically start talking to the new modules.

TDD Again   You should be wrapping all calls to standard SAP functions in specialized methods *anyway* as part of the TDD process. As mentioned back in Chapter 2, that is a lot of work, but it not only makes the code testable but also future proofs it as described here.

In theory, this means you don't have to touch any existing code whatsoever (open/closed principle). In reality, of course you will have to because nothing in life is perfect, but this will involve minor tweaks here and there as opposed to major surgery all over the place.

Industry Solutions

In the previous section we talked about standard SAP modules that "are not there" in S/4HANA, though really they still are. However, there are some areas that have indeed been totally removed—some of the so-called industry solutions (e.g., the apparel and footwear solutions).

Those who follow the history of SAP might find that quite surprising—industry solutions used to be separate add-ons, then they were all merged into the core, and now lots of them are gone again. I presume the idea is that eventually they will all be back in the S/4HANA core; it is just that many have not been rewritten yet. It's like the hokey pokey—you put the industry solution in, you take the industry solution out, you shake it all about.

At this point you might be saying, "I don't have an industry solution—what's that got to do with me?", and those industries that don't have their industry solution in S/4HANA yet will not be converting anyway, so what in the world is this section about?

Well, if you work in an organization that sells sausages, then you would imagine that none of your custom code would reference anything from the IS-OIL solution for the fossil fuel industry. Indeed, there should be no such references, but you might be surprised how many there actually are.

It is no great mystery how this seemingly strange situation arises—often when a programmer has to create a Z data element, or function module, or class, they think to themselves, "Has this already been created before—am I reinventing the wheel?" Sometimes they go searching for—and find—a data element or function module or what have you that is an exact match for their needs and they just reuse the existing object.

The problem is that in any list of existing objects the ones with a slash at the start of their name, like /BEV1/, will appear before any standard SAP objects, and the standard SAP objects will appear before any Z objects.

Reusing your own Z objects is obviously safest, as standard SAP objects might change (except for the very small number of "released" function modules) and industry solutions might vanish in a puff of smoke, as we have seen with S/4HANA.

Therefore, the nearer to the start of a list something is the more unwise it is to use it, and at the same time the more likely it is to be chosen *because* it is at the start of the list. The /BEV1/ example is a fine one—all the industry solutions are at the start of the list due to the forward slash at the start, and then when the second letter is considered, the letter "B" is at the start of the alphabet, and due to this all throughout the world a vast number of objects from the industry beverage solution are reused in companies that have nothing at all to do with making or selling drinks.

The remote ATC check will highlight all such usages. At that point, you can create an identical Z copy. Far better would be not to reuse industry solution components in the first place.

Conclusion

This chapter was all about what you should do to ensure your custom code will continue to work after you make the inevitable conversion to S/4HANA.

First of all, you heard about the logic behind making such changes over a protracted period, as part of the TDD process, rather than all at once in one huge push.

Then, you heard about the various automated checks that are available to help you during the conversion project.

Lastly, assorted specific issues that you will find during the conversion project were addressed, together with how the various checks can help in each area.

As you have seen in this chapter, the effort involved in making sure your current code works in S/4HANA is far greater than, say, making sure code in a 4.7 release works in an ECC 6.0 release. However, all this pales into nothing compared to what we will talk about in the next chapter, which is making sure custom code works in ABAP in the Cloud.

Recommended Reading

SAP Blog on S/4HANA Custom Code Conversion:

```
https://blogs.sap.com/2017/02/15/sap-s4hana-system-conversion-custom-code-
adaptation-process/
```

CHAPTER 9

Ensuring Code Runs in ABAP in the Cloud

"In the cloud" is where everybody wants to be—at least in recent times—and as of 2019 (just when everyone thought ABAP was about to die as a programming language), ABAP has joined the cloud party.

The original situation was that although the core of S/4HANA in the Cloud was still written in ABAP, if you wanted to write a "user exit" equivalent or build a Z extension in the same way you used to write Z programs inside your on-premises SAP system, then you had to write that code in Java or JavaScript, and SAP would supply tools to make that process as easy as possible.

Converting over 30 years of custom ABAP code into Java or JavaScript did not appeal to many organizations, which is the reason why, to date, most conversions to S/4HANA have been of the on-premises variety, in which you can pretty much keep all your Z code, albeit with a lot of changes (as seen in the previous chapter).

Therefore, SAP added the option of using ABAP in the Cloud to build extensions to S/4HANA in the Cloud in addition to the other language options. That way *in theory* people would not have to rewrite those 30 years of custom code. However, those 30 years of code will not work until you rewrite it for the cloud, and converting custom code into the ABAP in the Cloud environment is different from converting code into the S/4HANA on-premises environment for two main reasons, as follows:

- Converting to S/4HANA code as described in the previous chapter only applies if you choose the on-premises option. You can use ABAP in the Cloud to build extensions for an on-premises S/4HANA system (and SAP would encourage you to do so), but ABAP in the Cloud usually only comes into play when you take the S/4HANA in the Cloud option.

© Paul David Hardy 2021
P. D. Hardy, *Improving the Quality of ABAP Code*, https://doi.org/10.1007/978-1-4842-6711-0_9

- If converting your Z code to S/4HANA seemed ten times more difficult than the upgrades you have encountered in the past, then changing Z code to ABAP in the Cloud is a million times more difficult. For most organizations, pretty much all the custom ABAP code needs to be rewritten.

At this point, you most likely are thinking, "If this so difficult and I most likely will not be using ABAP in the Cloud for the foreseeable future, and maybe never, then why should I care about this at all?"

Service with a Smile   ABAP in the Cloud is not a development environment embedded into the ERP system, but rather is only available as a service provided by the SAP cloud platform. SAP initially described this as Platform as a Service, but many have said it is actually Software as a Service.

At first glance, being able to write code that works on ABAP in the Cloud does not seem to be a very practical skill to have, but there are some companies that have jumped in with both feet and already have applications live using this environment (the company LEGO springs to mind). In addition, you just never know when in the future this concept will jump out at you from nowhere and you will be told, "Our new subsidiary in Outer Mongolia just went live with S/4HANA Cloud, please copy some of your Z code over so they can use it." The latter may not be very likely, but if you have a choice of two ways of writing something, and one of them works both right now and also in a potential future ABAP in the Cloud environment, then why not go for the future-proof option?

In this chapter, first you will get a general introduction to ABAP in the Cloud and why it is so very different than the traditional ABAP development environment you are familiar with. Then, you will move on to a list of the (seemingly) insurmountable obstacles that will be in your way when you try to move your custom code to ABAP in the Cloud. Lastly, you will take a look at some of the tools SAP provides to help you in your conversion efforts.

The General Concept

In this section, we will look at the major differences between a cloud ABAP development environment and an on-premises one.

First, you will see how SAP enforces a clear separation between custom and standard SAP code. Then, you will take a look at the new ABAP RESTful Application Programming Model (RAP), which, whilst not that different in concept from what went before, is very different architecturally. We will end the section with a look at the free trial account you can get right now to try out ABAP in the Cloud and what SAP's grand plans for the future of ABAP programming are.

Separation of Z Code and Standard Code

Up until now, the repository of custom ABAP objects has lived inside the core ERP system as citizens equal to the standard SAP code. With S/4HANA in the Cloud, that is just not possible—the code base is shared between dozens, if not thousands, of different organizations, and thus that code has to be identical for all of them.

Does that mean you can no longer write Z-style programs to enhance the standard SAP functionality in the way you always have in the past; e.g., write Z reports and then make them interactive so you can perform CRUD operations both on standard SAP business objects like sales orders and on your own custom business objects? Naturally, of course you can. If you could not then SAP would not have much of a customer base left.

As mentioned earlier, initially such things were achieved by using non-ABAP languages, and this is obviously not only still possible but in fact very popular using the so-called CAP (Cloud Application Programming Model) framework. In recent years, ABAP in the Cloud was added to the equation.

The idea is that standard SAP tables and standard SAP code live in one place in your database, and custom (Z) tables and custom (Z) SAP code live in another place, and they are separated by a wall of fire a thousand miles high with small gaps in it. To be more technical, your Z code can only contact the standard SAP code by means of stable APIs.

This means that the lifecycles of the standard SAP code and your Z code are totally decoupled. The theory is that the automatic upgrade of the standard SAP S/4HANA in the Cloud system every three months cannot possibly break your Z code and no changes to your Z code can break the standard SAP code base.

The RAP

The next gigantic change that was introduced with ABAP in the Cloud (and that was later also made available in S/4HANA on-premises) was the ABAP RESTful Application Programming Model (RAP). This is the only way you can develop applications in the ABAP cloud environment, and it is very different than anything that has gone before.

There are generally only two main sorts of programs in ABAP—those that perform CRUD operations on business objects like sales orders, and reports, which either just read data from those objects or are interactive and both read and manipulate those objects. There are now three different programming models available in ABAP for performing either task, as follows:

- Traditionally, you read your data directly from database tables, programmed business logic however you felt like doing so, and then output your results using a DYNPRO (Dynamic Program) screen or an ALV (ABAP List Viewer) report. Even when Web Dynpro came along, things were pretty much exactly the same.

- In recent years—since about 2015—the SAP Programming Model for Fiori has been the recommended approach. Here, you read the data from CDS (Core Data Services) views rather than directly from database tables, code the logic using the Business Object Processing Framework (BOPF), expose your application as a service using transaction SEGW, and then output the final result as a Fiori application using UI5.

- The latest innovation is the RAP—now you read data using CDS entities (as opposed to CDS views) and define the business object behavior using a special sort of CDS entity that points to a special sort of ABAP class that implements that behavior. Exposing this as a service has been drastically simplified compared to SEGW. In essence, in this programming model, there are no more traditional CDS views, no more BOPF, and no more SEGW (before many people had heard of any of those concepts). The UI layer remains as a Fiori application using UI5.

I could write hundreds of pages about this new programming model, but the pertinent part for this chapter is how your existing code gets reused (or not) in the RAP.

There are two flavors to the RAP, as follows:

- The Managed Scenario — This is a so-called greenfield implementation where all code is created from scratch and the CRUD operations are handled automatically by the framework. This is obviously irrelevant for the subject of code reuse.

- The Unmanaged Scenario — This is for when you *do* want to reuse existing code; e.g., custom BAPIs for CRUD operations. The idea is that you could reuse an existing model class and its associated database access class as-is, and the various existing methods (CRUD, derivations, validations, user commands [now called actions]) would be called by the relevant parts of the RAP behavior class.

As an example, I had a model class and associated database access class, and I used it in a DYNPRO application, and a Web Dynpro application, and in the Fiori programming model via the BOPF, and also in the unmanaged scenario of the RAP, and my classes were totally unchanged each time. Each new framework had to adapt to my class, not the other way around. After all, in life the business logic generally stays unchanged, but the technology that calls that business logic changes all the time, faster and faster.

Free Trial Account

The good news is that anybody can try out ABAP in the Cloud for themselves, just to see how strange it is, for free. You will have to share your trial account with a bunch of random strangers from all around the world—i.e., they can see any code you write, and you can see any code they write, but as this is only intended for messing around and learning and not for any sort of productive purpose that should not matter.

There is a link to a blog telling you how to set up such a trial account at the end of the chapter.

Sharing your development environment with a bunch of other programmers is nothing you are not used to, but they have always been the programmers in your own organization rather than completely random people!

The Future of ABAP Development

Just to freak you out completely, the grand vision of SAP for the future is to change the ABAP development methodology so that it is just like most other languages, like Java. In other languages programmers develop on their own machines and periodically (at least once a day) merge their changes with the code base in the central system. Thus, you could have a dozen developers working on the same object at the same time, later having to work out how best to merge their changes into the core and still keep that core code working.

This sort of thing is totally alien to ABAP developers and furthermore was always deemed technically impossible due to the huge footprint an ABAP environment requires. Nonetheless, great minds at SAP have been working on this, and some trials have been done. The idea is that you would not develop on your own PC but rather on a separate instance of the development environment in the cloud, and you'd use a tool like abapGit to store the "branches" that each developer creates and then merge them into a central SAP development system. After that point, the change and transport system (looking the same but based on Git under the covers) would move things to quality assurance and production just as before—but with the added possibility of an instant rollback if something goes wrong; e.g., failed unit test or syntax error in the target system.

Branching Out   When using tools like Git and GitHub (and indeed abapGit) the idea is that the developer takes a local copy of the application and that becomes a "branch" that stores their changes. Later, that branch is merged back into the main application (sometimes called a "trunk" to keep the tree analogy going).

Obstacles to Code Conversion

In this section, you will see why you cannot just cut and paste your Z code into ABAP in the Cloud.

It is possible that the more you read of this chapter the more depressed you will become, but the good news is that when I first had access to an ABAP in the Cloud system and tried to copy over some of my custom ALV reports and an application that maintained a custom business object, I was pleasantly surprised at how much I could reuse.

This was because I had designed everything—even small ALV reports—using the Model-View-Controller (MVC) pattern, and I had also adhered to the principle of "separation of concerns." To be more precise, I had specialized classes for business logic (e.g., derivations and validations), for database access, and for UI output. For reasons that will become clear during this section, the UI classes had to be thrown away, as did any database access methods that read standard SAP tables, but the business logic classes and database classes that read and wrote to Z tables could be copied over more or less exactly as-is (subject to the restrictions mentioned in the next sections).

The moral of the story is very clear—if you design your applications in a modular fashion with classes with single responsibilities, then the most important part of the code (the business logic) becomes "portable" to not only ABAP in the Cloud but also any new framework that may come along after it.

In this section, you will look at the various syntax errors you would get if you just did a straight "cut and paste" of a large existing program into the ABAP in the Cloud environment. You would most likely get syntax errors in the following four areas:

- Syntax errors when using assorted ABAP statements you have been using for years

- Syntax errors when using statements that invoke the SAP GUI

- Syntax errors when referencing standard SAP function modules or data elements

- Syntax errors when referencing standard SAP tables like VBAK or KNA1

Obsolete ABAP Statements

ABAP has been around since the early 1980s and has evolved considerably since that point. Most changes have been incremental in nature, but three large "waves" of earth-shattering changes to the ABAP language have occurred to date.

The first was in 1999, when object-oriented (OO) programming was enabled in the ABAP language. The second came in 2013, when improvements such as inline declarations and "functional" constructs were introduced to ABAP—enabling programming with half the lines of code than before. The third "wave" started in 2017 and is still happening at time of writing; this wave is not only not slowing down but actually increasing in speed and size as time goes on. That third wave of which I speak started at the time ABAP in the Cloud was introduced.

The major change that made a third wave was the RAP programming model, but, in addition, with each release there are changes in almost every area of ABAP, and (a) since January 2017 a new version of ABAP has been released every three months and (b) with every release SAP tries to beat its previous record as to how many improvements to the ABAP language it can pack in.

Traditionally, SAP has always been very proud that its code is downward compatible; i.e., when you moved onto a higher release of ABAP all the code that worked in the former release was 100 percent guaranteed to keep on working. That's not the case in other languages. Often, at work after upgrading our version of Java on assorted Java-based SAP systems (e.g., PI), we have had some areas stop working, and we've had to move back down to a lower version of Java to fix the problem.

This means that for 40 years assorted things have been added to the ABAP language, and nothing has ever been removed. I have been programming in ABAP for 20 years, and the other day I saw an obscure ABAP command in a production program, and I had no idea what it did. That was because it was declared obsolete 25 years ago and no one much has used it since. There are dozens of such archaic commands hanging around that you could use if you really wanted to, but you really should not; e.g., STOP. Have you ever used that command? Hopefully not.

Imagine if the rule was that car companies were forced by law to keep making their old models forever no matter how many new models they came up with. In that imaginary world you could still buy a Model T Ford if you wanted, but a more modern car would be far cheaper, have many more features (e.g., a seat belt), and go much farther per gallon of gas. In this fantasy world, the government would want to encourage people to only buy the newer models as they put out fewer emissions and so are better for the environment. Back in the real world, this is actually happening, with some countries intending to ban the sale of gas and diesel cars from 2030.

If the commands in ABAP were cars and SAP were the government, it could simply "ban" the commands by removing them from the language. That has never happened, which is why you still have the option to use monstrosities like logical databases.

As you saw in the previous chapter, S/4HANA is not 100 percent downward compatible, but that has more to do with modules' not being there as opposed to ABAP commands' not being there. Nonetheless, there has been an attempt by SAP to "chip away" at old ABAP commands to stop people using them.

The most obvious example is OO ABAP—inside any method there is a whole raft of obsolete commands you cannot use. One example would be WITH HEADER LINE. The idea was that all the former procedural code could work exactly as before, but after a short while all new code would be written using methods and therefore there would be no more header lines. Twenty years on, new procedural code is still being written every day with header lines, but nevertheless the idea was sound.

If you run the extended program check in ATC mode you will get some warnings if obsolete statements are detected. In the code inspector both the "ABAP Open Checks" and the "Code Pal" set of checks (which you heard about in Chapter 3) will highlight any ABAP statements that should no longer be used. Thus, during the TDD cycle all such statements should hopefully be removed.

With ABAP 19/08 (i.e., the release in August 2019), something that should have happened a long time ago started to occur. First off, the command PERFORM XYZ IN PROGRAM ABC now gives a hard syntax error. Thank goodness for that. That is such an unstable way of calling a routine—the signature could change in the target program and then all the calling programs would start causing short dumps, seemingly out of the blue.

Second, the normal syntax check now warns when a command is deprecated. Such commands can still be used but will give you a yellow warning every time you do a syntax check, and thus in ABAP in Eclipse there will be a little yellow light glowing next to such commands and warning text hovering above them constantly. The idea is that programmers will find this (constantly getting warning messages) so annoying they will stop using these commands just to get rid of the messages. At some stage in the future those warning messages will become hard errors.

Do as I Say, Not as I Do   When I told a programmer colleague that remote PERFORMS amongst other commands were going to be outlawed he (a) had a heart attack and (b) noted that if this were true then SAP programmers would have to rewrite 20 billion lines of their standard code base. As it turns out, they do not, because the new warnings and errors apply to custom code both old and new but only to standard SAP code written after a certain date.

Let us have a look at some of these obsolete commands that give out warning messages in the higher releases of ABAP and that will eventually cause syntax errors:

- STATICS — I would hope that you have never used this, or even encountered it. This is where you declare a variable inside a FORM routine in the place you would normally declare a local variable, using the STATICS command instead of DATA. A variable so declared becomes an odd sort of global variable in that the value is retained when you leave the routine and then call the routine again later. A horrible, confusing construct that has long deserved death.

- AT FIRST / AT LAST and the like — These commands were always a disaster waiting to happen because if the LOOP they were called in had any sort of condition limiting what rows were looped over then the AT FIRST or whatever would behave in a totally unexpected way. So, someone would add a condition to a LOOP that worked before and suddenly the program would go haywire.

- ADD, DIVIDE, and the like — This is a pity as I quite liked them. I much prefer ADD 1 TO COUNT to the new construct COUNT =+ 1 as even though they do the exact same thing the former reads much more like plain English.

- RAISE SOME_CLASSICAL_EXCEPTION — Those exceptions from function modules (and methods) that set the value of SY-SUBRC are no longer supposed to be used. Instead, you should use exception classes.

- PERFORM — That's right! SAP has finally bit the bullet and said no more FORM routines ever. So stop using them right now. It's hard, but it's not impossible.

Note that all the preceding techniques worked in slow motion; with the exception of the new syntax error for a remote PERFORM the idea was always to keep old code working and then push the developer to change their old habits over a number of years.

With ABAP in the Cloud, SAP had a once in a lifetime opportunity to say "nothing old fashioned allowed here," as the whole environment is not downward compatible in the least. SAP describes the version of ABAP that runs in the cloud by using the snappy title *"ABAP language scope version 5 (ABAP language for SAP Cloud Platform)."*

In the cloud, amazingly, PERFORM statements are still allowed (SAP must have had enormous pressure from some large companies), at least within local methods, but in general the obsolete commands give you a syntax error.

Examples of statements giving a syntax error in ABAP in the Cloud are as follows:

- EXPORT TO MEMORY

- WRITE TO

- COMPUTE

- TABLES — This statement creates what is in effect a global variable, and is thus deemed bad.

Finally, a little something to make your head spin. If you write the code in Listing 9-1 using ABAP in the Cloud you will get a syntax error.

Listing 9-1. Syntax That No Longer Works

```
DATA(current_user) = SY-UNAME.
DATA(current_date) = SY-DATUM.
```

Instead, you write the same thing as shown in Listing 9-2.

Listing 9-2. Reading SYST Variable in ABAP in the Cloud

```
DATA(current_user) = CL_ABAP_CONTEXT_INFO=>get_user_formatted_name( ).
DATA(current_date) = CL_ABAP_CONTEXT_INFO=>get_system_date( ).
```

Luckily, you can still read SY-SUBRC directly, but for most system variables you have to go through an API class. In addition, you can no longer write to system variables; e.g., saying SY-SUBC = 4 like you used to do in VOFM routines will cause a syntax error.

Class CL_ABAP_CONTEXT_INFO does not exist in lower releases (as there is no need for it), but it is good practice in your code, when you want to get a SYST variable (apart from SY-SUBRC), to use a specialized class, as that way you can replace the call with a test double during unit tests. That would be a class you would use everywhere so when you port your code to ABAP in the Cloud you would only have to make the SYST adjustment in one place and all your programs would then be OK.

No SAP GUI

The first thing to note is that you can only program in ABAP in the Cloud using ABAP in Eclipse (ADT). There is no SAP GUI available at all. This has several implications:

- Up until now, when creating some types of ABAP objects in ADT, the SAP GUI opened up "in place" inside Eclipse, and you used that to create your object. That obviously does not work anymore, which is why there has been such a big push in recent years to enhance ADT such that it can create more and more types of objects without having to resort to the SAP GUI.

- Commands like `CALL SCREEN` or a `MESSAGE` statement trying to directly output itself do not make any sense and so are disallowed.

- The ALV function modules and classes will not work, as they rely on `CALL SCREEN` statements.

Since the vast bulk of custom programs are either ALV reports or DYNPRO programs used to perform `CRUD` operations on standard or custom business objects, the obvious conclusion is that none of your current programs that have any form of output whatsoever can just be cut and pasted into the ABAP in the Cloud environment. Instead, all output in the ABAP in the Cloud environment will be on the console in ABAP in Eclipse for testing (the equivalent of `WRITE` statements) or use UI5 for real applications.

So for most traditional programs like module pools where the screen logic and business logic are all jammed together like a penguin colony the idea of copying that program directly into ABAP in the Cloud seems laughable. The effort of changing it (unscrambling the egg, as it were) would be equal to or greater than just rewriting the whole thing from scratch.

Referencing Standard SAP Objects

When programming in a traditional ABAP system, you can use any standard SAP object you like—domains, data elements, classes, functional modules, and so on. A lot of the function modules were "not released," which meant you were not supposed to use them, but that did not stop *anybody*.

Some function modules were also flagged as "obsolete" and thus triggered static check warnings saying not to use them. Even though the implication was that SAP was going to delete those function modules from the system at some stage, that never happened, and so people had no compunctions at all about continuing to use obsolete function modules. It did not help that the successor function (or class) you were supposed to use was often not mentioned anywhere.

As a result, even though using an unreleased or obsolete function module—or indeed any SAP data element at all—carried the risk that one day after an upgrade that standard SAP object would no longer be there, causing your code to have a syntax error, realistically that risk was so low (given SAP's commitment to downward-compatible code) that thousands of custom SAP programs all around the globe are peppered with standard SAP objects.

In ABAP in the Cloud the situation is very different. Every single one of the standard SAP objects is still there, but if you try to use 99 percent of them you get a syntax error. You cannot use any standard SAP object—data element, class, or whatever—unless it is on the "White List."

Terminology Changes   When you upgraded from SAP 4.7 to ECC 6.0 you would have seen a terminology change at various places in the ABAP development system such that the term *main program* was replaced with the term *master program*. SAP is wishing they had not made that change now—in 2020 terms like *master* and *White List* are deemed to be racist, and SAP has vowed to change such terms to equivalents that are not so emotive. Nonetheless, whilst the terms still exist it would be even more confusing for this book to refer to those things using different words than those in the current menu options.

Often, if you search for a standard SAP data element or function module you find 20 or 30 seemingly identical ones. With ABAP in the Cloud SAP had a once in a lifetime opportunity to get rid of all the "rubbish" and just provide the absolute minimum amount of standard objects for reuse by customer organizations.

When logged on to an ABAP in the Cloud system you can see in the tree on the left the list of released objects (the so-called White List), as shown in Figure 9-1.

> 🏢 Favorite Packages (?)
> ☆ Favorite Objects (?)
∨ ⚙ Released Objects (1,754)
   ∨ ⓖ Authorizations (4)
      ∨ 🔟 Authorization Fields (2)
         (X) ACTVT
         (X) TABLE
      > 🔟 Authorization Objects (2)
   > ⓖ Core Data Services (43)
   > ⓖ Dictionary (333)
   > ⓖ Source Code Library (1,372)
   > ⓖ Transformations (2)

Figure 9-1. *List of released objects in ABAP in the Cloud*

In the first iteration of ABAP in the Cloud there were very few released objects indeed. With each new release the list increases, but new objects are only added if they are deemed to be vital. As an example, some of the building blocks for ABAP Unit were not there in the first release, and since lots of people (like me) consider these vital, they were added.

The first thing you might think to yourself is, "I use lots of standard function modules in my Z code, so I suppose the obsolete and not released ones will not be on the White List in ABAP in the Cloud." How right you would be—not only is the use of obsolete function modules prohibited, not only is the use of non-released function modules prohibited too, but also *no standard function modules at all* are allowed! At this point, you are beginning to see what you are up against.

You can, however, create your own Z function modules.

Referencing Standard SAP Tables

I would imagine that in 99.9 percent of the custom programs you have written to date there are references to standard SAP tables like VBAK or KNA1 as well as to any Z tables you may have created. Indeed, many custom programs wrap standard SAP transactions, be they reports on one or more standard SAP tables, or custom wrappers for sales order maintenance, or some such. Naturally, those programs would be full of references to standard SAP tables.

Now, here's a funny thing (you may not find it so funny): as mentioned before, all the standard SAP tables live in one area of the database, and all the Z tables live in another area of the database, separated by a wall of fire. Let us say I want to refer to standard SAP table USR21 in my ABAP in the Cloud code. To my surprise, I get the error shown in Figure 9-2.

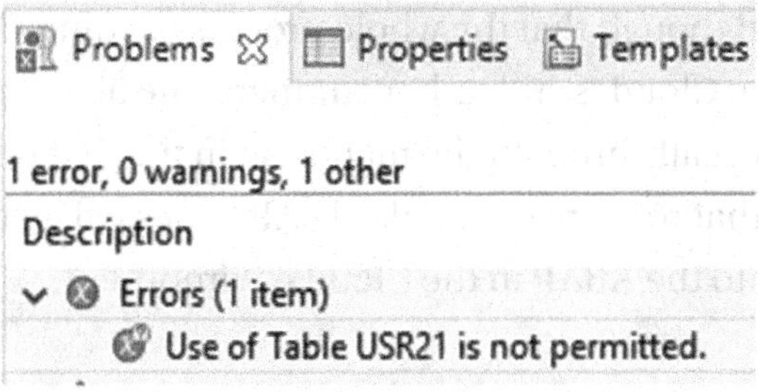

Figure 9-2. Unexpected error

You will note the error does not say that table USR21 does not exist, just that you cannot use it directly, because it lives on the other side of the wall of fire. How can you breach that wall of fire? In this case, you use a white-listed CDS view called I_USER. In Listing 9-3, the two statements are identical, but the first causes a syntax error, the second does not.

Listing 9-3. Two Ways of Trying to Access USR21-BNAME

```
DATA: ld_error   TYPE usr21-bname.
DATA: ld_allowed TYPE i_user-UserID.
```

So far so good—now try the same trick with VBAK; this time, you get the error "Type VBAK is Unknown." The ABAP in the Cloud system knows about USR21 as it is part of the standalone ABAP environment. It has no clue about VBAK, however, as that table is part of the ERP system.

All is not lost, however. For a very long time now external non-SAP systems have been able to read and write to an SAP system via use of the Remote Function Call (RFC) mechanism. Before the advent of ABAP in the Cloud you could write Java and JavaScript programs in the SAP Cloud Platform and the SAP software development kit (SDK) generated classes in those languages that could interact with the ERP system by wrapping BAPI calls to the ERP system.

It would be crazy if a JavaScript program could make BAPI calls to an SAP ERP system and an ABAP program written in the Cloud could not. So of course it can.

At the end of the chapter is a link to a blog that discusses how to call an ERP system via RFC from the ABAP in the Cloud environment. That example talks about connecting to an on-premises system, but the idea of defining a "communication arrangement" is the same whether the ERP system is on-premises or in the cloud.

It has to be admitted though that the whole process of communicating with an ERP system from ABAP in the Cloud is still rather cumbersome at the moment. It will get easier over time—I only really brought the matter up in the first place to highlight the fact that your custom code that references standard SAP tables will get syntax errors if you just "cut and paste" it into the ABAP in the Cloud environment.

The Mechanics of Code Conversion

In the previous section, you learned about the vast number of barriers in your way when trying to convert existing custom code to an ABAP in the Cloud environment. Nonetheless, as mentioned earlier in this chapter, if your applications are written using classes with single responsibilities and you have been regularly cleaning up all the static code check errors then it should be possible to reuse more than you might imagine.

In this section, you will look first at how SAP helps you do a remote check on your current development system to see what would break in the cloud environment, and then you will move on to the procedure for actually moving the code.

Remote Checks

In the previous chapter about S/4HANA, you were introduced to the concept of doing a remote ATC check from a standalone ABAP 7.52 system on the code in your development system to see what code would break when you converted to S/4HANA. In the same way, you can perform a remote check on your current custom code objects to see how many changes would be needed to port the code over to ABAP in the Cloud.

The procedure is exactly the same as for the remote ATC check for S/4HANA, but naturally you will use a different check variant—namely SAP_CP_READINESS_REMOTE. Confusingly, there is also a standard check variant with the name ABAP_VERSION_CLOUD_ DEV, which might fool you into thinking that is the one you want, but let us stick to the first one because that is what you are supposed to use.

SAP_CP_READINESS_REMOTE is not in the standard 7.52 system by default. To bring it into existence you have to import three SAP notes, as follows:

- SAP Note 2682626 — Code inspector check for restricted language scope version 5 (ABAP for SAP Cloud Platform)

- SAP Note 2684665 — Custom code checks for SAP Cloud Platform ABAP Environment

- SAP Note 2830799 — Custom code checks for SAP Cloud Platform ABAP Environment

As often happens when downloading SAP notes, you will get the ever popular "load the following notes into your system" dialog box. Just accept whatever is proposed.

Installing the first note is painless, but the second one will prompt you to do some "manual activities," which is always scary. Specifically, you will be asked to create a sub-package of package SYCM_MAIN called SYCM_APS. It is vital you do not ignore this step; otherwise, you will get syntax errors when the rest of the note is implemented. Then, amazingly, you will be prompted to create some text elements manually. You would think after 40 years SAP would have found a way to download text elements via SAP notes, but oh well, off to the SAP support portal we go to register some objects.

At that point, you will think you are done, but beware! There are some more manual steps hiding off the bottom of the screen where you cannot see them. Scroll down and you will find them. First, tick the green tick to import all the automatic corrections listed in the middle of the screen.

The instructions at the bottom of the screen tell you that you have to go into transaction SCI and navigate to the "management of tests" section and switch on certain entries, which are as follows:

CL_CLS_CI_CHECK_ENVIRONM_ONPR

CL_CI_TEST_ADMISSIBLE_4_CLOUD

CL_CLS_CI_CHECK_ENVIRONMENT

Then, in transaction SCI, you will select the menu option "Utilities ➤ Import Check Variants." That makes sure the new check variants actually exist. Then, it is time to create some more text elements manually, and that is the second note implemented. Agony though the process was, it is now done.

The third note requires a large number of other notes to be downloaded, but this is an automatic process. Then the horror begins again, and this time you have to create not only text elements but also data elements in the SAP namespace and add fields at the end of two standard SAP structures and add some data records to a standard SAP table.

The remote system is now ready to begin the check! You are finished! No, we are not.

Now you need to install some notes into the system to be analyzed (your development system), which needs SAP Note 2885486 installed; otherwise, the remote check will not work. Then add Note 2270689, which is so big you have to import it in the background using report SCWN_NOTE_DOWNLOAD. And then Note 2820873. Nothing good ever came easy. At the end of this process you have to run report RS_ABAP_INIT_ANALYSIS, which creates any missing DDIC objects.

At long last, you are ready to use transaction ATC in the standalone system to schedule a remote ATC check. The standalone system has been configured to analyze remote systems as opposed to itself, just as was the case in the previous chapter.

You create a remote ATC check run by creating a so-called configuration inside the "schedule runs" option of transaction ATC. You give this a descriptive name—I am just going to call mine ZABAP_CLOUD for example purposes and analyze a sales order-related package in the target system. The definition looks like Figure 9-3. You can tell it is a remote check because the "Object Provider" field is supplied with the name of the target system to be analyzed.

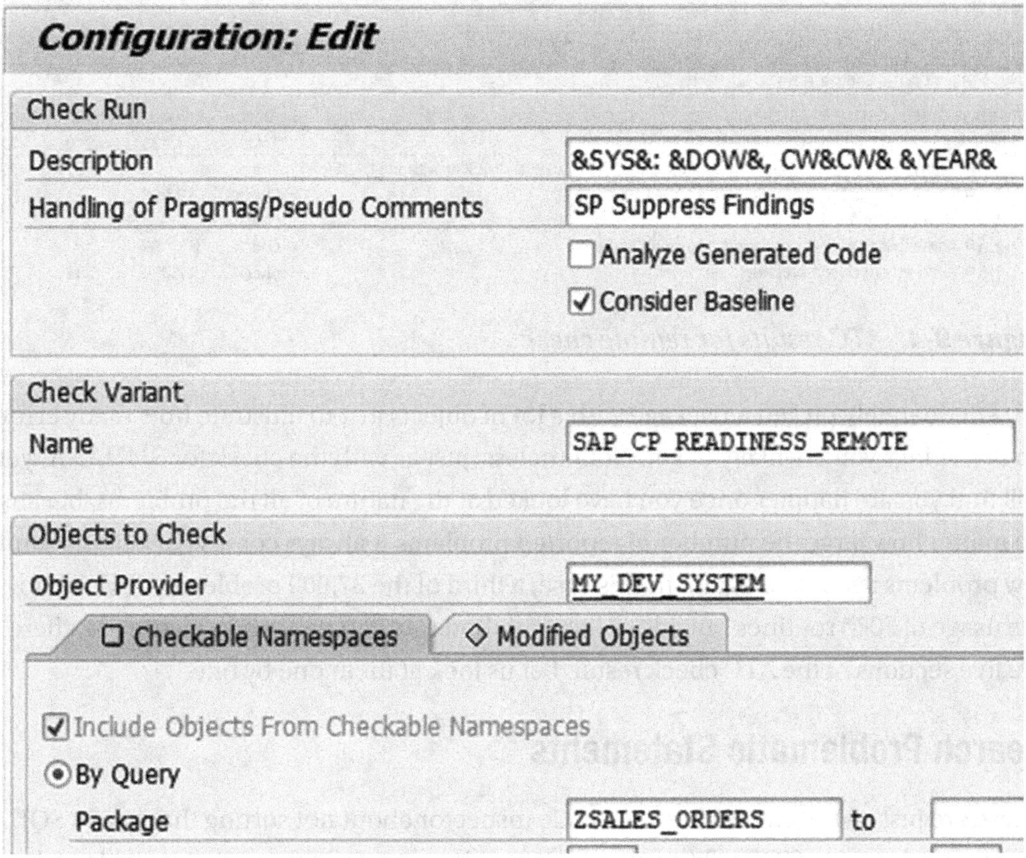

Configuration: Edit

Check Run

Description	&SYS&: &DOW&, CW&CW& &YEAR&
Handling of Pragmas/Pseudo Comments	SP Suppress Findings
	☐ Analyze Generated Code
	☑ Consider Baseline

Check Variant

Name	SAP_CP_READINESS_REMOTE

Objects to Check

Object Provider	MY_DEV_SYSTEM

☐ Checkable Namespaces ◇ Modified Objects

☑ Include Objects From Checkable Namespaces
⊙ By Query

| Package | ZSALES_ORDERS | to |

Figure 9-3. *Configuring a remote ATC check*

You save the new configuration and press the Schedule button, and then choose "execute in background"; running in the foreground would most likely cause a time out. If you look in SM37 in the remote system, you can see your background job running; it has 11 "phases" it needs to work through before it is complete. If you have chosen a package with a large number of Z objects, this could take some time.

When the job does finish, you go into the remote system and call up transaction SE80 and choose the option "ATC Result Browser." Then you select the analysis run that just finished, and the result will look like Figure 9-4.

Statistics: Check	Des...	Prio 1	Prio 2	Prio 3
▾ 🔢 Total	Total	37.430	349	224
▸ 🔲 Search problematic statements for result of SELECT/OPEN CURSOR without ORDER BY	Check...	3	11	220
▸ 🔲 Test for restricted language scope (ABAP version)	Check...	19.963		
▸ 🔲 Prerequisites for the test	Check...			4
▸ 🔲 Admissibility check for transport into cloud systems	Check...	89		
▸ 🔲 Whitelist Check (on-premise)	Check...	17.375	338	

Figure 9-4. *ATC results for remote check*

I deliberately picked a package with a lot of objects just to illustrate how many errors and warnings you are likely to get. Nonetheless, just as with the check for S/4HANA, you will find you are happier once you have looked at the nature of all the problems, because no matter how large the number of reported problems it always comes back to the same few problems again and again. In this case, a third of the 37,000 problems are down to the usage of FORM routines outside of local methods. As can be seen in Figure 9-4, there are five sections of the ATC check result. Let us look at them one by one.

Search Problematic Statements

These are just all the checks from the code inspector about not sorting the data in SQL statements by using ORDER BY or other means, plus assorted other existing static code checks, plus some red herrings. The upshot is that if you have your house in order by always doing the extended program check and code inspector, there will be nothing of any importance in this section.

Restricted Language Scope

The irony here in a section with the word *Language* in the title is that all the error explanations come out in German. Possibly that will have been fixed by the time you try this. In any event, the result here is split into 14 different sub-sections, and by clicking on each one you will see a list of what the ABAP in the Cloud system does not like. In Figure 9-5, you will see it has detected references to assorted SY variables.

Pri...	Check Title	Check Message	Obj. n...	Obj.	E...	C...	Pack...	1st Found	C...	R(	Referenced Object
⚡1	Test for restricted langu...	Syntaxfehler bei eingeschränktem Sprachu...	SAPM...	PROG		BU	ZSD...	11.12.2020			SY-DATUM
1	Test for restricted langu...	Syntaxfehler bei eingeschränktem Sprachu...	SAPM...	PROG		BU	ZSD...	11.12.2020			SY-UZEIT
1	Test for restricted langu...	Syntaxfehler bei eingeschränktem Sprachu...	SAPM...	PROG		BU	ZSD...	11.12.2020			SY-UZEIT
1	Test for restricted langu...	Syntaxfehler bei eingeschränktem Sprachu...	SAPM...	PROG		BU	ZSD...	11.12.2020			SY-DATUM
1	Test for restricted langu...	Syntaxfehler bei eingeschränktem Sprachu...	SAPM...	PROG		BU	ZSD...	11.12.2020			SY-DATUM
1	Test for restricted langu...	Syntaxfehler bei eingeschränktem Sprachu...	SAPM...	PROG		BU	ZSD...	11.12.2020			SY-UZEIT
1	Test for restricted langu...	Syntaxfehler bei eingeschränktem Sprachu...	SAPM...	PROG		BU	ZSD...	11.12.2020			SY-UZEIT
1	Test for restricted langu...	Syntaxfehler bei eingeschränktem Sprachu...	SAPM...	PROG		BU	ZSD...	11.12.2020			SY-DATUM
1	Test for restricted langu...	Syntaxfehler bei eingeschränktem Sprachu...	SAPM...	PROG		PE	ZSD...	11.12.2020			SY-MANDT
1	Test for restricted langu...	Syntaxfehler bei eingeschränktem Sprachu...	SAPM...	PROG		PE	ZSD...	11.12.2020			SY-DATUM

Figure 9-5. *List of problems relating to usage of SY variables*

If you click on any given line, you are taken into your development system to see the line of code where the problem occurs. By working through the 14 lists in this section you are given a clear understanding of what statements are not allowed; e.g., WRITE, OPEN DATASET, dynamic programming, SET PARAMETER, and so on. As mentioned earlier, by far the largest list of problems is related to the usage of FORM routines.

Prerequisites for the Test

In this section (which hopefully should be very small), you get objects the remote system could not analyze for whatever reason. You would have to manually check each mentioned object to see what (if anything) is wrong with it.

Admissibility Check

Half of this points at custom objects that have DYNPROS, which are of course not allowed in the cloud as there is no GUI. The other half is a list of object types that are also not allowed in the cloud—PIDs, transaction codes, REPORTS, search helps, and so on. Again, this is a good overview of things you have always taken for granted that are just not there in ABAP in the Cloud.

White list Check

This all revolves around usage of "forbidden objects"; i.e., objects that exist but are not on the White List and so you cannot use them. The types of forbidden objects are split up into sections. Some of the items on the first list of forbidden objects might surprise you; e.g., the function CONVERSION_EXIT_ALPHA_INPUT—but if you think about it, that function is GUI related. The list is also a bit inconsistent; e.g., data elements CHAR01 and CHAR04 are forbidden, but CHAR02 is fine.

The "Deprecated Base API" section is a list of data elements you cannot use anymore; e.g., BOOLEAN. For some of these there is an automated fix you can make after conversion, as mentioned in a later section. I think the idea is that when there are 20 billion different fake Boolean variables like XFELD and the like, SAP has decided to standardize on just the one.

In the list with the name "Not Released Application API," you will see all the references to standard SAP tables like VBAK and VBKD. As mentioned earlier in the chapter, these have to be accessed indirectly.

I would note that there are some errors that can be automatically fixed in ABAP in Eclipse by using quick fixes—but only after the code is in the ABAP in the Cloud system. A list of such quick fixes can be found via a link at the end of this chapter. For anything on that list it is a waste of effort to spend a week manually converting half a million pieces of code *before* conversion when you can convert them all at the touch of a button *after* conversion. You have exactly the same situation when converting code to S/4HANA. You cannot do the automatic conversions before conversion, because sometimes the quick fixes replace the current code with objects that do not exist in the prior development system.

The Conversion Procedure

Even if cutting and pasting your Z code into the cloud environment did work without having to change anything it would still be tedious—after all, in the past you used tools like SAPLINK and more recently abapGit to move code from one system to another.

The good news is that not only can you use abapGit to move code from one on-premises AP system to another, but you can also use that tool to transfer code from your on-premises system to ABAP in the Cloud.

Obviously, you need abapGit installed in your current development system; hopefully you already have that installed. Then, you need to isolate everything you want to transfer into a package (which can have sub-packages) and export that package to a GitHub repository.

You do this by creating a new repository on GitHub and then using abapGit in your development system to create a new online repository using the URL of the GitHub repository you just created. abapGit then duplicates the code in the specified package from your development system to GitHub. This is the exact same procedure as if you wanted to move that code to another on-premises ABAP system.

Okay, thus far Elvis has left the building; i.e., your development system. How does he get into the new building; i.e., the ABAP in the Cloud environment? The next step (and this is a once-off) is that your Eclipse version (which lives on your local PC) needs the abapGit plug-in.

Once you have Eclipse open, choose the menu option "Help ➤ Install New Software" and in the "Work with" box enter the URL http://eclipse.abapgit.org/updatesite/ as shown in Figure 9-6.

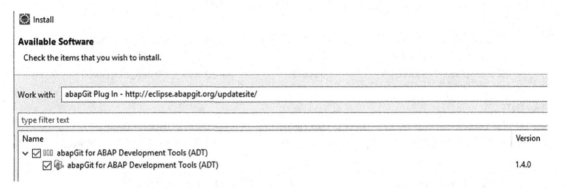

Figure 9-6. *Installing the abapGit plug-in for Eclipse*

You need to press the Next button a few times, accept the license agreement, and restart Eclipse, and then all will be well.

Now is the time to download your code from GitHub to your ABAP in the Cloud system. Create a new package in your cloud system to house the code you wish to download.

Next, at the bottom of the ADT screen, is a list of tabs—one of them is "abapGit Repositories." Navigate to that and press the green "plus" sign to link a new repository. On the next screen, enter the URL of the GitHub repository to which you just uploaded your code. On the screen after that, specify the target package—i.e., the package in the ABAP in the Cloud system where the code is going to live—and tick the box that says "Pull after link." Then, at the bottom of the screen, you will see a new entry with the package and URL and the status "Pull Running." Eventually, that will change to "Pulled Successfully," and you can right-click on the line to get the context menu. Choose "Show Object Log," and you will get a screen like that in Figure 9-7.

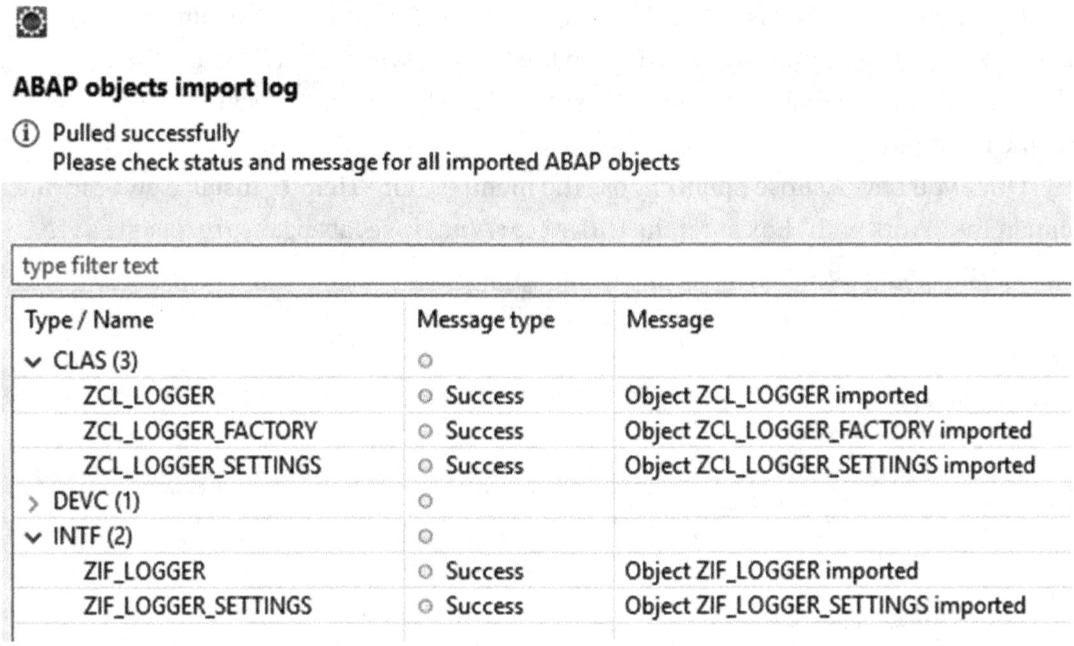

ABAP objects import log

ⓘ Pulled successfully
Please check status and message for all imported ABAP objects

type filter text

Type / Name	Message type	Message
⌄ CLAS (3)	○	
ZCL_LOGGER	○ Success	Object ZCL_LOGGER imported
ZCL_LOGGER_FACTORY	○ Success	Object ZCL_LOGGER_FACTORY imported
ZCL_LOGGER_SETTINGS	○ Success	Object ZCL_LOGGER_SETTINGS imported
› DEVC (1)	○	
⌄ INTF (2)	○	
ZIF_LOGGER	○ Success	Object ZIF_LOGGER imported
ZIF_LOGGER_SETTINGS	○ Success	Object ZIF_LOGGER_SETTINGS imported

Figure 9-7. *Importing code into ABAP in the Cloud using abapGit*

Then, you navigate to the imported objects and see all the errors, as in Figure 9-8.

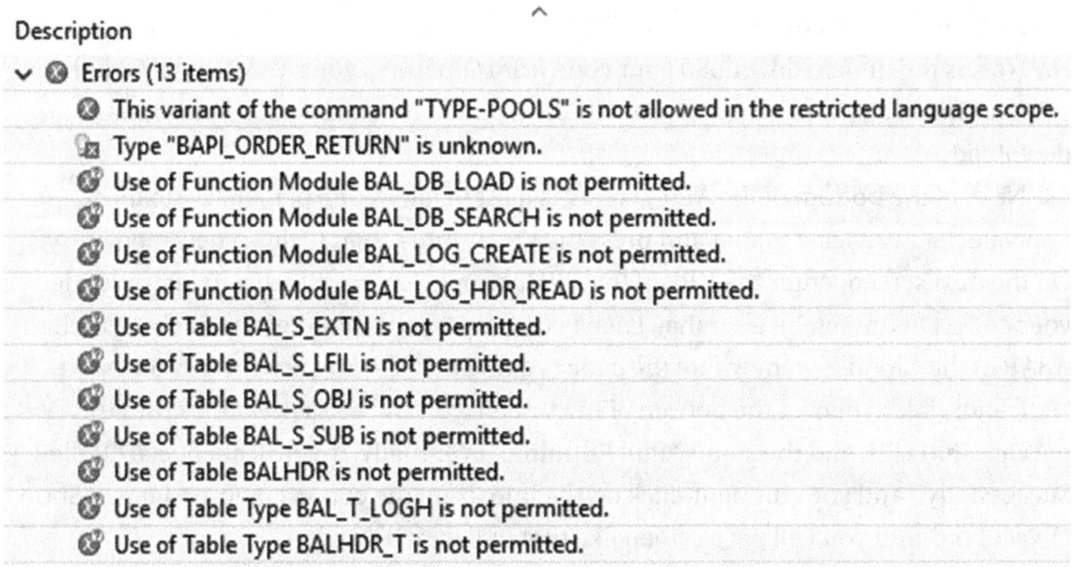

Description

⌄ ⊗ Errors (13 items)
  ⊗ This variant of the command "TYPE-POOLS" is not allowed in the restricted language scope.
  🔒 Type "BAPI_ORDER_RETURN" is unknown.
  ⊗ Use of Function Module BAL_DB_LOAD is not permitted.
  ⊗ Use of Function Module BAL_DB_SEARCH is not permitted.
  ⊗ Use of Function Module BAL_LOG_CREATE is not permitted.
  ⊗ Use of Function Module BAL_LOG_HDR_READ is not permitted.
  ⊗ Use of Table BAL_S_EXTN is not permitted.
  ⊗ Use of Table BAL_S_LFIL is not permitted.
  ⊗ Use of Table BAL_S_OBJ is not permitted.
  ⊗ Use of Table BAL_S_SUB is not permitted.
  ⊗ Use of Table BALHDR is not permitted.
  ⊗ Use of Table Type BAL_T_LOGH is not permitted.
  ⊗ Use of Table Type BALHDR_T is not permitted.

Figure 9-8. *Looking at the errors in the imported objects*

Once the code is in the ABAP in the Cloud system, you can use conversion-related ADT quick fixes to automatically fix a load of problems; e.g., you can automatically replace all usages of REFRESH with CLEAR and so on. There are a big bunch of such automated quick fixes, and more come out all the time.

One point to note is that those conversion-related quick fixes will only appear during an ATC run, not during normal code editing, and you can only do an ATC run on activated objects. Also, you cannot activate objects with syntax errors. This is what is known as a catch-22 situation—you can only automatically fix the errors if there are no errors to be automatically fixed, which is obviously crazy.

So, in order to get around this problem and perform the automatic adjustments, you will have to activate all the code that needs to be fixed. The system will try to stop you because there are syntax errors, but if you choose the "Activate anyway" option when told about those errors during activation you will be good to go.

Conclusion

In this chapter, first you were introduced to the general concept of the ABAP in the Cloud environment and how it differs quite substantially from traditional on-premises ABAP development systems.

Then, you got very depressed by reading about the myriad reasons why your current custom code cannot work "as-is" in the cloud environment.

Lastly, we ended on a more upbeat note by looking at the tools SAP provides to help you overcome all these problems and successfully migrate custom code from an on-premises system to an ABAP in the Cloud system.

On that subject (SAP tools to check and convert code), thus far in the book we have looked at all the standard tools available. But what if they are not 100 percent sufficient for your needs? In the last chapter, you will see how to plug that gap by creating your own custom checks and fixes.

Recommended Reading

SAP is pushing really hard to get people to adopt ABAP in the Cloud, and as part of this there is a regular series of truly excellent blogs published on the SAP Community Website. I would recommend not only reading the listed blogs but also "following" the authors so you can stay up to date with advances in this area, which come along regularly as this technology is so new.

Restricted ABAP in General:

```
https://blogs.sap.com/2020/07/23/restricted-abap-and-sap-s-4hana-on-premise/
```

Setting up a Trial Account for ABAP in the Cloud:

```
https://blogs.sap.com/2019/09/28/its-trialtime-for-abap-in-sap-cloud-
platform/
```

Calling the ERP system from ABAP in the Cloud:

```
https://blogs.sap.com/2019/02/28/how-to-call-a-remote-function-module-in-
your-on-premise-sap-system-from-sap-cloud-platform-abap-environment/
```

Setting up a Remote ATC Check in regard to ABAP in the Cloud:

```
https://blogs.sap.com/2018/10/02/how-to-check-your-custom-abap-code-for-
sap-cloud-platform-abap-environment/
```

Converting Code to ABAP in the Cloud:

```
https://blogs.sap.com/2019/11/11/how-to-bring-your-abap-custom-code-to-sap-
cloud-platform-abap-environment/
```

Quick Fixes for ABAP in the Cloud Available in ADT:

```
https://blogs.sap.com/2019/10/01/semi-automatic-custom-code-adaptation-for-
sap-cloud-platform-abap-environment/
```

CHAPTER 10

Creating Your Own Custom ATC Checks

SAP provides some fantastic tools for automated static code checking, the most prominent of which is the ATC (ABAP Test Cockpit), which is powered by the code inspector. However, there are bound to be things that any given organization needs to check that are 100 percent specific to their needs.

Such checks will not be in the standard system, so in this chapter you will learn how to code any new checks you can dream up and have them seamlessly integrate with the standard SAP ATC tool.

Keeping to a chronological view of the world, this chapter will be organized into three sections that in effect deal with the past, present, and future.

- First, the Ghost of Christmas Past will talk about what some developers have been doing up until now to increase the range of available ATC checks via open source GitHub projects.

- Then, the Ghost of Christmas Present will tell you in detail how to create a custom ATC check in your ABAP system to look for and highlight any organization-specific code problems you may have.

- Finally, the Ghost of Christmas Yet to Come will discuss the concept of custom ABAP in Eclipse plug-ins and how they can take ATC checks to a whole new level—promising a very bright future indeed.

Open Source ATC Projects

In Chapter 2, during the discussion of TDD, we talked about two open source projects that you can download from GitHub in order to import extra ATC checks into your development system. It is worth recapping that subject here. To install those open source

© Paul David Hardy 2021
P. D. Hardy, *Improving the Quality of ABAP Code*, https://doi.org/10.1007/978-1-4842-6711-0_10

projects, you will need to install abapGit into your SAP system first, which you can do by following the instructions from the following URL:

`https://docs.abapgit.org/guide-install.html`

Once abapGit is installed, you can use that tool to download extra ATC checks from the following repositories:

- `https://github.com/larshp/abapOpenChecks`

- `https://github.com/SAP/code-pal-for-abap`

"ABAP Open Checks" is the older of the two and was created by Lars Hvam Petersen, inventor of abapGit. The checks relate more to the appearance of the code than to functional correctness; i.e., they highlight areas where the code is possibly difficult to understand and hence maintain.

Some years later, this concept was taken further when "Code Pal for ABAP" was created by SAP employees (though as an open source project to which anyone in the world can contribute). The "Code Pal" concept is based on the "Clean Code" principles made famous by Robert Martin (Uncle Bob) in his 2009 book by the same name and adapted for ABAP as per the following style guide:

`https://github.com/SAP/styleguides/blob/master/clean-abap/CleanABAP.md`

The code base of "ABAP Open Checks" is updated on a regular basis, but the "Code Pal" project at time of writing is still quite new and as such there is a new major release every month. Thus far, there are only 11 contributors, mainly from SAP but also including Lars, who created the "ABAP Open Checks" project.

As these are open source projects, there are several points worth noting, as follows:

- These are community projects, and thus even if SAP employees are contributing there is no official support from SAP. If something you download does not work or causes a short dump, you have to fix it yourself.

- You can of course report bugs on the relevant GitHub site by opening an issue, and someone will look at that bug in due course. It would be far better, however, if when you encounter such a bug you investigate and fix it yourself and then post the solution on GitHub—you can even create a "pull request" where you submit the fixed code, which can then be merged with the core project code base once approved by the project owner.

- You can make suggestions for new checks. However, after you have read this chapter you will know how to create such new checks yourself, and if you so desire you could propose your new check as an addition to the open source project.

The good thing about the ATC checks is that you only activate the ones you think are worthwhile, be they standard SAP ATC checks or the ones you have gotten from an open source project. No two organizations will ever agree on what checks are good and which ones are pointless. In fact, no two developers will ever agree on this matter; your team will have to come to some sort of consensus.

In this rest of this chapter, we will concentrate on the scenario whereby you have identified a recurring problem in your custom code that is a problem for you personally but may not be a problem for every single SAP customer in the world. Hence, you will want to create a custom ATC check to look for your specific problem.

Custom Code Check Example

We will start with a simple example, perhaps not that realistic, just to get you used to the procedure for creating custom ATC checks. As you will see, once you know the basic procedure it is not going to be very difficult to move on to much more complicated real-life examples, as all you will need is to be able to program in ABAP! Anyway, let's get started with the simple example.

As you know, in many places in an ABAP program if an operation has been successful (for example, a SQL read on a database table or a read on an internal table) then the system variable gets set to zero.

There are two ways you can check for this:

- `IF SY-SUBRC = 0`

- `IF SY-SUBRC IS INITIAL`

The two statements are functionally identical. The initial value of `SY-SUBRC` is indeed zero. However, many people hate the second variant with a passion and say that anyone who uses that variant should be put to death. For the sake of argument, let us say that you feel the same way and want to create a custom ATC check in order to hunt down and destroy all usage of `IF SY-SUBRC IS INITIAL`.

In this section, we are going to work from the bottom up, starting with the building blocks you need to build a custom ATC check:

- Understanding the ATC interface

- Creating an ATC category class

- Creating an ATC custom check class

Next comes creating documentation for the custom checks so the end users (programmers) know what the check is for, and of course TDD gets a mention as always.

We then move on to coding the actual check class, and how to propagate the error message to the ATC should the check fail, and we end with how to attach your new check to the code inspector so it can be added to your default check variant.

Interfaces

There are many places in standard SAP where you configure (via the IMG) the system to call a function module, and that function module is called dynamically. If the function module has the wrong "interface" or "signature"—i.e., input and output parameters—then the standard program will dump.

Examples of such function modules include BI extractors, custom function modules called from variant configurations, and, most commonly, F4 search help function modules. The problem, of course, with such Z function modules is that the programmer has to manually create the signature (usually by copying it from somewhere else) and can of course potentially get it wrong, leading to a short dump during a dynamic call of the function module.

With the move from function modules to object-oriented classes, the potential for error goes away because the class in question has to implement an interface (in the SE24 sense of the word), and thus the possibility of cut and paste errors goes away. Put another way, the implementing class inherits an unchangeable signature.

The importance of such interfaces has been stressed throughout this book. An interface in OO terms is a declaration of what a class (or group of classes) can do; i.e., what services it can perform for the caller. Sometimes you even have an interface with no methods or attributes at all (which seems crazy) that is just a declaration of the purpose of the class—these are so-called marker interfaces. One example is IF_SERIALIZABLE_ OBJECT, which indicates a class can be uploaded/downloaded via XML/JSON. SAP recommends that most classes implement this interface.

In the specific example addressed in this chapter, we wish to indicate that our Z class is going to be used for an ATC check. Such a class does indeed implement the "marker" interface IF_SERIALIZABLE_OBJECT, but more importantly also implements the interface IF_CI_TEST to indicate it is going to be used by the ATC.

Interface IF_CI_TEST

As you know, when a class implements an interface it has to provide code for all the methods in that interface, even if that implementation is just a blank method. In this case, the methods are as shown in Figure 10-1.

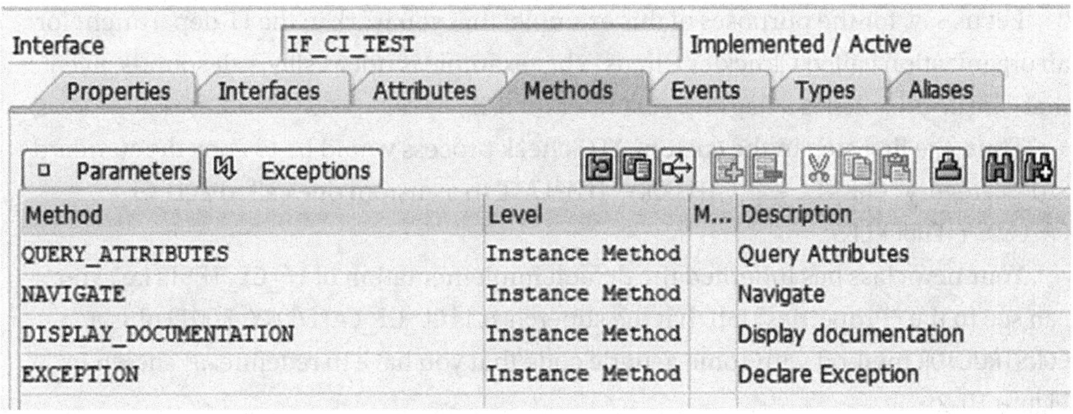

Figure 10-1. *IF_CI_TEST methods*

Earlier in the book when the subject of interfaces reared its ugly head, it was mentioned that sometimes a base class is created using the interface with code that would be the same in most classes that implemented the interface, and that subsequent classes would inherit from the base class, and this is what is happening here. In the default implementation of this interface (CL_CI_TEST_ROOT), one of the methods causes short dumps when you call it and two do nothing, so in the next sections you will see what needs to be done to improve that situation.

Creating a Category Class

In transaction SCI, if you take the menu path *Code Inspector ➤ Management of ➤ Tests* (the last word of that menu path is called *Checks* in ABAP 7.52 and up), you will see a list of the technical names of all the check classes that are currently available in the code

481

inspector. These will be the standard checks supplied by SAP, plus any open source lists of checks you have downloaded, plus any checks you have created yourself.

You will see that the naming convention for all the standard SAP check classes is that they start with the prefix "CL_CI_". If a class has the word "category" in its name it means it is not a check class at all but rather a container for grouping one or more check classes. Typically, you would only have one category for your own list of custom checks.

There is no need at all to reinvent the wheel here. SAP has done most of the work here for you, and in every step in this process you just need to copy SAP standard classes and redefine the 5 percent you need to change for the current task at hand. SAP wants you to inherit from the standard classes; otherwise, they would have made those classes final and you *would* have had to reinvent the wheel.

Let us say, for the purposes of this example, that you work in the IT department for an organization called Chuckles Circus. That example is not as silly as it sounds given that Cirque du Soleil is a flagship customer for SAP.

Thus, the first step in the custom ATC check process would be to copy the standard SAP "category" class CL_CI_CATEGORY_TEMPLATE to a custom one called ZCL_CI_CATEGORY_CHUCKLES.

Your new class has inherited the default implementation of IF_CI_TEST (i.e., you can see in the "Properties" tab that the superclass is CL_CI_CATEGORY_ROOT) plus a CONSTRUCTOR method with some generic code that you have to redefine, as shown in Figure 10-2.

Class/Interface	ZCL_CI_CATEGORY_CHUCKLES		Implemented / Active				
Properties	Interfaces	Friends	Attributes	Methods	Events	Types	Aliases

Parameters Exceptions Sourcecode				□ Filter
Method	Level	Visibility	M...	Description
<IF_CI_TEST>				
QUERY_ATTRIBUTES	Instance Method	Public		Query Attributes
NAVIGATE	Instance Method	Public		Navigate
DISPLAY_DOCUMENTATION	Instance Method	Public		Display documentation
EXCEPTION	Instance Method	Public		Declare Exception
CONSTRUCTOR	Instance Method	Public		Constructor

Figure 10-2. *Custom category class*

Inside your redefined CONSTRUCTOR method you have to set three class attributes, as follows:

- The description, which will appear in the SCI configuration list. You could hard code this, but I notice that "Code Pal" uses a standard SAP class to read the actual name of the current class, so that is the way forward. Hard coding is always bad. Thus, add a new method to your custom category class called GET_CLASS_DESCRIPTION and code it as described later.

- The category, which means the higher-level category in which this new set of custom checks will appear. As such, this is always set to CL_CI_CATEGORY_TOP so that it appears under the standard SAP tree of code inspector checks.

- The position — If this is "001" the new category of checks will appear at the top of the SAP standard list of checks (as do the "Code Pal" checks); if set to "999" the new category will appear at the bottom (as do the "ABAP Open Checks"). In this case, we will pick "999" as well to put the new category just above the "ABAP Open Checks" (if they are installed). You can have multiple categories with the same number.

As a result, the redefined CONSTRUCTOR method and the GET_CLASS_DESCRIPTION method copied from the "Code Pal" example end up looking like Listing 10-1.

Listing 10-1. Redefined CONSTRUCTOR Plus Added Method

```
METHOD CONSTRUCTOR.
  super->constructor( ).
  description = get_class_description( ).
  category    = 'CL_CI_CATEGORY_TOP'."#EC NOTEXT
  position    = '998'.

ENDMETHOD.
 METHOD get_class_description.

    TRY.
        result = NEW cl_oo_class( myname )->class-descript.
```

```
    CATCH cx_class_not_existent.
      "This should be impossible
      "We are talking about the name of the current class
      result = 'Description Not Available'(001).
  ENDTRY.

ENDMETHOD.
```

The MYNAME attribute is inherited from CL_CI_CATEGORY_ROOT, and its value is set in the constructor of that class. The GET_CLASS_DESCRIPTION method that you created in your class needs to be defined as PROTECTED so it can be inherited if need be, and has one RETURNING parameter typed as a string. The only reason for putting this logic in a separate method is because if the method call to CL_OO_CLASS fails it raises an exception, and the needed exception handling would "pollute" the constructor method.

The end result is that a new entry appears in the SCI transaction's list of check classes at the bottom, as seen in Figure 10-3.

☑ ZCL_AOC_CHECK_95	ℹ	095 - Object / Class member access
☑ ZCL_AOC_CHECK_96		096 - Check Editor Lock is set
☑ ZCL_AOC_CHECK_97		097 - Check Selection Screen Texts
☑ ZCL_AOC_CHECK_98	ℹ	098 - Combine empty catches
☑ ZCL_AOC_CHECK_99	ℹ	099 - Minimum number of WHENs in a CASE
☐ ZCL_CI_CATEGORY_CHUCKLES	ℹ	Custom ATC Checks for Chuckles the Clown

Figure 10-3. *New category class appearing in SCI list*

Later on, you will "activate" the category class by ticking the box to its left, but that would be pretty pointless right now due to the fact that as yet there are no custom check classes within that category.

Creating the Actual Custom Check Class

Both open source check-class projects stick to the convention of using the term "category" in the name of the category class, but otherwise they both deviate from how SAP names things. SAP uses the term "test" in the class names, and both open source projects use the term "check." I would imagine this is because the standard SAP ones were created when the menu path to look at these classes ended with the word "test," and the newer ones were created when the menu path ended with the word "check." Moreover, when SAP changes the menu path name again both terms will be out of date.

The "Code Pal" check classes all start with a Y and are in the format Y_CHECK_ SOMETHING, where the SOMETHING is as descriptive a name for the check as can fit in the remaining characters available. "ABAP Open Checks" uses the format ZCL_AOC_CHECK_ XX, where XX is a number so you have to look at the text description to see what it is checking for.

So, when you create your first custom check class, you have several naming conventions to choose from, or you could create your own, as it clearly does not matter.

One possibility is to start with the SAP convention and put a Z on the front; i.e., ZCL_ CI_. I don't feel the burning need to add either the word TEST or the word CHECK in the name as the CI in the name stands for code inspector, and therefore this prefix indicates a check class. You always have to be aware that there are only 30 characters available in an ABAP class name, and thus prefixes should be kept to the absolute minimum needed.

So, in this case the class to be created will be called ZCL_CI_SYSUBRC_IS_INITIAL— that is 25 characters long, and the chance of a name conflict with a future class from one of the open source projects is virtually non-existent.

The more important question is which class your new check class should inherit from. The superclass is always going to be CL_CI_TEST_SCAN. Are you going to have a base class that inherits from that class, and add all your reusable custom things there, or are you going to inherit from that class directly? If you are going to have dozens of custom check classes, then having your own base class makes a lot of sense. However, to keep things really simple for this example, you are going to create the custom ATC check by copying the standard template class CL_CI_TEST_SCAN_TEMPLATE to your new class ZCL_CI_SYSUBRC_IS_INITIAL. You can get much more fancy later on once you understand the basics. After copying, do not forget to change the class description—that step is easy to forget. The class description should be what you want to appear in the SCI list of code inspector checks.

CL_CI_TEST_SCAN_TEMPLATE inherits from class CL_CI_TEST_SCAN, and naturally so does the class you just copied from it. Thus, your new class has inherited about 20 billion attributes and methods—it is just as well you did not have to create everything from scratch. There are some things you have to change from the template, of course, but not very many, which will leave you free to concentrate on the important bit; i.e., new custom code.

First up, create an exact duplicate of the GET_CLASS_DESCRIPTION method from the category class using the exact same code as in Listing 10-1. The MYNAME variable is set in the exact same way as before.

Next, you need to change the constructor. The template class' constructor is full of commented code that sets a small number of attributes, and you need to change that code to set the actual attribute values. This is going to be very similar to what you did when changing the constructor of the category class. In this case, the attributes are as follows:

- The description — This will appear in the SCI list describing the check. Because it is bad to hard code this, the same trick as in the last section will be used.

- The category — This will be the name of the category class created in the last section, so that the code inspector knows what category to list this check under. I have not yet found a miracle solution to avoid hard coding that name here.

- The version — This starts at "000," and you are supposed to increase this number whenever you make a change to this class, but I doubt anyone ever does.

- Two attributes flags (which are optional) — What this means is that if this flag is TRUE then the programmer gets a pop-up box in SCI where they can configure certain values for this check; e.g., maximum nesting level if checking for cyclomatic complexity. We will not be using such attributes in this example.

The end result is shown in Listing 10-2.

Listing 10-2. CONSTRUCTOR Method of Custom Check Class

```
METHOD constructor.

  super->constructor( ).

  description = get_class_description( ).
  category    = 'ZCL_CI_CATEGORY_CHUCKLES'.
  version     = '000'.

*  HAS_ATTRIBUTES = 'X'.            "optional
*  ATTRIBUTES_OK  = 'X' or ' '.     "optional

ENDMETHOD.
```

Just by writing that code your new check class magically appears in the list of available checks in transaction SCI, as shown in Figure 10-4.

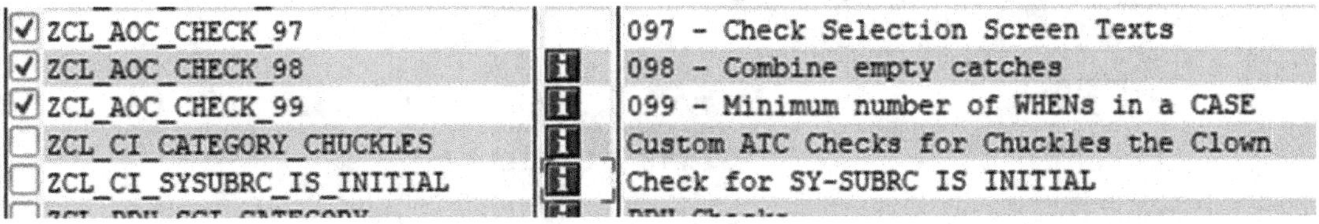

☑ ZCL_AOC_CHECK_97	097 - Check Selection Screen Texts
☑ ZCL_AOC_CHECK_98	🛈 098 - Combine empty catches
☑ ZCL_AOC_CHECK_99	🛈 099 - Minimum number of WHENs in a CASE
☐ ZCL_CI_CATEGORY_CHUCKLES	🛈 Custom ATC Checks for Chuckles the Clown
☐ ZCL_CI_SYSUBRC_IS_INITIAL	🛈 Check for SY-SUBRC IS INITIAL

Figure 10-4. *New check class now appears in the SCI list*

Creating Documentation

In the chapter on user-friendliness, you heard about the need to be friendly to developers as well as to end users and add documentation to all your ABAP classes. Here, it becomes even more important. When the end user (a developer in this case) clicks on the little blue information icon to the right of the class name in transaction SCI (as highlighted in Figure 10-5), or when creating a code inspector variant, the developer is expecting a description of the check to pop up and would be really surprised if it did not.

What SAP is expecting you to do is go into transaction SE61 to create the documentation. For both the category class and the check class you are supposed to create documentation of type "Class Attribute" (CA) with the same name as the class and a suffix of "0000," as shown in Figure 10-5.

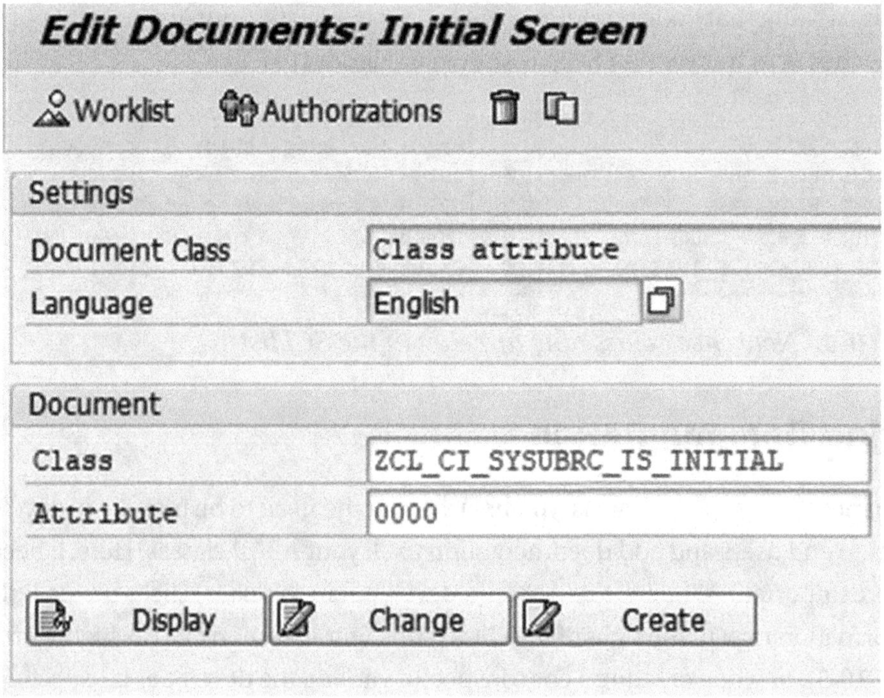

Edit Documents: Initial Screen

🖎 Worklist   👥 Authorizations   🗑 🗐

Settings

Document Class	Class attribute
Language	English 🗗

Document

Class	ZCL_CI_SYSUBRC_IS_INITIAL
Attribute	0000

📄 Display | 📝 Change | 📝 Create

Figure 10-5. Creating documentation for use in the code inspector

Realistically, there is not much you can say about the category class apart from a general description of why you felt the need to write any custom checks in the first place. However, for each actual check class you need to write a detailed description of what the check is for, why the situation being checked for is bad, and what is a better way to write the code.

This documentation will be automatically read by method DISPLAY_DOCUMENTATION, which calls function module DOCU_GET_FOR_F1HELP to look for the "CA" entry in SE61 with the name of the class. The open source projects do something a bit fancier and redefine that method to take you to the web to see the documentation, but I am a big fan of doing the least possible work to get something working, and so reusing the standard SAP documentation method seems at first glance to be the way forward.

However, since I am a firm believer in documenting every custom SE24 class, it seems wasteful to duplicate the class description documentation; i.e., have it available in SE24 by pressing the Documentation button and also have a separate SE61 "CA" entry with the exact same text.

Thus, I could not help but redefine the DISPLAY_DOCUMENTATION method, copying the standard SAP code, cleaning it up a bit, and changing it from using the class attribute (CA) identifier to using identifier CL for "Class." This way, the description of the check only has to be stored in one place. You just define the documentation straight from SE24 when you create the class and need not bother with the extra SE61 step.

In Listing 10-3, you can see some standard SAP code t I copied and then made minor changes to. I started with the standard SAP code in the method in the superclass that displays the documentation. In my new version, the code attempts to get the standard class documentation (CL) first in the system language and then (if that did not work) in the "master language"; i.e., the language it was created in. Then the standard text display function is called to show the documentation. All the constants like CLASSIC_SAPSCRIPT seen in the listing are defined in the superclass CL_CI_TEST_ROOT.

Listing 10-3. Redefined DISPLAY_DOCUMENTATION Method

```
METHOD if_ci_test~display_documentation.

  DATA: header          TYPE thead,
        text_lines       TYPE tline_tab,
        dummy_info      TYPE help_info,
        dummy_functions TYPE STANDARD TABLE OF editexcl,
        object          TYPE dokhl-object,
        language        TYPE sylangu.

  object(30) = myname.

  CALL FUNCTION 'DOCU_GET_FOR_F1HELP'
    EXPORTING
      id      = 'CL'
      langu   = sy-langu
      object  = object
    IMPORTING
      head    = header
    TABLES
      line    = text_lines
    EXCEPTIONS
      OTHERS = 1.

  IF sy-subrc <> 0.
    SELECT SINGLE masterlang
```

```
      FROM  tadir INTO language
      WHERE pgmid    = 'R3TR'
      AND  object   = 'CLAS'
      AND  obj_name =  myname.

  IF sy-subrc EQ 0.
    CALL FUNCTION 'DOCU_GET_FOR_F1HELP'
      EXPORTING
        id     = 'CL'
        langu  = language
        object = object
     IMPORTING
        head   = header
      TABLES
        line   = text_lines
      EXCEPTIONS
        OTHERS = 1.
  ENDIF.
ENDIF.

IF sy-subrc  = 0.
  CALL FUNCTION 'HELP_DOCULINES_SHOW'
    EXPORTING
      help_infos        = dummy_info
      overlay_header    = header
      classic_sapscript = classic_sapscript
    TABLES
      excludefun        = dummy_functions
      helplines         = text_lines
    EXCEPTIONS
      OTHERS            = 1.
ENDIF.

IF sy-subrc <> 0.
  MESSAGE
    ID sy-msgid TYPE 'S' NUMBER sy-msgno
    WITH sy-msgv1 sy-msgv2 sy-msgv3 sy-msgv4
    DISPLAY LIKE sy-msgty.
ENDIF.

ENDMETHOD.
```

Testing Your Class

As an experiment, using the Class Browser I picked one custom check class from the "Open ABAP Checks" project and one from the "Code Pal" project and in both cases pressed the Local Test Classes button. I was very happy to see unit tests there in both cases, with test doubles to simulate the code's being checked. Then with great trepidation I choose a standard SAP check class and once again pressed the Local Test Classes button—once again unit tests were there, although not done "properly" using test doubles. Nonetheless, the moral is clear—all the existing ATC check classes have automated unit tests and were thus presumably developed in a TDD manner, and you should do the same thing to facilitate testing your class.

Coding the Actual Check

You code the actual check by redefining the RUN method in your custom check class. There are two halves to this. First, you code an analysis on the source code being passed into the RUN method in order to detect the bad code the check is designed to detect. Second, if you find what you are looking for, you are one up on U2, and you then call the INFORM method, passing in details of the problem, which will then show up in the code inspector results.

If you look at the RUN result, you will see it has no parameters. Incoming data arrives by way of member variables. The template class we used as a base for your new class has already redefined the RUN method to give a load of helpful comments as to how the procedure is supposed to work.

At this point you need to recall how the ABAP compiler thinks of ABAP code—it breaks each program down into statements and tokens. A statement is something like RETURN or IF SOMETHING GT SOMETHING—i.e., a series of words ending with a period. A token is a brightly colored bird with a huge bill—oh, hang on, that's a *toucan*. A token is in actual fact a representation of each of the words within each statement.

You often need to analyze several different statements at once—when looking for identical blocks of code, for example, or checking if a SELECT/ENDSELECT loop has an EXIT statement in the middle of the loop. In our example, we are just checking each statement individually to see if we have IF SY-SUBRC IS INITIAL in that statement.

In the RUN method, there are two tables: one for all the statements and one for all the tokens. The tokens table looks like Figure 10-6.

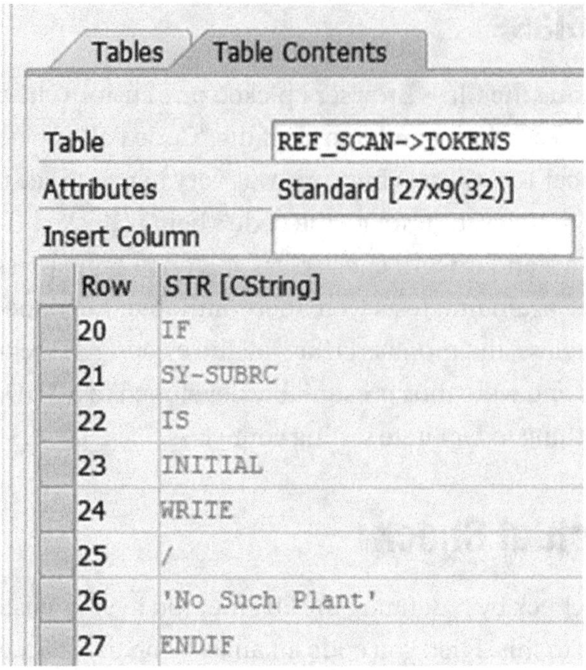

Figure 10-6. *Tokens table*

From looking at Figure 10-6, you can probably guess that it is not going to be too difficult to identify the pattern we are looking for. The only gotcha is that you have to compare several lines of the internal table at once, but that is not a very unusual programming task. As an aside, nothing to do with ATC checks, there are even some built-in functions in the HANA database that perform this sort of task (looking at multiple rows at once) during a SQL query.

In this case, we are dealing with an internal table, so you need to query the TOKENS table to identify the statements where the bad behavior has been coded. You will also need the STATEMENTS table so as to identify the line number with the problem in the program being checked. That way, the developer can jump right into the program from the code inspector at the exact point where the code needs to be changed.

Therefore, the algorithm will be as follows:

- Loop through all the statements. Ignore the ones that do not have SY-SUBRC anywhere inside them.

- If SY-SUBRC is mentioned, then make a note of which token number the SY-SUBRC is in and then check the entries before and after that token to see if the "evil" pattern we are looking for is there.

- If the evil pattern is detected, then notify the code inspector of the fact by calling the INFORM method.

The resulting code is shown in Listing 10-4.

Listing 10-4. Code for Custom Check

```
METHOD run.

  CONSTANTS: lc_code TYPE sci_errc VALUE '0001'.

  DATA: error_count      TYPE sci_errcnt,
        line_as_string   TYPE string,
        subrc_found      TYPE abap_bool,
        subrc_position   TYPE sy-tabix,
        column_in_error  TYPE token_col.

  "Make sure we have some source code to check!
  IF ref_scan IS INITIAL.
    CHECK get( ) = abap_true.
  ENDIF.

  IF ref_scan->subrc NE 0.
    "Something really bad has happened
    RETURN.
  ENDIF.

  "Look at every statement to get the row/column number
  "NB you have to loop into STATEMENT_WA - standard SAP code assumes you do
  LOOP AT ref_scan->statements INTO statement_wa.
    CHECK statement_wa-from <= statement_wa-to.
    DATA(statement_position) = sy-tabix.
    "Looking for SY-SUBRC
    CLEAR: subrc_found,subrc_position.
    LOOP AT ref_scan->tokens
    ASSIGNING FIELD-SYMBOL(<token>)
    FROM statement_wa-from TO statement_wa-to.
      IF <token>-str = 'SY-SUBRC'.
        subrc_found     = abap_true.
```

493

```abap
      subrc_position = sy-tabix.
      EXIT."From Loop
    ENDIF.
  ENDLOOP.
  IF subrc_found EQ abap_false.
    "Nothing to see here, move on
    CONTINUE."With next statement
  ENDIF.

  DATA(token_plus_1) = subrc_position + 1.
  DATA(token_plus_2) = subrc_position + 2.

  READ TABLE ref_scan->tokens
  ASSIGNING <token> INDEX token_plus_1.

  IF sy-subrc NE 0.
    CONTINUE.
  ELSEIF <token>-str NE 'IS'.
    CONTINUE.
  ENDIF.

  READ TABLE ref_scan->tokens
  ASSIGNING <token> INDEX token_plus_2.

  IF sy-subrc NE 0.
    CONTINUE.
  ELSEIF <token>-str NE 'INITIAL'.
    CONTINUE.
  ENDIF.

  "If we have goten here, the problem has been detected
  DATA(bad_token_number) = subrc_position.

  DATA(include_program) = get_include( p_ref_scan = ref_scan ).
  DATA(line_in_error)   = get_line_abs( bad_token_number ).
  column_in_error       = get_column_abs( bad_token_number ).
  error_count           = error_count + 1.
  line_as_string        = line_in_error.   "Type Conversion
  "Let the world know something is wrong
```

```
    "You have to INFORM them
    inform( p_sub_obj_type = c_type_include       "PROG
            p_sub_obj_name = include_program
            p_position     = statement_position
            p_line         = line_in_error
            p_column       = column_in_error
            p_errcnt       = error_count
            p_kind         = c_note"It's a comment/note
            p_test         = myname            "Is Michael Caine
            p_code         = lc_code           "Dummy Value
            p_suppress     = '"#EC GET_A_LIFE'
            p_param_1      = line_as_string ).

  ENDLOOP."Statements

ENDMETHOD.
```

Coding the Error Message

At this point, if you run a code inspector check on a sample program with the problem you are checking for, then the bad code will indeed show up in the code inspector, but with the cryptic message, "Program XYZ does not exist."

That is not much help in analyzing what the problem is, so you need to redefine the method GET_MESSAGE_TEXT. In this method, you can pass in anything you feel is helpful in the IMPORTING parameter P_CODE, and the message to be displayed will be passed out in EXPORTING parameter P_TEXT.

In this case, we are just passing in a dummy value of "0001," which will appear in the report as the Message Code number on the line preceding the diagnostic. The resulting diagnostic text will be a message to the effect that programmers should not use SY-SUBRC IS INITIAL. There is no need to do anything exotic here. In the code inspector, if the developer is puzzled by the short text of the ATC check message and wants extra information, then they can always press the blue information icon and get the documentation for the class as a whole.

Since the message is hard coded, Listing 10-5 doesn't look very impressive. In real life I would use a text symbol or set the error text using a MESSAGE INTO statement so the text could be translated into other languages.

Listing 10-5. Defining a Code Inspector Message

```
METHOD get_message_text.

  p_text = 'Prefer SY-SUBRC = 0 to SY-SUBRC IS INITIAL'.

ENDMETHOD.                              "GET_MESSAGE_TEXT
```

Nonetheless, the results appear as desired, as can be seen in Figure 10-7. In this case, the result appears in the "Information" column because earlier we passed C_NOTE to parameter P_KIND in Listing 10-4. If we had passed in C_ERROR, then it would be in the red column.

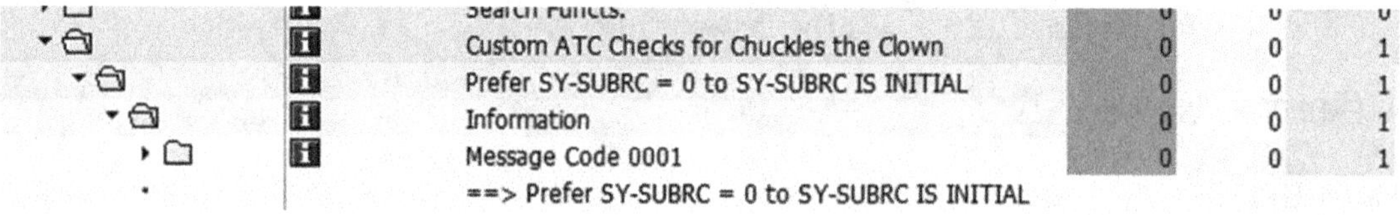

Figure 10-7. *Custom check is shown in code inspector*

Adding the Class to the List of SCI Checks

In the SCI transaction, you can now make your new check available for "consumption"; i.e., bring it to life so that developers can add your new check to their default code inspector variant.

This is as simple as bringing up the list of checks in SCI via the *Code Inspector ➤ Management of ➤ Tests* menu path, finding your category and check class, and ticking the box to their left, as shown in Figure 10-8.

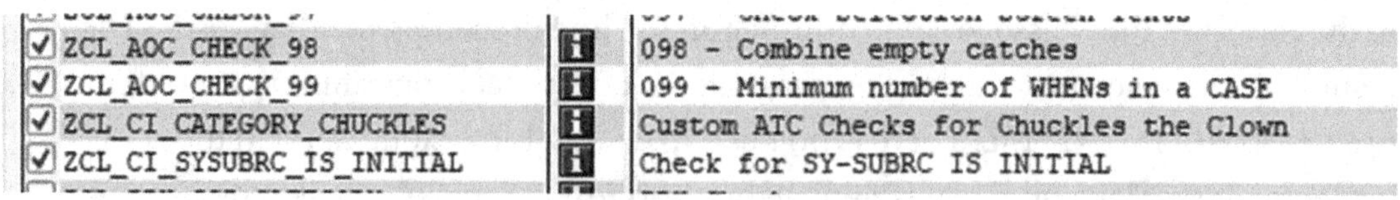

Figure 10-8. *Activating your custom check classes*

When you press Save, you will be asked to choose a transport request to store the change you just made. This never made any sense to me—where would you be transporting that change to? You only do the checks in the development system.

In any event, after you have made that change, the new check category and check will appear in transaction SCI when you create or maintain a "Check Variant," as shown in Figure 10-9.

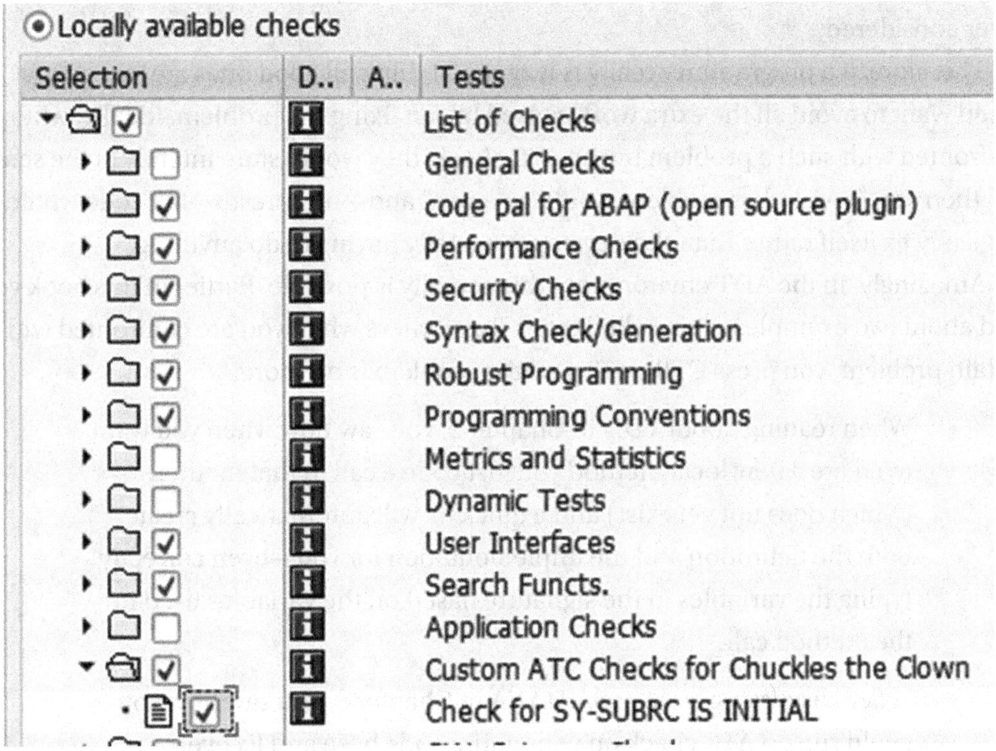

Figure 10-9. *Adding the new check to your Default Check Variant*

At this point the job is done—whenever you run the code inspector on any Z code hereafter your new check will be considered.

Custom Checks in ABAP in Eclipse

Now is the time to talk start talking about ABAP in Eclipse (ADT) again. That might seem like a bit of a non-sequitur at first glance, but bear with me.

As you have seen, if there is some sort of bad coding practice you don't like you can code a custom ATC check in order to look for that problem and highlight it. The idea is that a developer will run all the ATC checks and when presented with the findings actually care enough to do something about it; i.e., manually change the code.

As you have seen throughout this book, many developers just can't be bothered to do this. Why? Because it is boring, it is a chore, it is a bit too much like *hard work*. The fact that not fixing the code will come back to bite them later on and give them (or someone else) a hundred times more work than fixing it in the first place would have taken is never considered.

Therefore, if a programmer really is lazy (and I think all good ones are) then they would want to avoid all the extra work caused by not fixing the problem. Ideally, when confronted with such a problem by the ATC check, they would stare intently at the screen and then say, "I wish that problem would go away," and—hey presto—the code would magically fix itself rather than the developer actually having to do anything.

Amazingly, in the ADT environment this actually is possible. Earlier in this book you read about two examples of so-called quick fixes, where when you are confronted with a certain problem, you press CTRL + F1 and the problem is no more.

- When reading about TDD in Chapter 2, you saw how when you want to create a new local method you just code a call to that method (which does not yet exist) and a quick fix will automatically create both the definition and the implementation for you—even correctly typing the variables in the signature based on the variables used in the method call.

- When discussing code in S/4HANA in Chapter 8, you saw how you could run an ATC check on your entire code base and fix every single occurrence of certain problems—the ORDER BY problem, for example—all at once with the touch of a button. There could be thousands of places where you normally would have had to manually change the code.

The whole Eclipse framework works off plug-ins. The ADT itself is one big plug-in, and with every release more "quick fixes" become available (though what exactly is available is also dependent on your back-end version of ABAP).

It is not only SAP staff who write ABAP plug-ins. There are already six or seven open source ABAP plug-ins for ADT. More come out every year, and of course they get better with each version. The most relevant one for the purposes of this chapter is "ABAP Quick Fixes" by ABAP developer Lukasz Pegiel:

```
https://marketplace.eclipse.org/content/abap-quick-fix
```

You go into Eclipse, choose the menu option *Help => Eclipse Marketplace,* and search for the word *ABAP*. A result list like Figure 10-10 will appear.

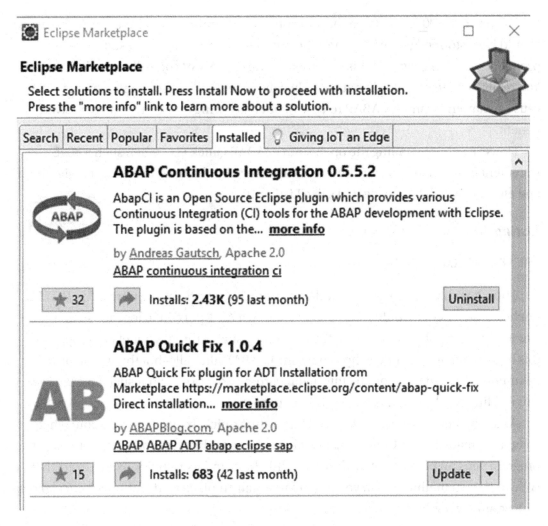

Figure 10-10. *Open source ADT plug-Ins*

Just click Install or Update and you are done—new quick fixes will automatically start appearing.

As an example: 30 years ago the ABAP statement in Listing 10-6 would have been normal.

Listing 10-6. MOVE Statement

```
MOVE 'EQ' TO S_WERKS-OPTION.
```

However, the MOVE statement became obsolete round about the year 2000. Everyone should have stopped using it on the spot, but they did not, and as a result there are probably a million usages of this statement in various ABAP code all around the world. You really need to change all that code (because eventually obsolete statements will cause syntax errors in new ABAP releases), but it is boring and there is no perceived benefit.

However, after installing the open source "ABAP Quick Fix," when such a MOVE statement is detected you can choose to automatically change it to a "direct assignment," and after being fixed the code looks like Listing 10-7.

Listing 10-7. Corrected MOVE Statement

```
S_WERKS-OPTION = 'EQ'.
```

Thus, it is all well and good to code a custom ATC check for the phrase IS INITIAL, but how much better would it be to code your own ADT plug-in to look for such a situation and enable a quick fix of it? Sadly, doing such a thing is out of the scope for this book—you do not code Eclipse plug-ins in ABAP after all—but there is plenty of documentation out there on the internet regarding how to go about such an exercise; you will find two links at the end of this chapter.

As an intellectual exercise, I picked an existing quick fix and thought about whether it could be made better. Currently, if you have the same block of code many times in your program you can pick one of the blocks, highlight it, and use a quick fix to extract that code to its own method. Then you have to manually replace all the other identical blocks with your new method.

It occurred to me that since there is an open source ATC check to identify such duplicate code blocks, then maybe this could be taken further, and an ADT plug-in could be developed to automatically replace all such blocks with the new method. Then, to shoot for the stars, as it were, what if this could work across multiple programs?

I asked the author of the ATC check in question if such a thing was possible, and he said it was—in theory. I said that was all I needed to know. Half an hour later he came back to me and said he could not rest until he had gotten such a thing working in real life. At time of writing there is no such plug-in—yet—but the point of the story is that the sky is the limit. You are not limited in what can be achieved in this area by technology, but rather purely by the bounds of your imagination.

Conclusion

The prior chapters were all about increasing the quality of ABAP code by using existing tools and methodologies. To end the book, you heard about possible ways to go beyond this.

First, you looked at how various developers both within and outside of SAP have created open source projects to establish their own ATC checks to expand the limits of what is currently possible. Then, you looked at a detailed example of how to create your own custom ATC check.

Lastly, you took a look at how to go further yet again, by using ABAP in Eclipse (ADT), where it is possible, to write plug-ins that not only look for whatever problem you want to find, but also automatically correct it.

Recommended Reading

Creating an ABAP in Eclipse (ADT) Plug-in (Christian Drumm):

`https://blogs.sap.com/2014/08/27/creating-a-abap-in-eclipse-plug-in-using-the-adt-sdk/`

Code Snippets for Creating an ADT Plug-in (Matthew Billingham):

`https://blogs.sap.com/2020/06/05/a-few-code-snippets-while-developing-an-adt-plugin/`

Index

A

T

Printed in the United States
by Baker & Taylor Publisher Services